THE COMPLETE BOOK OF

PETS
& PETCARE

THE COMPLETE BOOK OF
PETS
& PETCARE

The essential family reference
guide to pet breeds and petcare

DAVID ALDERTON ✦ ALAN EDWARDS
DR PETER LARKIN ✦ MIKE STOCKMAN

HERMES
HOUSE

CONTENTS

This edition is published by Hermes House

Hermes House is an imprint of Anness Publishing Limited
Hermes House, 88–89 Blackfriars Road, London SE1 8HA
tel. 020 7401 2077; fax 020 7633 9499; info@anness.com

A CIP catalogue record for this book is available from the British
Library.

Publisher Joanna Lorenz
Editorial director Judith Simons
Project editors Sarah Ainley, Gilly Cameron Cooper, Fiona Eaton
Designer Michael Morey
Special photography John Daniels
Illustrator Julian Baker
Indexer Helen Snaith
Production controller Pedro Nelson

Previously published as three separate volumes, *The Ultimate
Encyclopedia of Cats, Cat Breeds & Cat Care, The Complete Dog
Book*, and *The Ultimate Encyclopedia of Small Pets and Petcare*.

10 9 8 7 6 5 4 3 2 1

PREFACE

◆ BELOW
Before picking up a mouse, allow it to sniff your hand first. It will soon come to recognize your scent, and will realize that it is not in danger when being handled by you.

Pet-keeping is something that appeals to people of all ages, and is an activity that can literally change your life. Scientific research has now confirmed that having a pet can prove highly beneficial for both our physical and mental health. In an evermore stressful world, pets provide a relaxing focus set apart from daily worries. For children, the fascination of looking after a pet can trigger an interest in the natural world, and will help to encourage a sense of responsibility.

This book covers the characteristics and care of the major pet groups. Not only are there the obvious choices, such as dogs, cats and small mammals, birds and fish, but also herptiles and invertebrates, which have increased rapidly in popularity in recent years.

MAKING A CHOICE

When it comes to choosing a pet, there are a number of factors which must be considered at the outset. You may find the idea of owning a dog appealing, but if you live in an apartment in the centre of a city, without access to a garden, then this is unlikely to be a good option because of the amount of regular outdoor exercise dogs need. It is no coincidence that over recent years, largely as a result of lifestyle changes, smaller pets have become increasingly popular. These are often less demanding than dogs or cats in terms of care, exercise and the level of attention needed.

Although cats can be kept indoors on a permanent basis, many people dislike the idea of keeping a cat permanently confined. This has, in turn, led to a change of circumstances for the ever-popular rabbit, which used to be kept almost exclusively outdoors in a garden hutch. But since interest in keeping rabbits as pets within the home has grown, manufacturers are now providing equipment intended specifically for house-rabbits, which can be litter-trained in a similar way to cats.

◆ ABOVE
In many parts of the world, cats have become more popular as pets than dogs, thanks to their adaptable natures.

6

◆ BELOW
Pet tortoises have been known to live for over
160 years, but it is impossible to age them reliably
as adults, unless their date of hatching is known.

It is among the herptiles – the reptiles and
amphibians – that the pets with the longest
lifespans are found. Some herptiles look very
spectacular, while others can become very tame.
Invertebrates, too, have grown in popularity over
recent years, thanks in part to the novelty value
of their bizarre appearance. Fish also offer scope,
both for the home aquarium and the garden pond.
Few pets are easier to maintain than the goldfish.

This book has the advantage of allowing you to
compare the needs of pets in different groups, and
also examples within each category. This will help
to ensure that you make the right choice at the
outset, and can expand your interest, perhaps by
taking part in pet shows.

Other small mammals, such as hamsters, guinea
pigs, chinchillas and even rats and mice, are also
becoming better-known among pet-seekers, and
although they are often regarded as children's
pets, there are many enthusiastic breeders of all
ages who keep them for show purposes. This has
helped to ensure there is now an increased range
of colours and varieties to choose from.

The same applies in the case of the budgerigar,
which is also popular both as a pet and outdoor
aviary occupant. An outdoor aviary offers plenty
of scope. If you are interested in gardening
and keeping birds, then you can combine your
interests and construct an attractive planted aviary
where non-destructive birds, such as finches, can
be housed. If you are seeking a talking companion
other than the budgerigar, you could try another
member of the parrot family, but bear in mind
that, just like dogs, parrots are naturally social
and will require a lot of attention if they
are not to become bored and destructive.

◆ RIGHT
Rabbits are a good choice of
pet for older children. They
will not usually bite when
being picked up, although
they may scratch with their
claws if they feel they are
slipping out of your hold.

CATS

Despite its obvious liking for comfort and human company, the domestic
cat has many of the same characteristics as its wild relations. It shares the lithe
muscularity of a body built for stalking and hunting and a fine-furred pelt with
the big roaring cats of jungle and savanna. In fact, there are smaller wild
species that have at times left their feral state to cohabit with humans. At this
level, the boundaries between wildness and domesticity remain fluid.
For although the domestic feline appears to have a smaller brain than its wild
counterpart, if forced by circumstance, it can quite easily revert to the
free-roaming, independent life of a wild predator.

INTRODUCTION

Members of the cat family Felidae range from the great, roaring cats such as the lion and tiger to the small domestic cat. They are separated into different genuses (family sub-divisions), not because of their size but because of differences in their anatomy. These enable members of the genus *Panthera* to roar, while the small cat genus *Felis* cannot do so. Early in the 1900s there were more than 230 species in the cat family, but now there are fewer than 30. Many have become extinct because cats have always been hunted and killed by humans for their fine pelts.

ORIGINS OF DOMESTIC CATS

There is a close relationship between the wild and the domestic cat but it is uncertain which wild sub-species of the *Felis* (small cats) genus actually made the leap into domesticity. Wild cats are widely distributed worldwide and they vary considerably in appearance and habits, but experts generally agree that the most likely wild ancestor of the domestic cat is of European, Asian or African origin.

♦ LEFT AND BELOW
The European wild cat (*left*) was thought to be the ancestor of today's domestic cat because of its tabby markings, but this is now considered unlikely because of its instinctive wariness of people. The more likely contender is the African wild cat (*below*).

THE PATH TO DOMESTICATION

As humans developed agrarian society, based on crops that attracted rodents, kittens were tamed and put to work on the land as a form of pest control.

But it was in ancient Egypt, around 3,500 years ago, that cats were elevated to a status above rodent-catcher. Cats were revered as symbols of fertility and, in some households, they were even mummified in death.

The domesticated cat appeared in the Far East around 2,000 BC, possibly derived from the Asian desert cat. In Europe, the Romans valued cats as symbols of liberty, and they smuggled them from Egypt to their northern conquests to be used for mousing.

In fact, the domestic cat has probably been saved by its abilities as a hunter. With the fall of the Roman Empire the cat lost popularity, and for more than 700 years after the first millennium, cats were associated with witches and evil, and were widely persecuted. The domestic cat found favour once again in the 1600s, but it was not until the 1800s that serious interest was taken, in the form of exhibitions at country fairs and shows.

CAT ANCESTRY

The wild ancestors of today's domestic cat were among the first carnivores that evolved during the late Eocene and early Oligocene periods of pre-history over 35 million years ago. But it was another family of carnivores, the dogs, Canidae, that became the first animal companions of human beings. Stone Age man took advantage of the dog's superior sensory

powers to help him hunt, and this provided a sound basis for an ongoing relationship. It was not until people graduated into a more settled agricultural way of life that cats became part of the domestic scene.

Small feline skeletons have been found in Stone Age archaeological sites, usually with the remains of other small wild animals such as badgers, which suggests that the cats were killed for their meat or pelts. The first evidence of cats actually living in some tentative relationship with humans was found in a New Stone Age site in Jericho in the Middle East, dating from about 9,000 years ago. However, it is unlikely that domestic cats, living in a relationship with humans similar to that of today, emerged until around 3,500 years ago in ancient Egypt.

CLASS MAMMALIA

ORDER HERBIVORA (Herbivores) — ORDER CARNIVORA (Carnivores)

Family Felidae (Cats)

Panthera (roaring cats) including lion, leopard, tiger, snow leopard, jaguar, clouded leopard

Felis (small cats)

Acinonyx (cat with non-retractable claws)

cheetah

Felis manul
Manul[2]

Felis sylvestris libyca (African wild cat[3])
Felis sylvestris sylvestris (European wild cat[1])
and many other small cat species

1 May have bred with the early domesticated cats that reached Europe
2 A possible ancestor of longhaired cats
3 The most likely ancestor of most domestic cats

◆ ABOVE LEFT
The leopard is in a different genus from the small cat not because it is bigger, but because the anatomy of its larynx enables it to roar.

◆ RIGHT
Every member, big and small, of the cat family is built to be an efficient killer. The tiger, the largest of the *Panthera* species, is one of the most powerful predators of all.

The lion is another roaring cat of the genus *Panthera*. However, it is quite clearly in the same family as the domestic cat, with its flexible, muscular body, a typically short, rounded head, and large eyes.

The cheetah is in a separate genus because it has non-retractable claws. However, it is closely related to the puma (also known as the mountain lion or cougar), which can retract its claws.

11

Choosing the
Right Cat

Many households are entirely suitable for a cat, or even a companionable pair of cats, but it is important to consider the effects a cat will have on the household. Although they are known for their independence of character, cats do need care and attention. A normal, healthy cat may live for fourteen years or more, and you need to consider whether you can stand such a long-term responsibility and commitment. Cats may all be roughly the same size and shape, but they vary a great deal in temperament, interests and needs. Before you buy a cat, it is wise to look at your lifestyle and home, and consider the type of cat that will happily fit in with it.

◆ FACING PAGE
Ragdoll kittens like these will grow
into calm, good-natured adults that
enjoy comfort and should adapt
happily to an indoor lifestyle.

◆ LEFT
A lively Ocicat may not be of the
ideal temperament to be confined to
an indoor life.

WHY CHOOSE A CAT?

The cat's adaptability and independence make it a very practical pet for the modern working household. Cats do not have to be taken for walks; they self-clean and self-exercise. Some can happily adjust to a life spent totally indoors in a high-rise apartment. Depending on their character (and breed type if they are purebred), they can also learn to live with other domestic pets. For many people, though, it is the beauty of the cat that is so alluring. A cat on watch at a window, on the prowl or playing in the garden, or simply as a soothing, sleeping presence, is a graceful and rewarding, easy-care asset to the home and family.

THE RIGHT CAT

The choice of cat depends very much on personal preference for a particular type of cat, for long or short fur, or a particular coat colour and pattern.

✦ ABOVE
Cat and bird, as well as dog and cat, are legendary enemies, but it need not be so. Cats can be persuaded to live harmoniously with other domestic pets.

✦ LEFT
A pair of farm kittens on an old tractor wheel look irresistible. They may grow up to be much-loved pets, but will probably also earn their keep as valuable mousers.

A purebred cat with
a pedigree will cost
considerably more to
acquire than a non-
pedigreed animal,
and caring for it may
be a lot more time-
consuming.

A major determining factor is how
much you want to spend. At the top
end of the price scale are cats whose
parents and grandparents can be traced
through long pedigrees back to the late
1800s. At the other end of the scale are
unplanned litters of non-pedigreed cats
which may be picked up for free. In
between are cross-breeds – a random
or deliberate result of a mating between
different breeds, or the unplanned
mating of one pedigreed partner with
a non-pedigree. At a fraction of the
cost of a true pedigree, you could have
a cat with the aristocratic qualities of
its purebred mother and the resilient
health of its father, or vice versa.

Size is not an issue. Unlike dogs,
domestic cats do not vary greatly in
size – there is no feline equivalent of
the Great Dane or the tiny Chihuahua.
Living-space restrictions do not
generally present a problem as cats are
very adaptable. Allowances need to be
made for some active breeds, but most
cats can settle into a small apartment as
happily as into a large house.

THE PEDIGREE OPTION

Buying a purebred dog from a
reputable breeder has long been
accepted. However, it is only
comparatively recently that interest in
pedigreed cats has become established.
Until about 30 years ago, there was a
scarcity of breeders and, with the
exception of Blue Persian and Siamese
breeds, pedigreed cats were not readily

◆ ABOVE
Feral cats can be picked up for free on many
a Mediterranean island, but they need
particularly careful medical attention.

◆ BELOW
The non-pedigree from a known background is
cheap and likely to be balanced of character and
sturdy of health.

available. This situation has been
radically redressed by the cat fancy
(the world of pedigreed cats) being
much more active in its publicity.
The showing and breeding of cats
with a known ancestry has become
a popular hobby, making a much
greater range of breeds available.

A key advantage of buying a
pedigreed kitten from a reputable
breeder is that there are safeguards
woven into the transaction.

OFF THE STREETS

Cats that have been abandoned
by their owners, or that have been
born on the streets, carve a life for
themselves as strays. They revert
to a feral (wild) state, form
colonies with other cats, and breed
prolifically. It is perfectly possible
to adopt a stray or feral cat you
have found on the streets. One
might even adopt you. However,
they have been exposed to a host
of infections and diseases, so
thorough medical examination
and inoculation is particularly
important. You will also need to
spend more time with a stray to
help it bond with you and adjust
to a settled way of life.

LONGHAIR OR SHORTHAIR?

Having a longhaired cat requires you to set aside some time every day to groom it, to keep the coat free from tangles and matting. At the other extreme, the almost hairless Sphynx cat needs extra care as it is very susceptible to temperature change and skin problems.

If you are living in a hot, humid climate, a longhaired cat (even if it sheds its cold-weather coat) is not a wise choice unless it is to live in an air-conditioned home. The coat of a Sphynx does not adapt at all to climatic changes, and the cat would need to be kept in a centrally heated environment in cold winters.

If you are allergic to cats, it will probably make no difference whether you have a longhair or a shorthair. Most human allergies to cats are due to the proteins in the scurf (dander) or in the dried saliva covering the hair.

◆ ABOVE
The Maine Coon Cat is a breed with a semi-longhaired coat, which will not need as much extra care as the long fur of a Persian cat.

◆ BELOW
The fur of the Devon Rex cat is fine and wavy and can be so delicate in places that it is broken just by the cat's own grooming. Grooming should be with a very soft bristled brush.

FUR TYPES

Longhair: soft guardhairs up to 12.5 cm (5 in) long

Semi-longhair: soft guardhairs varying between 5 cm (2 in) and 10 cm (4 in) long

Shorthair: maximum about 5 cm (2 in) long

Hairless: suede-like coat with no guardhairs

Curly hair: short, soft, often delicate fur with rippled effect

Wirehair: short, bristly coat

BODY TYPES

Cobby: short-legged, stocky body; round, flattish face with small ears, such as the Persian

Muscular: sturdy, medium to compact build; medium length legs and tail; round face, medium ears, such as the American Shorthair

Oriental: long, lithe body; long, slender legs and tail; wedge-shaped face; large, pointed ears, such as the Siamese

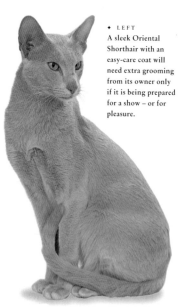

◆ LEFT
A sleek Oriental Shorthair with an easy-care coat will need extra grooming from its owner only if it is being prepared for a show – or for pleasure.

◆ RIGHT
This Persian cat has a splendid long coat that requires a lot of attention. If it lived in a hot climate, however, it would not develop such a full "show" coat.

GENDER AND AGE

If cats are neutered (altered), there is little difference in behavioural terms between a male and a female. However, a neutered male may be a little more indolent than a female. If you already have a cat in your home, it may be worth going for the opposite sex in your new cat. The established resident is more likely to defend its territory aggressively against a cat of the same sex.

Once sexual urges have been quelled by the neutering process, cats are likely to exhibit their true breed characteristics more strongly. The Siamese cat's attachment to its owner is accentuated, for example, and the Persian becomes even more placid and comfort-loving.

Male cats are generally larger than females. On average, a full-grown, neutered male cat tends to be a little heavier than an entire male, with an average weight of between 5 and 7.5 kg (11–16½ lb). Females are usually about 1 kg (2.2 lb) lighter. The largest pedigreed variety is the Maine Coon Cat from the north-eastern United States. Male Maine Coons have been

RIGHT
A kitten will adapt to your lifestyle more readily than an older cat, simply because it has not yet fully developed its mature character.

known to reach about 10–12.5 kg (22–27½ lb) in weight. The smallest, or most dainty breed is the Singapura (the "drain cat" of Singapore) at about 2.7 kg (6 lb), but breeders take care to make certain that their cats fall within the minimum weight range to ensure successful breeding.

ABOVE
Male cats are usually bigger than their female equivalents, although if they have been neutered (altered), they may be a little more indolent.

CHOOSING AN ADULT CAT

It can be easier to give a new home to an older cat than to a kitten. This is especially so if the cat is obtained from a major welfare source which has carried out rigorous health checks. (With a kitten from a private home, the onus of the initial health checks is usually left to you.) An older animal will be more settled in its ways and certainly have an established temperament. A poor temperament due to the cat coming from an environment where it was unhappy, can improve with changed circumstances, but you do not have the fresh start you would have with a kitten. Male cats that have only recently been neutered (altered) may carry some battle scars from their fighting days, but this is a purely aesthetic consideration.

RIGHT
Although the Singapura may have evolved into one of the smallest breeds because of its tough background on the streets of Singapore, it is a sturdy animal.

ABOVE
Deciding to take in an adult cat that you have found in a cat sanctuary or home may save the animal from being humanely put to sleep, and it will soon learn to be content in its new, welcoming environment.

WHERE TO FIND A PEDIGREED CAT

Some breeders advertise in local newspapers. This is a rather hit-and-miss source as there are no guarantees that they are reputable. Some unscrupulous breeders produce kittens of the most popular breeds purely for profit. They may show little concern for either the future welfare of the offspring, or for the breed as a whole.

A far better idea is to ask at your local veterinary surgery or clinic for information on those in the area who specialize in various breeds. Often, if one breeder has no kittens available at the time you want one, he or she will recommend another. Some breeders operate on a large scale and have big catteries, while others are "front parlour" breeders, who may be interested in breeding from just one pet queen. Either can be a good source; the best way to find out about them is by recommendation via a vet

or a local breed club. It is also valuable to visit cat shows well before you actually buy. Here you will find enthusiastic owners and breeders who will explain the advantages and disadvantages of their favourite breeds and let you know of available stock. Find out about cat shows from one of the specialist cat magazines.

♦ ABOVE
The charms of a pedigreed kitten are displayed by these two White Persians. If you want information about where to buy cats like this, the best place to start is the breed club.

♦ BELOW
The Supreme Show is where you can see the best examples of all the pedigreed breeds in the United Kingdom. There are cat shows in most countries at breed club, local and national levels.

VISITING THE BREEDER

Some breeders house their animals in an outside cattery, others within their homes. A reputable breeder will not hesitate to allow a prospective owner to visit. The advantage of the house-reared litter is that the kittens are socialized earlier. They have greater contact with day-to-day noise, humans, and perhaps other animals such as dogs. On the other hand, the disinfection and restricted contact routine of a first-rate cattery reduces the risk of disease and infection. Kittens from a good cattery will be handled and socialized, but this process cannot be as complete as if they were raised within the home. Beware of the unscrupulous cattery owner rearing kittens solely for financial gain. Conditions can often be substandard.

Usually, you need to make an appointment to see and select from a litter of kittens, but it is also possible to book a kitten in advance of delivery if you are drawn to a particular cat. By visiting the breeder, you can assess the general environment and conditions in which the kittens have been brought up in the first few vital weeks of their lives. If you ask the right questions and see the rest of the litter, the mother, and possibly the father, you will be able to build up a complete picture of the kitten's heritage – its breeding line; how long its relatives have lived; how big it is likely to grow; what it will look like as an adult. In addition, you can lay the foundations of an ongoing relationship with the breeder, who, if reputable, will be available for advice and help in the years to come.

A pedigreed kitten will not usually leave its breeder's home until it is twelve to fourteen weeks old. By

this time it should be properly house-trained, inoculated and used to being handled. If it has been brought up in a family environment, it may already be happy with dogs and children. But if it has not been in an ideal environment, it may have difficulties bonding with a new owner. In this case (and with a non-pedigreed kitten only) it may adapt more easily if it is taken away at seven or eight weeks.

A kitten ready for handing over to a new owner should have been gently weaned and introduced to a suitable diet of fresh, canned and dry foods. It should have been registered with one or more of the many registering bodies worldwide and the registration documents and pedigree

should be ready to take away. There may also be a health insurance policy that lasts about six weeks – enough time to let the new kitten settle into its new home.

The cost of a pedigreed kitten depends very much on the breed; seek guidelines from the individual breed clubs. It is possible to spend a great deal of money on rare, new varieties while the well-established, popular varieties are less expensive. Kittens of show quality are priced more highly than those of lesser quality.

♦ BELOW
Kittens being prepared to leave their breeders for a new home. If they have become used to a friendly family environment from birth, they should settle down quickly.

SELECTING A HEALTHY ANIMAL

A kitten from a responsible breeder will have had trips to the vet for inoculations against cat flu, feline infectious enteritis, and possibly chlamydia and feline leukaemia. It will have been wormed and its coat will be free from parasites (such as fleas) and fungal lesions (ringworm).

The queen passes on natural immunity to the diseases to which she is herself immune, through colostrum (first milk) during the kitten's first few days of life. This immunity is effective until the kitten is six to ten weeks of age, when it must be replaced by the artificially acquired immunity provided by inoculations. Before the age of eight or nine weeks, it is best not to interfere with the immunity acquired from the mother.

It is not advisable to take the kitten home before inoculations start if you have other cats. They might be carriers of feline diseases to which the mother of the kitten is not immune

◆ ABOVE
You may be tempted to buy both of these kittens. They have grown up together so are likely always to be friendly. They will enjoy playing together – and you will enjoy watching them. Make sure both are neutered, however!

◆ BELOW
At nine weeks old these non-pedigreed kittens could be taken from their birth home. However, some cat associations recommend they are left until 12 weeks, after the first vaccination course has finished.

and against which, therefore, the kitten has no protection. The certificate from the vet confirming first or complete vaccination carries with it the important implication that the cat is in good health – otherwise the inoculation would not have been administered.

WHAT TO LOOK FOR

The prospective owner can make his or her own immediate checks when selecting a kitten. If you are able to view the entire litter, look for the individuals with evenness of growth and solidity of muscle tone. Male kittens may already be showing a larger skeletal frame than the females. The kittens will be heavy for their size, and their spines should be well-fleshed and not feel ridged and bony.

If you see the litter shortly after feeding the kittens will probably be sleepy, but if they are inclined to play you can assess sociability. Frightened, unsociable kittens rush to hide and show fear and displeasure with trembling, bad language or claws – or maybe all three at once! The sociable but sleepy kitten purrs and almost certainly demands that its tummy is tickled. The playful kitten in good health has stamina and a spring in its step. It is alert and may already be displaying intelligence and leadership in play. Rather than you doing the choosing, a particular kitten may well choose you, inviting you to play, and ending up going to sleep on your lap.

The kitten's nose leather should be naturally slightly warm and a little damp. It should not be hot and dry, or have any discoloured discharge from the nostrils. Breathing should be deep and natural with no rasping or snorting. Eyes should be clean and bright with no discharge, tears, staining or redness. The mouth should show nice light-pink gums with no furring to the tongue or ulceration. Ears should be clean and free of wax.

COAT INDICATORS

Clean kitten fur has a lively feel with a warm, naturally wholesome scent, with no evidence of parasites, rough patches or lesions. The most common ectoparasite is the flea, which leaves gritty, granular droppings. Typical sites for these droppings are just above the base of the tail, between the shoulder blades, under the chin and in the armpits. Excessive infestation of fleas may cause a lack of liveliness, and also indicate that the animal may be worm-infested.

Signs of worm infestation are commonly a staring, harsh coat and a bloated abdomen. In severe cases, the kitten may show signs of anaemia and

♦ ABOVE
This Chocolate Silver Tabby Ocicat not only has fine tabby markings, but his clear, bright eyes suggest he is in peak health.

diarrhoea. Check under the tail for staining or signs of soreness, which indicate diarrhoea.

CHECKING AN ADULT CAT

The health check for the older cat is much the same. You need to check that male cats have been neutered (altered). If this has happened recently, they may show some battle scars, but this will only affect their appearance. The most likely place for wear and tear to show is in the mouth. Teeth may be missing or broken, and the gums may show signs of disease, but this can be treated by your vet, who may advise home dental care.

Whatever the age of the kitten or older cat you are thinking of buying, however sweet and charming it is, if you have any doubts about its health, and especially if you have other cats, do not take it home with you.

♦ BELOW
A confident stride, intelligent interest and a perky tail indicate that this 15-week-old Ocicat is a cat of sociable, playful character.

Creating the Right Environment

The domestic life is one in which a pet cat can feel secure in the knowledge of where the next meal is coming from. If you also provide an exciting and stimulating environment in which it can rest comfortably and where there are opportunities to climb and play, your cat will be a well-adjusted and rewarding companion. The financial outlay of buying the right equipment for your cat may seem high, but it is the first step in ensuring it leads a contented life.

◆ FACING PAGE
Cats may be independent and perfectly able to survive without humans, but as this ginger cat shows, they adapt well to a warm home and loving care.

◆ LEFT
A non-pedigreed cat sports his new flea collar.

SETTLING IN

Acquiring a cat should not be contemplated on a whim but with an awareness of the animal's continuing needs throughout its life in your home. Thoughtful preparation and planning before a new cat arrives is essential if the transition between old home and new is to be stress-free for both you and your pet. A cat needs time and space in which to adjust, and will settle down more easily, too, if all the right equipment is there when it arrives.

FORWARD PLANNING

This will be a new and strange environment for your cat, so before you collect it, check its diet with the breeder or cattery so that you know what it likes to eat and drink and can have some food ready.

The journey itself may be the first time in a kitten's short life that it has no other feline company. Even an older cat can be disorientated. While

travelling, talk to the animal in a calm voice. Do not be tempted to let it out of its carrier (in a car, for example) unless you have a companion with you who can restrain it.

THE ARRIVAL

A new arrival is a novelty and family and friends will want to be introduced, to stroke and play with the cat, especially if it is a kitten. This exciting time makes particular demands on

+ TOP
The first sortie in the new home. The cage should be kept to hand so that the kittens can be put back in it until they become used to their new environment, and any other animals in the home can be surveyed from the safety of the pen.

+ ABOVE
A young ginger cat has settled happily in the cat basket. A favourite blanket brought with it from its first home is an additional comfort.

+ LEFT
A Siamese half-breed kitten explores the new home. It is important to let kittens explore in their own time, but supervision is advisable in case they become stuck or locked in a cupboard.

EQUIPMENT CHECKLIST

Not all the following are essential; those that are, are in heavy type.

+ **bed and bedding**
+ **litter and litter tray (pan)**
+ **2 food bowls**
+ **water bowl**
+ **carrier**
+ collar
+ harness and lead
+ identity tag
+ cat flap

◆ RIGHT
Gradual, supervised introductions over the course of a few weeks have enabled this Irish Wolfhound and Chinchilla to feel at ease with each other. However, such close proximity would not be advisable with a pet mouse!

◆ BELOW RIGHT
Kittens will quickly seek out the most comfortable places to relax; if you do not want them in your bed, you need to keep the door shut!

children who, without realizing the implications, may treat the new animal like a toy. However, try to make sure there are not many people around when the new arrival is introduced. It is tempting to rush straight into the living room and let the cat out of the carrier. Instead, take it immediately to where its litter tray (pan), sleeping space, food and water bowls are going to be permanently positioned. Such items are part of a familiar routine, which will be comforting. A drink and a little food may be all that is wanted.

EXTENDING TERRITORY

A kitten will want to explore and take in all the new sensory experiences of this new environment. It must be allowed to do this in its own time, and if that means that it wants to scurry about under a kitchen cupboard, out of sight, so be it. Eventually it will emerge and continue its exploration. Allow the kitten to do this at leisure. However, supervision is wise, in case it becomes locked in a cupboard or stuck on a high shelf. Handle the cat calmly and gently. Over-enthusiastic handling

can be very disorientating and may bring out the defence mechanisms. Being bitten or scratched does not endear anyone to a new pet, but from the kitten's point of view it was probably justified. By all means stroke the cat as it passes and talk to it. The reassurance of the human voice helps bridge the gap between old and new

homes. When a new cat is tired, it will probably find its bed on its own and it should be left to sleep undisturbed. Cats and kittens sleep more than any other mammal on a daily basis and, for a kitten, adequate sleep maintains and encourages the assimilation of food and enhances correct growth.

If you already have another cat or a dog, confine the new arrival to a small area at first – or even a cage – so that it can get used to where its food, water and litter are in peace, and the animals can adjust to one another in their own time. A cage in the kitchen or living room will provide security for the new arrival and quickly allow it to adjust to any other animals in the household and vice versa.

If you have a baby in the house, it is a good idea to put a cat net over the pram or cot. A cat is unlikely to harm the baby, but could be attracted to a warm, sleeping body and may want to curl up alongside it.

HANDLING AND HOLDING YOUR CAT

If you watch a mother cat, you will see how she picks up a tiny kitten by taking hold of the loose skin at the back of the neck and gently lifting. The kitten then demonstrates one of its inborn reflexes, which is to curl up into an apparently lifeless ball. It will not move until its mother puts it down. This loose skin, which becomes far less apparent as the kitten grows, is the scruff or nap. The action of picking up a cat in such a way is called scruffing. While it is possible to lift your cat in this way, scruffing should normally only be considered if absolutely necessary – if instant control is required, for example, when the cat is at the veterinary surgery. For less flexible adult cats especially, it can be an unnerving experience, particularly as they freeze when scruffed.

It is far better to pick up your kitten or cat by placing one hand under the chest, supporting the

♦ LEFT
An established resident cat has become accustomed to a new arrival, and the two now provide extra warmth for each other.

backside with the other hand and then lifting. In this way the animal feels completely secure, with no limbs left dangling. This total support technique is essential if you are holding the cat for any length of time. As you and your cat become more confident, you can try different holds. Avoid tucking

the cat under your arm with its body, back legs and tail dangling like a ragdoll. This leaves most of its weight unsupported and puts a great strain on the internal organs. Many cats do not like being held for too long, and should be gently let down if they start to wriggle.

♦ RIGHT
Avoid surprising the cat when you are about to lift it. When it is relaxed, support the top of the hind legs with one hand and the chest with the other.

♦ FAR RIGHT
When holding or carrying a cat, keep the back end and legs supported. If the cat starts to wriggle, let it down gently; never force it to be held against its will, unless it is necessary.

BEDS AND BEDDING

During the initial settling-in period, a new kitten or cat should be able to settle down within easy reach of both litter tray (pan) and water. A simple cardboard box placed in a draught-proof spot with an old pillow and blanket is ideal. Then, if there are accidents, or if the cat's bedding becomes parasite-infested, everything can be burnt and little is lost.

Acrylic bedding is widely available, hygienic and easily laundered. Woollen materials, particularly if knitted, are not suitable as claws may become caught. Some cats seem also to be addicted to wool-sucking and chewing and this can cause congestion in the throat or digestive system.

Once the new arrival has settled in, you may want to provide a permanent bed. This can be made of wicker, moulded plastic or padded fabric, but it must be easy to wash and disinfect. Any bedding should be changed regularly. Very soon a collection of cushion beds, old jumpers, carpet-covered houses and other oddities will be adopted. Place these strategically where the cat likes to sleep at different times of the day.

◆ ABOVE
A cat is not fussy about the design of its bed. The advantage of a cardboard box is that if it becomes soiled or worn out, it can be easily replaced.

◆ LEFT
The owner's bed is often a favourite spot, especially if it has comfortable quilts and cushions.

◆ LEFT AND RIGHT
There is now such a range of pet beds available that you can choose one to match your decor. Whether you go for an enclosed, draughtproof and portable model or an open version, the easy-to-wash factor is the most important consideration.

LITTER AND LITTER TRAY

A kitten or cat needs access to a litter tray (pan) if it is not able to go outside when it wants to. The tray may become redundant once a kitten is fully immunized and has learnt to use its cat flap into the garden, although it is preferable to encourage your cat to stay in at night. Even when very young, kittens are inherently clean and will not soil their bed. If a cage or crate is being used during the settling-in period, it should be large enough to contain a litter tray.

There is a wide range of products available, from basic plastic trays to covered models with entrance flaps and filters to minimize odour. The key point about litter trays is that they must be easy to clean, and tough enough to withstand frequent washing and disinfecting. They should also be in a position that is easy to clean. Toxoplasmosis is an infection that can

◆ LEFT
The most important consideration when buying a litter tray (pan) is that it should be easy to clean. Use a scoop to remove faeces independently, rather than changing all the litter in the tray every time.

scrape the litter over any faeces deposited, which is does instinctively. Sawdust, woodshavings, cinders, ash and newspapers are not advised; nor are some pine-wood products that can be irritants.

◆ BELOW
The ultimate litter tray (pan) is not only draughtproof and private for the coy cat, but helps contain odours.

◆ ABOVE, LEFT TO RIGHT
Clay, wood and paper-based litters: some are highly absorbent, others are superfine and form clumps when wet.

be shed in a cat's faeces without the cat showing any signs of disease. It is, however, a hazard to humans, especially pregnant women. Disposal of faeces less than 24 hours after passing, and regular cleaning of litter trays with plenty of water and detergent, is effective in the control of toxoplasmosis. Some household products contain ingredients, which, although fine for use in the home, can be toxic to cats. The staff at your vet's should be able to advise on these.

LITTER OPTIONS

The various litter products available should be acceptable to the cat, reduce odour and absorb urine. It should also be easy for the cat to

◆ ABOVE
Kittens are instinctively clean. This feral kitten was abandoned by its mother and when a litter tray (pan) was provided, automatically began to use it after being shown it once.

FEEDING EQUIPMENT

If you already have perfectly suitable dishes, special purchases may not be necessary. The most practical choices are made of hard plastic, ceramic or stainless steel. All equipment should be easy to clean and disinfect. Discard cracked or chipped ceramic bowls, as germs may be harboured in the cracks. Once any container, new or old, has been allotted to the cat, it should not be used for anything else. Many people feed their cats in the kitchen; if there are dogs around, it is also likely that the cat is fed on

TOXOPLASMOSIS

Toxoplasmosis affects many animals but cats are the only ones that shed the parasite in their faeces. This only happens for a short time after the cat has become infected and the faeces are only infectious after 24 hours or more. In most cases there are no visible signs of disease or illness in the cat. The infection is carried in the cat's faeces and in 24–48 hours can pass on to humans. Unless their immune system is not functioning properly, humans contracting the infection are unlikely to become ill, but if a pregnant woman is infected, there is a 40 per cent chance that her baby will also be infected. Of these infected babies, 15 per cent may spontaneously abort or acquire some abnormality.

◆ Wear gloves when gardening in an area frequented by cats

◆ Cover children's play areas, such as sand-pits, when not in use

◆ Empty litter trays (pans) on a daily basis and clean regularly with plenty of water and detergent

◆ Use a separate set of feeding equipment for the cat and do not use it for humans; clean regularly

◆ ABOVE, LEFT TO RIGHT FROM TOP LEFT
The cutlery for serving the cat should be exclusively for this purpose; plastic lids to cover unfinished tins prevent the food from drying up and the smell from spreading; a simple plastic bowl; a metal bowl; a plastic combined water and food bowl; an automatic feeder.

a working surface. In either case it is especially important to maintain strict standards of hygiene to guard against the risk of toxoplasmosis (see box). The feeding area must be easy to clean and disinfect regularly. This is also important for the cat because it has a highly developed sense

of smell and will reject food that has become tainted and hardened. For the same reasons, put down fresh water at least once a day. A closed-off eating area is advisable if you have crawling babies or toddlers.

For the busy owner whose lifestyle makes feeding the cat at regular times uncertain, automatic food bowls with timer switches are available. The cover automatically lifts to reveal food at pre-set times. A water bowl is kept topped up with water from a reservoir, but you do need to remember to change the reservoir frequently.

◆ RIGHT
It is more hygienic to put your cat's food on the floor rather than on a working surface where food is prepared for humans.

CARRIERS

It is essential to buy, rather than borrow, a cat carrier. You will need it not only to bring the cat or kitten home, but also for visits to the veterinary surgery – and anywhere else for that matter. Any visit to the vet will quickly reveal that very many owners have great faith in their pets' ability not to escape! They arrive with all sorts of contraptions for carrying their cats; sometimes with nothing at all to restrain an animal which may be in pain, very frightened and, invariably, highly stressed.

SIZE CONSIDERATIONS
Do not be seduced into buying a sweet, kitten-sized carrier; consider the future and purchase accordingly.

◆ ABOVE
Large cat carriers provide plenty of room for your cat and can double up as pens for the settling-in period. They are, however, awkward to carry.

◆ LEFT
A top-loading wicker basket which could double as the cat's permanent bed.

That cute little fur-ball is going to turn into a considerably larger adult. A carrier of around 30 cm x 30 cm x 55 cm (12 in x 12 in x 22 in) should last into the cat's adulthood. For an extra-large male, it might be wise to go to the next size up. Cats prefer to be in a fairly snug environment if they are experiencing a rare and disturbing event such as travelling, but they do need to be able to turn around and stretch out a little. They also like to be able to see out so that they feel a little less trapped.

If the journey is going to be a long one (over an hour or two), have a carrier that can take a small litter tray (pan) as well as clip-on water and food bowls. However, if you are likely to have to carry the cat very far, for example when attending shows, remember the larger the carrier, the more awkward it is to carry. Strained shoulders and backs are not uncommon among exhibitors.

♦ BELOW
An easy-to-clean plastic container that might
cause loading and unloading difficulties.

♦ BELOW
A collapsible cardboard carrier that can be
dispensed with after being used to carry an
infectious animal.

WHAT IS AVAILABLE

Basic cardboard carriers, preferably coated with plastic, are bought flatpacked, and, when assembled, are suitable for transporting a sick and possibly infectious animal, as they are inexpensive and can be burnt after use. However, they are not suitable for more regular use as they cannot be cleaned and disinfected effectively, and are not durable. Traditionalists choose wickerwork baskets, which come in various shapes, and usually have leather straps and a handle. These are attractive and could double as the cat's permanent sleeping quarters – at least the cat would be less likely to panic if travelling in its own bed.

Openwork wire baskets, especially with the wire covered with white plastic, have veterinary approval because they are so easy to disinfect and the cat is easily visible. The top opening is secured by a separate rod pushed through rigid loops. Moulded plastic carriers with strategically placed ventilation holes are available in a great range of designs, are easy to dismantle for thorough cleaning, and

reassembling is no problem either. Clear moulded plastic (Perspex) carriers with airholes are a less worthwhile investment as the plastic tends to crack and degrade over time. If carried in sunlight, its occupant can quickly overheat.

The most practical designs are those with top access; they are less stressful both for cat and handler.

The cat can be grasped from above and removed without a struggle. With a front-loading carrier, the often frightened animal has to be recovered from the back of a tunnel. It can also be difficult to put the cat back inside.

♦ BELOW
If you want your cat carrier to look distinctive
or decorative, you could paint it with an
appropriate design.

COLLARS, HARNESSES AND LEADS

A collar is not necessarily merely decorative. A tag may be attached to it so that the cat can be identified if it gets lost or injured. An identity tag may be a simple engraved disc or a screw-topped cylinder containing a roll of paper with the cat's name, owner's address and telephone number, and sometimes the vet's emergency number. Magnetic tags that allow your cat exclusive entry to its cat flap can also be fitted on collars.

Most collars come with a bell, which rings when the cat moves and will reduce the death toll among garden birds and other potential hunting targets. Some collars are impregnated with an anti-flea substance, but keep a careful check on your cat when you first put one on it, as they can cause an allergic reaction. Signs of irritation around the neck or eyes are the main indications of allergy. A flea collar should never be combined with any other form of flea control.

Collars have two main disadvantages. If worn continuously, as they should be if they are carrying any form of identification, they will damage the fur around the neck,

◆ BELOW
A soft collar with a bell attached will help you find your cat, and will drastically reduce its hunting successes by warning birds of its presence.

◆ ABOVE
A soft, padded flea collar with a bell and an elastic section. Flea collars should only be used on cats over six months old. They may cause an allergic reaction in some cats.

◆ ABOVE
A soft leather collar with the all-important elastic section. Any collar you buy should have this, for if the collar is caught the elastic will stretch, allowing the cat to escape unharmed.

◆ ABOVE
Fabric collars, which can be cut to size without fraying, are useful for kittens and small cats. They are cheap enough to be changed regularly, or even to have a selection of different colours.

especially that of longhaired cats. This can be unsightly and is considered unacceptable by many exhibitors; although most show judges realize the reason for marks around the neck, they may still penalize the cat. Secondly, there is always the fear that the collar can become caught when the cat is hunting in trees or shrubs. However, if it is made of soft leather, suede, or soft fabric and has an elasticated insert, this will stretch if the collar catches, and the cat will be able to free itself. The collar should always be adjusted so that it will slip over the cat's head in an emergency, but not loose enough to allow the front leg to slip through and the collar to lodge under the armpit, which could cause injury.

GOING FOR A WALK

Cat leads are only necessary if you intend to take your cat for walks or if you are taking it to a strange house and need to keep it under control. Some cats actively enjoy this, particularly Siamese. It is not unusual to see this breed travelling on public transport on a lead. However, most cats are naturally resistant to wearing any such controlling apparatus and will fight against it, especially if they become frightened. To take them on a bus or train on a lead rather than in a carrier is foolhardy under any

circumstances. If the cat panics, it could either become tangled and hurt itself, or escape. If a lead is worn on a more suitable outing, it should be no more than 1 m (3 ft) long, and have a fitted harness rather than a collar for attachment. This not only allows more control and comfort, but is more secure. Cats are great escapologists, however, and even the most carefully fitted harness may prove insecure.

Introduce your cat to a harness and lead as early as possible. Put the harness on first by itself, and just for a short time each day. After you have done this for a few days, attach the lead for a short time, several days running, but just leave it trailing. When the cat seems relaxed about the lead, try walking it, first indoors for brief spells, then in the garden, and then in a street where the cat can get used to traffic and people, but do not overdo it!

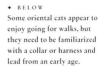

◆ LEFT
Magnetic tags double as a means of identity and a "key" to enable the wearer to go through its cat flap.

◆ BELOW
Some oriental cats appear to enjoy going for walks, but they need to be familiarized with a collar or harness and lead from an early age.

◆ LEFT
Identity tags can be simple metal discs engraved with the owner's name and telephone number, or an information-packed barrel containing the owner's address and the vet's address and emergency telephone number.

EXTRAS AND TOYS

Play for a young cat is just as essential for its well-being as it is for a human child. It is particularly important for the owner to play with the cat if it is the only one in the household. Through play, muscles are exercised and conditioned, the brain is kept alert and the eyes bright. And if the owner joins in, it strengthens the bond between the feline and its adopted human family.

At the very least your cat should have a scratching post, which it can be encouraged to use instead of the furniture and soft furnishings. A cat will naturally use surfaces such as the bark of a tree to sharpen and control the length of its claws – they are its main means of defence, and also provide grip when climbing. You can make an indoor scratching post yourself by binding a stout fence post with heavy-duty sisal string or cotton rope, and attaching it to a suitable base. A strip of old carpet is an alternative, but this is not as effective for the cat, as it frays quickly, creates a great deal of fluff, and needs to be

renewed regularly. If you do not mind your cat equipment taking over the home, feline climbing frames of varying size and complexity are readily available. Some are over 2 m (6 ft) high, with circular supports covered in sisal rope, carpet-covered perches, houses and barrels. They are likely to be found at cat shows, or through advertisements in specialist cat magazines and larger pet stores.

PLAY WITH A PURPOSE

A cat's play is orientated to the hunting process. When a cat swoops after a leaf in autumn, that leaf is an imaginary bird. The ping-pong ball just visible behind a chair leg is a mouse to be stalked, pounced upon and batted around. The screwed-up paper hurled into the air, caught and thrown away to be chased and sent flying again, is being

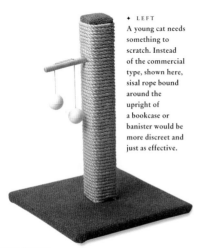

♦ LEFT
A young cat needs something to scratch. Instead of the commercial type, shown here, sisal rope bound around the upright of a bookcase or banister would be more discreet and just as effective.

♦ ABOVE
Being ten months old does not mean that this youngster has grown out of shredding curtains for fun.

♦ BELOW
Kittens enjoy playing with someone, especially if they are an only cat; they will soon become bored playing on their own with a ball.

◆ LEFT
The perfect combination for a family cat –
company, care, attention, and a game that seems
to be tailor-made for cats. Be careful of any
electrical connections, though.

hunted. Even in an apparently sterile
environment, a cat will find a scrap
of paper, a lost button, or a shadow to
play with. However, do be careful of
everyday household objects like the
odd button or needle and thread.
Swallowed thread can do even more
damage than a needle as it cheesewires
its way through the bowel.

Do check that any cat toys you
buy are reasonably solid. Some cheap
imported toys may have small plastic
bits that could fall off and be
swallowed. Some plastic materials that
are safe for children can be toxic to
cats. All that is needed can be found in
the home: paper scrunched into a ball
and thrown by the owner for retrieval
up and down the stairs; a paper
"butterfly" tied to a piece of string
and dragged around for the cat to
chase, or suspended from the back
of a chair to bat. Some cats are
particularly fond of hide-and-seek.
For group play, nothing is better than
the great game of the ping-pong ball
rolled around the carpet between
family members and friends, and
pursued by your cat.

◆ BELOW
A clockwork mouse is a poor
substitute for the real thing,
as it has to be wound up, but
it is less messy
for the
owner.

◆ RIGHT
You will probably need a continuing
supply of replacement balls as they are
constantly being batted out of sight.

◆ ABOVE
Cats are nature's most efficient predators: a
fabric mouse filled with delectable catnip may
not last long in the grip of this young Ocicat.

◆ RIGHT
Here's a soft, friendly chap to dig your claws
into. Let's hope the bear's eyes are well secured
so that the kitten does not swallow them.

Care at Home and Away

A cat instinctively knows its physical limits; it can also, through learned behaviour and training, avoid potentially dangerous situations. The wise owner strikes a balance between giving the cat the freedom it needs, being aware of the dangers it could face, and protecting it from them.

◆ FACING PAGE
A mother introduces one of her kittens to the outside world. She will teach it survival and hunting skills.

◆ ABOVE
A well-cared-for ginger and white non-pedigree is completely relaxed at home and away.

CONTROLLING A CAT'S TERRITORY

If you live in an apartment block or in a busy urban environment, or your cat is frail or a valuable pedigree, it is perfectly feasible – and acceptable to most cats – to keep it indoors all the time. In some parts of the United States, vets actively recommend this for cats in urban environments.

Because of the balanced pet foods now available, modern cats do not need to go out to supplement their diet by hunting. Outdoor exercise is also unnecessary, as long as the owner provides toys and plays with the cat.

Although cats are nocturnal by nature, it is really unwise to allow much-loved pets to stay out at night. Train them to stay in from an early age and make sure there is always a clean litter tray (pan) available. This training also ensures that they are equally happy if kept indoors for long periods.

The outdoor cat's tendency to roam and exposure to the dangers of traffic, fighting and infection from other cats, can be reduced at a snip – that is, by being neutered (altered). The sex-drive of a calling queen or an active

♦ ABOVE
A Burmese is attracted to the outside world. Some cats are freedom-loving and do not like being kept indoors.

♦ RIGHT
A ginger kitten has taken over the best armchair. An indoor cat needs plenty of toys and active input from its owner if it is not to become bored and substitute the upholstery for a tree.

THE MAKING OF AN INDOOR CAT

The consultant, a breeder of Maine Coon Cats, does not let his cats out until they are well over six months old – two to three months after they have been neutered (altered). The cats are trained to litter trays (pans) and so, when they are eventually let out, it is not long before they rush back in to use their usual toilet facilities. Because they are neutered (altered), their hunting and roaming instinct is greatly curtailed and they seldom stray beyond their familiar garden.

♦ LEFT
A Persian has the comfort-loving temperament suited to an indoor life, and its long coat is easier to care for inside.

tom cat will override any considerations for road safety. The unneutered male cat can hunt over an area of about 11 km (7 miles). His desexed counterparts will probably exercise territorial rights over maybe 200 m (217 yds) at most.

DANGERS IN THE HOME

There are dangers even for the cat that is kept indoors all the time. Those who live in high-rise buildings should erect netting across open windows and around balconies. The defences can be camouflaged by plants. Even within the house, cats should be allowed access to heights only if they are considered safe. A specific danger area is a staircase with openwork bannisters from which a kitten could launch itself into space – not necessarily landing on its feet. Kittens should be supervised as they explore.

THE ALLURE OF MACHINES

The warmth, the smells and the movement of washing and drying machines attract a cat's attention. Always make sure that the appliance's doors are kept closed when not in use. Before you turn the machine on, check that there is no cat curled inside. The smell of food in a fridge is also enticing. At least if it were to be inadvertently incarcerated, a cat would survive there for some time, as long as there was sufficient air available. It would not, however, survive for long in a freezer. Fifteen minutes would probably be long enough to cause irreversible hypothermia.

PLAYING WITH FIRE

Burns and scalds, sustained by cats exploring the source of interesting food smells, are not unusual and are sometimes very severe. Cats have been known to dance across the hot rings of an electric cooker, badly damaging their paws.

Electric cables are potential playthings, so make sure no wires are loose or exposed, and if you spot your cat chewing them, conceal the cables beneath a carpet, or cover them with a catproof material such as thick, loose rubber or plastic tubing. A cat will nose around drawers and boxes packed with interesting oddments – but here too, are potential dangers such as pins and paper clips. Tasty, pingy elastic bands may be fun to pick at and chew, but could cause choking and suffocation, and the same goes for lengths of wool or cotton, or plastic film. Cats are also attracted to olives, the stones of which are just the right size to become stuck in a feline throat. Open fireplaces should always be guarded, even when a fire is not lit, for cats like climbing up chimneys and may become stuck or break a limb, or at the very least emerge soot-covered. Electric and gas fires can be equally dangerous. One cat owner was faced with a fire in her living room and some very frightened kittens, after the combined weight of the litter of kittens toppled a highly flammable chair against the bars of a gas fire.

◆ LEFT
A very cosy scene for mother and kitten – however, open fires should always be kept guarded unless you are in the room to keep an eye on your cat.

◆ ABOVE
The washing machine has just been turned off and is still warm, making it a possible spot to curl up in for an undisturbed sleep.

◆ ABOVE
The deliberate leap from the table is well within this cat's capability, but a kitten could hurt itself if it fell or jumped from such a height.

ACCESS TO THE OUTSIDE WORLD

It always used to be common practice to put the house cat out at night, so that it could carry out its rodent extermination duties, and to avoid mess in the house. Effective rodent control and the availability of litter trays (pans) have made this unnecessary. Now a cat's freedom is more likely to be dependent upon human work patterns. However, unless you have pedigreed cats which you keep for exhibition and show, or your living space necessitates an indoor lifestyle, you can allow your pet various degrees of access to the outside world.

Some cats automatically confine their territories to the back garden. Others may develop an awareness of the traffic in their area, and avoid rush hours, for example. However, it is difficult to be sure of their abilities, and even quiet streets can be dangerous because of the occasional,

unexpected vehicle. For these reasons, and the risks of territorial fighting and exposure to infection, it is worth exercising some form of control over your cat's freedom to roam.

♦ ABOVE
A Brown Burmese selects a high vantage point from which to survey the surrounding territory.

♦ LEFT
A cat will soon learn to use its cat flap with confidence. The flap swings shut when the cat has passed through.

CAT FLAPS

Cat flaps are cat-sized windows that are fitted about 15 cm (6 in) from the base of a door. The most practical design is one that is gravity-loaded so that the door automatically closes after entry or exit, and with a clear plastic window so that the cat can look through it before venturing outside.

Flaps are a boon to the indoor/outdoor cat that is not afraid of operating the flap and whose owners are not always home to obey the cat's every whim. They allow both cat and owner a degree of independence from each other. The main disadvantage of cat flaps, particularly when there is no such feline control, is that neighbours' or feral cats will soon learn to use them, particularly if delicious food is known to be available on the other side of the flap. This could lead to disease or infection being brought into the home, or territorial fights, or both. One way of overcoming this is to have an electronically operated flap that allows entry only to cats wearing the appropriate collar and gadgetry – usually in the form of a magnetic tag that doubles as an identity tag.

Alternatively, you can allow your cat limited freedom and, for example, lock the flap at night when you are unable to keep an eye on unwanted visitors. It is useful to buy a flap that can be locked to prevent your cat from going out at certain times, or other cats from coming in. Your cat will soon become used to whatever routine you set.

When you introduce your cat to the cat flap, spend some time encouraging it with your voice and showing it how the door works. Put the cat on one side and call encouragingly from the

A tom cat prepares for his nocturnal prowl. Many of the small rodents that cats hunt are active as night falls, and this also seems to be a prime time to look for a mate.

other. After a few tries, it will know exactly what to do by itself. However, it is not unusual for some cats to steadfastly refuse to use a flap – particularly if the flap was introduced after the cat. The same goes for flaps on covered litter trays (pans).

OUTDOOR CONFINEMENT

Indoor living can be safely supplemented by a secure outdoor area. Areas of a garden can be fenced in with wire or plastic mesh like a fruit cage, or a purpose-built shed or pen can be provided. Climbing plants can be trained to cover the sides to soften the appearance, but take advice on which plants to choose – some are poisonous to cats.

A pen can be constructed in the garden or as an extension to the house (with access via a cat flap). It should be sturdy in structure with wire or plastic mesh stretched between a solid wood frame, and roofed. Features could include a covered shelter and an outdoor play area with logs, shelves and playthings to keep the cats amused. Such pens are commercially available. In extreme cases, or with very small areas, whole gardens are secured around the perimeter to prevent cats from escaping and, more importantly, other cats from getting in. You can make a framework of stout posts to a height of say 3 m (9 ft) and attach wire netting between them. If the netting is loosely fitted the cat will not be able to climb up it and there will be no need to roof in the top. The base of the wire should be buried or well secured.

✦ ABOVE
A lithe hunter like this Brown Burmese will be a joy to watch in your garden.

✦ RIGHT
Cats are often attracted to the shelter and warmth offered by parked cars, so always check beneath your car before you drive away.

✦ FAR RIGHT
Cats enjoy fresh air and sunshine from the safety of an outside pen.

IN THE GARDEN

To watch a cat move and play in a garden is a source of delight, but there are dangers. Cats can swim, but are not generally renowned for their ability in this area, and there are cases of accidental drowning each year. The simple solution, in the case of a garden pond, stream or swimming pool, is to cover the water with very fine mesh or to erect a barrier to make the area inaccessible to the cat.

Cats do have a wonderful righting ability which enables them to almost invariably land on their feet when falling from a height. However, vets regularly see cats that have been badly injured as a result of falls. If a cat lands on an unyielding surface, it is likely to injure itself if the fall is more than 3–4 m (9–12 ft), which is equivalent in height to the first storey of a house. The same applies if they fall out of trees. The most common problem with cats climbing is that they become absorbed in either hunting or exploring and end up on a branch too small to turn around on and escape.

◆ LEFT
Thirst, reflections and goldfish are all good reasons for cats to be interested in water. They are not renowned for their swimming skills, however, and a net over the garden pond is worth considering.

◆ BELOW
Another sticky situation for an exploratory kitten. At this stage of their development, adventurous kittens should be supervised.

This is when the rescue services are called in. Discourage habitual climbers by placing wire netting around the base of favourite or particularly dangerous trees. However, the determined feline may just look for another tree.

◆ LEFT
When maturity and wisdom have taken the place of adventure and curiosity, a garden can be a great place for sunning and relaxation.

*Points to check on your preliminary
visit to a cattery:*

✦ are there individual runs?

✦ are the runs and houses inside
or outside, and are they are
adequately heated?

✦ are the pens sheltered, clean and
safely out of the reach of dogs if
they are taken in too?

✦ are the beds and bedding
disposed of or thoroughly
disinfected for each new resident?

✦ are the feeding bowls sterilized
between residents?

✦ do the staff seem happy, bright
and animal-loving? Do they have
any qualifications?

✦ is there plenty for your cat to
watch?

✦ do the runs have appropriate
sneeze gaps between them? Are the
partitions impervious?

✦ are there climbing posts
permanently available?

✦ how often are the cats visited
during the day?

✦ are the kitchens clean?

✦ is there access to a vet at all times?

✦ ABOVE
This boarding cattery
has outside pens. If
you have an indoor
cat, will it be happy
and warm enough
here?

✦ LEFT
On your preliminary
visit to a cattery you
could check other
residents to see if
they look contented.

owner will ask of you, most
importantly whether the cat is in good
health and has up-to-date vaccination
status. The cattery should have details
of your vet's name, address and
telephone number, and your own
contact address and telephone
numbers while you are away. You will
be asked for details of special dietary
requirements for your cat, and will
need to sign a consent form regarding
appropriate treatment in the case of
illness, and your acceptance of any
necessary veterinary bills.

✦ RIGHT
Check there is enough sneezing distance
between one pen and another, just in case one
inmate develops an infection.

TRAVELLING TIPS

If you anticipate regular travelling with your cat – to shows, for example – it is worth introducing travelling at an early age. Any length of journey can be very stressful for a cat, and you should try to create as secure an environment as possible within the carrier. Some cats – especially Siamese – can complain loudly throughout a journey: they are distressed because they feel trapped. This can be very distracting for the driver. A vet can administer a tranquillizer, but this should be avoided if possible. Because of the stress factor, it is not advisable to subject a pregnant cat, or a nursing mother and young kittens to travelling.

If there is no room for a litter tray (pan), lay some form of absorbent padding – absorbent kitchen paper, or a baby's nappy (diaper) – on the base. Avoid newsprint, especially if you have a light-coloured cat whose fur might stain. Spread one of the cat's usual sleeping blankets or towels on top, and add a favourite toy.

✦ LEFT
A pedigreed cat is going off to a show. As it is travelling alone with the driver, the carrier will have to be firmly secured on the back seat of the car.

✦ BELOW LEFT
A Seal Point Siamese emerges from its lightproof and draughtproof container.

COMFORT IN TRANSIT

Seasoned cat show travellers suggest that the cat carrier should be placed as far away from the engine as possible, away from engine noise, and from direct blasts of dry air from heaters and fans. Some carriers have a specially designed cover to keep out light and draughts. Otherwise, on cold days, you can cover the carrier with a blanket or towel. Do make sure there are sufficient gaps for ventilation. In the early days of cat shows, owners would send their prize animals by train in such carefully sealed baskets that on occasions the cats arrived dead from suffocation.

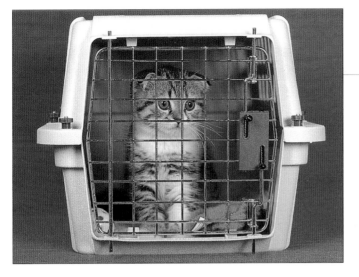

BOOK AHEAD

Before booking a bus or coach journey, always contact the company you intend to travel with well in advance to check their regulations on the transportation of animals. Companies have different rules and it may not be possible for your cat to travel with you, if at all. In the United States, for instance, the Greyhound bus line does not permit pets. You will almost certainly have to pay a fare for your pet. Few companies consider them as hand baggage.

AIR TRAVEL

Commercial airlines have well-established regulations for the transportation of pets. These conform to International Air Transport Association (IATA) regulations. It is vital to contact the airline offices at least a month in advance of the travel date to ascertain requirements. You may be required to buy a carrier that has to be ordered by mail from a specialist supplier. In any event, the carrier should be of a strong, rigid material, stable and well-ventilated. There needs to be a handle for ease of carrying, and a door that can be locked to guard against anyone opening it.

♦ ABOVE
A sturdy carrier suitable for an air journey has a ridge around it to guard against the ventilation holes becoming blocked.

A label carrying the owner's name and address, together with instructions for any feeding or watering that might be necessary should be securely attached. If the journey is to be a long one, and the carrier is not big enough for a litter tray (pan), line the base with plenty of absorbent towelling or a disposable nappy (diaper).

Some airlines allow a cat in its carrier to stay with its owner in the passenger section. Usually, though, your cat will be housed with other animals booked on the flight in a special area of the hold which provides an environment with heat, light and air-conditioning, according to IATA regulations.

♦ LEFT
For short journeys – to the vet, for example – two cats are company for each other. On longer hauls, this would constitute overcrowding.

Nutrition and Feeding

If you give your cat a well-balanced diet, it will radiate good health. It will be contented, alert and active, with bright eyes, a glossy coat and a moist nose. Regular feeding and a variety of textures and flavours may also contribute to a contented and healthy cat.

◆ FACING PAGE
Dinner is served on a plate, but if
the owner were to disappear, this
cat would adapt to finding its own
food in the wild.

◆ ABOVE
Two can be company when it
comes to meal-times, as long as
each cat obtains its fair share.

EATING HABITS

The cat is a carnivore which means that its natural diet consists of the prey which it eats. The cat's teeth and whole dietary adaptation are geared towards the consumption and digestion of entire insects, small rodents, birds, amphibians and fish. While cats do eat some plant matter, they have specific requirements for certain nutrients that can only be found in animal tissues. For this reason, meat must form at least part of a cat's diet. For an owner to try to impose a vegetarian diet would be cruel.

Nutrients are the part of the food that provide energy or raw materials from which the cat builds or replaces its tissues. Unless they are provided in the correct quantity and balance, the cat will not be able to maintain a normal, active life. Nutritional requirements vary at different stages of the cat's life cycle, which is why commercial cat foods are now available for kittens, adults and senior cats. The belief that feeding a cat well makes it less likely to bring its prey into the

house, or that keeping the cat hungry will make it become a better mouser, is ill-founded. A cat does not need the incentive of hunger to hunt; the healthier it is, the more successful it will be as a hunter.

◆ LEFT
A leopard with its natural prey. Even a domestic cat will appreciate the occasional raw bone.

◆ BELOW
Abandoned kittens enjoy a balanced diet and security at a cat welfare home.

ROUTINE

Feed an adult cat once or twice a day. Serve the food in the same place at around the same time each day. A mixture of canned and dry food is a good idea, for variety, and so that the cat uses its jaws and teeth on the dry food. For the correct quantity, follow the manufacturers' recommendations on the can or packet. An adult 4 kg (8 lb) cat generally needs around 400 g (14 oz) of canned food per day or about 50 g (2 oz) of dry food, depending on its lifestyle. Cats with freedom to roam will need more than an indoor cat, and more may be required during cold weather. Avoid giving snacks between meals. If your cat asks persistently for more, check the quantities are within the above range, but do not feed on a demand basis. If concerned, ask your vet's advice. Overeating and obesity do occur in cats, although to a lesser extent than with dogs. Do not leave food, especially canned food, lying around for long. It dries, begins to smell, attracts flies, and generally offends the cat's acute senses of smell and taste. Clear away any uneaten food immediately, and wash specially designated utensils and bowls thoroughly. Feeding your cat tidbits from the table is not recommended. Cats readily form anti-social habits, and pester you at meal-times.

◆ LEFT
A meal served at room temperature is eaten with gusto. Cold food straight from the refrigerator may be rejected.

◆ ABOVE
A Siamese can persistently ask for more food in a very loud voice. Some indoor/outdoor cats do need more food in cold weather, or simply because they are more active than indoor cats.

◆ RIGHT
A cat takes its meal on a worktop, so that the house dog does not steal its food. Ideally, the area should not be used for human food preparation. A windowsill is more suitable.

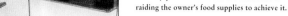

A Balanced Diet

Within its diet the cat requires a
balance of proteins, carbohydrates,
fats, vitamins, minerals and water.
If you give your pet meals at regular
times, and offer a variety of fresh and
commercial cat foods following the
guidelines below, it should get all that
it needs without the addition of any
dietary supplements such as vitamin
pills. Read the labels of commercial cat
foods to check the nutritional contents.

PROTEINS FOR STRENGTH

Proteins are made up of amino acids
which are the building blocks of the
body. They are not only used for
growth and repair, but they can
be metabolized to provide energy.
The amount of protein in a cat's diet
depends on its age. As cats become
less active with age, they need a less
protein-rich diet. In addition, their
livers and kidneys have reduced
efficiency and are less able to flush out
the toxic by-products produced from
the body's breakdown of proteins.
A kitten, however, because it is
growing and building up muscle mass,
needs around 50 per cent of protein
in its diet, compared with over 30 per

♦ BELOW
Natural instinct is the driving force for a cat
to hunt, not hunger. Feeding your cat a healthy
and adequate diet will not stop it hunting, and
could improve hunting performance.

♦ BOTTOM
A pair of Singapura kittens clearly have
sufficient animal fats and tissue in their diet
to provide them with an abundance of energy.

cent for a young adult. These levels are
around 20 per cent more than those
required by a dog of comparable age.
The cat's digestive system processes
proteins so efficiently that only 5 per
cent of total protein absorbed is lost
through waste products. Regular
ingestion of protein must occur or the
cat loses weight and condition. In the
wild, feral cats acquire essential amino
acids through a variety of captured
animals. Protein-rich foods are meat,
fish, eggs, milk and cheese. Today, all
nutritional needs are covered in the
commercially available, scientifically
formulated cat foods.

FATS FOR ENERGY

Fats are the second major source
of energy for cats and should form
a minimum of 9 per cent of the dry
matter of the diet. The cat can digest
up to 95 per cent of the fat it
consumes; any excess is stored
beneath the skin to provide insulation
and protection for the internal organs.
However, an imbalance between
intake and fat used up through normal
exercise can lead to an excess of fatty
deposits and obesity. Fat is broken
down in the body to fatty acids, which
are important in the formation and
maintenance of cell membranes
throughout the body. In addition, fat
also provides fat-soluble vitamins to
the cat, including vitamins A, D, E and
K. Some fatty acids are essential to the
cat's diet, and are almost entirely
absent from vegetable foods. They
come from animal fat and tissue.

CARBOHYDRATES FOR BULK

Carbohydrates are the major energy
source for most animals, but the cat
can, in fact, survive without them.

◆ LEFT
Night vision can be helped by vitamin A.
This should be provided by a balanced diet
that includes some liver, for example.

◆ LEFT
The teeth of the wild
cat and its domestic
descendants are
geared to killing and
eating small animals.
A vegetarian diet
would not be
appropriate for
your cat.

The cat's main natural food sources, birds and mice, are relatively low in carbohydrates, apart from what is found in the stomachs of the prey. However, carbohydrates are a considerably cheaper energy source than protein-rich meat and fish, and are therefore usually incorporated into most commercial cat foods.

Carbohydrates can provide a beneficial boost of readily available energy at times of growth, pregnancy, nursing or stress. They are also a useful source of fibre, which, although not digested by the cat, provides bulk in the faeces. A wild cat would obtain fibre from the fur, feathers or stomach contents of its prey, but the domestic cat obtains it from most commercial cat foods in the form of cellulose or plant fibre.

Carbohydrates should not make up more than 40 per cent of the diet.

MINERALS AND VITAMINS

Proteins, fats and carbohydrates are macronutrients, whereas vitamins and minerals are micronutrients – they are required in only small quantities. A cat synthesizes vitamin C for itself, and therefore needs no

extra. Vitamins A, D, E and K work together to refine the bodily functions, and they should all be present in a healthy, balanced diet, together with the vitamins of the B complex. An excess of vitamins can be harmful. Cats fed exclusively on liver,

for example (which they love because of the high fat content), may be getting an overdose of vitamin A which is stored in the liver. This can lead to serious arthritic problems involving the legs and spine, even in young cats.

◆ ABOVE AND ABOVE RIGHT
Commercially available snacks, such as these biscuits and milk-flavoured
drops, should be given in ones and twos, as an occasional treat, not in
bowlfuls as a main meal.

◆ RIGHT
A determined
attempt to reach the
treats at the bottom
of the jar is likely
to end in success.
It is wise to keep
cat-friendly food in
sealed containers in
cat-proof cupboards
if you do not want
your pet to help
itself at will.

Minerals need to be available in the correct amounts which, in turn, have to be correct in relation to each other. The daily requirements even of macro minerals (which include phosphorus, calcium, sodium, potassium and magnesium) are measured in milligrams (one thousandth of a gram). Trace or micro minerals are also necessary, but daily requirements are measured in micrograms (a millionth of a gram). A cat that has a regular and balanced diet is unlikely to suffer from mineral deficiency, and supplements should not be necessary.

Calcium and phosphorus, for example, are both present in milk, and are very important for the growing kitten. Kittens fed on an all-meat diet and deprived of adequate supplies of milk will develop serious bone abnormalities because they are receiving too much phosphorus (present in meat protein), and not enough calcium. For many years, Siamese breeders weaned their kittens on to a meat and water diet in the belief that milk caused diarrhoea. As a result, bone problems often occurred.

♦ BELOW
A pedigreed cat not interested in its food could be ill or simply not hungry. It may also be bored with the same meal served up yet again and be yearning for variety.

♦ ABOVE
Greek feral cats fend for themselves on the harbourside, their diet of fish supplemented by scraps thrown by tourists from the tavernas.

♦ ABOVE
A raw meat treat for a kitten exercises its jaws, cleans its teeth, and reminds it of its natural diet. It is a good idea to serve it outside!

FOOD SOURCES

You can supplement your cat's canned or dry commercial food for the sake of variety. It is obviously more time-consuming to prepare special meals, but leftovers and scraps can introduce different tastes and textures with minimal effort and preparation. It is essential, however, to have an idea of the benefits and drawbacks of certain foods, and the danger of an unbalanced diet, such as too much liver and vitamin A. If you want to feed your pet exclusively on home-prepared foods, it is advisable to discuss this with your vet, particularly with regard to types, variety and amounts.

FRESH MEAT

A house cat may traditionally have lived off table scraps and odd bits of meat and fish thrown out for it – which probably provided perfectly good nutritional levels. The feral cat will eat a small rodent in its entirety, including bones, innards and muscle and will benefit from all the nutrients these contain.

If you want to feed your cat on raw meat, this must be supplemented with other foods, such as pasta and vegetables for carbohydrates, minerals

◆ LEFT
A Red Tabby tucks into a meal served up on
a plate. It is important, for reasons of hygiene,
that the plate is reserved especially for him.

and fibre, that will provide the equivalent nutritional content of the bones and intestines of the naturally caught rodent.

The best meat, irrespective of type, has a valuable protein content of about 20 per cent. It is best served raw or lightly cooked as many of the vitamins can be destroyed, and the proteins denatured in the cooking process. Protein decreases and fat content increases as the cuts of meat become cheaper. Fat is not a problem, as the cat is well able to digest it and convert it into energy.

Poultry can be served, giblets and all, but make sure the bones are removed, as they become brittle with cooking and could be dangerous. Large pork or lamb bones, however, can provide a cat and kittens with hours of gnawing pleasure and also help to develop jaw strength, keep the teeth clean, and reduce the risk of dental problems in old age. Generally, avoid meats with additives and high salt content such as ham, bacon and sausages. Offal, such as liver and heart, is rich in minerals such as iron, but is also rich in vitamin A, too much of which can cause serious arthritis.

FISH

Uncooked fish has a protein level of over 10 per cent, while fish roes have a high protein level of 20–25 per cent. Raw fish should only be a rare treat, however, as it contains an enzyme that destroys some essential B vitamins. This could result in a variety of symptoms affecting the nervous and gastro-intestinal systems and skin. Oily fish, such as herring or sardines, is highly nutritious and is also higher

in fat, making it a better choice than white fish. A weekly meal of oily fish may help a cat to cope with the fur balls that collect in its stomach, as well as providing fat-soluble vitamins.

VEGETABLES

Cats on a diet of commercial cat food do not need vegetables. Sometimes they eat grass, which is considered to be a natural emetic and possibly

a source of minerals and vitamins. Vegetables are often included in commercial or home-prepared foods as a cheap source of protein and fibre.

DAIRY PRODUCTS

Milk provides fat and protein, as well as lactose (milk sugar), all of which can be beneficial during periods of growth, pregnancy, lactation or stress. Cheese and milk provide useful minerals such as calcium and phosphorus, but are not part of the cat's natural diet, and should be an occasional treat. Too much can cause diarrhoea, particularly in an older cat. Eggs mashed or scrambled are full of protein and vitamin A, but should not be fed raw as they contain an enzyme that can also destroy some essential B vitamins.

◆ ABOVE
Oily fish, such as pilchards or sardines, are nutritionally better for the cat than white fish.

◆ LEFT
Milk is a nutritious treat, but should be offered occasionally. In an older cat, it can cause diarrhoea.

PREPARED CAT FOOD

Over the last few decades, there has been a tremendous revolution in feline feeding methods. Today there are commercial foods available that cater for all stages of a cat's life. These are available in dry, semi-moist or canned forms, and, in addition, there are deep-frozen foods which come the closest to fresh meat or fish. If the commercial foods are manufactured by reputable, well-known brand names, you can be sure that the contents displayed on the wrapper are balanced. If they are marketed as complete foods, they are complete, and the only necessary addition is drinking water. No vitamins, minerals, or other supplements are necessary. However, cost does increase with quality, and the most expensive varieties are those that are scientifically researched and geared to the dietary needs of cats in each of the three major stages of development: kitten, active adulthood, and old age.

Do check the labels for additives (preferably minimal), ingredients and breakdown of nutrient content. Bear in mind, however, that while the average protein content of a can of

◆ ABOVE
Dry food (10 per cent moisture) can be kept longer when opened and left longer in the bowl than wet food, without becoming tainted.

◆ ABOVE
Semi-moist cat food has a moisture content of 40–50 per cent, and so the cat will require less supplementary water than with a dry-food diet.

◆ ABOVE
Canned food (75–85 per cent water) dries and spoils if not eaten immediately. Supplementary biscuits provide exercise for the jaw.

food may be only 6–12 per cent, this is usually the total content per 100 g (3.5 oz) of food, rather than being calculated on a dry-weight basis. About 10 per cent protein in canned food is equivalent to over 40 per cent dry weight, and is therefore acceptable.

If your cat is fed an exclusively dry diet, fresh water should always be available and changed at least once a day.

WATER

Water is vital for many functions within the body. A cat can survive for 10–14 days without food, but a total lack of water can result in death within days. The daily intake depends very much upon factors such as the moisture content of the food and the climate or temperature. Cats are not great drinkers, and many will hardly seem to drink at all, as they obtain most of their needs from their food. Fresh meat and canned food are made up of about 75 per cent water, whereas dry food contains only about 10 per cent. Because of the domestic cat's evolution from desert dweller (the African wild cat), the kidneys are extremely efficient at conserving water. However, fresh water should be always available, especially if your cat eats dry or semi-moist food.

◆ LEFT
Meat is meat to these two cats; acceptable food has been found, and it will save a great deal of time and bother for their owner if they have the same thing all the time. Some cats appear to demand variety, but it is not essential for good health.

SPECIAL NEEDS

A great deal of research has gone into specialized diets for specific conditions such as heart disease, digestive disorders, lower urinary tract disease, and obesity. If you think your cat needs a special diet, seek the advice of your vet. Most of the diets are only available on prescription.

THE ELDERLY CAT

In young and adult life, cats need protein for growth, to replace worn-out tissues and also as a significant energy source. As cats grow old, they become less active, vital organs start to deteriorate, and their need for protein is reduced.

If you maintain the cat on the same diet it had when it was young and active, there will be an excess of protein. This throws strain on the kidneys and liver, as the protein has to be broken down and eliminated from the body. If the kidneys are not fully functioning due to age, the body tries to maintain the status quo by increasing thirst, and the cat starts to urinate more. This flushes out some of the toxic products, but at the same time removes some essential vitamins and minerals.

Elderly cats in general require a protein level that is reduced from 40 per cent dry weight to about 30 per cent. There needs to be a corresponding increase in fat levels to ensure that sufficient non-harmful energy is available, but not in quantities that might cause obesity. Carbohydrates (such as starches and sugars) should be avoided, as these are more difficult for the elderly cat to digest and can cause diarrhoea and other problems. Sometimes weight loss is noted in an

elderly cat even though appetite has not diminished, or may even have increased. In such circumstances, consult your vet, as this may be due to a condition such as hyperthyroidism, which can be treated.

◆ ABOVE
Perhaps its owner has left stale water in the cat's bowl. In any event, the movement of the drips makes this a far more exciting way to drink.

◆ LEFT
An elderly cat's diet should supply easily assimilated protein in the right quantities to sustain energy but not overload the system.

◆ ABOVE
An active adult cat needs – and can assimilate – a higher level of protein in its diet to fuel its lifestyle than an elderly cat.

MOTHERHOOD

The first sign of a cat's pregnancy will
probably not be a noticeable increase
in abdominal size but a demand for
more food. If the queen is in good
condition at the time of mating, she
should not need extra food until about
the last third of the pregnancy (seven –
nine weeks). By this time the foetuses
will be growing in the womb and space
is at a premium, so the cat needs
frequent small meals, up to four times
daily. The total quantity should only
be increased by about one third. Top-
quality, nourishing food of low bulk is
of special importance at this time.

NURSING

To maintain the amount of milk
needed for her kittens, a nursing
queen will certainly at least double her
normal food intake. Food should be
of high quality and low bulk – in other
words, as much energy and nutrients
packed into as small a volume as
possible. These requirements are most
easily met by some of the special
high-energy diets specially devised for
nursing queens. Alternatively, kitten
food can be used.

THE KITTENS

Kittens suckle from their mother
exclusively for the first three or four
weeks of their lives. As they become
more aware of their surroundings they
may start to nibble at their mother's
food, a sure sign they are ready for

weaning. The queen will happily
continue to nurse her litter to some
extent well into their third month of
life. However, by the time they are
about eight weeks old, the greater part
of the kittens' diet will usually be

provided by the owner. There is a fine
line between allowing the kittens to
gorge themselves, which may cause
digestive problems, and giving them
enough to maintain healthy growth.
The weaning process should be

◆ L E F T
The young, active adult cat often cannot last a whole day before the next meal and will need an extra snack in-between.

◆ B E L O W
A Persian kitten matures over four years and frequent, nutritious meals need to be given during this time.

gradual, and the kittens fed little and often, with small quantities of high-protein food well chopped so as to be easily consumable. The easiest method of weaning is to use one of the readily available, well-established kitten foods, either in the dry or canned versions.

During the actual weaning process, canned foods are probably preferable, as the kittens may be attracted by the meaty smell. However, the dry foods are just as nutritious and have proven success. Do plan feeding times carefully so that mother and kittens may eat the extra meals in peace, away from other animals or disturbance in the household.

HOW MUCH, HOW OFTEN?

At about eight weeks old, kittens should be fed little and often. If you are feeding dry kitten food (which can be left out for longer than canned food), you can try providing it on a continuous basis for the kitten to nibble as required. Such a routine should be avoided, however, if your kitten shows a tendency to be overweight. Four or more meals a day for the kittens is normal, and can be gradually reduced to about three meals by the age of three to four months, and two meals at six months.

THE YOUNG ADULT

The feeding regime can gradually be reduced to one main meal as the kitten reaches adulthood at nine to twelve months of age. However, young, active cats will become very hungry if they have to wait 24 hours between meals. Many owners therefore offer a snack in the morning, with the main meal at night. If this is done, it is important to ensure that the main meal is reduced in quantity by the equivalent of the earlier snack, so that too many calories do not lead to weight problems. Most breeds of cat reach their adult size at about a

year of age, although some of the longhaired breeds continue to develop until they are about four years old.

If you do have a slow-maturing cat, it is essential to ensure that adequate food of high quality is available throughout the growth period. A routine of two or three meals a day with a dry-weight protein value of over 30 per cent should continue over the growth period in order to maintain peak development.

◆ B E L O W
These 12-week-old kittens are likely to be demanding three meals a day.

Grooming

Cats are fastidious animals and devote a large part of their waking hours to grooming themselves. A little extra help from their human friends is required by longhaired and semi-longhaired cats. Even for shorthairs, the grooming process is important. It can be a pleasurable, bonding and rewarding experience for both cat and owner. Extra grooming also contributes to general health, for it stimulates the blood vessels just below the skin and improves muscle tone.

◆ FACING PAGE
A ginger cat uses his paw to clean the parts the tongue cannot reach. The paw stimulates secretions from the glands on the head, which it then transfers to other parts of the body.

◆ ABOVE
A satisfied customer – a Burmese Red – poses for photographs after a grooming session.

THE NATURAL WAY

The cat is well-equipped to groom itself: tongue, teeth, paws and claws are all pressed into service. The cat's tongue has a rough surface which, combined with saliva, helps to remove grit and sticky substances from the fur. Even though cats are very flexible, there are areas they cannot reach directly with the tongue – so the front paws are licked and used rather like a face flannel (washcloth). As the coat dries, the cat nibbles the fur back into place with its small incisor teeth and removes any foreign matter that the washing process failed to dislodge.

The back claws act almost like a wide-toothed comb and remove larger objects from the coat. The front paws stimulate slight oily secretions from glands around the head, and transfer them to other parts of the body during grooming. The cat is preening its coat with its own perfume, which can then be used to mark territory.

◆ ABOVE
A fluffy silver and white kitten shows her remarkable flexibility as she grooms her hind leg. Careful grooming is particularly important with long fur, to remove any matting that could lead to a skin infection.

CHANGING COATS

In the natural state, the cat sheds its coat once a year, usually in spring. However, the process is dependent on light and temperature. In warm, artificially heated and illuminated homes, indoor cats tend to shed throughout the year. It does not happen in one vast shedding of fur, but in discreet areas across the body so that hair loss is hardly noticed – except on the owner's carpets, furnishings and clothes.

When self-grooming at any time of the year, the cat dislodges loose fur, some of which is swallowed. This gradually builds up into a fur ball (hairball) which can eventually solidify into a pellet in the cat's intestine. Most cats automatically bring up a small fur ball every few days or so, but sometimes one can become stuck, causing loss of appetite and a rundown condition. In extreme cases, a vet may need to operate to remove the obstruction. The fur ball problem can strike at any time, although longhaired cats are most at risk. The occasional meal of oily fish may help ease the passage of the ingested hair.

◆ LEFT
A Silver Tabby licks a front paw so that it can then use it rather like a face flannel (washcloth) to wipe its face.

◆ BELOW
The grooming process is completely absorbing for these two kittens. As well as being necessary, grooming is an activity that cats enjoy.

HUMAN AID

A feral cat in good physical condition usually keeps itself reasonably well-groomed. Domestication and selective breeding have resulted in changes to the cat's coat, such as longer hair, that sometimes require more maintenance than the cat is able to provide for itself. Assistance is then needed from the owner. Older cats, too, may lose the motivation and energy to groom themselves and welcome extra help.

You can remove some of the loose dead hairs which accumulate just by stroking a cat. The polishing action gives the coat a beautiful sheen. Some experienced owners claim that the best time to groom a cat is just after washing the dishes, for if your hands are very slightly damp, stroking is even more effective. Thin rubber gloves have a similar effect in removing loose hair.

EQUIPMENT

The grooming equipment you need depends on the type of coat your cat has. You will also gradually discover what works best for your pet. If you have a pedigreed cat, ask the breeder's advice. First-hand experience, especially from a breeder who keeps show cats, can save time and money.

Start regular grooming as a part of a kitten's routine as soon as it comes into your household. An older cat may need some encouragement to submit to the experience, but will probably soon enjoy it immensely, if you are gentle. Choose a quiet time in the cat's observed routine, make sure all you need is accessible and settle the cat on a towel on your lap. It is pointless trying to restrain a cat that just wants to play; scratches are far less likely if the cat is relaxed.

◆ CLOCKWISE FROM BELOW
Narrow/wide-toothed grooming comb, flea comb, ball-tipped brush, slicker tail brush.

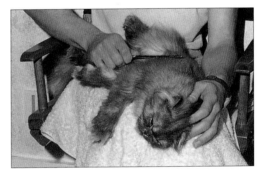

◆ LEFT
A longhaired cat is lying down on a towel specially reserved for its grooming. Having a waste (trash) bin nearby is also a wise move.

◆ BELOW
Finish off a grooming session with a stroke and hear that cat purr. Stroking also removes any stray loose hairs and gives a final polish.

GROOMING A SHORTHAIRED CAT

Supplementing the self-grooming of a shorthaired cat is really only absolutely necessary if you are showing. But an extra groom, say twice weekly, does help keep loose, dead hairs under control and off the furniture. It is also a good opportunity to check for fleas, or the onset of any ear or dental problems. In addition, the activity is pleasurable for both cat and owner. The process is, of course, far simpler than for a longhaired cat. Grooming aids can include a metal

CHECKLIST

+ towel
+ rubber-bristled brush
+ wide-toothed metal comb
+ natural, soft-bristled brush
+ flea comb
+ chamois leather or velvet glove
+ cotton wool
+ ear cleaner
+ eye wipes

comb with round-tipped teeth, a soft, natural-bristled brush to settle the fur, a brush with stiffer bristles (a rubber brush is essential for Rex cats, as it does not scratch the skin), and a polishing cloth of silk or chamois leather. Start the grooming

session by gently stroking the cat to relax it. Use the stiff brush first, brushing very gently along the lie of the fur, to loosen the dead hairs and dirt. Brush the whole body, but be especially gentle in delicate parts around the ears, armpits and groin,

+ BELOW LEFT AND RIGHT
When grooming is finished, it's time to rest and watch a friend finish off his tail. Cats often groom together if they have the opportunity; it is an important social activity.

+ ABOVE
A soft-bristled brush settles the fur after any static triggered by the use of a metal comb.

♦ BELOW
A rubber brush is not only gentler on the
shorthair's skin, but the cat seems to relish the
feel of it, too. It removes not only dead hair but
dandruff as well.

and under the belly and tail. Next, use
the metal comb to extract the dead
hairs. It may set up some static in the
coat, causing fur to clump together or
the guardhairs to develop a wispy life
of their own. This will be corrected
with the soft-bristled brush, and a
final polish with the chamois leather,
velvet or silk.

A DRY SHAMPOO

It is rarely necessary to wash a
shorthaired cat unless it is a pale-
coloured exhibition cat, or unless
the cat has become greasy – from
sitting under a car, for example. Some
exhibitors give their shorthairs a bran
bath to remove excess grease, dirt and
dandruff. Warm a good five or six
handfuls of natural bran flakes in
the oven to a comfortable hand-hot
temperature. Rub these over the cat,
avoiding the face and inner ears,
working the hands thoroughly

♦ LEFT
A final sheen is
encouraged on a
shorthair's coat by
stroking it with a
chamois leather or
velvet glove. A silk
scarf would do the
job just as well.

through the coat; then simply brush
it all out with a soft brush. A coat that
is predominantly dark will take on a
shine immediately; pastel blues and
creams may take a couple of days
before their texture and shine reach
the peak of perfection.

♦ RIGHT
A contented and very sleek
Red Burmese following
a full grooming session.

GROOMING A LONGHAIRED CAT

Longhaired cats, whether they are Persians or semi-longhairs – the so-called self-grooming breeds such as the Maine Coon Cat or Norwegian Forest Cat – all need considerable grooming help from the owner. This is true whether the animal is purebred or not. Longhaired cats pick up dirt and debris in their coats, and they need help to keep the fur clean and free from tangles. This must be done daily. If not, the hair mats, particularly in the armpits and groin, and can become uncomfortable. A severely matted coat is unyielding and prevents the cat from moving with ease. Any movement results in individual hairs being pulled. The build-up of fur leads to deterioration in the general condition of the coat and a much greater likelihood of hairballs.

Grooming procedures are more elaborate than for the shorthairs. Start with the wide-toothed comb with blunt teeth to ease out tangles and debris. Try the comb on yourself before you try it out on the cat. If it does not feel sharp on your head, it should be fine for the cat. To deal with obstinate knots and tangles, sprinkle them with unscented talcum powder and ease them free with your hands. A sprinkle of talcum powder also helps pick up excess grease and dirt. It should be brushed out thoroughly at the brushing stage. Make partings in the tail, and brush each parted section sideways. Finish with a well-earned stroke in all the right directions.

1 Use the comb gently to ease out any tangles, knots and twigs. Sprinkle with talcum powder once a week. Do the underbelly and legs first.

2 Brush the body fur firmly in sections against the lie of the fur towards the cat's head. Brush thoroughly to remove talcum powder, if you have used it.

3 Use the fine comb for the neck fur. For Persians, the fur should be combed upwards to form a ruff beneath the chin.

CHECKLIST FOR SHAMPOO AND GROOM

+ towels
+ wide-toothed metal comb
+ fine comb
+ natural-bristled brush
+ unscented talcum powder
+ feline or baby shampoo
+ shower attachment
+ hairdryer

+ RIGHT
A Maine Coon is groomed fit for going on exhibition.

SHAMPOO AND STYLE

Washing a cat is time-consuming, but essential if you are to show your cat. Unless the idea is introduced during kittenhood, a cat may object to being bathed, so it is helpful to have two pairs of human hands.

Make sure the room is warm, free of draughts, and escape-proof. A large, flat-based kitchen sink is ideal. Allow plenty of clear space around the sink, with a stock of dry towels nearby, and one on the draining board. Have all you need at hand before you start.

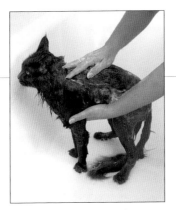

1 Fill the sink with warm water to about 5cm (2in). Talk soothingly to the cat all the time. Using a shower attachment, test the water first, then wet the fur thoroughly. Apply a little shampoo and work into a lather. Make sure no shampoo goes near the cat's eyes, nose or mouth.

2 Rinse thoroughly and repeat the shampooing process. If you are using conditioner, put a drop on the back and work it through the coat with the wide-toothed comb. Rinse thoroughly and then squeeze down the whole body, legs and tail to remove excess moisture.

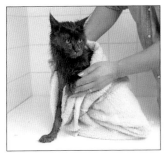

3 Lift the cat from the sink and wrap it immediately in a towel. Rub gently to absorb most of the water. You may need several towels!

4 Set the hairdryer on low. Do not direct the airstream too close. Lift and comb the fur as you dry (this is easier if the dryer is on a stand), and stop when the fur is still slightly damp and tacky. If your cat objects to a hairdryer, do not persist, but resort to towels, brushes and patience.

5 Use the soft-bristled brush against the lie of the coat, lifting and brushing as you go. Separate any knots gently with the fingers. Pay particular attention to the flow of the tail plume. Make sure the leg fur is well separated, and that the fur on the underparts, particularly in armpits and groin, does not become curly. On Persians, work up the dramatic ruff of fur around the neck.

ATTENTION TO DETAIL

EYES

The discharges that accumulate in the corners of the eyes can be removed carefully with your finger. Short-faced cats are prone to show tear stains beneath the eyes, which can be cleaned with a special preparation available from pet stores or the vet's surgery.

MOUTH AND NOSE

A dark brown or black tarry secretion on the cat's chin indicates an excess production of sebum from the hair follicles, which is used in scent marking. A similar condition, known as stud tail, can occur around the base of the tail. Veterinary treatment is usually necessary. Recurrence may be prevented by cleansing with special anti-bacterial shampoo from your vet.

TEETH AND GUMS

Keeping your cat's teeth clean reduces the risk of gum disease which has escalated with the advent of modern

◆ LEFT AND
BELOW LEFT
Daily cleansing of the area around the eyes is particularly necessary with Persian cats. This kitten is being introduced to the idea at an early age. A cotton wool bud (swab) dampened with tepid water is used, and the area is gently wiped with absorbent tissue.

◆ BELOW
A cat is more inclined to allow its teeth to be cleaned if the toothpaste is flavoured with chicken, fish or meat.

cat foods. If tartar can be kept under control, the risk is reduced. Some vets give cats a general check-up once or twice a year, and if necessary, perform a scale and polish under general anaesthetic. The alternative is for the owner to clean the cat's teeth once or twice a week. Special toothbrushes that fit over your finger and cat food-flavoured toothpastes make the job easier, but do not necessarily guarantee

◆ ABOVE
The owner cleans tartar from the outside surfaces of the kitten's teeth. The cat's rough tongue will take care of any tartar build-up on the inside surfaces of the teeth.

not fully retracted either. Trimming the
nails will help. Outdoor cats should
have only their front claws clipped, so
that they are not completely disarmed
if they meet an enemy, and will be able
to climb should escape be necessary.

If claw clipping is necessary, ask
the vet to do it, for a mistake could be
dangerous. On light-coloured claws, a
dark blood vessel can be seen. Cutting

this (called cutting to the quick) causes
copious bleeding and pain. Declawing,
or onychectomy, is considered an
unnecessary mutilation in the United
Kingdom. It is widely practised in the
United States, and is often carried out
at about the same time as sterilization.
It is a major operation that removes
the cat's main means of self-defence,
and should be reserved for indoor cats.

success. Just before feeding time, you
could try wrapping a piece of fabric
sticking plaster around the index
finger. Smear this with a little wet cat
food, and gently try to rub against the
teeth while holding the head.

EARS

If ears appear soiled on the inside,
wipe them out gently with a soft
absorbent tissue on your finger,
dampened with olive oil, liquid
paraffin or ear cleaner from the pet
shop. Never clean further than you
can see, and do not use cotton wool
buds (swabs). An abundance of dark
brown, dry waxy material may indicate
mites, in which case veterinary
treatment is necessary.

CLAWS

Some Siamese cats and their
derivatives, such as Balinese, Oriental
Shorthairs and Oriental Longhairs, are
unable to retract their claws completely
and are therefore ill at ease on hard,
uncarpeted floors. Elderly cats of any
breed may have similar problems. The
nails continue to grow and, because
older cats take less exercise, are not
worn down. Due to stiffness, they are

♦ RIGHT
A thorough self-groom for this cat will
help keep fleas and parasites at bay, and
in warm weather, help it keep cool. The
saliva takes the place of sweat in
humans, evaporating
and cooling the cat.

♦ LEFT
A Burmese-cross
is having its nails
trimmed with a nail
clipper custom-made
for cats. Clippers
designed for human
nails may split cats'
claws. Only the very
edges are trimmed.
If you are at all
uncertain about your
skills, it is wise to ask
the vet to do this job.

SHOWING

A cat has no particular interest in whether it goes to a show or not, but its owner can gain a great deal of satisfaction from having a prize-winning animal and becoming part of the cat-showing circuit. Shows provide an arena for the serious cat breeder or committed owner to display their stock. Some shows also feature more relaxed classes for ordinary household pets.

THE REWARDS OF SHOWING
Showing your cat is an expensive business, even if the animal has championship potential. The rewards are likely to be pride in your – and your cat's – achievements, a rosette and perhaps a silver cup or a supply of commercial cat food rather than prize money. Apart from the cost and maintenance of your pedigreed cat, there are equipment and travelling costs as well as high entry fees to consider. However, for the committed cat fancier – the person who is

◆ LEFT
A White Persian at an American cat show sits with its rosettes in a decorated pen.

◆ BELOW LEFT
Cat shows provide an opportunity for like-minded people to compare notes and make friends.

interested in breeding and showing pedigreed cats – there are many rewards. Cat shows present an ideal opportunity to find out more about the various breeds. You will become part of the cat fancier's network, check out the latest breeds and cat products, make friends and fill your social calender with cat-related events.

Whether your cat enjoys the show or not is debatable. Most cats are so adaptable they will tolerate being confined to a pen for the best part of a day. Others may have a shy or timid nature, or may be particularly active; in either case it would be unfair to subject them to the show scene. If you introduce a kitten to showing at an early age, it is more likely to adapt. Some cats even appear to relish the attention and admiration from passers-by. If you are taking your cat to a show for the first time, keep a close eye on it: if it is unhappy, it will not hesitate to let you know.

ENTERING A SHOW
First go to a show without your cat; it will be much easier if you have a clear idea of noise level, numbers, conditions and how the event is run.

◆ ABOVE
The whole family can be involved – and may prevent the cat from becoming too bored.

◆ LEFT
It may be very boring and rather noisy to sit in a small pen at a cat show all day, but the impressive display of rosettes suggest that this cat is worth breeding from.

The organizing bodies usually publish an annual list of the shows under their jurisdiction, which you can buy for a small fee. The publication should have the name and address of a contact for the show to whom you should apply for a schedule – allow about three months before the event.

The schedule contains the rules under which the show is operating, the classes that can be entered and the qualification requirements for each class. There will also be an entry form, as well as details of the entry fees charged. Read it all meticulously. If you get something wrong, you could be refused entry on the day.

WHAT HAPPENS AT A SHOW

Show style and rules vary from country to country, and according to the size of the show. Individual breed clubs organize their own events, which tend to be small-scale, informal, friendly occasions. Others may be organized by major registering bodies, or may be compound affairs, with separate shows running concurrently.

When you arrive with your cat at a European show, including all British shows, you will probably have to have your cat checked by a vet (vetted-in); in some countries it is left to trust that your cat is in good health and has all the necesary inoculations. For vetting-in you will need to produce the cat's up-to-date vaccination certificates.

Next, find your allocated pen, which is where the cat will stay for the duration of the show. Check the security on the cage and attach the cat's show identification label (known as a tally). Setting the cat in the cage is termed benching, and all the information you need about this is in

the show rules, including what you can and cannot put inside the pen. Fresh drinking water must be in the bowl at all times, but food and toys may not be allowed until judging has finished.

Depending on the individual show style, either the judges go around the pens or the cats are taken to a judging arena where they are assessed, with the winners being announced or posted on a results board.

WHAT THE JUDGES LOOK FOR

The judges check each pedigreed cat against the standard of points for its breed that are set by the show's governing body. (Standards of points

are published and can be bought from the relevant organizations). A maximum mark is set for each aspect of the cat, such as the head, tail or coat. This will vary according to the breed and will often differ slightly between one registering body and another. If you want to ask a judge about your cat, it is fine to approach them on the day, after judging has finished. Judges are almost certainly successful breeders in their own right and will have a lot of sound advice to give; don't dismiss them just because they have not given a high award to your cat. Contrary to popular belief, judges hate down-marking exhibits.

♦ ABOVE
The early cat shows at the end of the 1800s were dominated by Persians and domestic shorthairs in the United Kingdom.

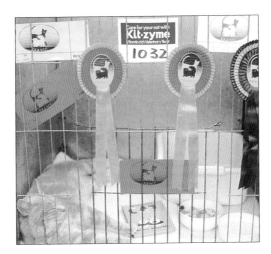

♦ LEFT
Now all that prodding and poking is over, and the rosettes are up, maybe a chap can have a nap.

Behaviour and Intelligence

The average cat is considered to be fairly intelligent, but compared with dogs
its repertoire of party tricks appears paltry. Dogs, as pack animals, will obey
understood commands in order to seek the approval of, or a reward from,
the owner, who is considered to be the dominant pack leader. The cat is
a more solitary animal and may well understand what it is supposed to
do but choose not to comply.

◆ FACING PAGE
A kitten practises looking intelligent
in front of a mirror. Cats do not have
colour vision to the same extent as
humans, but they can recognize
mental alertness when they see it.

◆ ABOVE
The cat has the body and the build
of a hunter – and a temperament and
instinct to match.

THE ART OF COMMUNICATION

What a cat is inclined to do and what it can do are quite different. By nature and inclination, for example, cats move gracefully, daintily and sedately, yet their bodies are designed for speed and movement. When establishing a relationship with your cat, bear in mind that it will do what you ask not because it considers you dominant, but because it feels inclined to do so.

A well-balanced cat is used to being handled by its owner, and is alert, independent and inquisitive. If a cat is timid, dependent and constantly seeking attention, it may have suffered misuse or lack of socialization when it was young (6–16 weeks).

LEARNING FROM YOUR CAT

Communication is a two-way process; if you are alert and observant, you will notice subtle nuances in your cat's voice and body language. Listen to your pet in the context of its activity at the time and you may be able to link certain sounds with meanings such as hunger or contentment. Vocalization

♦ RIGHT
A well-balanced cat – confident, alert and relaxed.

and vowel sounds – miaowing – vary from cat to cat. Siamese tend to be very vocal and "talk" to their owners, other cats speak hardly at all. Purring – which can be done breathing in or out and for remarkably long, unbroken periods – is generally an indication of contentment. Kittens start to purr from approximately one week of age; they purr when they are feeding and their mother knows that all is well. It is believed that each kitten has a distinctive and unique

♦ ABOVE
A cat may be comfortably settled on its owner's lap, but its ears remain pricked and alert.

♦ LEFT
A good stretch helps keep the cat's streamlined body supple and awake, in a state of readiness for action.

purr so that the queen is able to instantly recognize which of the offspring is communicating.

Fear, anger and dissatisfaction are expressed by spits, hisses and snarls. The pitch of a growl drops when a cat is hunting to become a low hypnotic rumbling. Some cats "chitter" and salivate in anticipation or excitement when they catch sight of something to hunt. Strained, high-intensity yowls are reserved for inter-cat communication, and are especially noticeable in a female on heat.

BODY LANGUAGE

When a cat feels good, its ears are erect and forward-pointing, and its whiskers are relaxed. At rest on a familiar lap, it may purr and "knead" its paws, opening and closing them just as it did against its mother's breast when it was suckling.

If its whiskers bristle forwards, ears turn back, pupils narrow to slits, and fur, particularly along the spine and tail, stands on end, the cat is spoiling for a fight. The fur extension may be accompanied by an arched back so that the cat looks as big and menacing as possible. Wide eyes and flattened whiskers and ears are signs of fear. Whiskers are highly sensitive organs of touch and are sometimes used to make friendly contact with another cat.

BASIC INSTINCTS

Cats are nocturnal and may spend up to 16 hours in any one day resting, if not actually asleep. As hunters, they are conserving their energy for the quick bursts of power needed to pursue their targets. Their overwhelming instinct when they go out is to hunt small creatures. This can even be detected in the play of young kittens with toys and leaves. Hearing, sight and smell are geared to the demands of stalking and hunting and these senses are much more acute than they are in humans. Tactile whiskers supplement the other senses, acting as sensors to feel close objects. They may also be used as a friendly whisker-to-whisker gesture with other cats. Cats are sociable and will establish a relationship with other animals or become part of the neighbourhood cat community if they

are allowed outside. This community is hierarchical, with the unneutered (unaltered) males and females reigning supreme, and highly territorial.

GENTLE MARKING
Both male and female cats gently assert their territorial rights by rubbing their heads against objects and humans. They leave traces of a scent that is secreted by glands located at various parts of the body, but particularly around the ears, neck and at the back of the head. The scent is also released from between the paw pads when a cat scratches a tree to sharpen its claws.

♦ ABOVE
As this cat rubs its forehead against a chair, a scent is released that proclaims the chair as part of the cat's own territory.

♦ ABOVE
At still only a couple of weeks old, this kitten has not begun to acquire trust or domesticated patterns of behaviour; it is still in its feral state, expressing fear and aggression at intruders.

♦ LEFT
A cat pounces. Its specially adapted eyes, with their wide angle of vision, are able to make the most of limited light, enabling a cat to detect the slightest movement in dim light.

TERRITORIAL RIGHTS

The cat instinctively carves out a social and hunting territory for itself. This behaviour is most marked in the unneutered (unaltered) male, whose main purpose in life is to pass on his genes to future generations. He may extend his territory to cover an area of as much as 10 km (6 miles), maintaining his position in the social hierarchy and priority access to any local females by fighting. His life can be violent and short.

An unneutered female can fight as effectively and as viciously as the tom, as she develops and defends her hunting territory. From about four months of age, she periodically attracts all the males in the neighbourhood and regularly becomes pregnant.

DOMESTIC IMPLICATIONS
For the domestic neutered (altered) cat, its own home and garden are the focal points of its territory. An unneutered cat will extend the area

✦ ABOVE
A cat sprays to mark the boundaries of what it considers to be its territory. If the cat – whether male or female – has been neutered, the smell is unlikely to be obvious to humans.

✦ LEFT
Two cats demonstrate their affection for each other by rubbing their foreheads together. Other signs of friendship may include licking each other or brushing whiskers.

and challenge the neighbourhood cats. Kittens that are brought up together usually co-exist happily unless there are too many cats in the household, which could result in some territorial marking. If an adult cat is introduced into a home where there are cats already, care and sometimes expert guidance is needed. Among neutered cats, territorial rights may be resolved by some violent vocals, body language, and the establishment of non-violent dominance. If the cats are unneutered, it is a different story.

SPRAYING
The cat marks the boundaries of its patch with a spray of concentrated, very strong-smelling urine. It will also

◆ OPPOSITE
A male Burmese goes
hunting: it could
roam as far as 10km
(6 miles) in search
of food and female
company if it is
not neutered.

◆ BELOW
Son, aged six months, is keen on keeping close
to his mother. The dominant, unneutered
female, however, is not always this complacent,
and often asserts her independence.

◆ RIGHT
A kitten begins
to explore outside,
ready to take its
place among the
local community and
hierarchy of cats.

do this if it feels threatened or
insecure, for example, if strange
visitors or animals come into the
house. The most common and the
most pungent spraying comes from
unneutered males, but entire females
spray, especially when they are on
heat. Neutered cats also spray, but
the odour is usually less offensive.

In extreme situations, the marking
may involve dropping faeces away
from litter trays (pans). This is not
simply dirty behaviour, but
dysfunctional, and the causes must
be established. A cat that constantly
re-marks its territory is trying
to reassure itself that it is worth
something. The wise owner checks
with the vet for medical advice.
Home treatment of attention and
affection may solve the problem. If
the behaviour continues, you may be
referred to an animal behaviourist.

THE EFFECT OF NEUTERING
Neutering (altering) dramatically
reduces a cat's urge to exert territorial
rights. Territory becomes confined to

an area around the home (although
this will still be robustly defended by
a neutered cat of either sex).

In a neutered, or castrated, male,
the means of producing the hormones
that fuel sex drive – the testes – are
removed. Castration takes place
ideally from four months of age.
It is done under general anaesthetic.
No stitches are needed, recovery is
complete within 24 hours, and there is
no discernible traumatic effect on the
cat. Long-term, however, the animal's
territorial, sexual and hunting
behaviours are modified. A female

is neutered or spayed by the removal
of her ovaries and uterus, or womb,
so that she cannot become pregnant.
She no longer comes on heat or
attracts all the local males. The
operation is ideally carried out from
four to five months of age. Once the
cat has recovered from the anaesthetic,
she is usually fine. Long-term she
may become more friendly and placid.
Desexed animals do tend to convert
their food more efficiently, and
may be less active. If they start to
look plump, some attention to diet
may be necessary.

◆ RIGHT
Two neutered (altered) Burmese, who have
known each other since kittenhood, are happy
to share their limited territory of house and
garden amicably.

BEHAVIOURAL PROBLEMS

◆ BELOW
The areas between a cat's eyes and ears are often more sparsely covered with fur than elsewhere. On this cat, however, the extreme baldness may be a sign of stress and be due to excess rubbing.

It is sometimes difficult to recognize symptoms of stress in the solitary, individualistic feline. Some breeds are more nervous than others. Highly strung Orientals, for example, can react very badly to strange situations, and even the first visit to a cattery may change the personality. Stolid domestic shorthairs may be equally upset, but are more likely to react aggressively – by hissing, scratching and biting. Cats probably show stress to a greater extent than dogs, but the first signs are sometimes too subtle for us to notice.

SYMPTOMS OF STRESS
When feeling vulnerable, a cat withdraws into itself, and cold aloofness is one of the first clues to its condition. A cat about to go into battle tries to appear as large as possible, but in distress it tries to become mouse-sized. Fur is flattened, tail is curled round and the cat crouches. If the situation continues, the cat starts to shake. Salivation, vomiting and defecation can also be signs of nervousness and tension.

A cat may react actively or passively when it is frightened. Typical, active signs are pupil dilation, arching back, piloerection (the hair stands on end) and hissing. A cat may react to any

attempts at reassurance, such as vocal intonations or body contact, with further aggression.

Passive symptoms of fear are more subtle and harder to detect. The cat may hide or try to appear smaller, placing the ears back and becoming immobile. A timid cat will start at the slightest movement or unexpected noise. This

may be because it was abused as a kitten, or simply because it lacked proper socialization. If you breed, it is important to socialize your kittens to prepare them for everyday household life and noise.

DEALING WITH FEAR
Mild fear may be overcome by the owner. A timid cat needs a safe, quiet place to retreat to, such as a covered bed. Avoid forcing your attentions on the cat – wait for it to approach you. Always move slowly, speak to it softly and evenly and keep strangers or strange situations at bay until it has become more confident.

It is important to identify the cause of a cat's fear so that you can deal with it. This may not always be easy, unless

◆ ABOVE
An aggressive cat seeing off an unwanted visitor. Neutering makes a cat more placid.

◆ LEFT
A timid cat crouches or hides when feeling threatened by the slightest noise or an unexpected situation.

it is obvious – a one-off visit to the vet, for example. There may be an ongoing situation, such as mild teasing behaviour by a child, or persistent noise or confinement. Once the cause is established, it must be removed and the cat's confidence regained.

It may be that you can persuade the cat to overcome its fears. Cats have a highly developed flight response and when faced with any threatening situation, such as being trapped in a carrier or a car, their immediate reaction is to try to get away. You may be able to control this with soothing words or by gradually making the cat realize it needn't be afraid by exposing it little and often to the situation.

After an initial shock reaction, cats often settle down in catteries or veterinary hospitals after about 48 hours. If they are handled, however gently, during that time, they may

associate the handling with the initial fear and bridle every time anyone approaches to feed them. Left alone, they usually calm down and soon start to make overtures to the very people that they hated the day before.

DEALING WITH AGGRESSION
If a cat that is normally calm and well-behaved suddenly starts to scratch and bite, it may be ill, bored or frightened, and the underlying cause should be addressed. It is important to train a kitten from the beginning that aggressive behaviour is unacceptable, even in play. A firm no, immediate cessation of play, and a light tap on the nose whenever it bites or scratches should correct this behaviour. Do remember that a cat likes its independence, and if you impose your attentions on it when it does not want them – for example, if it is asleep – it may react instinctively by attacking you.

♦ A B O V E
A kitten in listening mode. It is important to talk encouragingly to your pet when it has behaved well, and never shout at it or hit it. A firm, quiet "no" and a tap on the nose should be sufficient to stop any mischief.

♦ A B O V E
Scratching is fun for the kitten, but does not do the soft furnishings much good. Provision of a scratching post and a little training should solve the problem.

♦ A B O V E
Play with your indoor cat as often as you can to ensure it gets enough exercise and attention, or its boredom could turn to destructive tendencies.

TRAINING AND LEARNED BEHAVIOUR

Switched-on, intelligent cats will soon learn to manipulate doting owners. They can also be trained to produce predictable repeatable behaviour. The degree of training depends very much on the amount of time the owner has to spend with the cat. A kitten's play is, in fact, its instinctive means of acquiring hunting and survival skills.

Although many hunting actions are instinctive, they are also learned from other cats. Solitary, hand-reared kittens do not learn to hunt.

Each kitten is an individual with a unique temperament and balance of skills. In encouraging and extending a kitten's play, you can observe the strengths and weaknesses in its temperament and skills repertoire. Observing and enhancing natural

◆ LEFT
A Bi-colour Ragdoll kitten has retrieved a toy. It may take it back to its owner for it to be thrown again.

traits is the secret behind the methods of successful animal trainers. All cats show skill at balancing and spacial awareness, but some are much better than others. A kitten may pick up a piece of crumpled paper and bring it to its owner to be thrown again. You can encourage repetition of this trick with a tasty tidbit and pretty soon you will be boasting about your "retriever" cat!

You can train your cat to conform to certain household standards, using spoken commands which the cat is well able to understand and respond to.

ESTABLISHING COMMUNICATION

The first step in training is to establish communication between cat and human, and a kitten should be given a name as soon as possible. If an adult cat joins the household, it is advisable to retain its existing name even if you dislike it. If you use the cat's name repeatedly when you are attracting its attention, it will soon learn to respond. From there it is easy for the cat to learn certain command words. Repetition of the verbal message, spoken firmly in a low voice, and

◆ LEFT
Each kitten is an individual with its own strengths, weaknesses and special skills. This kitten's speciality seems to be acrobatics.

◆ RIGHT
Kittens and young cats enjoy playing hide-and-seek – as long as they are found quickly, congratulated and cuddled.

◆ LEFT
The intelligent cat helps itself to a treat.

best sofa, say "no", gently but firmly, take it to the scratching post, and place its paws on the post. If the cat uses the post, give it some praise and a stroke.

never shouted, is the key. Avoid shouting, for this can traumatize a cat and lead to behavioural problems.

SAVING THE FURNITURE

A cat scratches a tree – or your furniture – to sharpen its claws, to mark its territory, or just for the satisfying feeling. If you want to conserve your furniture, therefore, provide your cat with a scratching post, and, as an extra incentive, rub some catnip into it. Whenever the cat begins to assault the curtains or the

USING THE CAT FLAP

Practice and encouragement is also the key to training a cat to use a cat flap. Make sure the door is at a comfortable

height for your cat and that the flap swings easily. Place some tempting food on the far side of the door and gently push the cat through. Then open the flap slightly and call the cat back. Repeat a few times and the cat will soon learn to operate the flap itself.

◆ ABOVE
To dissuade a cat from nibbling your houseplants, provide it with its own pot of cat mint. You could also try wiping the leaves of plants you want to protect with a solution of lemon juice and water.

◆ LEFT
A cat enjoying the companionship of its young owner. Although independent, most cats are social animals and prefer to have company.

◆ ABOVE
Here's a positive response to an owner's call. From the look of expectancy and the line of the tail, it is probably supper time.

◆ LEFT
Boy and kitten play together. This is important for both – the child learns to be gentle and kind to animals. The kitten does not become lonely or bored and hones its hunting techniques.

Breeding from Your Cat

The vast majority of people are quite content to own a cat, or cats, and leave it at that. Their animals are neutered (altered) and live the life of non-reproductive felines that simply grace the lives and homes of their owner. There are other people who become deeply involved in breeding cats as a hobby – it is rarely a profitable business. The amateur cat breeder may be rewarded by a handful of exquisite and charming kittens that may or may not be perfect pedigrees, but he or she is also taking on an expensive, time-absorbing, and often frustrating commitment.

◆ FACING PAGE
A Singapura mother and her kitten demonstrate the rewards of breeding in their beauty and character. The breed was developed from the "drain cats" of Singapore.

◆ ABOVE
A pale coat combined with darker points at ears, nose, tail and paws – seen to great effect in the Siamese – is known in breeding circles as the "Himalayan factor".

THE REWARDS OF BREEDING

◆ BELOW
The ultimate reward for a breeder is to produce a pedigreed cat of such perfection of type and temperament that it becomes a national Supreme Grand Champion like the Cream Colourpoint Longhair, Rosjoy Rambo.

Think carefully of the implications before you decide to let your cat have kittens. Whether you are giving your non-pedigree a chance to be a mother before having her neutered (altered), or planning to propagate a pedigree line, the process can be both time-consuming and expensive. Perhaps the most important consideration of all is to be sure that you will be able to find good homes for the kittens. If not, or if the prospective buyers change their minds, you must be prepared to give them a permanent home yourself.

Most people who breed from their cats are dealing with pedigrees rather than random-bred animals, with a view to continuing or improving on pure-bred lines. For the cat lover, the pedigree cat world is one of absorbing interest and beauty. It is also a stimulating environment where you will learn a great deal; your rivals will often become your best friends.

THE COMMITMENT

Those who go into breeding pedigrees thinking they are going to earn a lot of money from selling them are going to be disappointed. Even the most experienced and reputable breeders are lucky to break even over the course of any financial year. There are veterinary bills to pay for both mother and offspring, stud fees, special diets for the pregnant and nursing mother, heating for the kittens, veterinary testing and inoculation, and registration and advertising costs.

A heavily pregnant and nursing cat needs attention. The queen may not deliver her kittens at a convenient time and place during the day. This may happen in the early hours of the morning, and she may need some help from you, especially if it is her first litter. There may be deaths to deal with, especially in a first litter, which will be extremely distressing for everyone concerned.

Kittens may be lovable and cute, but they can also be destructive and get in the way. They need to be watched and cared for, and prepared for going out into the world. You should raise a pedigree litter for love and interest rather than money, and preferably when you already have some experience as an owner.

HOW IT ALL BEGAN

Breeding pedigreed cats on a serious level did not take place until the 1800s. The first cat show, held in London in 1871, set a trend for exhibiting, which in turn led to a more calculated approach to breeding. The organizer, an artist and author called Harrison Weir, set guidelines for breeding which became the basis for standards throughout the world, although different countries set their own rules. Most of the cats in the early shows were domestic shorthairs and Persians.

◆ BELOW
After a particularly awful day, with kittens into everything and apparently multiplying, many a cat breeder wonders, "Why am I doing this?" One look at this trio of bi-colours would probably answer the question.

Diminutive yet powerful Singapuras are the
pedigreed version of the Singapore alley cat. The
best examples were selected and bred to produce
a pedigree which is increasing in popularity.

♦ BELOW
If your breeding
programme produces
a line-up of six week-
old Blue and Cream
Persians like this
one, you should have
no difficulty finding
a home for them.

It was not until the 1880s that Asian
breeds were introduced to western
Europe. The first Siamese cats were
exhibited in Britain in 1885. By this
time, breeders in Europe and America
were setting up their own breeding
programmes. They drew from the best
British pedigreed stock and their own
indigenous cats. The first American
cat show was in New York in 1895.

A NEW BREED
There are now more than fifty
internationally recognized breeds, and
several others that are recognized as
established and distinct breeds in some
countries but not in others. The
purpose of breeding may go beyond a
desire to produce kittens for show or
for sale, or even to keep a pedigree line
going. Careful and well-informed
selection of the queen and the stud can
improve the type. Instead of waiting
for the natural processes of evolution
to select the fittest of a species, a
breeder can speed up the process.
Picking the healthiest and most
well-formed examples of indigenous
street cats, and mating them, for
example, led to the development of
standard types of British, American
and European shorthairs. Breeders can
also try to create a new variety of cat –
a new colour variation of an
established breed, or a new breed
altogether. However, this is an area
that should be left to the experts who
have built up an in-depth knowledge
of feline genetics, for mutations do
sometimes occur. To establish a new
breed takes many years. Only after
several matings can a breed be proved
to produce healthy offspring of
consistent type, and only then can
it be officially registered.

READY FOR MATING?

It is quite obvious when a female is ready for mating. She starts what is known as "calling" – although this can be more like shrieking or wailing in some breeds, such as Siamese. Some Persians content themselves with dainty little mews and miaows. The female displays some brazen behaviour, rolling and dragging herself around the floor, flicking her tail and raising her rump to expose the slightly reddened area beneath. She may also lose interest in her food. If her behaviour fools you into thinking she is unwell, try picking her up by her neck folds (as an interested tom would do) and stroke along her back. If she responds with pleasure, pads her feet and raises her tail, she is definitely in season.

The average age of sexual maturity in a female is around six months, but cats of oriental origin such as Siamese and Burmese can be as early as fourteen or sixteen weeks. British Shorthairs and Persians do not start calling much before ten months. Generally, tom cats become sexually mature a month or two later than females of the same breed. The time of year also has an

◆ ABOVE
A Siamese female in season rolls around and thrashes her tail. Siamese are notorious for announcing their sexual readiness with loud and strident calling.

◆ BELOW
A Bi-colour Seal Point Ragdoll tom has taken a fancy to a Ragdoll and Turkish Van cross. If they mate successfully, their kittens will be very pretty, but they will not be pedigreed stock.

effect on the first call. If due in
autumn or winter, it may be delayed
until the warmer months of spring.

The cycle is approximately 21 days
and females may come into oestrus
(on call) for about three to ten days.
They continue to be fertile until at
least fourteen years of age.

It is best to let the young queen run
through the first couple of cycles –
until she is at least a year old – rather
than put her to stud immediately. This
gets the system going and reduces the
risk of problems at birth.

CHOOSING THE MALE

Many breed clubs publish a stud list
of proven males, but the breeder
from whom you bought the female is
likely to know of suitable mates. An
experienced breeder is also likely to
know about genetically compatible
lines, and even if you have some
ideas of your own, it is important to
take expert advice.

If you go to a show to look for
potential partners, do not be tempted
to go for the stunning new male
Grand Champion. Other breeders
may be clamouring to use him, but the
wiser choice would be his father. Not
only has he proved himself to be the
sire of outstanding stock, but with a

maiden queen it
is wiser to use an
experienced stud for
the first mating.

RENDEZVOUS

Before committing
yourself to a
particular stud,
visit the breeder
to check the
conditions in which
the maiden queen is to
be kept. This is an opportunity also to
ask vital questions about the number
and the supervision of matings.
Documentation on the participating
animals that needs to be exchanged
varies according to the conditions for
entry to stud, but for your female
include the following:
◆ pedigree
◆ registration and/or transfer
◆ up-to-date vaccination certificate
◆ current test certificates showing
negative status for both feline
infectious leukaemia and feline
immunodeficiency virus (FIV).

The stud owner may require
the tests to have
been carried out
within the last
24 hours,
although
others accept
tests within the past
five to seven days.
The conditions and fees
should be agreed before
taking the queen to the
stud. Conditions of the
mating might include
an agreement that no
males from a resulting
litter will be used for

◆ LEFT
Whatever the breed, it is
important that the male
is neither monorchid
(one testicled) nor
cryptorchid (hidden
testicled): this Korat is
fully endowed!

breeding, or for the pick of the litter
to be substituted in lieu of a mating
fee. It is usual for there to be another
free mating should the queen fail to
become pregnant.

On a more informal level, the stud
owner should want to know the pet
name of the cat and the diet she is
used to.

◆ BELOW
The ideal Tabby stud should not only
be of first-class type, but have clear,
well-defined markings.

THE MATING

When the young queen starts to call, contact the stud owner. Both animals must be in good health, and have their nails clipped beforehand.

The journey to the stud usually takes place on the second or third day of the call. The stud's owner prepares for the arrival of the queen by thoroughly disinfecting the entire stud run and the queen's quarters. The queen is settled in her quarters within the stud run, where the stud can "talk" to her. This enables the queen to become accustomed to the stud's presence, and prepares her for mating.

At a quiet moment, the stud's owner releases the queen from her quarters. If all goes to plan, she crouches ready to receive the male; he grasps her by the scruff with his teeth, and taps her rump with one of his back legs until she raises it and flicks her tail over. The first entry of the male induces ovulation in the female and may result in fertilization, though subsequent matings are more likely to do so. (Note that your queen is likely to remain fertile for several days, so keep her in when she returns home.)

When sexual climax is reached, the female utters a strange cry that is only ever heard at this time. As soon as he withdraws from the female, the male moves away as the female turns on him with tooth and claw. She then rolls around, washing furiously for a couple of minutes. Only after she has done this is she calm again. Several matings need to take place over two or three days to try to ensure that the female becomes pregnant.

The stud owner supervises matings so that no harm comes to either stud or queen, but, in many cases, the male and female soon develop a bond. They are then allowed to run together and mating can take place freely. It is very common for the queen to take over the stud's bed and to assume matriarchal dominance. At the end of her stay, the stud owner will provide a certificate giving details of:

+ the stud's pedigree
  + number of matings observed
    + dates of matings
    + expected date of litter arrival
    + the agreed stud fee and conditions.

+ BELOW
The queen and tom go through preparatory rituals before mating takes place, but once the male has ejaculated, he moves out of the way to avoid a sharp cuff from his partner.

+ TOP
A female does not ovulate (release her eggs) until the moment of mating. One of the triggers is the male taking hold of the queen's neck fur; this also has the practical effect of keeping her in one place.

THE PREGNANCY

◆ BELOW
Towards the end of a pregnancy, most cats
require more rest than usual, and this Persian is
relaxing before her confinement.

The average gestation period for cats is between 63 and 68 days. Occasionally, healthy kittens are produced, even at 61 days. Kittens produced at or before this time usually require very specialized nursing, as key systems have not fully developed. Some females carry their kittens for as long as 70 days. In this event, the kittens may be larger than normal.

SIGNS OF PREGNANCY
The first indication that a cat is pregnant (or in kitten) is when she does not come on heat two or three weeks after mating. Soon after this, there will be visible signs of pregnancy: the nipples become rather swollen and take on a deep coral-pink tone, a process that is called pinking up. Very experienced breeders may know a cat is in kitten a few days in advance of this, as there is sometimes a ridging of the muscles of the cat's stomach. A vet is able to confirm a pregnancy by feeling the cat's abdomen after three or four weeks.

ANTENATAL CARE
A pregnant cat should be encouraged to maintain a normal lifestyle. You can increase the amount of food you give her from about the fifth week of pregnancy, and introduce a vitamin supplement. In a feral state, a cat gorges itself as it does not know where the next meal is coming from. Your cat will let you know how much food she wants. Seek veterinary advice if you are in any doubt.

Climbing, jumping, running – and hunting if the cat is free-range – are all normal physical activities, even for a pregnant pedigree. Do remember, however, that allowing a pregnant female free range may expose her to other dangers. She may slow down a bit towards the end of her term, but activity ensures that good, strong muscle tone is maintained. This is essential for a natural, successful birth.

After about four weeks, the queen's stomach starts to distend, the nipples become very prominent, and she begins to look pregnant. By around 28 days, all the kittens' internal organs have formed, and the embryos are about 2.5 cm (1 in) long. The skeleton develops from about 40 days, and at 50 days, the kittens quicken – show signs of movement. Look for rippling, sliding motions along the mother's flank; they are most noticeable when she is resting.

About a week before the birth, the queen starts looking for a nesting place. It is a good idea to prepare a cardboard-box house for the queen with lots of plain paper inside for her to tear up. If this is not done, she will do her best to get into wardrobes (closets), drawers, airing cupboards – anywhere warm and draught-free.

◆ LEFT
Given a choice, your queen would probably nest in a most inconvenient spot. A kittening box is ideal for both mother and owner, but do make sure the cat is used to and comfortable with both the box and its location well before the birth.

THE KITTENING

Birth is an exciting but messy business, which is why there should be a lot of padding in the kittening box, and the area beneath and around the box should be easy to clean and disinfect without disturbing the inmates too much.

About 24 hours before the actual birth, the queen enters the first stage of labour. Outward physical signs are very few. There may be the odd faint ripple along the flank of the cat, and experienced breeders will note that her breathing through the nose has become shallow and rapid on occasion. Close examination reveals a flickering of the nostrils during these early, very faint contractions. Towards the end of this process, a small mucous plug may be found in the bedding, or adhering to the hair close to the cat's vulva.

The next stage can take quite a long time, depending on the number of kittens. It is important not to panic: as long as the queen shows no signs of physical distress, all is going well. During this second stage, the classic signs of major contractions are clearly visible. The queen is breathing deeply and her whole abdomen seems to shudder and ripple downwards.

Eventually, a membrane sac containing a kitten and fluid starts to emerge from the queen's vulva and it may be possible to see the kitten's head within the sac. Sometimes the sac will burst at this point when it is said

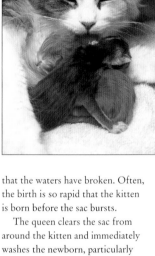

♦ ABOVE LEFT
A newborn kitten has just emerged and broken free from the protective sac of amniotic fluid.

♦ ABOVE RIGHT
Mother's first task is to take her newborn kitten and wash it thoroughly, especially around the nose and mouth to clear respiratory passages so that it can breathe – and utter its first cries.

MIDWIFE EQUIPMENT

- ♦ disinfected, blunt-ended scissors
- ♦ sterile surgical gloves
- ♦ kitchen towels
- ♦ hot water
- ♦ ordinary towels
- ♦ towelling face cloths
- ♦ water-based lubricant

♦ LEFT
One week old, blind, deaf, hungry – and not at all domesticated.

that the waters have broken. Often, the birth is so rapid that the kitten is born before the sac bursts.

The queen clears the sac from around the kitten and immediately washes the newborn, particularly around the nose and mouth. This prompts the kitten to get rid of any amniotic residue from its respiratory system and it will often begin to cry. By this time secondary contractions have expelled the placenta (afterbirth), which the queen will instinctively eat. In a feral state, this would provide her with food and nutrients during the first couple of days after kittening when she needs to recover. Hormones in the placenta promote milk secretion, and also help the uterus to contract, preventing a haemorrhage, which is a normal occurence after every birth. In the wild, such haemorrhaging could lead a predator to the kittens' nest. The queen also chews through the umbilical cord. In a straightforward birth, the queen, even a maiden queen,

◆ BELOW
Three weeks old: eyes are open and mobility is
improving. The kitten can now try some finely
chopped cooked meat or kitten food to
supplement the milk from its mother.

◆ BELOW
A non-pedigreed litter has settled down after
the trials of birth.

will usually cope with everything.
However, it may be that you will
have to assist on occasions. For this,
a range of equipment should be within
easy reach.

BREECH BIRTH

It is normal for some kittens to be
born backwards, with hind feet being
presented first. If the rump and tail,
rather than the stretched-out hind
feet, are presented first, this is a
breech birth and can be a problem.
It is so easy to become impatient and
want to get your hands in the nest to
help out, but the real need to do this
should be very carefully weighed up.

If the queen is contracting strongly,
it is likely that she will be able to birth
the kitten quite normally. This way
round is just a little more difficult,
as the head is not widening the birth
passage so that the rest of the body
can slide through. However, if the
waters have burst, and the kitten is
taking a very long time to be born,
there is a risk of brain damage or still-
birth and the kitten should be helped
out as quickly as possible.

If the legs are coming first, quickly
slip on the surgical gloves and smear
a little of the lubrication around the
vulva. Never pull on any part of the
kitten – it is an extremely delicate

organism capable of being very easily
damaged. As the queen's contractions
push the legs further out of the vulva,
use index and middle finger to
"scissor" the legs right next to the
opening of the vulva. As the
contractions cease, the natural effect
is for the legs to be drawn back into
the vulva. The breeder's fingers will
hold the legs in position until the next
set of contractions. Then as more of
the legs appear, use the index and
middle fingers of the other hand to

repeat the process. Generally, once the
hips have emerged, the queen can do
the rest by herself.

In the case of a rump or tail breech
birth, you may need to gently insert a
lubricated finger beside the kitten and
hold it as a hook. But it must be
emphasized that, in most cases, the
queen knows what is best and can
manage by herself.

APPARENT STILL-BIRTH

Sometimes a kitten will be born
apparently lifeless. This may not be
the case; it may not be breathing and
be in a state of shock. If the queen
does not immediately rasp away at the
kitten's face, it is your job to do it.
To clear any excess fluid from the
nose and lungs, hold the kitten in your
hand with index finger going over and
supporting its head. Gently swing the
kitten downwards two or three times
and then wipe and stimulate the face

around the nose and nostrils. At
the same time, rub its little body
vigorously. In most cases this will get
it going but you may have to resort
to mouth-to-mouth resuscitation.

It may be that the kitten has
suffered some form of foetal distress
during the birth process and has, in
fact, died. The cause may be more
serious, and a dead kitten should be
laid aside carefully for a post-mortem
examination to establish the cause.

QUEEN DISTRESS

Even very experienced queens may
become distressed and unable to birth
their kittens. Because of this possibility
it is wise to let your veterinarian know
when the kittens are due. The most
common form of distress is the lack of
strong contractions. The vet may inject
the queen with oxytocin, a hormone to
improve contractions. If this does not
work, birth by Caesarean section may
be the only option. This is done very
rapidly and with the minimum amount
of anaesthetic, so that the queen is
well able to look after her kittens.

One of the reasons why it is
essential to examine the breeding
record of the bloodline from which
a queen is obtained is to check for
any predisposition to the need for
Caesarean sections.

POST-NATAL CARE

While it is rare for a healthy queen to
encounter problems after pregnancy,
a close watch should always be kept for
the following conditions:

- ◆ Pyometra: an infection of the
  uterus characterized by a thick,
  off-white discharge. This condition
  is not serious if caught quickly and
  treated with antibiotics. In a serious
  form it will mean that the queen
  will have to be spayed.
- ◆ Eclampsia (milk fever): caused by
  a dramatic fall in calcium levels
  in the queen who will begin to
  convulse. An immediate intra-
  muscular or intravenous injection
  of calcium from the vet brings
  immediate recovery.
- ◆ Mastitis: the queen's mammary
  glands become hard, lumpy and hot
  due to an infection. Treatment is
  with antibiotics. Temporary relief
  can be given by the use of warm
  compresses on the affected area.
- ◆ Lack of milk: the queen's milk can
  dry up if she doesn't have
  sufficient wholesome food and
  drink; or the kittens are not
  suckling vigorously enough; or
  through mastitis. A homeopathic
  remedy such as Lachesis or
  hormone treatment may result in
  a return of the milk supply. If not,
  the kittens may have to be hand-
  fed until they are weaned. This
  means two-hourly feeds with a
  commercially available substitute
  milk. The vet may know of
  breeders who are specialists in the
  techniques of hand-feeding.

ABNORMALITIES

Defects are rare. They include:
- ◆ cleft palate or hare-lip
- ◆ lack of eyes
- ◆ heart defects including hole
  in the heart
- ◆ umbilical hernia
- ◆ intestines on the outside.

GROWING UP

If the litter is strong and healthy, the queen will require no assistance from you for the first two to three weeks. However, do change the bedding regularly (provided this does not upset the mother) and make sure the mother has plenty to eat: she may need three times as much as usual. The kittens' eyes open at around a week old and they will stop hissing at you every time you pick them up.

It is important to handle the kittens from the start. Encourage them to become used to the human voice and contact by picking them up and stroking them gently and regularly, and crooning to them. Experts used to advise that queens and their newborn kittens should be kept in a warm, dark, secluded place. However, this is just about the best way to make kittens nervous of people and activity. Once the kittens are weaned they can be introduced into the wider home environment and visitors, even if this is from within the sanctuary of a kitten pen. Social contact increases their confidence to tackle new situations when they leave home at 12 to 16 weeks of age.

EATING HABITS

The mother guides her kittens to her teats. They knead the teats with their paws and then start to suckle. The colostrum milk of the first few days is rich in the mother's antibodies and nutrients which protect the newborn kittens from infection. The kittens should be gradually weaned off their mother's milk. There is no specific time when this starts to happen, though they may begin to eat their mother's food at three to four weeks. It is not unusual for a kitten to remain

✦ BELOW
Seven weeks old: these three look harmless enough, but at this age they will be learning to hunt and fend for themselves through play.

on mother's milk for the first five weeks. Kittens must be fully weaned by 12 weeks, when they are ready to go to a new owner. They are actually capable of lapping water and of being on a solid diet by about six weeks.

The first solid food should be high-quality canned kitten food, finely

✦ BELOW
Nine weeks old: active, strong and independent enough to venture outside – but not until it has had its first vaccinations.

minced (ground) cooked meat or poultry, or flaked white fish. Variety will encourage broad taste and good habits in later life as well as a balanced diet. Avoid dried food at this stage, and feed the kittens small quantities four to six times daily at three to four weeks of age, gradually reducing to three or four times daily from then on.

Until they begin eating solid foods, the kittens do not need to use the litter tray (pan). The mother cleans them herself. You may find that the kittens simply copy their mother and use the tray

◆ LEFT
A Siamese mother shows
her kitten exactly where,
when and how to use the
litter tray (pan). It is
unlikely that the kitten
will need any extra
training from its owner.

◆ BELOW
Some are more interested
than others in the prospect
of solid food. One of
these Siamese kittens
may be reflecting on the
warmth and comfort of
its mother's breast.

without any help from you. If not,
you can try placing the kittens in the
tray immediately after each feed. The
tray should be in a quiet spot where
the floor and surroundings can be
easily cleaned and disinfected. From
this moment until the kittens leave
to go to their new homes, your

management of the environment is
extremely important. Where there
is a lack of hygiene, there is a risk of
disease and infection. The kittens may
also form bad habits which they will
carry with them to a new home.
Such a situation would be a poor
advertisement for a breeder.

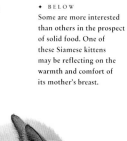

THE ART OF SELECTION

◆ LEFT
Cinnamon is a recessive gene to black and is carried on the same gene locus as chocolate.

The colour range in a litter is determined by genes inherited from the parents, and whether those genes are dominant or recessive. Each kitten will inherit genes from both parents, but in a unique combination.

Genes are found in pairs. Black is dominant to chocolate and cinnamon, so a cat with one black gene will be black, whereas if it has no black genes it will be chocolate or cinnamon. Within this same pair, chocolate is dominant to cinnamon, so a cinnamon cat must have two cinnamon genes (a cat with one gene for chocolate and one for cinnamon will be chocolate in colour). The dilute gene, which dilutes the pigment of a cat from black to blue, chocolate to lilac, cinnamon to fawn, or red to cream, is recessive. In

order for a cat to be a dilute colour it must have two dilute genes.

A tabby pattern is carried by the agouti gene which gives each hair a dark tip and alternate bands of light and dark colour. A non-agouti gene blocks the production of the light band in each hair, so producing a solid-coloured coat. White fur is the product of a gene which carries no pigmentation at all.

◆ ABOVE RIGHT
The lineage of this Blue Abyssinian would have included two dilute recessive genes and a black gene.

◆ RIGHT
This Exotic Shorthair must be female as she is a tortoiseshell – a colour produced by the presence of one red and one 'not red' gene.

COLOUR MUTATIONS

Black The first colour recessive mutation from the ancestral grey/brown agouti. Produces an extremely dark, solid colour perceived as black

Chocolate Recessive gene to black creating a dark brown

Cinnamon Recessive gene to black and chocolate. Carried on the same gene locus as chocolate, producing a light-brown colour with a warm (almost red-tinted) tone

Orange Sex-linked gene (carried on the X chromosome, so females XX can have two such genes, males XY can have only one).This alters black, chocolate and cinnamon to an orange (red, auburn, ginger) colour. Females are not sterile

Dilution Very often known as the "blue" gene as the presence of the recessive dilution with black creates a grey (lavender-blue) individual. Also affects other colours. Alters the

structure of the pigment cells
Dilution + black = blue
Dilution + chocolate = lilac
Dilution + cinnamon = fawn
Dilution + orange = cream

Tortoiseshell The presence of the orange gene plus black and its recessive colours of chocolate and cinnamon creates the two-coloured tortoiseshell female, i.e. black, chocolate and cinnamon tortoiseshells. In combination with the dilution gene the pastel blue-cream, lilac-cream and fawn-cream are created. The rare occurrence of the tortoiseshell male is probably due to the presence of an extra X chromosome. The males are usually sterile

Inhibitor Dominant and, as its name suggests, inhibiting – this gene reduces ground colour, e.g. the rufous colour of the brown tabby to the pewter ground of the silver tabby, or converting a self cat to a smoke

Dilute modifier Dominant gene, the presence of which is still disputed. Creates a rather dull brownish-grey colour known as caramel. It has no effect on the dominant colours black, chocolate, cinnamon or red. Probably originated in Chinchilla Persian stock and is to be found in several breeds of pedigreed cat

Full colour and its recessives Recessives to full colour are Burmese, Siamese, and blue-eyed and pink-eyed Albinos.
Burmese affects black, reducing it to a lustrous brown, or sable.
In the Siamese cat, black becomes a warm-toned seal.
Albinos are almost completely lacking in pigmentation (the blue-eyed version) or entirely without pigmentation (the pink-eyed version). Both may be completely or incompletely light-sensitive. Extremely rare in cats, although a race of Albino Siamese was discovered in America

Everyday Health Care

A cat is a survivor, and if it is injured, will often keep going regardless, making it difficult to spot if anything is wrong. Getting to know your cat's character, giving it regular checks, and understanding a little about the strengths and weaknesses of its body will help alert you to the first signs of illness or injury. Vigilance and care will keep the vet's bills down, too. If an emergency arises, knowing how to deal with it may save your cat's life and increase its chances of a full recovery.

◆ FACING PAGE AND RIGHT
Two images of cats in prime condition. Bright eyes, alert expressions and a proudly carried tail are all indicators of sound physical and mental health.

HOW TO TELL IF YOUR CAT IS SICK

The cat's coat is a barometer of health. It reflects the quality of its diet and general condition, and should be gleaming and free from dandruff. The healthy cat's eyes are bright and clear with no discharge, redness or blinking. The tissue around them is pale pink in colour rather than red and inflamed. Nose leather is cool and slightly moist from the cat's tear ducts, and licking also keeps the nostrils moist.

Often, it is only by knowing your cat and understanding how it normally behaves, looks and reacts within its usual environment that you can tell if anything is wrong. You are the mirror of your cat's health, so do not be afraid to mention anything abnormal that you have noticed, no matter how small. The vet may only see your cat once a year and does not know its normal character or behaviour. Particular points to look out for are changes in eating or drinking habits.

SIGNS OF A SICK CAT

The first sign that your cat is not well may be a change in its normal behaviour or appearance that may only

✦ ABOVE
A Red Tabby is interested in the life going on around it, as every healthy cat should be.

✦ ABOVE
An alert expression, pricked up ears and a glossy coat suggest that this cat has a balanced diet and a healthy, contented life.

✦ LEFT
A cat playing is in character – if it were suddenly to become uninterested in playing and listless, this would be a sign to the owner of possible ill health.

WHEN TO CALL THE VET

If your cat is displaying any of the following symptoms, call the vet immediately:

✦ blood in vomit, urine or faeces

✦ excessive thirst

✦ swollen and tender abdomen

✦ high temperature

✦ vomiting and diarrhoea together

✦ bleeding from penis or vulva

✦ straining when it tries to pass urine

✦ shallow, laboured breathing

✦ after a road accident

be perceptible to you. If a normally friendly cat shows signs of aggression, or an outgoing animal suddenly becomes withdrawn, timid and shy, look for other signs of illness. Lack of response to being called may be due to fever or temporary deafness caused by ear mite infestation.

COAT

A stary, ungroomed look to the coat with abnormally raised fur is a general indication of ill health.

STOOLS

If you still have cause for concern, check the cat's stools: they should be firm and without extreme or pungent odour. If you have an outdoor cat, confine it if possible and provide a litter tray (pan), so that you can make this check.

Where cats have access to dustbins, diarrhoea may be caused by a stomach upset resulting from eating contaminated food, but could be a sign

UNDERSTANDING YOUR CAT'S ANATOMY

The cat's skeleton provides support and protection for the vulnerable, internal organs. The entire feline skeleton is strong but light, as befits its function as a hunter.

The coat normally comprises a dense, soft undercoat covered by coarser hairs which are known as guardhairs. The density of the fur adds further protection to the skin (epidermis) from which it grows.

Skin consists of many layers of cells. These are constantly reproducing to compensate for the loss, caused by sloughing, of the cells which die and are shed from the surface as scurf.

TAIL Tail bones are joined by a complex machinery of small muscles and tendons, making the tail capable of a great range of movement. This enhances balancing potential and has also developed as a barometer of the cat's emotional state.

EYES Deep, large eye sockets facing forward protect the eyes. Binocular vision gives the depth of focus needed by a hunting animal in order to judge distances accurately.

HEAD is that of a typical predator, with a strong skull protecting the brain. It is capable of a wide range of movement due to the very flexible neck.

EARS Large, cup-like outer ears collect a vast range of sound. This is helped by tiny muscles which give the ears great flexibility of movement. The inner ear assists with balance.

BACK The back muscles are well developed to allow the cat to carry heavy weights over long distances. The spinal column ranges from the closely positioned bones of the chest to the longer, heavier lumbar vertebrae which support the weight of the body organs.

PELVIS is fused to the vertebrae of the lower back, and these are also linked to the progressively smaller bones of the tail.

TEETH are those of a typical predatory carnivore – canine teeth, or fangs, for killing; incisors for gripping; heavy, sharp molars for chewing and tearing. This process is helped by a very flexible lower jaw arrangement which allows sideways movement so that the tearing process becomes very efficient.

FRONT LEGS are capable of some rotation so that the pads can be presented to the face, for use in the washing process.

PAWS are long so that the cat actually walks on its fingers and toes which are supported by the sensitive fleshy pads. Claws are capable of being retracted.

BACK LEGS Movement is restricted to backwards and forwards only. The way in which the knee opposes the position of the elbow at the front, allows for the enormous spring which gives the cat the ability to pounce.

of something more serious, especially if it is persistent. Constipation, causing the cat to strain, can also be a problem, especially if there is any blood in the stools.

EYES

If the third eyelid – the haw or nictitating (blinking) membrane – is visible, it indicates an infection or that there is a foreign body in the eye. Any signs of redness or inflammation or excessive and persistent, thick, yellowish discharge are cause for concern. If either pupil appears dilated, or does not react to bright light, this needs prompt veterinary attention.

EARS

Clear wax in the ears is normal, but a dark brown waxy deposit may indicate ear mites that need veterinary treatment. Look out for seeds, such as grass seeds, too. A seed may lodge in the ear and enter the ear canal, making the cat shake and scratch its ear. The wall of the ear canal and flap (pinna)

is extremely delicate and vulnerable to damage in fighting situations. A puncture to the pinna often results in a haematoma (a large blood blister) that could become infected if not

treated. If the ears are very hot, the cat may be running a temperature, but before rushing to the vet, check this is not due to your cat lying in the sun or next to a radiator!

+ ABOVE
An owner gently holds back the ear to check that there are no scratches on the pinna (the inner lining of the outer ear). Also check for dark, waxy deposits.

+ ABOVE
As part of the regular care routine, make a random check in the fur by parting it until you can see the skin.

+ LEFT
As in humans and other animals, the state of a cat's eyes can indicate problems elsewhere in the body. This cat's eyes are those of a radiantly healthy animal.

SICKNESS

Light vomiting is very often no cause
for alarm. It may be due to the cat
having bolted down its food too fast,
a reaction to something it has caught
and eaten, to grass that it has
chewed to clear its system out, or
a physiological response to remove
hairballs. Persistent vomiting,
however, especially if it contains any
blood, is important, and is reason
enough to check with the vet.

TEMPERATURE

A good indication that the cat has a
raised temperature is if the ears feel
hot. A rectal thermometer is needed
in order to take a precise temperature
reading, which should be 38–38.5°C
(100.5–101.5°F). Unless you have
been taught how to do this properly,
it is best left to a professional.

PULSE

Key pulse points in a cat are located
under the forearms (armpits) and
back legs (groin). The pulse rate may
vary between 120 and 170, depending
on how active the cat has been
recently. The average is 150.

REGULAR CHECK-UPS

The caring and wise owner checks the
pet regularly to make sure it is in top
condition. Early signs of conditions
such as mite infestation or fleas will
prevent more serious problems
developing later. The check-up can
be at a time when you are relaxing
with your cat, or if it is one that
needs regular grooming, as an integral
part of the grooming routine. If a cat
does show any signs of ill-health or

♦ ABOVE
Modern cat food does not give a cat's teeth the
exercise and cleaning power that would come
from hunted food. It is therefore important to
check them regularly.

discomfort, you can go through the
checking points described on the
previous pages. Then, if you do need
to take it to the vet, you can give a
detailed report on anything unusual
you have noticed.

FUR AND BODY

One good reason for grooming your
cat regularly, even if it is a shorthair,
is that you will be quickly alerted to
any lumps, or signs of attack by fleas,
ticks, mites or lice. If the grooming
process rakes out some grit-like dirt,
check further. Comb the cat over
moistened absorbent paper. If the grit
leaves a red stain, these are the blood-
gorged faeces of fleas. If not, the cat
has just been rolling in the garden.

Small, raised grey or whitish lumps
indicate ticks. These can irritate the
cat considerably as the tick's head is
buried deep into the skin, leaving only
the body visible. They should be
removed as soon as possible but great
care has to be taken to ensure that the
head is removed as, if left behind, an
abscess or sore can develop.

EARS, NOSE AND MOUTH

Check that ears are clean and free
of dark waxy deposits and seeds.
Even minor scratches need to be kept
clean to prevent infection. Check for
broken or discoloured teeth, swollen
gums and bad breath, and make sure
there are no lumps (enlarged glands)
around the neck.

PAWS

The claws of an indoor cat need to be
checked regularly in case they need
clipping and to prevent them from
ingrowing. Also check for any
soreness or wounds on the pads.

STANDARD TREATMENTS

However hardy your cat is, it runs the risk of being struck down by a killer virus infection unless it is inoculated and boosted on a regular basis. If a cat contracts one of the diseases for which preventative vaccines are available, it is very serious, for there is no treatment that can be guaranteed to save it. All a vet can do is to treat the symptoms and minimize suffering, and hope that your pet's natural immunity will fight the illness.

INOCULATIONS
In the first few days of its life, a kitten's resistance is boosted by the antibody-rich colostrum that is the mother's first milk. Although this is replaced by normal milk after the first few days, this also contains some antibodies so, as long as the kittens are feeding, the mother's immunity will pass down to them through the

milk. As soon as weaning starts, this natural protection diminishes. From now on, immunity has to be built up actively by the kitten and will no longer be acquired passively from the queen. Active immunity can be built

up by exposure to infections or, more safely and securely, by inoculations. Taking your cat to the vet to be inoculated is a vital part of routine care. Inoculations are given at 9–12 weeks; the kitten is then kept in for a week or two to prevent exposure to infection while the aquired immunity from the vaccine becomes effective. Inoculations subsequently need to be boosted every year. Some kittens or adult cats may feel a little under par for a few days after first inoculations or the annual booster, but it is rare for there to be any major problems.

FREEDOM FROM WORRY
Over the past 30 years, there have been enormous steps forward in the prevention and cure of feline ailments. The diseases that used to pose the greatest risk to pedigreed and non-pedigreed felines alike, are no longer a problem if the regular, recommended inoculation programme is followed.

◆ LEFT
Six-week-old kittens may be introduced to new social experiences, but three weeks before their first vaccination they must not be exposed to other cats in the outside world.

◆ BELOW
A stray cat with its single-kitten litter.
The mother's tough and probably deprived
lifestyle may have limited her ability to
produce a bigger litter.

◆ BELOW
A kitten receives its first vaccination at six
to nine weeks of age. It will have to be kept
indoors for another two to three weeks after
it has received its second vaccination.

WHICH INOCULATIONS?

Recommendations regarding
vaccinations vary in different
countries. In the United States, for
instance, where, in urban areas, owners
are often advised to keep their cats
indoors, both cat flu viruses, feline
infectious enteritis (feline distemper)
and rabies are considered the core
inoculations. Those against chlamydia,

WHAT TO DO WHEN

◆ 9 weeks: first vaccination

◆ 12 weeks: second vaccination

◆ 16 weeks: spaying for females

◆ 4–6 months: neutering
(altering) for males

◆ 6 months: start flea treatment

◆ monthly (after 6 months):
renew flea treatment

◆ every 6 months: worm treatment

◆ every year: booster vaccinations
and check-up

feline leukaemia virus and feline
infectious peritonitis are often
considered necessary only for cats
likely to be exposed to risk in the
outside world. However, bear in mind
that your cat could escape and come
into contact with one of the diseases
you decided not to inoculate against.
Take your vet's advice.

THE KILLERS

The most serious infections are: cat flu
(viral rhinitis), which encompasses
two viruses that affect the cat's upper
respiratory tract; feline infectious
enteritis; chlamydia; and feline
leukaemia virus. Rabies should be
added to the list in countries where
the disease is known to exist. Although
these are not the only viruses to affect
the cat, these are the major viral
conditions that have wrought havoc
in the past among domestic cats.

Effective vaccines against cat flu
and feline enteritis have been around
for several years. A vaccine to treat
the leukaemia virus is a more recent

addition. As yet, in the United
Kingdom, where rabies does not exist,
the vaccine can only be administered by
authorised vets to cats that are going
to countries where the disease exists.

GENERAL CHECK-UP

The vet will only inoculate your cat if
it is in good health, so do not take it
if it is below par for any reason. At
the same time as the annual booster
vaccinations, ask the vet to give your
cat a check-up – to look at ears, teeth,
gums and general condition. With
luck, this will be the only time the vet
sees your cat. You can also stock up
with treatments for worms and fleas.

◆ BELOW
A Chocolate Silver Ocicat kitten at 15 weeks
old has had all its vaccinations, and is
independent of its mother.

NEUTERING

♦ BELOW
A recently spayed female shows the shaved area
where the incision was made. There is a slight
possibility that the fur may grow back a
different colour in this area.

Neutering, altering or desexing not only prevents reproduction but also the inconvenience of the female cat coming into heat (oestrus) or calling. In the female cat this is called spaying. In the male the operation, castration, reduces the tendency to spray and also the odour of the male cat's urine.

The operation has the effect of modifying behaviour associated with sexual desire and establishing and marking territory. The result is that the desexed cat is usually more stable and affectionate, and bonds more easily with the family. Recent work in Britain and the United States has shown that the operation in either sex can be carried out earlier than was previously thought with no ill effects.

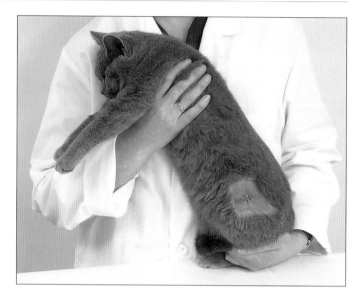

♦ BELOW
A recently spayed female shows the shaved area where the incision was made. There is a slight possibility that the fur may grow back a different colour in this area.

Some rescue organizations now desex kittens before they are homed at 8–12 weeks, but the majority of vets prefer to carry out the operation when the kitten is older, at 4–6 months. As both operations are carried out under a general anaesthetic, no food or water can be taken for about 12 hours beforehand. The operation cannot be reversed in either sex.

CASTRATION

The operation involves the removal, under anaesthetic, of the cat's testes. Tiny incisions are involved and usually no stitches are necessary. Within 24 hours the cat will usually be back to normal. Both kittens and adult cats can be castrated. If you consider giving a home to a stray tom, castration will

♦ LEFT
Burmillas are generally known for their good nature, but any aggressive tendencies will be further modified by the desexing process.

ensure that he settles quickly, is less aggressive, less territorial and less likely to roam. This also means that he is less likely to pick up infections and be involved in traffic accidents.

SPAYING

Female cats do not miss motherhood, and as they no longer have the urge to roam when coming into heat, and will not be targeted by unneutered (unaltered) toms, they gain security. Spaying involves the removal of the cat's ovaries (where the eggs are produced) and womb (uterus) to prevent her coming into heat. She should not be on heat at the time of the operation. A small area of fur is shaved on the abdomen and an incision made, which is later stitched. The spayed female cat will recover quickly but she will appreciate care, warmth and light meals for about a week, until the stitches are taken out.

HOW LONG WILL YOUR CAT LIVE?

◆ BELOW
A Blue Bi-colour Persian father seems to
contemplate the continuation of his pedigreed
line with one of his kittens.

From about the age of ten to 12 years, a cat may begin to show signs of growing old. This may not be immediately apparent as the slowing down process is very gradual. Internal organs may not work as well as they once did and joints may become that little bit stiffer. Over time the cat seems to restrict its activities, is far less playful and becomes a creature of sedentary habits. Particular health conditions associated with old age, such as diabetes or arthritis, can require constant supervision and medical intervention.

The oldest cat recorded was a tabby called Puss who was said to have lived for 36 years. The oldest pedigreed cat on record is Sukoo, a Siamese who died in 1989, at the age of 31 years. These are exceptional ages, however. Most cats live for about 14–16 years and a few may reach 20 years.

Neutered (altered) cats have a slightly longer lifespan than those which remain unneutered (unaltered). This is particularly true of male cats. An unneutered tom will fight to defend territory and the resulting injuries and infections may shorten his life. Females lead a much quieter life, and a career spent having kittens, in an environment in which her condition is well-maintained, appears to have little effect on the female's longevity.

As it grows older, a cat's physical responses slow down and its joints become stiff. This has the effect of reducing suppleness and agility, and grooming will become more difficult as the cat's flexibility is reduced.

THE DEATH OF YOUR CAT

Very old cats settle into a routine that reflects their capabilities. It seems

important for cats to maintain dignity, and this can be very difficult when the efficacy of their bodily functions is being challenged by old age. Your cat may die in its sleep but this does not happen very often. If the cat is suffering from chronic pain or can no longer respond to its natural instincts, you need to consider how kind it is to keep it alive. A vet can end the cat's life painlessly on the request of the owner: the cat is injected with an overdose of anaesthetic which literally puts it to sleep. Euthanasia can be regarded as the final gift to a much-loved animal that has shared your life.

◆ RIGHT
The start of a long relationship: this kitten
will probably live long enough to be a
companion for its young owner throughout
her childhood and teenage years.

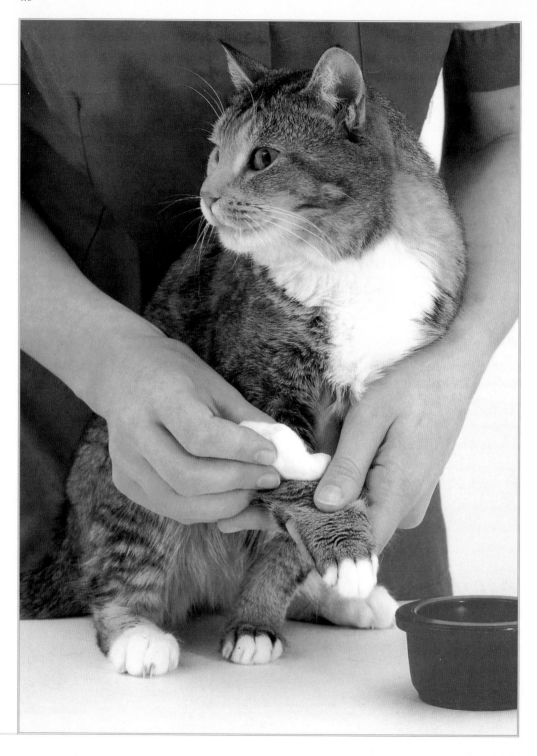

Injuries and Ailments

Cats traditionally live longer than dogs. Twenty years is not unusual. If you provide a balanced diet, the correct inoculations and regular check-ups, there is no reason why your cat should not live a long and happy life. However, illness or injury can strike at any time, so it is important to keep an eye open for any unusual behaviour in your pet that might indicate all is not well. In most cases of injury or disease, you will need to call the vet, but much can also be done at home in the way of first aid and general nursing.

HOME NURSING

A sick cat should be confined in an area that is warm and free from draughts, quiet and capable of being easily cleaned and disinfected. The first two requirements are relatively easy to fulfil, whereas the third could cause some problems. Many modern homes are carpeted throughout which makes disinfecting difficult. If there is not a separate utility room with a floor that is easily cleaned, you should consider buying a large, plastic travelling carrier which comes apart so that every part can be thoroughly cleaned.

Use a disinfectant agent recommended by your vet – it is most important to avoid any substances containing coal-tar, wood-tar, phenol, cresol and chloroxylenols. These

◆ LEFT
Special syringes, available from your veterinary practice and some pet shops, will help you administer medicines.

◆ BELOW
A warm, comfortable bed and plenty of tender, loving care are essential when nursing a sick cat.

agents are fine for use with people but can be lethal for cats. If a condition is seriously infectious to other cats, you should set aside some old clothes and shoes to wear when handling the sick

cat, and wash thoroughly afterwards. Always dispose of any used bandages or applicators promptly. Thoroughly clean up any vomit or faeces without delay and disinfect the area carefully.

BEDSIDE MANNER

You can help your cat's recovery tremendously with care, love and attention. Spend time talking quietly, maintaining appropriate physical contact without being overwhelming, and ensuring that its bodily needs are catered for. The cat may not be able to do anything for itself and, therefore, feeding, watering, grooming and assisting with toilet procedures become your responsibility. While this is very time-consuming, the bond you have already achieved with your cat will grow even stronger. The veterinary nurses (technicians) will help if you need advice on the various techniques involved with the grooming, feeding and toileting of a sick cat.

ADMINISTERING MEDICINES

Your vet will always give advice and instruction on how much and how often you should administer any medication your cat needs for treatment. Medicinal preparations come in several forms – liquids, pills, capsules, drops and lotions. The secret of administering any of these

successfully, and with least disturbance to the animal, is to have confidence in your ability to do so. However, some cats will object tooth and claw to having any foreign object forced into their mouths. If this is the case with your cat, you will need to ask someone to assist you and, if necessary, wrap the cat securely in a towel to help immobilize it.

Liquid medicines can be given using a plastic syringe obtainable from your vet or from most pet shops. After use it should be cleaned thoroughly and then stored for future use in a sterilizing agent such as one of those used for baby feeding equipment. Draw up the amount for one dose into the syringe. Holding the cat's head firmly, gently insert the syringe between the lips, at the side of the mouth. Push the plunger gently so that the cat receives the dose slowly and gradually, allowing it time to swallow. This reduces the risk of any liquid going into the lungs, which could cause pneumonia to set in rapidly in the case of a sick cat. Pill poppers, which look like elongated syringes, are available if you have

difficulty opening your cat's mouth. The pill is placed into the popper and a plunger pushes the pill to the back of the cat's tongue. Direct the instrument towards the palate rather than pressing on the tongue. Hold the cat's mouth closed and stroke its throat until it has swallowed.

DROPPING IN

Most preparations designed to be dropped into the eyes or ears are supplied with a dropper or a dropping nozzle. If not, droppers can be purchased from chemists (drugstores). Always carefully read the directions about how and when to apply the medication, before using.

The membranes of the eyes and ears are very delicate and it is most important for the cat to be held securely. Another pair of hands makes the job much easier.

With eye drops, one drop is usually sufficient. For ear drops, hold the pinna (ear flap) firmly to open the canal, and place two or three drops into the ear, then massage gently. Ear drops are usually oily and overdoing the drops results in a greasy head.

ADMINISTERING TABLETS

1 Hold the cat's head firmly, with your fingers on either side of the jaw, and gently pull the head back until the jaws open.

2 Talking quietly and encouragingly to your cat throughout the process, drop the pill or capsule at the back of the cat's tongue.

3 Hold the mouth closed and massage the throat until a swallowing action shows that the pill or capsule has been ingested.

ACCIDENT AND INJURY

Emergency treatment is often required for accidents within the home. Do not assume that a cat or kitten will automatically know its physical limits or be able to tell, for example, which plants are poisonous. It might well be able to fall from any angle and regain its footing, but only within certain heights. A cat falling from a balcony is just as likely to sustain serious damage as any other animal. Cats can be as vulnerable to accidents as children, and you should keep a constant eye on safety in your home.

It is valuable to know what on-the-spot treatment you can give before the cat receives veterinary attention. In extreme situations, this could make the difference between life and death. A cat that is very frightened or in pain may instinctively withdraw, and scratch and bite if handled. If this

WHEN TO WORRY

✦ obvious or suspected injury from a fall (usually 4m/12 ft, or more), or from a road traffic accident

✦ obvious fractures or dislocations

✦ profuse bleeding

✦ choking or respiratory distress

✦ severe burn or scalding

✦ collapse or a fit lasting more than a few seconds

✦ injuries to or foreign body in the eye

✦ LEFT
A cat is so intent on stalking a moving leaf or insect that it may end up on a branch that cannot support its weight and fall.

happens, talk calmly and keep the cat as warm, comfortable and confined as possible until professional help is available. As with any emergency, the first rule is not to panic and the second is to rely on your common sense. However inexperienced, you will learn by careful observation to recognize the real emergency. Prompt first aid is all that is needed, but if you are in the least doubt about the seriousness of any condition, seek professional help immediately. All veterinary practices have to offer a 24-hour emergency service. Phone the surgery number first to check for any special emergency arrangements, or at least to give the surgery advance warning of your imminent arrival.

A cardboard box is a good carrier in an emergency; if an injured cat is placed on a board serving as a stretcher, it could easily fall off. Keep the cat warm by covering with a blanket and call the vet immediately. Try not to panic and handle the cat as gently as possible.

THE FIRST-AID KIT

✦ sterile pads and dressings

✦ bandages: 2.5 cm and 5 cm (1 in and 2 in) widths

✦ stretch fabric adhesive strapping

✦ lint padding or cotton wool roll

✦ cotton wool balls (uncoloured)

✦ antiseptic wipes, cream and lotion (as recommended by your vet)

✦ small, blunt-ended scissors

✦ tweezers

✦ nail clippers

✦ non-prescription soothing eye drops

✦ ear cleaner

✦ liquid paraffin

✦ kaolin mixture

✦ antihistamine cream

✦ rectal thermometer

✦ water-based lubricant

✦ eye dropper

✦ 5 ml (1 tsp) plastic syringe

✦ sterilizing agent

✦ Elizabethan (medical) collar

✦ surgical gloves

✦ suitable carrier or box

IMMEDIATE ACTION

What should you do in an emergency? If the cat is in a situation where further injury could occur, such as a busy road, move the animal carefully. Depending on the position of the injuries, try to grasp the cat gently by the scruff and support its weight with the other hand. Put it in a suitable box or carrier. If the cat is unconscious, take precautions against choking by clearing any blood or vomit from the mouth and pulling the tongue forward. The head should be below the body level when the cat is lying down so that any fluids can run out.

If there is severe bleeding try to stem it by putting a pressure bandage (like a tight bandage) over the wound. This works well in areas such as the limbs. Otherwise, try applying finger pressure to the wound.

CHOKING

If a cat is fighting for air and gasping for breath, wrap it in a blanket or towel to immobilize it, and try to look in the mouth to see if there is any obstruction. While someone is calling the vet, you could try to dislocate the object by shining a small torch down the gullet and pulling the object out with a pair of tweezers. Take care you are not bitten. If a sharp object has been swallowed the problem should be dealt with by a vet. If the cat swallows a length of string or thread, do not pull it out. Leave it or tie the exposed end to an improvised collar so that it is not lost on the way to the vet.

FOREIGN BODIES

If grit, seeds or other objects become lodged in a cat's eyes or ears, you may be able to use ear or eye drops or olive oil to float them out. Do not use tweezers in these areas. A cotton bud (swab) can sometimes be used gently to remove foreign bodies in the eye.

If potentially dangerous substances such as oil, paint or chemicals are spilt on a cat's coat, wash them off immediately with a dilute solution of mild detergent or soap and water. Patches of fur that are badly soiled should be cut off carefully and the area washed with soap and water.

◆ ABOVE
A cat that roams freely may have a more active and varied life, but it also runs a greater risk of accident and injury than the indoor pet.

◆ BELOW
Although cats can swim – and Turkish Van cats like this one are supposed to have a particular love of water – they will drown if enough water enters the lungs.

HOW TO RESUSCITATE A CAT

There is no point in being squeamish if the cat's life is to be saved. A feline kiss of life is difficult to administer and will require coming into intimate oral contact with either the cat's nostrils or mouth. The instinct to save life is very strong so, for most owners, this aspect of resuscitation will not pose a problem.

1 Clear the airways of any vomit or blood and check that the tongue is pulled forward. Hold the cat's head gently backwards and blow into the nostrils. If the nostrils are restricted in some way, pinch the cat's mouth open with your fingers pressing both cheeks to create a restricted opening, take a deep breath and blow into the mouth. Do not overdo it, as a cat's lungs are very much smaller than a person's.

2 Between each breath, gently massage the chest to allow the air to trickle out, and maintain a rubbing motion on the cat's chest to try to stimulate heartbeat. Keep on with the mouth-to-mouth process until the cat can breathe regularly by itself. It may be that this form of resuscitation does not work, in which case heart massage is the last option.

3 Heart massage may damage the cat. A delicate rubbing motion will just not stimulate the heart into beating so, with the cat on its side, preferably supported on a blanket or towel, press downwards firmly on the chest just behind the front leg, about once a second. In some cases, ribs have been broken in elderly animals, but the cat has survived. If this does not work, at least you know that you have done everything possible.

RESUSCITATION SITUATIONS

A completely collapsed cat which may appear dead can sometimes be resuscitated if you act swiftly. The condition most frequently occurs with a newly born kitten. It is very simple to assess if there is still a heartbeat by feeling for a pulse in the armpit. If no pulse is found it does not necessarily mean that brain death has occurred, and you may still be able to resuscitate the animal by gently massaging the chest between finger and thumb and holding the head down.

HEART ATTACK

There has been a recent increase in the number of cats, especially pedigreed cats, who collapse and die of a condition called cardiomyopathy, of which there are various types. An apparently healthy cat may suddenly keel over and die. This condition is thought to run in families, but the mode of inheritance is unclear and is the subject of much research worldwide. Sometimes, in mild cases, massaging the chest between finger and thumb does help.

ELECTRIC SHOCK

A cat can sustain an electric shock as a result of chewing through electrical flexes and cords. Switch off the electricity immediately to prevent further shock. The vet's advice should be sought as severe burns to the gums and lips can result.

DROWNING

It takes very little liquid to cause drowning. All that is required is enough for the lungs to be filled so that oxygen is unable to enter the bloodstream. Patting the cat's back may be all that is needed to expel the water from the lungs but, more often, drastic measures have to be employed, such as swinging the cat by the hind legs in an attempt to get the liquid out. Then resuscitation can begin (*see box*).

ANIMAL BITES

The cat that roams freely outside is much more likely to come into contact with other animals than the house-bound feline. Fights over territorial rights around the home are likely. The bite of any animal, including other cats, dogs, rodents and snakes, can be dangerous, as many bacteria are carried in the mouth.

It may not be immediately obvious that your cat has been bitten. Usually a cat that has been hurt will find a quiet, secluded spot to lick its wounds, quite literally. This is the cat's own first aid, as its saliva contains a natural antiseptic. You may not discover a

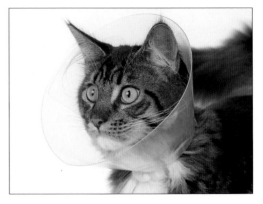

◆ LEFT
An Elizabethan (medical) collar is attached around the neck to prevent a cat from reaching back or down to lick a wound or medical dressing. The cat's owner then has to take on all grooming responsibilities.

IMMOBILIZING A CAT THAT IS FRIGHTENED OR IN PAIN

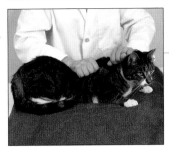

1 Place the towel on a table and the cat on the towel. Place one hand firmly on the cat's neck to control its head. Press the other firmly on the cat's back so that it lies down.

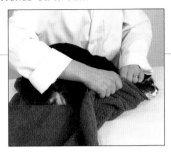

2 Keep one hand firmly on the cat's neck so that the head is under control throughout. With the other hand, bring the towel over the cat's neck, legs and body so that the legs are restrained.

3 Still keeping a firm but gentle hold on the cat's neck, tuck the towel underneath the cat's body. Do not forget to talk to your pet in a calm voice all the time you are doing this.

hidden bite until you actually touch the site of the wound and the cat reacts. Keep the cat warm and comfortable and seek advice. Delay could mean that the cat will develop infection which will make treatment more complicated and, therefore, more traumatic for the cat. Wounds will need regular cleaning and bathing with a suitable antiseptic.

ABSCESSES

Any untreated puncture wound is liable to become infected and result in an abscess, which is a large, pus-filled swelling. Without treatment, the abscess may eventually burst, with a real risk of septicaemia (blood

poisoning) due to toxins from the untreated abscess entering the bloodstream. The original puncture wounds soon heal, so the correct treatment will involve a trip to the vet so that the abscess can be lanced, allowing it to drain properly.

Septicaemia is serious, as it is with people. The onset is rapid and within hours a cat can be running a very high temperature. This may be followed by fits, sickness, a rapid fall of temperature to sub-normal level, collapse and death.

The greatest cause of an abscess is a bite or claw puncture from another cat. Such wounds are invariably sustained during a fight, so the most

common abscess sites are around the head and neck, paws, and at the base of the tail.

SNAKE BITES

Many snake bites can be poisonous and may be followed by swelling around the wound, progressive lethargy and hyperventilation which may be accompanied by fits, followed by collapse and coma.

Once the wound site has been identified, try to apply a tourniquet above the punctures as quickly as possible (*see box*). The most likely site of a bite is on the leg, near the paws, in which case the tourniquet should be applied to the upper leg. If the wound is around the face or neck, then there is little that can be done.

When applying a tourniquet to a snake bite, the aim is to prevent the venom entering the bloodstream. However, remember that the application of a tourniquet cuts off the blood supply to the limb. The tourniquet should therefore be slackened every two to three minutes to ensure that the tissues are kept alive, even if this results in releasing a limited amount of the venom into the bloodstream. If this is not done, there is a possibility of such severe tissue damage that the limb would have to be amputated.

TO APPLY A TOURNIQUET

1 Place a loop of soft, narrow fabric, such as a stocking or a tie, around the limb, on the heart side of the wound site

2 Insert a pen, pencil, piece of cutlery or thin, strong stick between the skin and the fabric loop

3 Twist the fabric until it is tight enough to cut off the blood supply below it

4 Loosen the tourniquet for a few moments every two or three minutes and then re-tighten

5 If there is any swelling, apply a cold compress by wrapping a few ice cubes in a cloth, or (an athlete's tip) use a packet of frozen peas

6 Gently wash the affected spot with a recommended antiseptic, diluted to the manufacturer's instruction

7 Any bleeding should stop. If it does not, the tourniquet is not tight enough

8 Try to bandage the wound and take the cat to the vet as soon as possible. The wound may need stitching

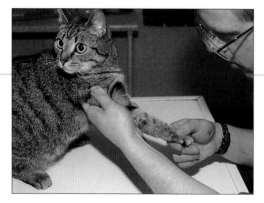

◆ LEFT
A vet feels a cat's leg for any breakages in the bone or internal swellings that might suggest a sprain or arthritis, to find the cause of a limp.

STINGS

It is the cat's nature to chase and pounce on insects regardless of any danger. A single wasp sting is not too alarming but remember the wasp is able to sting repeatedly. Although a cat moves fast, a wasp tangled in the cat's fur can sting a number of times before it can be brushed off. In contrast, the bee leaves the sting behind in the cat. The bee sacrifices itself when it stings, and the full quota of bee venom is left behind. Stings can occur in the mouth or throat if the insect is swallowed. This will cause swelling, and breathing and swallowing might be restricted. If external this is unpleasant and painful; internally, it can be dangerous.

The cat may show an alarming allergic reaction to a sting. If the swelling has been caused by a bee sting, the actual sting remnant may be visible. This must be removed if possible, with tweezers. Whether the sting is internal or external, the cat should have veterinary attention without delay.

As a first-aid measure, external stings by bees or wasps may be treated with a commercially available antihistamine cream or lotion. If this is not immediately available, simple home remedies can be used. Bee stings can be treated with alkaline substances such as bicarbonate of soda, whereas wasp stings respond to the application of an acid such as vinegar. The cat should not be allowed to lick at any of these substances.

POISONING

Cats are great wanderers and they may well walk through any range of toxic materials. Transferred to the mouth through washing, such substances can easily cause poisoning, and burning to contact areas. Thorough washing of paws with a mild shampoo followed by thorough rinsing will alleviate some of the pain before the vet is involved. Vomiting, lassitude, apparent blindness, convulsions and collapse are all signs of poisoning. If such symptoms occur, seek veterinary aid immediately.

It is inadvisable to try to find a way of easing the animal's suffering yourself beyond keeping the cat warm and quiet. Take a sample of the substance if you know what it is, or note the name, so that an antidote may be found quickly if available. Your vet will have access to the national poison hotline. In some countries, where stray animals are a

◆ ABOVE
Give a cat a toy to play with in the garden, and with a bit of luck, this may distract it from pursuing the local wildlife.

◆ ABOVE
A vital nerve was severed in this cat's foreleg. The cause was barely visible – a tiny puncture in the skin, perhaps from a barbed wire fence or an animal bite. There was no improvement after a month, and the leg was amputated, but the cat continued to lead an active outdoor life.

BANDAGING A LEG

1 One person should hold the cat, and the other apply the dressing. Place lint over the injured area and hold it in place with your hand.

2 Use the bandage to bind the lint into position by taking it down over the paw and back up again; then wind it around the leg.

3 Continue winding the bandage firmly (but not so tight that the blood supply is cut off) and evenly around the entire length of the leg.

4 Split the end of the bandage leaving two ends long enough to take back around the leg in opposite directions. Tie the two ends together.

5 Tape adhesive bandage over the end of the paw and back up again as before. Wind around the entire length of the leg.

6 Keep the cat indoors for as long as the dressing is on. Change the dressing regularly as advised by the vet, or when it becomes grubby or loose.

nuisance, cats and dogs are sometimes deliberately poisoned by those who consider them pests.

If your cat returns home covered in motor oil, it is important to remove the oil from the coat immediately, as it could poison the cat's digestive system and result in kidney damage. Use a mild household detergent in lots of warm water, and seek veterinary advice if in difficulty.

SCRAPES AND BRUISES

Bruises are much less easy to detect than cuts, though you will suspect their presence if the cat becomes unusually unhappy about your touching the spot where the bruise is rooted. Similar signs are apparent if an abscess is developing on the site. As with human bruises, some come to the surface of the skin reasonably rapidly, whereas deep-seated bruising can take days to work its way out. Seek professional advice if

in doubt. Bruises and contusions respond very well to the application of *Hamamelis virginiana* (witch-hazel). Although such a remedy can be taken orally in very limited doses, it is better to prevent the cat from licking off any application by putting a medical collar around the neck.

STRAINS AND LIMPS

The cat may limp and resort to excessive washing of the injured spot. If you suspect something is amiss, first examine the paw carefully to see if there is a splinter or thorn in it, and remove it with tweezers if possible. Disinfect the area and keep your eye on the cat. Confine the cat indoors and, if there is no improvement, ask the vet to have a look at it.

If the problem is a strain, a cat will not rest of its own accord, and continued physical activity could not only aggravate the strain but also prevent it from healing.

BURNS

Cats attracted by cooking smells may leap on to unguarded cooking areas and even into ovens, and may be scalded by spilled hot liquid. A cat may also receive appalling burns, externally and internally, if it comes into contact with any of the lethal chemicals to be found in the house and garden.

Once the skin is burned, the body institutes its own first-aid regime. Body fluids are rushed to the affected area, and a blister forms protecting the underlying tissue. Do not burst the blister as the fluid in it helps to prevent infection. You can bathe the burn with ice-cold water until all heat has been taken out of the damaged area. Call the vet.

You can also apply a sterile, dry dressing loosely over the burn to keep out infection. Do not apply greasy substances – this would be like putting butter into a hot frying pan.

VIRAL INFECTIONS

Viruses need a host body to provide the energy they need to reproduce. Not all viruses cause disease. In the cat, pathogenic (disease-producing) viruses are responsible for such serious conditions as feline enteritis, cat flu and rabies. Some viruses, such as the one responsible for enteritis, are stable and resilient, surviving for long periods, while others, such as the flu virus, are readily destroyed by common disinfectants. Some viruses produce acute disease very quickly, while others have a long incubation period, like the feline immunodeficiency virus (FIV).

Even though you are able to protect your cat from many serious viral infections by means of vaccination, it is not yet universally common veterinary practice to inoculate against rabies or feline infectious peritonitis. Both vaccines are available worldwide but they are not necessarily universally licensed. In the United Kingdom, for example, the rabies virus is only used on animals intending to travel abroad; the rabies vaccination is mandatory as part of the "pet passport" scheme. The viral diseases that are effectively protected against by regular vaccination include feline enteritis and the flu viruses.

Infections are not necessarily the same as disease. Disease is any impairment of the normal functioning of the animal, and is usually, but not always, caused by infection. For example, cats will become infected with feline coronavirus, but may not show any signs of disease or illness at all. Infections are not always contagious, that is, they need not spread to other animals by contact.

CHLAMYDIA

Chlamydial organisms fall midway between viruses and bacteria (which, unlike viruses, are self-contained cells and do not need a host body) and are responsible for a disease of the upper respiratory tract in the cat, with symptoms very similar to those of cat flu. Minor outbreaks cause one or both eyes to become inflamed and to show an unpleasant discharge. More severe attacks also cause nasal discharge and a subsequent loss of smell and appetite. Chlamydia organisms are susceptible to similar antibiotics to which bacteria are sensitive. A vaccine has been available since 1991, and though the majority of cases are observed in households with pedigreed breeding stock, it is certainly known in the wider cat population.

INFLUENZA (VIRAL RHINITIS)

This is a distressing illness affecting the upper respiratory tract, which is caused by two main viruses, feline calicivirus and feline herpesvirus. Both viruses cause coughing and sneezing. Discharge from the nose and the eyes cause the cat great distress, and a rasping soreness in the throat discourages eating or drinking. Feline calicivirus often causes serious ulceration of nose, mouth and tongue. Feline herpesvirus may cause the nose, windpipe and lungs to become seriously inflamed, resulting in a lot of

✦ ABOVE
The acute conjunctivitis and corneal opacity in one of this Blue Tonkinese kitten's eyes are symptoms of chlamydia, a respiratory disease.

◆ RIGHT
A Lilac Cream Burmese-cross kitten has severe conjunctivitis – a symptom of feline flu.

coughing and sneezing. The cat that is kept warm and comfortable and is encouraged to eat and drink stands the greatest chance of survival. Antibiotics reduce the risk of secondary infections but do not attack the primary viruses. Effective vaccination against cat flu is the best preventative course.

FELINE INFECTIOUS ENTERITIS

This disease, a cat version of the distemper that infects dogs, is also known as feline panleukopaenia and feline parvovirus. The first symptom of this sometimes astonishingly rapid killer virus is usually a very high fever. The virus attacks rapidly dividing cells, particularly in the bowel. Symptoms may include unusually depressed behaviour, loss of appetite, vomiting, and a desire to drink but an inability to do so. Diarrhoea is not always present. Rapid dehydration sets in followed by coma and death. The rapidity of the disease, after its short incubation period, can mean that death occurs two or three days after vomiting starts, or even within 24 hours. The disease is highly infectious. Treatment is supportive: keep the cat warm and free from draughts, and administer rehydration therapy as advised by the vet.

FELINE LEUKAEMIA VIRUS (FeLV)

This virus first came to the notice of breeders of pedigreed cats in the early 1970s. Originally there were fears that it could be a health hazard to humans, particularly children. This is most certainly not the case – the virus cannot be transmitted except to another cat. To begin with, it was thought that particular pedigreed

breeds were more prone to the disease than other cats, but this has not been proven. All cats may be similarly and as rapidly affected when they come into contact with the virus. It was found that a far larger percentage of the normal domestic cat population was affected than expected, and many of these cats lived into old age. This made a nonsense of early veterinary advice that cats with feline leukaemia virus should be euthanased immediately.

Some cats do succumb rapidly to other serious and untreatable infections as the virus wreaks havoc with the cat's immune system, while others are less affected. If one cat is affected within a multi-cat household, it should be removed, as the virus is easily transmitted through saliva or blood. The infected animal could be moved to a single-cat household where it may live out its life without infecting others. Testing for the virus

is through a blood sample. It is possible for a cat to test positive and then, two weeks later, to show a negative result, only having had a passing contact with the virus. For some years, a vaccine countering this disease has been available in the United States, and since 1992, FeLV licences have been available in the United Kingdom.

Most breeders have all their animals, whether elderly, neutered (altered) or young breeding cats, regularly tested to show that they are FeLV-negative. Females are only mated to males which also regularly test negative, so that the kittens are automatically negative too. They can then be protected by vaccination. Many breeders leave this to the new owners. If there are other cats in your home, it should be done immediately. If the kitten is the only pet, inoculation may be left until it is a little older.

◆ RIGHT
Feline infectious peritonitis is carried in the
saliva and the faeces. It is essential to disinfect
litter trays (pans) regularly. The illness can
strike at any age.

FELINE IMMUNODEFICIENCY VIRUS (FIV)

This is a similar virus to the human immunodeficiency virus (HIV) which may lead eventually to acquired immunodeficiency syndrome (AIDS). The feline version cannot be passed on to a human being, and HIV cannot be passed on to a cat.

FIV progressively breaks down the cat's immune system. This leads to the cat becoming increasingly vulnerable to infections. Despite periods of apparently normal health, the cat slowly succumbs to minor illnesses which become untreatable. No vaccination exists at present.

FELINE INFECTIOUS PERITONITIS (FIP)

The virus that causes this disease is found in many cats and normally only occasionally causes a transient diarrhoea. However, in about 10 per cent of infected cats, the virus leaves the intestines, invades the blood

vessels and causes a severe inflammation – which is feline infectious peritonitis. The membrane which lines the abdominal cavity is called the peritoneum, and once the

◆ ABOVE
A cat is spending a night in the vet's pens
before surgery in the morning.

blood vessels of this have become infected and inflamed, treatment is extremely difficult, and often unsuccessful. As yet no definitive pattern to the progression of illness has emerged. The disease can be triggered in almost all age groups, even young kittens are susceptible.

Wet FIP is the most common form of the disease. Onset is usually rapid. Just 24 hours after appearing lively, playful, of good appetite and with normal litter-tray (pan) motions, a wet FIP sufferer will be lethargic, will not want to eat very much and will have sickness and diarrhoea. The coat is often staring and dull, but the most dramatic sign is the grossly distended fluid-filled abdomen. There is no cure. Euthanasia is the only option.

Dry FIP is a less common form of the disease and is often difficult to diagnose. The signs are similar to those of other illnesses. Terminally, the cat may have jaundice and show symptoms akin to cat flu, physical disorientation, blindness due to haemorrhages in the eyes and, finally, fits.

The presence of the virus is detected by antibody tests. Cats which show none are designated nil titre count. Over 80 per cent of show cats are seropositive, showing they have had some contact with the disease. Some cat breeders advertise their animals as nil (free) status, but most vets regard a low count as being relatively normal. Many cats, even with a very high titre count may seem normal. It is thought that a stressful situation, such as the introduction of a new cat into the household or a long journey, may tip a cat with a pre-existing viral condition into the full-blown illness.

FIP does not seem to be as infectious as was at first thought. The virus is carried in the cat's saliva and the faeces. Litter trays (pans) should be disinfected regularly and frequently using an agent recommended by your vet. Keeping cats in small, easily managed colonies, observing strict hygiene and, above all, maintaining a stress-free environment should help reduce the possibility of the disease flaring up. The virus is not able to survive very long outside the host and is very susceptible to disinfection agents. There is no vaccination available at present in the United Kingdom although it is available in some European countries.

RABIES

All mammals, including humans, are susceptible to rabies, and the bite of an infected animal is dangerous. Once infected, a cat may show signs of a radical alteration of appetite and voice, with unexpected aggressive behaviour. An inability to drink gives rabies its other name, hydrophobia – fear of water. Other signs follow – foaming at the mouth, swelling of the skull, jaw paralysis and disorientation.

Treatment is possible but must be started promptly after being bitten by a suspected animal. There is very little hope of any infected mammal surviving once the long incubation period of the disease has passed and symptoms have begun to show. Several countries are rabies-free, including the United Kingdom due to rigorous import regulations. Vaccination is available and standard in countries where rabies exists but, at present, in Britain it is only obtainable for animals that are to be exported.

FELINE SPONGIFORM ENCEPHALOPATHY

This disease is caused by a sub-viral protein that is capable of reproducing itself. It is similar to the bovine form (BSE) that has occurred in the United Kingdom and, to a lesser extent, elsewhere. The disease seems to be invariably fatal in cats, and is not diagnosable prior to death. It seems to have been transmitted to cats as a result of eating meat from cattle infected with BSE or sheep with scrapie. The cat develops abnormal behaviour, including failure to groom, and often drools with muscle tremors and an abnormal head posture. However, positive diagnosis is only possible on post-mortem examination.

◆ LEFT
One of the early signs of the feline form of BSE is a disinterest in grooming.

PARASITES

Being aware of the problems and facts about parasites is the first step in prevention. Routine care of any cat or kitten must include checking that the fur and skin are kept free from all parasites.

A parasite is an animal or plant that takes food and protection from a host animal or plant. It survives to the detriment of its host, causing loss of condition, and sometimes death. In some cases, such as ringworm, the parasitic condition of a host cat can be passed on to the humans it lives with.

Preparations to eradicate external parasites such as fleas, ticks, lice, mites and ringworm, as well as internal parasites including worms, are easily available. Seek veterinary advice,

◆ ABOVE
A cat is having its regular check for fleas, lice, and ticks. The check-up can be part of a weekly grooming routine.

◆ RIGHT
Excessive scratching may indicate that fleas or lice are present.

follow instructions carefully, and stick to a strict cleaning regime, and parasites should not be a problem.

FLEAS

The cat with fleas may scratch obsessively, particularly around the neck, and may groom the base of the spine vigorously and spontaneously. It may also worry at the entire length of the spine. Using the tips of the fingers and nails, groom the cat behind the ears, the neck, spine and base of the tail. If this reveals dark, chocolate-brown grit, put these on a damp tissue. If red leaches from them, they are flea droppings, which are largely made up of dried blood.

In severe infestations or where the cat is actually allergic to substances produced by the flea in its bite, patches of scabby skin may be found with the scabs breaking off to reveal sore-looking, slightly weeping patches. This clears up rapidly with the eradication of the fleas.

Fleas move very fast through the fur of the cat and are difficult to catch even if seen. A cat can be attacked by the cat flea, the dog flea and the human flea. They all lay their eggs in the cat's fur; many will drop out and hatch into larvae in cracks in the floorboards, in the weave of fabrics and in carpets. The larvae develop into fleas that immediately feed from any host that may wander by. A flea can live, with periods of feeding and resting, for up to two years, but two to six months is the norm.

Many anti-parasitic preparations, including powders, shampoos and sprays are available from pet stores, supermarkets and veterinary practices. With heavy infestations, both the cat and the environment have to be treated. Long-acting sprays are probably the most effective for the environment. For the cat, one of the easiest and most effective methods is an insecticide that is applied to a small area on the cat's neck. This spot application gives protection to the whole body for a month.

Modern parasiticides are very safe and some are available that can be applied to very young kittens. Your vet will advise on the most appropriate products for young cats.

TICKS

Ticks, like fleas, are blood suckers. However, unlike fleas, they live permanently on the cat. This parasite is normally rural in distribution, but the hedgehog tick is common in urban areas. The tick burrows its head into the host animal's skin, and gorges itself on blood. It can sometimes reach the size of a haricot bean, then drop off to complete its life cycle with no further damage to the cat. However, it could move on to other animals in the home. Removal of a tick requires

precision, to avoid the head parts remaining buried in the skin. The cat itself may be irritated by the tick's burrowing and knock it off, leaving its head behind. This usually sets up chronic infection followed by an abscess or sore which is difficult to heal. A vet can use substances to relax the tick's hold before removing it. A home equivalent is surgical alcohol (or any form of alcoholic spirit). The whole tick is then carefully removed with tweezers or a custom-made tick remover (available from pet stores).

Tick bites can be responsible for a bacterial disease called Lyme disease. This occurs in Britain, but is more widespread in the United States. Symptoms include a reluctance to jump followed by acute and recurring lameness, a raised temperature, lethargy and swollen lymph nodes, particularly around the head and

limbs. Blood tests confirm the cause, and treatment is a four to six week course of antibiotics. Lyme disease should not occur if ticks are prevented. Most flea preparations also prevent tick infestation.

LICE

Fortunately, lice infestation is uncommon on cats, but poor condition and extremes of age make individuals susceptible. There are three types of louse which are known to occur on cats, one blood-sucking, and two which bite. Telltale signs are some scratching, usually not very excessive, combined with dry skin which shows an unusual increase of scurf or dandruff. The lice may be seen quite easily with the naked eye. The eggs, or nits, are laid directly on the lower third of the hair and seem to be glued in place. Anti-flea preparations are effective.

♦ ABOVE, LEFT AND RIGHT
As a preventative measure against fleas and lice, apply an anti-parasite insecticide once a month. Part the fur on the back of the neck and squeeze on the required amount of medication.

◆ BELOW
Incessant scratching of the head and ears is a
sign of ear mites, and could aggravate the
problem if not treated quickly.

MITES

Four groups of mites affect the cat's skin and ears. The harvest mite appears in the autumn (fall). The cat is affected by the larvae which tend to settle in areas where the fur is thin, such as between the toes, on the underbelly, in the groin and around the lips and nose.

The orange larvae are just about visible to the naked eye. They set up irritation which the cat vigorously attacks with teeth and claws, thus creating more irritation. The sores which develop are round, damp and surrounded by scabby skin. Mite infestation is highly contagious and treated with insecticidal preparations.

The ear mite is commonly transmitted from cat to cat. Irritation is sometimes severe; the cat shakes its head, holds the ears almost flat, and scratches furiously. This often leads to secondary infections arising from self-inflicted trauma. Evidence of ear mites is a dark brown tarry substance

in the ears. Because of the ear's delicacy, it is wise to ask your vet to carry out initial treatment. The owner can then cleanse the ear gently.

Cheyletiella mites cause a condition known as "walking dandruff", and are less common. They often seem to cause little irritation to the cat though

there may be more scratching and grooming than usual. Excessive dandruff is the usual sign. The mite normally lives on the wild rabbit and can also affect people (rashes appear on chest, stomach and arms). Treatment is with parasiticides – for both cat and human!

One fortunately rare form of mange is caused by a burrowing mite. It is usually found around the head, starting at the base of the ear. There is severe irritation, hair loss and general lack of condition. Blood poisoning can occur in severe cases. Antibiotic treatment is necessary for any secondary infections, while the actual skin damage is treated with the use of parasiticidal preparations.

RINGWORM

Ringworm is caused by a fungus, and can affect humans, especially children. The name comes from the shape of the lesions seen on the skin in humans, which are circular, red, scaly and very itchy. In the cat, particularly the

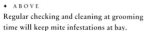

◆ ABOVE
Regular checking and cleaning at grooming
time will keep mite infestations at bay.

◆ RIGHT
A vet checks for ear mites as part of the
routine examination.

Persian, often all that is seen are tiny pimples and scurf on the skin. (Nevertheless, these cats can still be highly contagious.) At worst, moist, pink sores spread outwards. The fungal parasite lives on the hair and not on the skin, and causes the hair to break off. Ringworm can affect animals that are not in top condition, or that are young, and can be a major problem in longhaired show cats.

Diagnosis is initially by the use of special filtered light (Wood's Light), when about 65 per cent of cases will fluoresce. Laboratory tests are more reliable but take longer. The eradication process is long and tedious. The animals are treated with fungicides, both in the form of baths and external applications, and also tablets. The entire environment, human and animal, has to be carefully cleansed to eradicate all spores. There is no simple answer to the problem. Professional advice on procedure must be taken and, if necessary, the local environmental health department consulted. In the United States and in the United Kingdom, research is aimed at improving diagnostic tests as well as treatments. Considerable headway has been made in the production of a vaccine, but at present only cuts down treatment time.

MAGGOTS

Flies may be attracted to animals by the presence of discharge from wounds, or diarrhoea, and lay their eggs in the fur. Fly strike, as this situation is known, is particularly common in cats in poor condition, such as those in feral colonies. The maggots burrow into the skin and form tunnels which can run for considerable distances. Toxins produced to aid burrowing are absorbed by the cat and cause toxaemia (blood poisoning). If you find maggot infestation on your cat, clean it as thoroughly as possible using soap and water and contact the vet without delay.

BRONCHITIS

Infectious bronchitis is sometimes caused by a parasitic bacterium that lodges in the respiratory tract of animals. The parasite itself does not normally cause disease, but certain strains of the parasite do cause bronchitis. In a dog, this may appear as kennel cough. A cat on the other hand may cough and sneeze, with or without running nose and eyes. Normally, the disease is self-limiting. However, in very young or elderly cats, or those with other debilitating diseases, it can be persistent and troublesome to clear. The organism is sensitive to several antibiotics.

◆ BELOW LEFT
Thinning and bald patches on the hind leg of a Blue Burmese could be signs of ringworm.

◆ BELOW RIGHT
The mark on the head of this Lilac Tonkinese kitten is confirmed as ringworm. The fungal parasites live on the hair, and not on the skin, causing the hair to break.

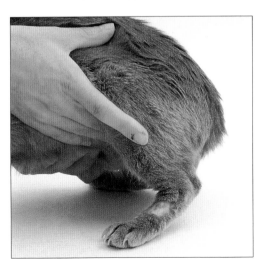

WORMS

The cat is affected by two groups of internal, parasitic worm – roundworms and tapeworms. Effective worm treatments are available, without prescription, from pet stores and supermarkets. However, experience has shown that these may be difficult to administer with total accuracy. Routine worming treatments – and advice – are best obtained from your vet. Worming preparations which give multiple protection to the cat are now available, either as tablets or injections. Regular, correctly spaced treatments will keep your cat worm-free. These are often supplied at the same time as the annual booster vaccination, but may need to be given every six months.

ROUNDWORMS

Roundworms include ascarids, hookworms and lungworms. Infestations are difficult to spot unless the attack is severe, in which case, especially with ascarids, a ball of living worms may be voided. If you suspect infestation, you will probably need to take a faecal sample to the vet for accurate identification. Ascarids and hookworms live in the small intestine. They have very similar life cycles but whereas the ascarids are free-floating and feed on food in the process of digestion, the hookworms attach themselves to the lining of the intestine and suck blood. Symptoms are, therefore, slightly different. In a severe ascarid infestation, the cat will have diarrhoea, the coat will be lank, and the cat will generally look uncomfortable. Often the belly is distended ("pot belly").

The main symptom of hookworm infestation is anaemia, which in a cat is most obvious on its nose leather and gums. The gums appear excessively pale, almost white. There is a general

♦ LEFT
A vet checks gum and tongue colour for any undue paleness that could indicate anaemia and possible hookworm infestation.

lack of energy and the cat may become very thin.

The intermediate host of the lungworm is the slug or snail, which could be eaten by a cat. However, it is more likely that they will be eaten first by birds or rodents and the infective larvae reach the cat through eating them. Nevertheless, infestation is quite rare. After a complicated journey through the cat's intestine and lymph nodes, the larvae become adult worms, which eventually enter the lungs via the bloodstream. As a result, respiratory symptoms occur, similar to bronchitis or pneumonia.

TAPEWORMS

Tapeworm diagnosis is relatively easy. Segments of tapeworm containing eggs are shed and attach themselves to the fur around the anus. They look like grains of rice. Tapeworms require intermediate hosts and the flea fulfils this role in relation to the most common tapeworm to affect the cat. Flea control is therefore important. Flea larvae eat the secreted tapeworm segments that contain the eggs. The infective stage of the tapeworm is reached as the adult flea preys on the cat for a blood meal. If the cat catches and swallows the flea, as it may do

while grooming, the process is completed. The infective stage of the second most common tapeworm to affect cats develops in the livers of small rodents. The infected livers and other intestinal parts will almost certainly be consumed by a cat, if it catches one of these animals.

The way to prevent infestation by tapeworms is to eradicate fleas, and discourage your cat from hunting. Both may be impossible targets, but although tapeworms continue to be a problem, their presence does not seem to affect cats much beyond diarrhoea in the case of very heavy infestation.

♦ RIGHT
The abdomen of a cat being palpated; a distended belly may indicate roundworm infestation.

◆ BELOW
Keep an eye open for roving cats using your
garden as a toileting area. Your animals may be
free of diseases such as toxoplasmosis, but
visitors may not be.

TOXOPLASMOSIS

Toxoplasmosis is caused by
microscopic organisms called coccidia.
The organisms can infect humans,
although symptoms of illness are
rarely felt. If a pregnant woman is
infected, however, the foetus may
be affected, resulting in spontaneous
abortion or brain damage to the baby.
The disease may not even affect the
cat in any recognizable form, although
it may cause a chest infection in
young cats. In older cats there may
be gross loss of condition, digestive
disorders and anaemia. Eye problems
are not uncommon.

The immature egg of the parasite
is passed in the cat's faeces, so that
potential contact with any faecal
matter when changing and cleaning
litter trays (pans) must be countered
by a rigid routine of hygiene. Oocysts
passed by the cat with toxoplasmosis
take at least 24 hours to become
infective, so litter trays (pans) must
be changed as soon as possible after
use and rubber gloves worn.

Small children should be kept away
from litter trays (pans) at all times.
You should also frequently clear away
the faeces of any neighbourhood
cats that visit your garden and use
it as a toileting area.

AREAS AFFECTED

EYES

Conjunctivitis is relatively common in the cat and can vary from a relatively mild infection, often called "gum eye" by cat breeders, to more serious conditions such as that caused by the chlamydia organism.

Gum eye is mostly seen in kittens just after their eyes have opened at about seven to ten days, up until the age of about three weeks. The eyes appear to be firmly glued together with a discharge and this may be due to a mild viral infection. Usually, the mother cat will wash the eyes open, but sometimes you will have to help her. To do this, bathe the kitten's eye(s) with a sterile pad soaked in cold water. Always work from the corner of the eye nearest the nose outwards. Should the gum eye persist over a couple of days, seek professional advice.

EARS

A blood blister called a haematoma can occur on the ear flap (pinna) due to excessive shaking and rubbing caused by irritation. Without skilled treatment, a deformed pinna will result in cauliflower ear.

NOSE

Nasal discharges are usually due to viral infections like cat flu and should be treated by the vet. Certain breeds of cat (Persians, in particular) have restricted nostrils, and the flattening, or foreshortening, of the face causes kinking of the tear duct. The cat will probably always have eye and nasal discharges that have to be constantly attended to by the owner. Rarely, a cat may show an asthmatic condition, having become allergic to

one or more of the thousands of substances it encounters each day. Again, your vet should be able to diagnose and may even pinpoint the allergen. Long-term treatment may be necessary.

CHEST AND LUNGS

Inflammation of the fine membrane that covers the lungs and inside of the chest cavity is called pleurisy. Cats may have fluid in their chests for various reasons, ranging from heart failure to injuries. Usually, the fluid is sterile, but it may become infected with certain bacteria, either blood-borne or from a bite or wound. Breathing becomes increasingly difficult, and any sudden exercise results in panting and a wide-eyed, very distressed appearance. The condition needs urgent veterinary attention, and despite chest drains and antibiotic treatment, many cats do not respond, and die of the condition known as pyothorax.

SKIN

Cats can sometimes develop a type of acne, in which blackheads appear on the chin. These are caused by excessive production and secretion of

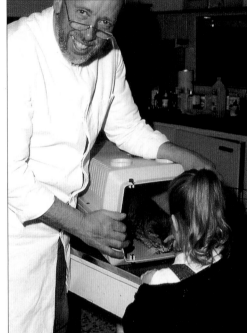

sebum, which lubricates the hair.
The pores through which the sebum
is released may become blocked.
When it occurs on the top of the
tail it is known as "stud tail". Both
conditions should be treated with
antibiotics and anti-inflammatory
drugs. If your cat has a predisposition
for these conditions, keep both
areas scrupulously clean to prevent
recurrence and, if in any doubt,
consult the vet.

Even the best groomed cat can
be affected by dandruff. When it
strikes, even a shorthaired cat needs
to be bathed and a conditioning
agent used. If the scurf persists
despite your best efforts, there
may be something actually wrong
with the skin itself.

DIGESTIVE SYSTEM
Constipation and diarrhoea often
occur during the life of any
otherwise healthy cat. There are

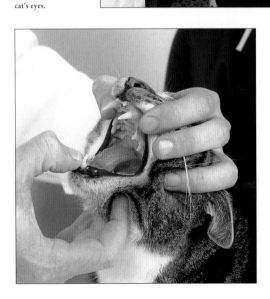

◆ ABOVE
The vet palpates
(feels) the cat's
abdomen to make
sure that it is neither
swollen nor tender,
and also the glands
around the neck and
top of the legs to
make sure they are
not enlarged.

◆ RIGHT
The vet administers
ear drops to a cat
with a sore ear.
The ears are very
delicate, so it is
always preferable
for the vet to check
them initially if
you think there
is a problem.

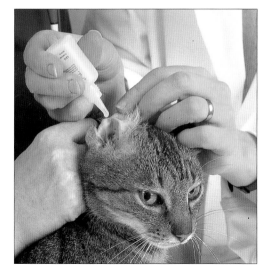

many reasons why a cat becomes constipated. Fur balls (hairballs) are a usual cause, but sometimes a diet with insufficient bulk or roughage may be the problem. Introduce some bran or other cereal into the diet, or add a little liquid paraffin to the food. If the condition persists, take the cat to the vet. It may indicate a more serious condition, such as megacolon. If too much liquid paraffin is used, the cat will have diarrhoea.

There are feline preparations on the market, but home-made remedies can often be just as effective. These involve a mild diet of bland food which does not upset the system. Try feeding the cat cooked white meat and white fish, bulked out with simple boiled rice or pasta. Some cats adore natural yogurt. Another remedy is to sprinkle dehydrated potato granules on the food – it may seem an unorthodox treatment, but it does work.

With both constipation and diarrhoea, the anal glands, which are situated on either side of the anal opening, may become blocked, infected and swell up. Clearing them out can be done at home, but it is not pleasant and does require some skill, so it is probably better left to a professional.

In addition to being uncomfortable for the cat, excessive diarrhoea or straining can cause a condition called anal prolapse. This can easily be recognized – a small section of the bowel protrudes through the anal opening. Do not attempt do anything about this yourself; it will require a qualified vet to put this back into its proper place immediately, and it may even take a stitch or two to secure it.

THE BREEDS

THE PERSIAN CAT

All Persian cats – known officially as Longhair Persian type – have the same basic physical shape and conformation. Their faces are flat with short noses and small ears. Their bodies are broad-chested with sturdy legs and large paws, and they all have a soft, thick fur coat with a distinctive ruff around the neck, and a full, low-slung tail. Persian longhairs come in many different colours and patterns. In some countries, such as the United States, the colour variations are considered as varieties of the same breed, but in Britain, each different colour is listed as a separate breed. Persian cats are among the longest-known pedigreed cats. Longhaired variations of wild species may have spontaneously occurred in colder regions in the heart of Asia, and then gradually become established with subsequent interbreeding. The ancestors of today's Persians were probably stocky, longhaired grey cats brought to Europe from Persia (now Iran) in the 1600s and silken-haired white Angora cats from Turkey (a different type from the modern Angora breed). Today, there are over 60 different colour variations of the Longhair Persian type.

◆ ABOVE
The Red Colourpoint is one of the newer, patterned varieties of Persian cat, but it has the voluptuous fur and cobby body, the short nose and small ears of the type.

BLACK PERSIAN

Black Self Persians are thought to be one of the earliest Persian breeds to have been officially recognized as long ago as the 1600s. Today, however, they are not at all common. The show standard insists on a solid, dense coal-black coat, with no hint of rustiness, shading, markings or white hairs. Kittens often show some grey or rusting, and if this continues beyond six to eight months, it is not considered acceptable. To maintain its lustrous black coat, the cat needs to be kept in cool, dry surroundings free from direct light. A damp atmosphere and bright sunlight seem to fade the black – one breeder retired her show cat so that it could enjoy the sunshine. Like many Persians, the Blacks are affectionate and dignified, although they have a reputation for being more playful than the White Persian.

BREED BOX	
Coat	thick, lustrous; full frill at neck and shoulders
Eyes	copper or deep orange; rims black
Other features	nose leather and paw pads black
Grooming	demanding; thorough, daily
Temperament	placid

◆ LEFT
A fully mature Black Persian with a superb coat of solid colour, of the right density and length, and striking, deep copper eyes.

◆ ABOVE
A Black kitten shows great promise as a future show cat. Even though a certain amount of rustiness is accepted in kittens, this youngster already has a superb dense black coat.

BLUE PERSIAN

At the end of the 1800s, Blue Persians became extremely popular as pets of the wealthy, and were specially bred to be sold for high prices. They became particular favourites of European royalty. Queen Victoria of England acquired two Blues, Princess Victoria of Schleswig-Holstein was an enthusiastic breeder, and King Edward VII presented medals for the top prize-winners of the day.

One reason for the Blue's popularity may have been because it was thought to be the nearest in colour to the original Persians brought to Europe by traders in the 1600s. The genetic mutation of the breed we know today may well have arisen on the Mediterranean island of Malta – which is why it is sometimes called the Maltese Blue. The blue-grey colouring is a dilution of black. The blue comes from a lavender sheen which adds a brightness to the pale coat. This is very much in evidence with the show cat, which is ideally an even, medium to pale blue, with no shading, markings or white hairs.

◆ LEFT
The Blue was one of the first Persian cats to be established as a breed. In the late 1800s, it became a fashionable asset for the wealthy and aristocratic.

A dark, slate-grey coat is considered very undesirable. Because of its long, distinguished history of careful breeding, the Persian Blue is often used as the standard Persian type against which other Persian breeds are compared. For this reason, it is sometimes included in breeding programmes to improve the type of other varieties.

The Blue has a reputation for being a very affectionate and gentle cat that enjoys close human companionship.

BREED BOX

Coat	thick, dense, silky; full frill at neck and shoulders
Eyes	copper or deep orange; rims blue-grey
Other features	nose leather and paw pads blue-grey
Grooming	demanding; thorough, daily
Temperament	placid

◆ LEFT
A Blue with a well-earned aristocratic air. Its evenly coloured coat with a lustrous sheen offsets glorious copper-orange eyes.

BI-COLOUR

In the early days of pedigree breeding, any longhaired cat with a patch of white was regarded with horror. However, there were so few animals without a white spot on the belly or neck, that to fill classes at shows, the Bi-colours were allowed to compete. These solid-coloured cats with white undersides, muzzles, chests, legs and

◆ ABOVE
A Blue Bi-colour is an example of the many variations of the breed. They are available in all the colours accepted for the Self colours such as Red, Cream and Chocolate.

BREED BOX	
Coat	thick, dense, silky; full frill at neck and shoulders
Eyes	deep orange or copper
Grooming	demanding; thorough, daily, especially the white parts
Temperament	placid

◆ LEFT
A beautifully groomed black and white Bi-colour in full coat shows the distinct white patching that is highly desirable in show cats.

feet, were placed along with the Tortoiseshell and Whites, in an "any other variety" category. Eventually, breeders began to consider them seriously as a variety in their own right. The ideal standard is for the white patches to be balanced and even, with a dapper and clearly defined inverted V shape running over the nose.

◆ BELOW
A black Tortie and White displays well-mingled markings, clearly defined white patches, and an exceptionally fine longhaired coat.

TORTOISESHELL AND WHITE

The classic Tortoiseshell's black and red (or its dilute colours) are offset by patches of dazzling white – as long as the cat is well and frequently groomed. In America this variety is called a Calico after printed calico (cotton).

◆ BELOW
Tortie and Whites occur in as many different colour combinations as the Tortoiseshells themselves. This is a dilute colour – Blue Tortie (Blue-Cream) and White.

BREED BOX	
Coat	particularly long and silky; full frill at neck and shoulders; full, bushy tail
Eyes	orange or deep copper
Grooming	demanding; thorough, daily, especially the white parts
Temperament	placid

The English version of this name was Chintz, but this is no longer used. The American standard requires well-defined patches of colour, but in the United Kingdom, any degree of white is acceptable, from some on all four legs, chest and belly, to the van pattern.

CHINCHILLA

In 1882, a fine-boned, silver Angora-type female cat with no markings was mated with a similarly coloured, non-pedigreed male. Their daughter became the mother of the

◆ LEFT
When a Chinchilla moves, the coat appears to sparkle, which is why the breed is sometimes described as ethereal or fairy-like.

BREED BOX

Coat	thick and dense, like swansdown
Eyes	emerald or blue-green; visible skin on eyelids black or dark brown
Other features	nose leather brick-red; paw pads black or dark brown
Grooming	demanding; needs constant attention
Temperament	placid; often livelier than other Persians

first Chinchilla title holder, whose body was exhibited in London's Natural History Museum.

The undercoat of the Chinchilla is pure white. The coat on the back, flanks, head, ears and tail is tipped with black. The tipping should be evenly distributed to give the characteristic silver sparkle. The legs may be slightly shaded with the tipping, but the chin, ear furnishings, stomach and chest must be pure white. Tabby markings or brown or cream tinges are undesirable. There has been great controversy about the required size of a Chinchilla; the breed

is sometimes described as fairy-like, but this is not to do with size – Chinchillas are usually medium-sized and quite solidly built.

◆ ABOVE
The Chinchilla's emerald or bluish-green eyes are outlined in black, creating an eyeliner effect.

GOLDEN PERSIAN

Golden cats may well have occurred as an offshoot of Chinchilla breeding in the 1920s. However, the modern breed became established following an explosion of American imports of Chinchillas into Britain in the 1970s, combined with a New Zealand import from American bloodlines. On the back, flanks, head and tail

the undercoat must be sufficiently tipped with seal brown or black to give a golden appearance. An apricot undercoat deepens to gold, while chin, ear furnishings, stomach and chest are pale apricot. The general tipping effect may be darker than that of the Chinchilla, and tipping on the tail may be heavier than on the body. Legs may be shaded, but the back from paw to heel should be solid seal brown or black. Kittens often show tabby markings or grey at the base of the undercoat.

◆ LEFT
The Golden Persian, originally called the Golden Chinchilla, has the same striking dark rims around the eyes.

BREED BOX

Coat	dense, silky
Eyes	emerald or blue-green; eye rims seal-brown or black
Other features	nose leather brick-red outlined with seal or black; paw pads seal or black
Grooming	very demanding; thorough, needs daily attention
Temperament	placid, but often livelier than other Persians

135

CAMEO

The Cameo was regarded as a delicious accident for a great many years, but towards the end of the 1950s, the breed was formally registered in the United States. The formula for creating Cameos turned out to be extraordinarily straightforward, with kittens of consistent colouring appearing in the first hybridization.

BREED BOX

Coat	thick, dense, silky; full frill at neck and shoulders
Eyes	large, round; deep orange or copper
Grooming	demanding; thorough, daily
Temperament	placid

Apart from Red and Cream Cameos, there are Blue-Cream and Tortoiseshell variations.

There are two levels of colour tipping to the fur. In the Shell Cameo, colour is restricted to the very tips of the fur to give a soft sheen like mother-of-pearl. The Shaded Cameo has heavier tipping, and normally occurs in the first crosses between a Chinchilla and a Red or Cream cat. In all Cameos, the undercoat should ideally be as white as possible with the tips shading to red or tortoiseshell in the Red series, and shading to cream or blue-cream in the Cream series. The deepest intensity of colour is most defined on the mask, along the spine from the head to the tip of the tail and on legs and feet. The light points occur on the frill, flanks, undersides and ear furnishings.

PEWTER

Breeding from Tortie Cameos produces cats with black rather than red, cream or tortoiseshell tipping. These cats are a relatively recent development and have their place as

BREED BOX

Coat	thick, long; full frill
Eyes	deep orange or copper
Other features	nose leather and paw pads brick-red
Grooming	thorough, daily
Temperament	placid

Pewters. They are very similar in appearance to Shaded Silvers but with orange or copper eye colour. Pewters are recognized in the United Kingdom only with black tipping. The coat is exceptionally long – almost to the point of obscuring the cobby build – with a full neck ruff ending in a frill over the front legs.

◆ ABOVE
Orange-copper eyes distinguish the Pewter from the similar Shaded Silver Persian. This cat's distinguished neck ruff descends satisfyingly deep to finish between the front legs.

COLOURPOINT (HIMALAYAN)

The catalogue of Persian longhaired cats until this point has been based on a solid colour cat modified by the introduction of the tabby pattern, sex-linked colour, silver or white patching. The pioneers of Colourpoint breeding fused the Persian type longhair with the Himalayan (which is why this breed is known in America as Himalayan) pattern of the Siamese cat. The result was a cat of Persian type with long hair and the restricted coat pattern of the Siamese. The points (mask, legs, feet and tail) are evenly coloured and there is a good contrast between the points and body colour. Light body shading, if present, should be confined to the shoulders and flanks, and should complement the

◆ LEFT
Cream Colourpoint Rosjoy Rambo, Supreme Grand Champion, has the wonderful blue eyes of a Siamese set against the red-gold cream of his fur.

POINT COLOURS

Individual organizations recognize point colours that include the Silver series and Red sex-linked Silver series. In Britain, the point colours are represented by four distinct groupings:
Solid point colours – Seal, Blue, Chocolate, Lilac, Red and Cream
Tortie point colours – Seal Tortie, Blue-Cream, Chocolate Tortie and Lilac-Cream
Tabby point colours – Seal Tabby, Blue Tabby, Chocolate Tabby, Lilac Tabby, Red Tabby, and Cream Tabby
Tortie Tabby point colours – Seal Tortie Tabby, Blue-Cream Tabby, Chocolate Tortie Tabby and Lilac-Cream Tabby
    In the United States, seven varieties are recognized:
Blue Point, Chocolate Point, Seal Point, Flame Point, Lilac Point, Blue-Cream Point, and Tortoiseshell Point.

points. The mask covers the entire face. It should not extend over the head, although the mask of a mature male is more extensive than that of a mature female. Kittens are born white and fluffy, the point colours starting to appear in less than a week.
    Attempts to transfer the Siamese pattern to Persian type were being made before World War II, but the cats were not shown until 1957 in California, and were only officially incorporated into the Persian breed by the Cat Fanciers' Association in 1984. Breeding lines have since expanded to develop the full range of point colours. The Colourpoint Persian has now outstripped the Blue in the longhair popularity stakes.

BREED BOX

Coat	thick, dense, no trace of woolliness; glossy; full frill over shoulders and continuing between front legs
Eyes	large, round; brilliant blue
Other features	nose and paw pad colour matches the point colour
Grooming	demanding; thorough, daily
Temperament	placid

◆ BELOW
The darkened points of the Siamese are blended with all the characteristics of the Persian Longhair. This cat is a Blue Colourpoint.

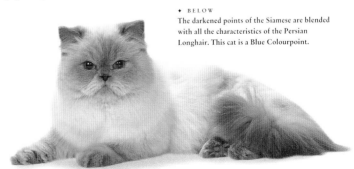

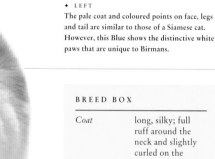

BIRMAN

The Birman falls somewhere between the Siamese and the Persian in its character, build and length of fur, yet it is very much a breed of its own. It also has the distinction of being the sacred cat of Burma.

All Birmans have colourpointed features – darker coloration on the ears, face, tail and legs. The original Birman was seal-pointed, but there are now blue, lilac, chocolate, and a wide range of tortoiseshell and tabby points. All are now regarded as different breeds, but share the same blue eyes, dark points, white feet, body shape and general temperament.

The Birman body has some of the mass of the Persian's, with thickset legs and a broad, rounded head. However, the body and legs are longer than those of a Persian, and the face is pointed rather than flat, with a longish, straight nose and relatively large ears.

The unique and most distinctive feature of the Birman is its paw design. Each forepaw ends in a symmetrically shaped, white glove. The show

BREED BOX

Coat	long, silky; full ruff around the neck and slightly curled on the stomach
Eyes	almost round but not bold; deep, clear blue
Other features	white mittens on forepaws; longer white "gauntlets" on rear paws
Grooming	relatively easy with regular brushing and combing
Temperament	gentle, individualistic, extremely loyal

◆ BELOW
The mask, tail and legs of Seal Point Birmans take their colour from the rich brown of Burmese soil, according to one legend.

◆ RIGHT
The Seal Point original has now been joined by many differently coloured varieties of the Birman, but all have clear sapphire eyes and a sweet facial expression.

standard is for the white to end in an even line across the paw and not pass beyond the angle of paw and leg. The white areas on the back paws taper up the back of the leg to finish just below the hock, and are known as gauntlets. These white finishing touches are the result of a rare recessive genetic trait.

TURKISH VAN

♦ RIGHT
A classically coloured auburn and white Turkish Van – this one has the unique distinction of winning the United Kingdom's Supreme Cat Show two years running.

Ancestors of the Turkish Van come from a rugged region in south-east Turkey, around the country's largest lake, the 3675km² (1419 square mile) Lake Van. This may be why this breed apparently loves water – and is sometimes called the Turkish swimming cat. It is not true that all cats hate water, but these cats will actually seek it out and seem to swim as a form of recreation. Turkey's

domestic cats are predominantly white with auburn markings. Even today, in Istanbul, you will see many street cats of this colouring.

On a visit to the Lake Van region in the 1950s, two English women bought a stocky white female cat with flashes of head colour and a full auburn tail.

♦ ABOVE
The "thumbprint" markings on the head of this auburn and white Van correctly (for the show standard cat) do not extend below the eyeline.

Their Istanbul hotel manager told them of another cat – a male with very similar markings. They took both cats back to Britain, and after four years were successfully breeding consistently patterned kittens. The two women returned to Turkey and bought another male and female to add to the new gene pool. The breed was first officially recognized in Britain in 1969 as the Turkish Cat, the name later being changed to Turkish Van.

Despite its fine coat and white colouring, no link with the Turkish Angora breed has been established. The Van is the more muscular of the two breeds, deep-chested with a long, sturdy body. Its legs are medium in length with neat, tufted, well-rounded feet. The tail is a *pièce de résistance*, a full brush in perfect proportion to the body and, of course, coloured and possibly faintly ringed. The cat has a long, straight nose and prominent, well-feathered ears.

The perfect coat is chalk-white with no trace of yellow, with coloured tail and head markings not extending below the eye line or the base of the ears at the back. There is a white blaze on the forehead and sometimes the occasional thumb-print of colour on the body. All colours are recognized (auburn and cream only in the United Kingdom).

Turkish Vans have reached the height of excellence, including the title of Supreme Exhibit at the United Kingdom's Supreme Cat Show.

BREED BOX

Coat	long, soft, silky; no woolly undercoat
Eyes	large, oval, expressive; light to medium amber, blue or odd-eyed
Other features	enjoys swimming; not prolific (litters of about four kittens)
Grooming	relatively easy; daily brushing and combing
Temperament	affectionate, intelligent; not particularly lively; may be nervous

♦ LEFT
The creamy-white Turkish Van is one of the two colours accepted by the United Kingdom's cat fancy, the other being the classic auburn and white.

SOMALI

◆ LEFT
An example of the Usual – or original colour –
with an undercoat overlaid with rich golden
brown and each hair tipped with black.

The Somali is the semi-longhaired version of the Abyssinian cat. Although the Abyssinian is a shorthaired breed, semi-longhaired kittens have occasionally appeared in their litters over several decades. In the United States it was eventually realized that a new breed was appearing spontaneously. The long fur was the result of a naturally long-established recessive gene within the breeding population. It may have been introduced via ticked tabby cats of unknown parentage in the breeding programme. These cats would have been introduced to sustain the breeding viability of the early Abyssinians, for the gene pool was extremely restricted at the turn of the century – a state of affairs that lasted well into the 1920s and 1930s.

BREED BOX	
Coat	soft, fine, dense; lies flat along the spine
Eyes	almond-shaped, slanting; outlined with a darker surround; amber, hazel or green, the richer and deeper the better
Other features	smiling expression
Grooming	easy if done regularly
Temperament	intelligent, lively, alert, interested; may be shy; freedom-loving (must not be confined indoors)

connections, the breed was named after the nearby African country of Somalia.

The coat pattern of the Somali is quite distinctive: it is ticked – with three two-colour bands of colour on each hair.

◆ LEFT
The Sorrel Somali is rather paler than the
Usual as the base apricot is ticked with
cinnamon rather than black.

Any fluffy Abyssinian kittens were initially regarded as below standard and banished to pet homes. Then an American breeder discovered that a longhaired Abyssinian at a humane society home had actually been sired by her own stud cat. The stud was tried out again to see if a consistent line of semi-longhairs could be produced – and the Somalis were established during the 1960s. Because of its Abyssinian or Ethiopian

◆ RIGHT
While the adult (left) shows full
colouring, it is not uncommon for
a kitten (right) to show greyish
roots, and this is quite acceptable
if you are showing a youngster.

RAGDOLL

When a Ragdoll is picked up it is supposed to go limp – and that is how it came to be named. There is a far-fetched story that the first Ragdoll kittens are said to have inherited this characteristic, together with an apparent resistance to pain, because their white semi-longhair mother, Josephine, had been injured in a road accident. It is more likely that the Ragdoll's docile nature arises from a happy coincidence of character genes. The breed was created in California in 1963. An early alternative name was Cherubim, while some variations are called Ragamuffins. Although the original breeder claimed non-pedigreed parentage, it is likely that Birman and Burmese genes were present somewhere along the line. However, in the majority of cats the dominant white spotting gene creates the look of the Mitted variety, while the one that produces a similar effect in the Birman is recessive.

The Ragdoll is a cat of powerful build, with big, round paws and a long, bushy tail. Its head is broad and wide-cheeked with a slightly retroussé nose

♦ BELOW
A Seal Colourpointed Ragdoll has distinct, deep brown points.

♦ ABOVE
A Blue Colourpointed gives a good overall impression of the breed's solid, powerful build. Colourpoints have the traditional pattern of complete coloured mask, ears, legs and tail.

and wide eyes of deep sapphire. The three recognized main groupings are Colourpointed, Mitted and Bi-colour. The Mitted has Colourpointed features contrasting with a pale body, plus white-gloved front feet and white rear legs to the hock or beyond. The Bi-colour is white on the chin, bib, chest and underbody with a triangular blaze over its nose.

BREED BOX	
Coat	dense, silky
Eyes	small, round, slanted; deep blue
Other features	goes limp when picked up
Grooming	easy; daily brushing with soft brush
Temperament	docile, relaxed, easy to handle; needs calm (so suitable to confine indoors)

♦ LEFT
White gloves on the forepaws and longer gauntlets on the rear legs are the distinctive features of the Mitted Ragdoll and bear witness to the probable Birman genes in the breeding programme.

♦ ABOVE
A triangular nose blaze denotes the true look of the Bi-colour Ragdoll. Bib, chest, underbody and front legs are also white.

MAINE COON CAT

The Maine Coon Cat is a fine working cat, as well as one of the longest established breeds. As the first part of its name suggests, it comes from Maine, America's most north-easterly state. This is a land of mountains, forests, lakes and inhospitable winters.

♦ LEFT
The Brown Tabby is the traditional Maine Coon Cat pattern. Individuals may take three or four years to reach the size and stature of this one.

BREED BOX	
Coat	thick, dense, waterproof; has an undercoat
Eyes	full, round with a slightly oblique aperture; all colours (including blue and odd-eyed in white cats)
Other features	big; good climbers; smallish litters (two or three kittens)
Grooming	coat rarely gets matted but regular brushing and combing advised
Temperament	intelligent, calm; freedom-loving (should not be confined indoors)

The Maine Coon Cat is appropriately powerfully built, with an all-weather coat and a reputation for being a wise and skilful hunter.

The second part of its name comes from the long tail and density of fur that have been compared to the similar attributes of the raccoon, an indigenous North American mammal. Like the raccoon, the cat is an exceptional climber. Another theory suggests that the lynx-like tufts on many a Maine Coon's ears are a result of genes inherited from the North American lynx, but this is unlikely. It is more likely that there is a touch of Angora in the breed. Local cats could have bred with Angoras that landed with sailors at the East Coast ports.

♦ BELOW
A Blue Maine Coon Cat shows the ideal head shape and feathered ears typical of the breed. It was once suggested that the ears were inherited from the North American lynx.

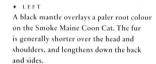

♦ LEFT
A black mantle overlays a paler root colour on the Smoke Maine Coon Cat. The fur is generally shorter over the head and shoulders, and lengthens down the back and sides.

BALINESE (JAVANESE)

Imagine a Siamese cat with a long, silky, flowing coat and a feathered tail, and you have an idea of the Balinese. It has the same dazzling sapphire eyes and large, erect ears as the Siamese cat – and comes in the same colour variations. However, the Balinese – or Javanese as some colours are called in the United States – tends to be a little less noisy than the Siamese.

Its names are probably inspired by the cat's graceful movement that is reminiscent of an Indonesian dancer. (Further confusion, however, arises because in Europe, the Javanese is the name given to what the British call the Angora!) The ancestry, however, is certainly Siamese. It is likely that in over 100 years of breeding Siamese cats, the recessive gene for long hair crept in and, in the 1940s, longhaired kittens began to appear in purebred Siamese litters. A Californian breeder

decided to take advantage of this tendency, and in the 1950s developed a fully constituted pedigree breed. The new breed was introduced to the United Kingdom and Europe in the 1970s. Soon, some remarkably beautiful animals were being bred.

◆ ABOVE
Balinese cats are found in all the same point colours as the Siamese. This Blue Point shows how the longer fur of the Balinese can have the effect of making a subtler transition between points and main body colour.

◆ LEFT
The mask of a Chocolate Point Balinese covers the whole face and merges into the ear colour, as is considered ideal in the breed as a whole.

BREED BOX	
Coat	medium length, fine, silky; lies mainly flat along the body; no woolly undercoat
Eyes	almond-shaped, slanted; alert, intelligent expression; clear brilliant blue
Other features	feathered tail
Grooming	relatively easy; regular gentle brushing and combing
Temperament	intelligent, lively, playful, loyal, affectionate but can be aloof

143

EXOTIC SHORTHAIR

The aim in breeding the Exotic Shorthair (known simply as the Exotic in the United States) was to produce a Persian cat without the long hair to reduce the grooming commitment. These shorthaired cats are judged in the Longhair Persian-type section, which can cause some confusion for newcomers to the showing scene.

In facial make-up and expression, body shape and even character, the Exotic Shorthair has all the characteristics of the Persian breeds, and is even available in the same colours and variations. It is a medium-sized cat with a short body, short, thick legs and large paws. The head is round, with a short nose and small, wide-set, round-tipped ears.

◆ ABOVE
Eyes complement the rich red of the Red Tabby's coat. Brilliance of eye colour is an important distinction for this breed in general.

◆ BELOW
A Silver Tabby shows off her eyes lined in black like a Chinchilla. Her shorter coat, however, appears more darkly tipped and the pattern more obvious than that of the longhaired Shaded Silver.

◆ ABOVE
Brilliant orbs of gold-copper are startling against the solid density of the Black Exotic Shorthair. The nose leather and paw pads are black.

BREED BOX	
Coat	medium, slightly longer than other shorthairs, but not long enough to flow; dense, plush, soft, full of life; not flat or close-lying
Eyes	large, round, bright; colour reflects coat colour
Other features	small, blunt ears, set wide apart and leaning slightly forward
Grooming	easy; thorough, daily brushing and combing
Temperament	gentle, affectionate, good-natured, inquisitive, playful

◆ LEFT
The coat of a Blue-Cream Exotic shows definite, but scattered areas of cream among the subtle shades of soft blue-grey.

BRITISH SHORTHAIR

All the essential characteristics of the British Shorthair type are often seen at their peak in the Black. This is because it was one of the earliest British Shorthair breeds to be selectively bred from the very best of British street cats in the 1800s. It was also one of the first to be shown at the first national cat show in 1871 at Crystal Palace, London.

The top-rate pedigreed Black should have a dense black coat from hair root to tip, with no hint of browning, stray white hairs, patches or tabby markings. This provides a striking backdrop for the large, round, deep copper eyes with absolutely no green.

Blacks are often used in breeding programmes to improve the type of other Shorthair breeds, particularly Tortoiseshell and Tortie and White.

BREED BOX	
Coat	short, thick, fine
Eyes	round; copper, no green
Other features	round-tipped ears; short nose; big round paws; nose leather and paw pads black
Grooming	easy; regular combing
Temperament	companionable, independent, freedom-loving

◆ LEFT
The densely coloured, short fur of the British Black Shorthair is inherited from ancestors reputed to be the familiars of witches, and the butt of superstition and legend during the Dark Ages and medieval times.

BRITISH SHORTHAIR COLOURS AND PATTERNS

Self colours:
White (blue-eyed, orange-eyed, odd-eyed), Black, Chocolate, Lilac, Blue, Cream, Red, Cinnamon and Fawn

Tabby:
Silver, Blue Silver, Chocolate Silver, Lilac Silver, Red Silver, Cream Silver, Black Tortie Silver, Blue-Cream Silver, Chocolate Tortie Silver, Lilac-Cream Silver, Brown, Chocolate, Lilac, Blue, Red, Cream, Brown Tortie, Blue-Cream, Chocolate Tortie and Lilac-Cream
Patterns – classic, mackerel or spotted

Tortoiseshell:
Black Tortie, Chocolate Tortie, Blue-Cream Tortie and Lilac Tortie

Patched:
Black Tortie and White, Blue Tortie and White, Chocolate Tortie and White, Lilac Tortie and White, Black and White, Blue and White, Chocolate and White, Lilac and White, Red and White, Cream and White

Smoke:
All self colours (other than white, cinnamon and fawn) and all the tortoiseshell colours

Tipped:
Sparkling white coat with the very tips of the fur dusted with the self and tortoiseshell colours. The Golden Tipped, the non-silver version, has black tipping

Colourpointed:
Colour restricted to the points which can be in all self, tabby, silver tabby, tortoiseshell and smoke colours. Cats have blue eyes

ORIENTAL SHORTHAIR

The ancestors of the Oriental Shorthairs are, like the Siamese, from Thailand. They are, in fact, just like Siamese cats but with all-over coat colour and pattern rather than the Siamese colourpoints on face, ears, tail and legs. The eyes of the Orientals are usually green rather than the blue of the Siamese, although in the solid White, they may be blue or orange (though the British standard rejects the orange-eyed). Virtually all colour and pattern variations are represented, except, of course, the colourpoints, making this one of the most diverse of all cat breeds and groups.

In the United Kingdom and Europe, the self colours were originally known as Foreign Shorthairs but the other varieties have always been

♦ ABOVE
A Red Oriental can show the tabby markings that come with its red genes, but preferably no white hairs at all. You can see this cat's Siamese heritage in its large ears and long, straight nose.

♦ RIGHT
A wedge-shaped face, both in profile and from the front, is characteristic. This Black also shows the long legs and neat oval paws so typical of the breed.

known as Orientals. Each different colour was given a separate breed category to enable the cats to be entered at shows, as they were excluded from the Siamese classes. In the United States in the 1970s, all the variations were grouped together in the one category of Oriental Shorthairs, and this broad term is now universal. However, the British cat fancy still classifies the colours and patterns as distinct breeds. There are four fundamental subdivisions: solid colours, shaded, smokes and tabbies.

The Oriental Shorthair type was developed during the 1960s by mating Siamese with indigenous cats such as the British, European and American Shorthairs. They have since only been outcrossed to Siamese, so have a very similar temperament. They enjoy human company generally, and do not like being left alone for too long.

BREED BOX

Coat	short, soft, fine, lying flat along the body
Eyes	almond-shaped, slanted; green with no flecks (except Foreign White – brilliant blue)
Other features	loud voice as in Siamese, large ears, big personality
Grooming	easy; can be "polished" with a soft glove
Temperament	intelligent, lively, inquisitive, active, need company

ORIENTAL COLOURS AND PATTERNS

Foreign White:
White with blue eyes (United Kingdom), or orange or blue eyes (United States)

Self colours:
Chocolate (Havana), Lilac, Black, Blue, Red, Cream, Apricot, Cinnamon, Caramel, Fawn

Tortoiseshell:
as self colours

Oriental Smoke:
any colour with a near-white undercoat

Oriental Shaded:
shaded or tipped with any colour with or without silver

Oriental Tabbies:
spotted, classic or mackerel pattern in all colours with or without silver

RUSSIAN BLUE

◆ LEFT
A Russian Blue gives an impression of making a complaint, but in fact its voice is so quiet that it is sometimes not even obvious when the queens are calling.

As befits a cat that is said to originate from the fringe of the Arctic Circle (and have a possible Norwegian connection, too), the most distinctive feature of today's Russian Blue is its double overcoat.

From the very start of the cat fancy, two types of Blue cat came into competition with each other at shows all over the world. The domestic British Shorthair was one; the other was known as the Blue Foreign. The names suggest a distinct difference in type between the two varieties.

Blue cats were reputed to have reached the West via merchant ships travelling from the port of Archangel in northern Russia, and became known as Archangel cats. Another import was a blue tabby from Norway. There were probably several other blues from other parts of the world that may have helped

◆ ABOVE
The Russian Blue has pronounced whisker pads, wide-set, pointed ears and a face more rounded than that of other foreign shorthairs. These combine to give the cat a gentle expression that reflects its nature.

◆ RIGHT
Top-quality coat texture is the single most important point that judges look for in a Russian Blue. It should be dense beneath and fine and short on top.

the true blue breeding programme. The type is also known as the Maltese Blue and the Spanish Blue. By the late 1800s, there were enough Blues bred to be shown at the early cat shows. Unlike the cats of today, though, these early Blues had orange eyes.

Later breeding programmes included the Korat and British Blue Shorthairs. Just before and after World War II, a bid to save the Blue from extinction led to the inclusion of a Blue Point Siamese in one breeding programme, and until fairly recently the occasional Siamese pattern was subsequently found in litters of

Russian Blues. Siamese characteristics are now regarded as unacceptable in the breed.

Imports of Blues were brought in from Scandinavia, and many good Russians went to the United States where the standard colour is a little lighter than that required in Europe.

There must be no hint of white or tabby markings on the perfect Russian Blue, but there is a silver sheen to its coat, as the slate-blue hairs often have transparent tips. A medium-sized cat, it combines sturdiness with grace. A gentle expression reflects its reputation as a quiet-spoken, affectionate animal.

An English breeder of Russian Blues maintained that the Russian type referred to a particular shape rather than the colour. Using a white, double-coated female found near the London docks, she began to develop Russian cats in other colours. The project appears to have died out in Britain, but there is a thriving colony of coloured cats in the Netherlands.

BREED BOX	
Coat	plush, heavy, double; brush-like from the body
Eyes	almond-shaped; green
Other features as hairs often have transparent tips	silver sheen to coat
Grooming	easy; gentle, regular brushing so as not to damage the double coat texture
Temperament	quiet, gentle, affectionate

BLUE BURMESE

The first Blue Burmese was sired in the United Kingdom by an imported American cat. It was the Burmese equivalent of its genetic cousin, the Blue Point Siamese. The ideal tone is soft, silvery slate-blue, with the silver effect more pronounced on ears, cheeks and paws. Nose leather is dark grey and paw pads are a lighter, pinkish-grey.

BREED BOX (ALL BURMESE)	
Coat	short, fine, glossy, satiny, close-lying
Eyes	wide-set, large, round; yellow to gold
Grooming	little extra grooming is necessary
Temperament	intelligent, active, inquisitive, adaptable, friendly

♦ LEFT
The density of a Blue Burmese's fur accentuates strong shoulders and a broad, rounded chest. The Burmese is quite a heavy cat for its size!

BROWN (SABLE) BURMESE

The Brown Burmese is the Usual or original colour, and should be warm and rich in tone with matching brown nose leather and paw pads. (The Chocolate, or Champagne, which was introduced later, is more of a milk-chocolate colour.) Some kittens have faint markings but these usually disappear as they mature. As with all the solid colours of Burmese, the fur lightens in shade on the underparts. Similarly, darker areas may be evident on the ears, mask and tail, like ghosts of the seal points of a Siamese.

♦ RIGHT
A Brown Burmese shows the breed's tendency to rotundity – unlike its compatriot, the lithe Siamese.

♦ RIGHT
The top line of the Burmese's eye slants towards the nose, while the lower line is distinctly rounded, giving the breed its unique expression.

BENGAL

◆ LEFT
A young Bengal shows off the muscular and athletic body it has inherited from its wild relations, and the spotted tummy so desirable in breeding standards.

The Bengal was developed in an attempt to combine the look of the wild Asian Leopard Cat with the temperament of the domesticated cat. Because this involved crossing domestic cats with the wild cats indigenous to south-east Asia, the breeding programmes have met with some controversy. To gain acceptance, it needs to establish that wild tendencies have been bred out, and that the new breed has the ability to reproduce a consistent type. The first Bengal litters born of wild/domestic parents (known as the F1 generation) tended to produce non-fertile males and only partially fertile females, and in some cases the temperament has been unstable. Most associations, therefore, do not allow these early generations to be shown, and they are often not suitable as pets.

Although the modern breed was pioneered in the desert state of Arizona in the United States during the 1960s, it is not registered as a championship breed by all American cat associations. Most of the American varieties are shades of brown. The Bengal is on its way to gaining provisional status in the United Kingdom, where spotted and marbled variations are being bred. There has been a huge increase in Bengal breeding lines throughout the world, possibly because of the high prices commanded by the kittens.

The concept of hybrids between small wild cat species and domestic varieties is not new. There is a record of a prototype Bengal at the London Zoo sometime before 1889, and at a Dutch cattery during the 1960s.

The modern breed is very striking: it is long, sleek and muscular with beautifully patterned fur. Its coat is its unique feature, quite unlike any other domestic breed, being more akin to the feel of a wild cat's pelt. Smallish, forward-pointing ears extend straight up from the sides of the broadly wedge-shaped head.

◆ ABOVE
This Leopard Spotted youngster is beginning to show the desirable patterns that will be clearly outlined in maturity, but at present are slightly masked by the woolly kitten coat.

◆ ABOVE
The Snow Spotted Bengal is a paler version of the spotted variety. The pale background colour is the result of the recessive Siamese gene, and is complemented by clear blue eyes.

BREED BOX

Coat	short to medium, very dense; and unusually soft to the touch
Eyes	oval, large, not bold
Grooming	regular stroking; some brushing
Temperament	active, playful, loves water

◆ LEFT
A Marbled Bengal displays the dramatic coat pattern and long, prowling bodyline.

BLUE POINT SIAMESE

The modern Siamese is long-bodied and long-limbed with dainty oval paws. Face on, its head from the tip of the large, triangular ears to the muzzle is a pronounced wedge shape. The Blue Point has a main body colour of icy white with hints of the pale bluish-brown of the points. The Blue was one of the early variations of the breed to gain acceptance. It is a dilute form of the Seal Point, the original Siamese cat.

The first breeding pair of Siamese reached Britain from Siam (modern Thailand) in 1884. The required standards then for what are known as Traditional Siamese (also known as Apple Heads, Opals or Thai Siamese) called for stockier cats, rounder in the head than later lines, with small ears, and dense and plushy coats. The cats also had a squint and a kink in the end of their tails, typical of the genetic inheritance of cats throughout south-east Asia, considered defects in the modern pedigree. The Traditional Siamese is still popular among those who seek a cat less extreme than those approved of today by show judges.

◆ RIGHT
The long, straight Roman nose and startling blue eye colour of the breed are finely demonstrated by this Blue Point.

BREED BOX (ALL VARIATIONS)	
Coat	very short, fine, glossy, close-lying
Eyes	almond-shaped, slanted; alert, intelligent expression; clear brilliant blue
Other features	loud voice, large ears, big personality
Grooming	easy; must be done regularly
Temperament	intelligent, lively, playful, loyal, affectionate but can be aloof

LILAC (FROST) POINT SIAMESE

As its alternative American name suggests, a main body colour with just a hint of off-white moves into the frosted blue-grey of the points. There is a touch of lavender in the point colour, meeting its match in complementary lavender-pink nose and paw pads. This is the dilute form of the Chocolate.

◆ RIGHT
A Lilac Point is carrying on a conversation even while it is being photographed. Siamese are the most vocal and extrovert of cats.

CORNISH REX

The first recorded Cornish Rex kitten was born in 1950 in Cornwall, England, to a plain-coated tortoiseshell and white female. The kitten was a cream classic tabby with white chest and white belly. Its fur was closely waved. It was mated with its mother, and the resulting

litter contained two curly-coated kittens. Because of the interbreeding of the early Cornish Rexes, the gene pool was restricted and the kittens became weaker. Most of the kittens had to be put down, but one survivor, the son of one of the original kittens, was mated to his daughter before she was exported to the United States. Her lineage was strengthened by outcrossed matings with other breeds, and then back-crossed to rex cats to recreate the recessive curly coat. The breed was officially recognized in 1967.

The Cornish Rex has an elongated wedge of a head that curves gently at the forehead. The muzzle is

◆ ABOVE LEFT
The Cornish Rex, with its crisply waved coat, is available in all colours and patterns, including this White and Black Smoke.

rounded, the chin strong and the profile straight. The ears are large and the body hard and muscular, with long legs, and a fine and tapering tail. The Cornish Rex comes in all colours, patterns and colour combinations.

BREED BOX	
Coat	short, plushy, silky; no guardhairs; waves, curls or ripples particularly on back and tail
Eyes	medium, oval
Other features	big ears
Grooming	gentle brushing, using fingers to set waves
Temperament	intelligent, thoughtful, active

DEVON REX

In 1960, another curly-coated cat was discovered in Devon, England, the neighbouring county to the home of the Cornish Rex. A curly-coated feral male had mated with a stray, straight-haired female, and the litter included one curly-coated male. As the curly hair gene is recessive and needs to find a matching one to emerge, the female must have had a compatible gene pool. However, the gene which caused the coat was quite different from that of the Cornish Rex – mating the two breeds resulted in only straight-coated offspring.

The Devon Rex coat is generally less dense than that of the Cornish Rex and, without careful breeding, very sparse coats can result. Physically, the Devon Rex is quite different from

◆ LEFT
The Devon Rex is affectionately described as having a pixie-like expression that reflects its mischievous character.

the Cornish. It shares the muscular build, slim legs and long, whip-like tail, but it is broad chested, and has a flat forehead, prominent cheek-bones and

a crinkled brow. All coat colours, patterns and colour combinations are allowed in this type.

BREED BOX	
Coat	very short, fine, wavy, soft; can have a rippled effect
Eyes	wide-set, large and oval; all colours
Grooming	requires very gentle stroking with a soft mitt rather than a brush
Temperament	extraordinarily playful; mischievous yet never unkind

DOGS

The dog has been man's best friend at work and play for thousands of years. No animal lover can fail to admire this versatile and endearing creature, combining as it does strength, personality, intelligence and a willing nature. This chapter brings together a practical care guide for all dog owners, and a useful reference to some of the world's best-loved breeds.

The chapter opens with advice on buying a dog and covers in detail every important topic that the responsible owner needs to consider. There is information on all aspects of dog care, with advice on everything from bedding types and everyday equipment, safety in the home, feeding and grooming, as well as more specialized sections on breeding, training, health care and basic first aid.

◆ FACING PAGE
The friendly nature of the English Setter makes him a natural family member, although, given the amount of off-lead exercise he needs, he may be happier with a home in the country.

◆ LEFT
This cheeky looking Shih Tzu is waiting for someone to throw him his ball. The ever-playful nature of dogs is one of their most endearing qualities.

INTRODUCTION

The dog is humanity's oldest companion. Human and dog came together thousands of years ago for mutual comfort and slowly developed the interdependence seen today – human's caring for the dog in return for continuing companionship and a great variety of working functions.

The gradual recognition of the many different ways in which the dog could contribute to the association has led to the development of an enormous variety of dog types. All varieties of dog are members of a single species; it is the most varied of any species known, ranging from the tiny Chihuahua to the massive Irish Wolfhound.

So close has the association of dog and human become that there are now probably only two breeds of truly wild dogs left, the Cape Hunting Dog and the Australian Dingo. Many countries,

◆ RIGHT
The Golden Retriever is one of the most popular companion breeds and has an impeccable working background as a gundog.

of course, have roaming packs of wild dogs that lead an independent existence, but these are invariably domestic dogs that have "gone wild" for one of any number of reasons.

To a remarkable extent, a dog of any breed can mate with another of any other breed and produce fertile offspring. This fact in itself has led to even more varieties developing over the centuries, as new functions and

fashions were thought up. There are something like four hundred known breeds in existence today. The precise figure is impossible to determine as previously unrecognized breeds continue to emerge, and types of the same breed are recognized as distinct; or conversely, varieties previously

◆ BELOW
This German Shepherd is a true companion and guard, always keen to please his owner.

◆ ABOVE
Dogs are inveterate game-players, always learning from their play.

◆ RIGHT
Dogs may learn to carry out all kinds of helpful tasks, including collecting and delivering items around the house.

◆ LEFT
The Great Dane is likely to weigh
more than 54 kg (119 lb) when mature.

◆ LEFT
A dog will roll on
to its back as a sign
of submission to
its owner or to
another dog.

considered as separate are combined
under the name of one breed.

As part of this continuing
evolutionary process, breeds have
also died out; several have disappeared
even in the last one hundred years or
so, possibly due to reduced fertility
or the particular type ceasing to be
fashionable. Loss of the traditional
function of a breed may be another
reason, but more often the breed has
changed in conformation to such an
extent as to be almost unrecognizable
as the original breed. The war dogs of
old, for instance, have developed into
the civilized mastiff types.

Although every breed of dog, in
the western world at least, is expected
to be domesticated, certain type
characteristics tend to persist through
many generations, and these are not
just characteristics of conformation.
Everyone realizes that if you buy a
Great Dane puppy, for instance,
small though it may be at eight weeks
old, it will grow into a very large dog.
If you buy a terrier of whatever breed,

it will display the terrier behaviour
characteristics, which it has inherited
from its working ancestors.

If you have decided to buy a dog,
look into all the breed characteristics,
and consider them carefully before
you decide which type of dog you
want to live with. A dog may live for
between ten and 20 years – it will be
yours to care for all of its life, which
is a good part of yours.

◆ LEFT
The young of every
breed are appealing,
but an owner's
responsibility may
last for over 15 years.

◆ RIGHT
Children and dogs
are good for each
other. Both have
much to learn from
their mutual love.

Choosing a
Suitable Dog

Many households are just not suitable for a dog. If you work long periods away from home, or even just very long hours, and if there is no-one else at home while you are away, you need to consider very carefully whether the comforts of coming home to a dog are not outweighed by the lack of company that the dog will have to endure, with all the potential behaviour problems that this may cause. Consider not just how the dog would fit into your own way of life, but how your lifestyle would affect the dog.

◆ FACING PAGE
Before getting a dog, it is
important to ensure that
you can provide it with
the environment it needs.

◆ LEFT
Border Collies make
highly obedient pets,
but without attention
they can become bored
and mischievous.

WHAT TYPE OF DOG?

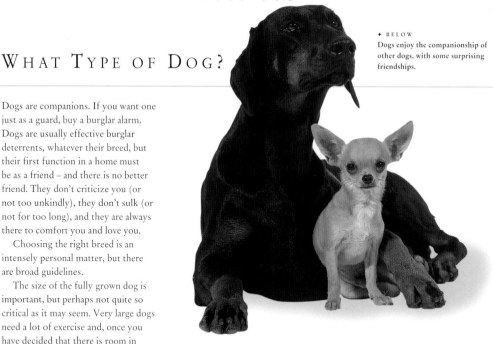

◆ BELOW
Dogs enjoy the companionship of
other dogs, with some surprising
friendships.

Dogs are companions. If you want one just as a guard, buy a burglar alarm. Dogs are usually effective burglar deterrents, whatever their breed, but their first function in a home must be as a friend – and there is no better friend. They don't criticize you (or not too unkindly), they don't sulk (or not for too long), and they are always there to comfort you and love you.

Choosing the right breed is an intensely personal matter, but there are broad guidelines.

The size of the fully grown dog is important, but perhaps not quite so critical as it may seem. Very large dogs need a lot of exercise and, once you have decided that there is room in your house for a large dog, exercise is the most important consideration. Most people, however, want a dog that fits reasonably into the home environment. A pair of Wolfhounds may be your ideal, but their bulk may make a small flat uninhabitable.

The Labrador Retriever, a dog which, if not overweight, will weigh when mature about 30 kg (66 lb), is the most popular dog in the United States and the United Kingdom, with 132,000 in the US and 32,000 in the UK. Second in the US is the Rottweiler, with almost 94,000 registered, and

◆ FACING
A common problem
with insecure dogs is
barking when they
are left alone. Once
established it may be
very difficult to
overcome.

◆ LEFT
Complete family
integration with
people and dogs all
joining in as many
activities as possible
will usually prevent
behaviour problems.

♦ BELOW
Some breeds, like the Border Collie,
spend hours looking for attention.
Ignore them at your peril!

♦ LEFT
Most dogs love
jumping for toys.
It can be a helpful
supplement to their
exercise when walks
are restricted.

breed – your veterinary surgeon sees
a wide variety of dogs every day.

Typically, the terrier types are
lively, not easy to train, but very
responsive dogs. They are good
with children if properly trained.

Toy dogs are usually better
companions for owners who do not
have young children. The dogs may be
upset by what they perceive as large
noisy humans rushing around. Their
fear may make them snappy, with
unhappy results. All toy dogs will be
happy with as much exercise as you
can give them, but they may be equally
happy with only a moderate amount.

Hounds need as much exercise as
possible. With this condition they make
very good house dogs who love their
comfort. Breeds in the other groups
vary, but, in general, the working
breeds are all better with an occupation
that keeps them out of mischief.

The gundog (sporting) breeds are
generally easy to train, and settle into
the human environment without
difficulty. They need exercise, and
lack of exercise shows!

Certain of the herding breeds,
typified by the Border Collie, are,

third the German Shepherd with 79,000
registered. In Britain the German
Shepherd is second (24,000) and the
Golden Retriever third (16,000). These
are all large dogs. By no means do all of
them live in large houses.

Breed or type behaviour is probably
more important in choosing a dog
than any other characteristic. It pays
to ask not just dedicated owners but
knowledgeable people outside the

or should be regarded as, specialist
working dogs. They demand more
attention than other breeds if they are
not to become neurotic pets. Outside
their traditional working function they
have become the outstanding type in
obedience work of all sorts. Provided
you are able to give sufficient attention
to them to keep their very active minds
occupied, they are among the most
rewarding of pets. But if you don't,
they will find something to occupy
themselves, and it will be trouble.

With so many breeds to choose
from, as well as crossbreds and
mongrels, there really isn't a typical
household pet these days.

♦ RIGHT
This charming
Bernese puppy will
make a beautiful
house pet, but he
will grow to 70 cm
(27½ in) at the
shoulder when
mature.

THE COST OF KEEPING A DOG

Can you afford it? Buying a dog is just the start. Very few puppies can be acquired for nothing. Almost everyone will want to sell the litter they have reared, even if only to try to recoup the cost of feeding the puppies to the weaning stage.

The cost of good pedigree puppies varies from country to country. In the United Kingdom, depending on breed, a puppy may cost from around £300, although probably the average price asked for a well-bred puppy of most breeds is between £400 and £600. In the United States asking prices are usually somewhat higher, from about $1,000 upwards. Australian prices are similar to those in the United Kingdom. Imported puppies in any country may cost a great deal more.

The initial examination by the veterinary surgeon, and the puppy's primary inoculations will be another expense, and you can spend as much as you wish on toys and other canine equipment – some essential, some not.

◆ LEFT
A fair return for the cost of keeping a dog may be the exercise it encourages its owner to take.

◆ BELOW LEFT
The superb grooming of this dog may be achieved either by a professional at considerable cost or through hours of work by its owner.

◆ BELOW RIGHT
The cost of keeping a toy dog is probably very little less than for a larger animal. Veterinary attention is much the same and fussy eaters need special food.

A substantial part of the cost of keeping a dog as a pet may be the cost of veterinary treatment. Veterinary surgeons are these days capable of administering sophisticated treatments of illness or injury, but they have no subsidy for the costs. If your dog ever needs complicated or prolonged veterinary treatment the cost may be astonomically high.

There are several pet insurance companies catering for veterinary treatments; each has its own approach, and dog owners would be well advised to study what each company offers before deciding which policy to buy.

♦ BELOW
Diet and exercise may both be critical to the
well-being of the older dog. Overweight dogs
are often reluctant to walk far; a few pounds off
works wonders.

♦ RIGHT
The size and breed of
a dog may not be an
accurate guide to its
demand for exercise.

The premium grade policies offer sums for the death of your dog, and for rewards to be offered if the dog is lost. They may include kennelling fees in case of your own illness, even holiday cancellation costs. The level of veterinary fees covered is variable on most schemes, and it may be worth discussing this with your vet. A vet should be able to advise you on the health areas likely to incur the greatest costs, and may also be able to suggest the degree to which your dog is at risk. All additions cost money.

Some insurance companies will offer a basic veterinary fee insurance as an alternative to the premium schemes. It will be up to you to decide which of the various forms of insurance best suits your own needs.

Most insurers offer a puppy scheme, sometimes with an incentive to transfer to the adult scheme when it expires. Many breeders will offer puppy insurance to buyers, either as part of or as an extra cost to the purchase price of the puppy.

Feeding costs vary greatly. In theory, the smaller the dog, the less expensive to feed, but this may be offset by the need for specialized, more expensive foods for small dogs with specific dietary requirements.

♦ ABOVE
Running with a
companion dog is
terrific exercise, but
be sure you are in
control.

♦ LEFT
Diets to rear healthy
puppies need careful
consideration. The
breeder will usually
offer sound advice,
but be wary of
bizarre feeding
regimes.

PEDIGREE OR NON-PEDIGREE?

Crossbred dogs, the most identifiable of which is the Lurcher, are usually not expensive to buy, which is an obvious advantage. They have their own "mutt" charm, and their apparent type may be just what you are looking for. But remember the tiny puppy may become an enormous adult. The best way to judge is to see both parents, but in the nature of things the father is likely to be "away on business" when the puppies are ready to leave.

It is not necessarily true that crossbred dogs are healthier than purebreds, as many people believe. Every veterinary surgeon can tell you of crossbreds or mongrels suffering from recognizable, inherited diseases.

The advantage of picking a purebred dog is that you know what you are getting. From a reputable breeder a Cocker Spaniel puppy will grow up into a Cocker Spaniel dog, of a size and weight that is within the breed norm, and with potential behaviour characteristics typical of the breed. There is, or should be, advice available to deal with whatever problems may arise as a particular feature of the breed.

There is no doubt that many breeds have inherited problems associated with that breed, although these have often been exaggerated in the press. It is up to the potential owner to enquire about these problems, and to take independent advice on their significance. It is worth bearing in mind that no species of animal, including human beings, is free from inheritable disease. Dogs may be less afflicted than most.

◆ LEFT
A lovable mongrel. Did his owners know how he was going to turn out? And have they the time and inclination to give that coat the attention it demands?

◆ RIGHT
Crossbred dogs are often the basis for new working types. A cross between two recognized breeds is likely to have characteristics somewhere between the two.

DOG OR BITCH?

◆ LEFT
Labradors, dogs and bitches, are notorious for the ease with which they put on weight.

Choosing whether to have a male or female – a dog or a bitch – is one of the early decisions.

Dogs tend to have a more "macho" outlook on life than bitches, and if that attracts you, the male of the species will be your choice. Dogs are

◆ RIGHT
The King Charles Spaniel is regarded by many as the ideal family pet.

possibly more outgoing, certainly on average a little harder to train, but often more responsive once trained.

They do not, of course, come into season twice a year, with the attendant bother of oestrous discharges, and the attraction of all the dogs in the neighbourhood. But don't forget that

it is the male dogs that are attracted, and if you have a male it could be yours that has to be dragged home each night from his wanderings.

On balance, if there is such a thing in this particular choice, the female is likely to make a better family pet. She is less likely to be aggressive, although dominance is as much a breed characteristic as it is related to the sex of the dog. Bitches are much less likely to try to wander for most of the year, and they are inclined to be more loving to their human family.

◆ BELOW
The Boston Terrier needs the minimum of grooming but likes its exercise.

◆ LEFT
The Rough Collie is a working dog; not for the lazy owner.

◆ FAR LEFT
The Airedale is a real terrier in every respect.

◆ BELOW
The Dachshund is a well-loved breed.

BUYING A PUPPY

Let us assume that you know more or less the type of dog you feel you can best live with. Even though you may have no intention of ever showing your dog, dog shows are good places to visit while you are finally making up your mind. Talk to the people showing and find out their views about the breed – you may find that many of the exhibitors are remarkably frank about the drawbacks as well as the virtues of their breed. In the long run it pays them to be so.

The next step is to look for the right breeder, not necessarily the top one in the breed, who would, quite fairly, expect a premium price for puppies of show standard. Top breeders, however, will often be the most genuinely encouraging to the potential new owner.

Many dogs are still sold through so-called "puppy farms" and pet shops. Neither is a suitable place to find a puppy. Young dogs cannot be treated as commodities to be traded at the convenience of their breeder, and serious health problems regularly arise from this form of mistreatment of young animals.

Take your time, and be prepared to wait to get the dog you really want. Above all, visit the kennels and make sure you see the dam with the puppies in the litter (and other litters), and, if possible, the sire. Make your own mind up about the conditions in which the puppies have been reared.

There is some argument about the right age to buy a puppy, although the general consensus seems to be that about eight weeks is right. Much before that may be too early to remove the puppy from the nest; leaving it later can give rise to socialization problems, with the time between six and eight weeks regarded by behaviourists as a critical period in the puppy's development. Certainly, if the puppy is much older than eight weeks, you need to be satisfied that it

◆ RIGHT
It is safe to let
prospective owners
handle the puppies
if they haven't been
handling other dogs.

◆ BELOW RIGHT
Retrievers tend to
have very large
litters, often ten or
more. Weaning can
start as early as three
weeks with suitable
supplements.

has been exposed to a sensible social environment and not simply left in its rearing kennel to make its own way.

Be honest with the breeder. If you are looking for a dog that you may later want to show, don't pretend that you are only looking for a pet puppy, in the hope that the price might be lower. Explain truthfully and carefully the life that the puppy will lead, especially its home environment. At worst, the breeder will explain why that may not be suitable for rearing a puppy; at best, you may get much good advice.

Never expect a guarantee that your puppy will be a show winner. Even though it comes from the very best show stock, with a pedigree as long as your arm, no-one, including the most experienced breeders, can pick a "cert" at eight weeks.

The breeder should provide you with the puppy's pedigree, and a

receipt for its purchase. If the breeder has already taken the puppies for their first inoculation, this may be included in the quoted price or regarded as an extra. You should ask.

You may be expected to sign a contract setting out the limitations of the breeder's liability in the event of the puppy later developing an inheritable condition. We live in a litigious society. Recent court cases have made it plain that if a breeder fails to warn a purchaser of conditions that are recognized in the breed, and the puppy later develops such a condition, the breeder may be held liable, even though he or she is unaware of the existence of the problem in that puppy, and has taken reasonable precautions to avoid the condition.

The contract you may be asked to sign must be reasonable, and it is likely to consist of a statement drawing your attention to the known inheritable diseases of the breed and an expectation that you will have discussed the significance of the condition with your veterinary surgeon. Your veterinary surgeon may be advised to make his comments in a written statement.

◆ BELOW LEFT

The best way to decide on the suitability of a
particular kennel is to see as many of their dogs
as possible, both at home and at work or in the
show-ring.

◆ BELOW RIGHT

Ex-racing greyhounds make wonderful pets,
but occasionally have problems socializing
after years in a racing kennel.

The breeder should provide a
feeding chart for the next stage of the
rearing process. It is worthwhile
discussing this with the vet when you
take the puppy for its first visit. Many
breeders give new owners sample feed
to start the puppy off in its new home.

You should expect a healthy puppy,
which has been wormed adequately,
probably twice, and is free from skin
parasites such as fleas or lice.

Most pet insurance companies have
short-term cover schemes, available to
breeders for issue to new owners when

they take home their new puppy. Ask
the breeder if he or she has such cover.
If not, arrange your own as soon as
you have bought the puppy. Puppies
are at their most vulnerable during the
first few weeks in their new homes,
and it can help to be prepared.

◆ LEFT
The age to
leave home is
a compromise.
A critical
socializing time
is about six
weeks, when
ideally the puppy
should meet its
new family, but
other factors
usually dictate
that eight weeks
is probably the
best practical age
at which to buy
your puppy.

CHOOSING A PUPPY

Never be fobbed off with excuses about the condition a puppy is in or its behaviour; and never buy a puppy simply because it's the last one left and you feel sorry for it.

It is often said that puppies choose their new owners, rather than the other way around, and there is much truth to this claim. An overly shy puppy may have socialization problems later, and the puppy that comes forward from the nest, asking to be chosen, is probably the right one.

The puppy must be alert and have bright, clean eyes. Its nose must be clean (but forgive a little crust of food), its ears must be free of wax, and its coat must be clean and pleasant to handle and smell. There must be no sign of sores or grittiness on the skin and coat. Black "coal dust" is usually flea dirt – fleas themselves are more difficult to spot. Examine all the puppies briefly to ensure that they have been well cared for.

Make sure there is no discharge from the eyes. Forgive a scratch or two on the face – puppies in the nest don't always agree.

The membranes of the nose must be clear and free of discharge. There must be no sign of a runny nose.

The inside of the ears must look pink and shiny, without inflammation or dark-coloured wax. It should not look sore.

Soreness or inflammation of the rims of the eyes, or eyes that are not completely clear, may be serious signs of present or potential disease.

The puppy's coat and skin should feel loose and soft. The skin should be free of sores.

Sturdy, strong limbs are a must for any breed, although if you fancy an Italian Greyhound don't expect him to be this sturdy.

Puppies should have a clean bottom. Signs of diarrhoea are obvious from a quick examination behind. The whole litter should be examined.

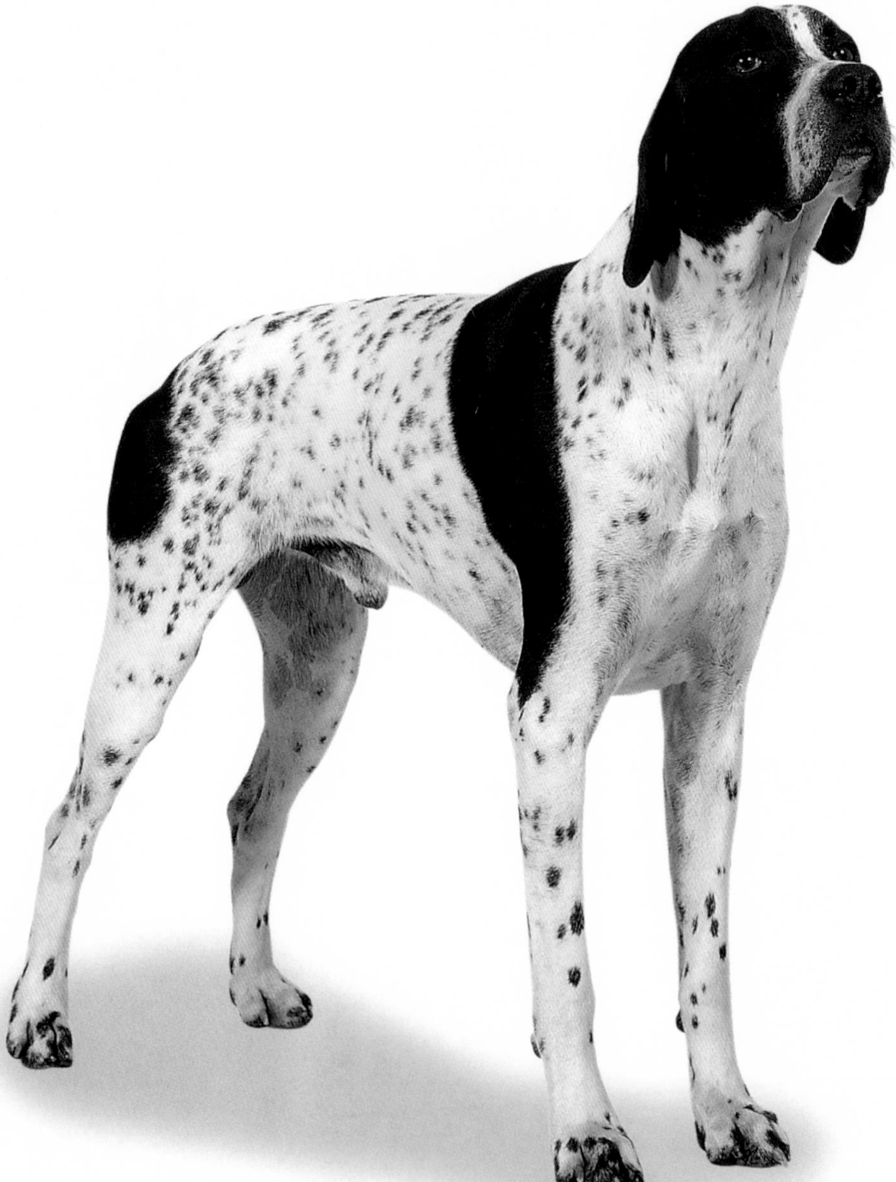

Creating the Right Environment

When you take a dog into your home, you are accepting an obligation to take care of all its needs. Tailoring your home to the needs of your dog is the first step towards achieving a hugely satisfying relationship between dog and owner. Provided your dog can feel safe and comfortable, with plenty of opportunities for play and exercise, he will quickly settle into a contented life as a well-adjusted family friend.

♦ FACING PAGE
This pointer requires plenty of exercise. Like all dogs, his home should reflect the needs and temperament of his breed.

♦ LEFT
Dalmatians are superfriendly dogs, but as adults they can be a handful to control, especially for children.

SETTLING IN

♦ LEFT
Puppies' curiosity
about new toys helps
to overcome their
awe of strange
surroundings.

Bringing home a new puppy or even an older dog is an important family occasion. Everyone wants to touch, hold and stroke the new member of the family, especially the children. But do take things slowly.

In the case of a puppy, this will be the first time away from the only environment he has known, and away from his mother and litter mates. The world is huge and very frightening.

Even for an older dog, there is still a lot of adjusting to be done. Bring him home when there are not too many people around, and introduce him to his new environment in as relaxed a manner as possible. Let him take time to look and sniff around, offer him a little something to eat, which he probably won't accept, and allow him to have a run around the garden. Bring your family and friends to meet the dog one or two at a time, and give him time to make friends before introducing anyone else.

At some stage you have to cause a little more trauma by taking the dog to the veterinary surgeon for a health check. If at all possible, take him to the vet on the way home from the breeder or kennels. If there should be a problem that necessitates returning the dog to the seller (fortunately, a very rare occurrence), it is going to be much easier if the family haven't met and already fallen in love with him.

Once the settling in process has begun, interrupt the dog's established routine as little as possible. For a puppy, follow the breeder's feeding

regime, giving the same number of feeds at the same time each day. To start with, give the food the dog is used to – the seller might have provided a "starter pack" – even if you have decided eventually to use a different type of food. Make any dietary changes gradually.

Clean water should always be available; show the dog where it is. Make sure that not only is the water bowl always full, but that it is washed regularly – dogs are messy drinkers, and the bowl soon gets dirty. Most dogs, some breeds more than others,

♦ RIGHT
Puppies hate
to be left alone
until they
are confident
that you will
quickly return.

SAFETY GUIDELINES ON TOYS FOR DOGS

The jaws and teeth of nearly all dogs are much stronger than you think, so toys should be very tough.

Fluffy dolls will be torn to pieces without fail so, if you must provide them, make sure that they do not have parts that can be detached and swallowed.

Balls are popular toys for dogs because the owners can throw them and join in the game. Fine, but make sure the ball is large enough not even to be half-swallowed by the dog. A dog being rushed to the veterinary surgeon choking on a tennis ball that is stuck in its throat is a common emergency.

The use of a bone as a toy is controversial. Most veterinary surgeons advise against it, unless

the bone is so big that the dog cannot break pieces off and swallow them. There is no doubt that a good chew at a bone is a dog's delight.

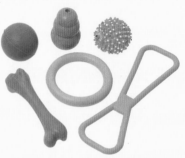

♦ ABOVE
Toys should be solid enough not to risk pieces being chewed off and swallowed.

are also very splashy drinkers, spilling more water around the bowl than they swallow. So choose your water-bowl site carefully.

The ideal water bowl may be made of ceramic or non-rust metal, but it must be non-spill, and preferably too heavy for the dog to pick up and carry around. If you start with a heavy bowl, the puppy will soon get the idea that this is not a toy to be picked up and carted around, and he will look for something else to play with.

Feed bowls may be much the same as water bowls, with the same idea: the dog should not regard the bowl as a toy. Apart from anything else, if the bowl gets carried around, you can never find it when you want to feed the dog!

The new dog's bed is very important – the bed is the dog's own special place. It is important to introduce the dog to his bed as soon as he arrives, and to insist that the bed is where he sleeps. This may be difficult but, if you give in and let him sleep on your

◆ BELOW
Puppies take great comfort from a hot-water bottle, but beware leaks from chewing. An alarm clock seems to soothe them at night.

bed "just until he settles in", you have lost the battle – and probably the war.

To make sure the dog uses his own bed, the best way is to shut him into a "bedroom" on the first night in his new home with no other options for a comfortable sleep but his bed. Make sure it is sited away from any draughts. Young puppies will miss their litter mates and perhaps their dam. A useful tip, if the puppy doesn't settle – that's if he is crying pitifully just as you are getting to sleep – is to provide him with

◆ LEFT
Hygiene is important for feed bowls. Never add another meal without first thoroughly cleaning the bowl.

◆ BELOW
Rawhide chews are usually an excellent substitute for bones.

comforters. Traditionally, these are a hot-water bottle and a ticking alarm clock; and like many traditions, they often work well.

Toys are important, whatever the age of the dog, but particularly for a young puppy. There is an enormous range on sale, from fluffy dolls that amuse the owner but soon become unrecognizable once the puppy has had a chance to tear them apart, to specifically designed training aids.

Some dogs are obsessive about a particular toy – this occurs more in the terrier breeds than in other types – but mostly dogs have a rather short attention span, dropping one object for another after a short spell of play. There is no certain winner. Each dog has a different fancy, but do provide choice for a puppy, bearing in mind safety guidelines.

BEDS AND BEDDING

The dog must have a bed of his own. From the owner's point of view, washability is the priority. Plastic beds made for this purpose are not expensive and easily cleaned, but they must have soft bedding for comfort.

Providing a mobile cage as a bed and a private place for your puppy has several advantages, not least of which is that there is somewhere to put the puppy when non-doggy friends, who may not appreciate dog hairs all over their clothes, arrive.

Cages may be the completely collapsible type, useful for folding and taking with you when you are travelling with the dog, or, probably better in the long run, the "sky kennel" type which is fastened by nuts and bolts around the middle. This enables the cage to be divided in half for travelling but provides a more permanent kennel for the dog to use at home.

There are plenty of choices of bedding. The most satisfactory from the hygiene point of view, as well as

♦ LEFT
Traditional wicker baskets look good until the dog starts to chew the edges. They are not easy to keep clean.

for comfort and warmth, is veterinary bedding, sold under a number of brand names, made of synthetic fur backed by a strong woven base. These veterinary beds may be machine washed, they stay dry as moisture goes straight through them, they are long-

lasting, and they are resistant (but not if the dog is really determined) to being chewed up. They can be bought or cut to any size, and using the principle of "one on, one in the wash", you can easily keep the bed clean and free from doggy odours.

♦ LEFT
Flexible dog beds seem to pass the comfort test. They are usually insulated against cold floors and are easily cleaned. They may be expensive and destructible by determined dogs.

♦ ABOVE, LEFT TO RIGHT
An old blanket is best in a bed rather than just on the floor; synthetic veterinary bedding is probably more hygienic than any other soft bedding; the bean bag is supremely comfortable and warmly insulating; a plastic basket is easily cleaned, but it does need a comfortable lining to be given the dog's personal accolade.

♦ LEFT
Dogs all appreciate a warm covering to lie on, wherever they choose to sleep.

◆ RIGHT
Dogs are thought to be colour-blind –
even though they may choose the
perfect background on which to pose!

BEHAVIOUR TIP

Dogs will often accept your rage if
it means you are paying attention
to them rather than ignoring them.
To ignore your dog is the most
severe punishment you can inflict
on him. So for peaceful nights for
you and your dog, make him sleep
elsewhere.

◆ TOP
The collapsible travelling cage has many uses at
home as well as away.

◆ ABOVE
An outside kennel must be dry, warm and of an
adequate size for the dog's comfort.

◆ RIGHT
An outside kennel and run must always be kept
clean (with wood this may not be easy). The run
is no substitute for proper exercise.

Cushions filled with polystyrene
granules are possibly the most
comfortable of all for the dog,
but they are less easy to wash than
veterinary bedding. Some dogs enjoy
chewing their bed and this results in
a myriad little polystyrene balls rolling
around the floor, which are almost
impossible to sweep up.

Still probably more used than
anything else is a square of old
blanket or a blanket off-cut. Nothing
wrong with them, provided you have
enough so that you can wash them
regularly, bearing in mind that they
leave a fluffy deposit which needs to
be removed from the washing machine
and they take forever to dry.

WHERE TO SLEEP?

The kitchen or a warm utility room
are the best places for the dog to sleep.
The kitchen floor often has non-
absorbent flooring, useful for a puppy

before he's able to avoid accidents.
Once he has become accustomed to
the kitchen, if it remains convenient to
you, it is possibly the best place for
him to stay. The kitchen tends to be
one of the warm places in the house,
and dogs like warmth.

Most dogs are not kennelled out
of doors. There is no particular reason
why they should not be, and if that is
your intention it must be instituted
from the start. Use plenty of warm
bedding and pay attention to draughts
and waterproofing. One problem with
outside kennels is that it becomes too
easy to ignore the dog. Few owners
would indulge in the outright cruelty
of neglecting to feed their dog but,
if the weather doesn't look too good,
plenty would put the walk off to
another day.

If a dog is to be confined in a
kennel, you must ask yourself if you
really want a dog. At worst, the kennel
must provide an adequate exercise
area, as well as the essentials
mentioned above.

HOME, GARDEN AND CAR SAFETY

◆ BELOW
The easiest way for a dog to get out of the
garden is via the gate. The gate must be rigid
and placed over a hard standing.

Of immediate interest to most new dog owners is the need to make the home and garden dog-proof. This may prove to be a difficult and very expensive undertaking.

You have a responsibility in law to keep your dog under control. This means that your garden must be fenced in such a way as to prevent the dog escaping. As the puppies of almost any breed other than the very smallest grow, so does their ability to jump over fences. There can be no hard and fast rule for the height needed to prevent this; even within the same breed, one will be a jumper and another never learn the skill. However, the minimum height for any dog-proof fence for anything but toy breeds will be 1 m (3 ft). Often, for dogs from the small terrier breeds, like Jack Russells, and the more agile larger breeds, this will not be sufficient. Plenty of dogs can scale a 2 m (6 ft 6 in) fence. A fence this high starts to make the garden look like Fort Knox, and the usual compromise is a fence of about 1.5 m (5 ft). If it is a wire fence, it must be tightly strung. Many gardens are close fenced to this height, and close fencing has advantages as a dog fence. Being unable to see the world outside often removes the temptation to investigate it.

There are two ways through a fence, even if it is in good repair.

One way is over the top, and the other is underneath. Dogs enjoy digging. You need to be sure that there is no way under. Wire fencing is particularly vulnerable to the tunnelling dog, unless it is firmly attached to some sort of hard, impenetrable base.

Preventing the dog from escaping from the house is usually a matter of care rather than built-in precautions. The perfectly trained dog will not push past his owner when the front door is opened unless required to do so; plenty of others in real life try to. The family has to learn to keep the dog shut in the kitchen when they answer the door – one reason for not restraining the dog's barking when

someone knocks at the front door; at least the dog is reminding you to shut him away. Downstairs windows, and occasionally upstairs windows, may attract the dog. It is a matter of vigilance unless you are prepared to barricade yourself in.

DOGS IN CARS

The idea of travelling with a dog in the car is very appealing. In the event, it sometimes becomes a nightmare. Part of the very earliest training for the puppy must be to learn to travel in a safe and socially acceptable way in the car. For the smaller breeds, a collapsible cage is ideal.

If your car is a hatchback, a dog guard is an obvious and sensible investment. It needs to be well fitting and strong enough to prevent a determined dog from climbing through it into the front of the car. There are dozens of dog guards

BEHAVIOUR TIP

Any response to unacceptable behaviour may be taken by the dog as encouragement. The only sensible response is not to take any obvious notice.

♦ ABOVE AND RIGHT
Dogs may escape despite precautions. Identity discs for collars should have a contact telephone number rather than names and addresses.

designed specifically for each make and model of car. They are advertised in the dog magazines or available from most of the larger dog shows.

Unrestrained dogs in cars cause accidents. If you are not able to use a dog guard or cage, the puppy must be taught to sit on the back seat and never to climb into the front. He will soon learn if you gently and patiently restrain him, and scold him firmly if he comes forward. It is one piece of training where the immediate "no" can work, but not if you sometimes relent and let him sit on the front seat. Harnesses, designed to clip to the rear seat belt fastening, are another way to keep the dog on the back seat.

Some dogs become "barkers" when in the car. This is dangerous and distracting, and steps to remedy it must be taken before the behaviour becomes totally engrained. Specialist advice may be necessary, but the first step is to restrain the dog, with a short lead, below the window level of the car. It's no good shouting at him to shut him up – the dog's response will be to redouble his efforts to be heard above his owner's voice.

Nutrition and Feeding

The diets of yesteryear, of home-mixed meat and biscuits, have long gone.
Nowadays, professional nutritionists produce feeds of a variety and quality
that should satisfy any dog in forms convenient enough to suit any owner.
Nutrition is a complex subject and there is a simple question: do you know
more about the nutrition of the dog than the experts? Teams of nutritionists
form part of a multi-million pound industry involving science, marketing and,
most importantly, competition between feed companies.
For modern dogs, palatability is considered to be of great importance,
and the professional feed laboratories spend a great deal of time getting
the flavour just right.

♦ FACING PAGE
It is important to
provide your dog with
a nutritious diet.

♦ LEFT
Follow the
manufacturer's guide
to quantity when
feeding your dog.

TYPES OF FOOD

Dogs are carnivores. Their digestive system, from the mouth through their intestines, is designed to cope with a meat diet. The dog's teeth are adapted to tear food into swallowable-sized chunks rather than to grind the food, and their stomachs can digest food in this state.

Dogs have probably evolved from animals that lived on a diet of other animals. However, as with the fox in modern times, meat was not always available to them, and the dog is able also to digest and survive on a diet that is mostly vegetable; but a complete absence of meat is likely to lead to nutritional deficiencies.

Foods, whether for dogs or humans, have to supply energy, from which, as well as being the means of movement, the animal's body derives heat, materials for growth and repair, and substances that support these activities. For dogs, this involves

a satisfactory mixture of the major nutrients – carbohydrates, fats and proteins – in proportions similar to those required for a healthy human diet; they must also have a sufficient intake of the minor nutrients – vitamins and minerals – in proportions that do differ significantly from the needs of humans.

Dog foods may be divided into several broad categories. For many years the so-called **moist diets** held the major part of the market. They are the tinned foods seen on every supermarket shelf.

Over the past few years other types of food have infiltrated the market. **Complete dry feeds** are becoming increasingly popular. They need minimal preparation – if so desired, they can simply be poured into a dog bowl and given to the dog. Only very slightly more demanding is to pour hot water on to moisten the feed.

Semi-moist diets are not intended to provide a balanced diet on their own. They hold a small but significant place in the market, largely, in all probability, because they involve some degree of preparation before feeding. It is still fairly minimal, involving the addition of carbohydrate supplements as a mixer, often some form of biscuit, to balance the nutritional quality of the food. This is a psychologically important exercise for the owner, who likes to think that he or she is doing something for the dog, as previous generations did when they mixed a bowl of table scraps with some meat and gravy. The one thing to remember is that too much mixing of modern foods can result in nutritional problems. What too often happens is that the concerned owner adds, not just a carbohydrate mixer, but high-protein feed as well, resulting in a diet that is unbalanced, with too much

♦ BELOW
If a dog is hungry and healthy, he will eat. If he is healthy but won't eat, he isn't hungry, so take the food away and let him miss a meal.

NUTRIENTS

The **major nutrients**, required in substantial quantities by every animal, include:

Carbohydrates, which provide the body with energy, and in surplus, will be converted into body fat.

Fats, which are the most concentrated form of energy, producing more than twice as much energy, weight for weight, than carbohydrates, and which will also convert to body fats if supplied in excess.

Proteins, which essentially provide the body-building elements in the diet.

The **minor nutrients** include the vitamins, minerals and trace elements, which, although critical to the animal's health, are required in comparatively small amounts. The vitamins are usually divided into two groups:

Fat soluble: vitamins A, D, E and K.

Water soluble: the B complex vitamins and vitamin C.

◆ BELOW
Each dog should have his own bowl, although the food is often more interesting on the other dog's plate.

◆ ABOVE
Heavy feed bowls make eating easier as they don't skid all over the floor.

protein. There is usually no harm; animals, like man, can deal with an astonishing variety of diet, but too high levels of protein can occasionally exacerbate an existing metabolic problem. There is an old adage: "When all else fails, follow the instructions." It is worth bearing in mind when feeding your dog.

One feature of all modern compound dog foods is that they will contain adequate minor nutrients, which did not always happen in the

meat and biscuit days. The outcome is that there is rarely any need for the proprietary feed supplements that are still widely advertised. Calcium, for instance, may have been lacking in some traditional diets, and a bonemeal supplement often used to be recommended. Such a supplement may today do harm in certain circumstances, such as pregnancy in the bitch.

Special diets are a development of the last ten or fifteen years. They are of two types: those that target healthy

dogs with special requirements – puppies, for instance, with special growth needs, especially active dogs, and older dogs – and those designed as supportive diets for various illnesses. There are kidney diets, for instance, which control the amount and type of protein the dog is given. These latter special diets are dispensed strictly under the control of a veterinary surgeon, many of whom are now trained specifically in the use of such diets.

◆ LEFT
Canned food must be used within twenty-four hours of opening and kept refrigerated. Cover open cans with plastic lids, and reserve an opener and fork just for dog food.

◆ LEFT
Dogs love bones but vets don't because of the risks of bowel stoppages or choking. Very large bones minimize such risk. Never give a dog a chop bone.

FOOD REQUIREMENTS

Dogs are adaptable creatures. They can, for instance, utilize protein foods, like meats, for energy if their intake of carbohydrates is deficient. They must, however, be provided with a minimum level of each of around thirty nutrients, including the vitamins and minerals, if they are to stay healthy. All the modern prepared foods, and the great majority of home-mixed diets, will provide an adequate supply of essential nutrients.

Some animal protein is essential to maintain a dog's health. A vegetarian diet for dogs can be devised but requires skill, although there is no doubt that dogs do not need the level of animal protein in their diet that is commonly provided.

Some fats are also vital in the diet, providing certain essential fatty acids, and acting as carriers for the fat-soluble vitamins.

Carbohydrates form the bulk of most diets, including normal dog foods, whether commercially compounded or home-mixed.

Provided your dog's diet has a reasonable balance of the major nutrients, and the foods are not themselves wildly out of the ordinary, the owner's concern need only be with the actual quantity given to the dog, and the total calorie provision.

Butcher's scraps, canned or fresh, is not a complete feed.

Canned chicken must be balanced with other foods.

Frozen chicken is an inexpensive way of providing meat protein for small dogs.

Commercial canned food may be a complete feed or mixed.

Rice is a source of carbohydrates for home mixing.

Dry complete feeds have become very popular.

Semi-moist feeds must be kept in sealed packets.

The traditional feed of biscuits with gravy.

Dog biscuits are not adequate as a dog's only food.

At first sight the figures in the table below suggest that the obvious, and cheapest, way to feed a dog is to give it biscuits alone. They offer the highest calorie content, weight for weight, of any food except pure fat, and dog biscuits are cheaper to buy than canned foods. But this is misleading because a diet that consisted solely of dog biscuits would be seriously deficient in protein, and it would be deficient in fats, vitamins and minerals.

AVERAGE CALORIE REQUIREMENTS FOR 24 HOURS

Growing puppies:	6 weeks	3 months	6 months
Terriers, mature weight 10 kg (22 lb)	330	530	700
German Shepherds, mature weight 30 kg (66 lb)	1200	1800	2600
Giant breeds, mature weight 50 kg (110 lb)	1950	2500	4000
Adult dogs:	maintenance:		
Terriers	400		
German Shepherds	1600		
Giant breeds	2400		

The table gives average amounts and should be regarded as a guide only. Take account of whether the mature dog on this level of food intake is gaining or losing weight. Puppies should gain weight steadily, without becoming too fat.

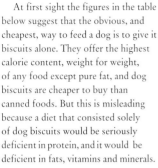

Meaty treats make excellent rewards.

Most dogs enjoy bone-shaped biscuits, and hard-baked (so safer) bones.

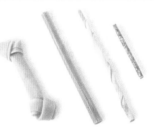

Chews made out of raw or processed hide are usually a safe substitute for bones.

Very nearly every dog loves chocolate, but only allow him to eat the canine variety.

Some biscuits include a charcoal variety, intended to help digestive problems.

Biscuit treats are produced in various flavours.

CALORIE CONTENT OF COMMON FOOD PER 100 G (3½ OZ)

Dog biscuits used as mixer feeds	300–360
Fresh meat	140
Soft, moist, complete feeds	320
Dry complete feeds	270

MANUFACTURER'S DECLARED CALORIE CONTENT PER 100 G (3½ OZ) IN THEIR RANGE OF CANNED FOODS (HILL'S SCIENCE DIET)

Canine Growth	136
Canine Maintenance	126
Canine Performance	140
Canine Maintenance Light	87
Canine Senior	117

SPECIAL DIETS

Quality of feed is particularly
important during puppyhood, to
provide nutrients for the rapidly
growing animal. Similarly, an in-whelp
bitch needs high-quality food if she
is to produce healthy puppies without
putting undue strain on her own
bodily resources. Pregnant animals
will deplete their own tissues to
provide sufficient nutrients for their
puppies both in the uterus and
afterwards when they are suckling.
A bitch with a litter of several puppies
will almost inevitably lose some
weight; her condition needs to be

◆ LEFT
Regular veterinary
examination of older
dogs will reveal the
possible existence of
nutritionally
controllable diseases.

◆ ABOVE
If puppies share
a bowl of food it is
difficult to be sure
they both get their
fair share.

watched carefully. There is no point,
however, in over-feeding the bitch
while she is pregnant.

There may be specific demands for
particularly active adult dogs, for the
older dog, and for the overweight dog.
Scientifically formulated diets are
designed to provide for these various
special requirements.

Several pet food manufacturers
provide prescription diets that, used
under veterinary supervision, aid in
the management of a number of
diseases. They are only obtainable
through a veterinary surgeon.

The range is wide and includes
products that may either contain
greater proportions of certain
nutrients than usual – one is a high-
fibre diet, for instance, which may be
of benefit in cases of diabetes, and in
fibre responsive intestinal problems –
or smaller elements of the normal diet.
Low-protein diets assist in the control
of chronic kidney disease, low-sodium
diets are used in the management of
congestive heart failure.

DAILY CALORIE REQUIREMENT FOR THE OVERWEIGHT DOG

Target weight	Scale 1	Scale 2
2.5 kg (5½ lb)	120	90
5 kg (11 lb)	200	160
7 kg (15½ lb)	275	220
10 kg (22 lb)	350	270
12 kg (26½ lb)	400	320
15 kg (33 lb)	470	375
20 kg (44 lb)	600	470
25 kg (55 lb)	700	550
30 kg (66 lb)	800	650
40 kg (88 lb)	1000	800

OBESITY

One of the commonest afflictions in the dog is simple obesity. Owners will frequently not see it and, once acknowledged, it may still be extremely difficult for them to understand that reducing the dog's food intake is not cruel. The obesity diet has its part to play by enabling the owner to feed a low-calorie diet to the dog, which will satisfy the hunger pangs while reducing his intake of nutrients.

This table indicates a suitable intake of calories for an overweight dog, with the target weight indicated in the first column. The diet needs to be balanced by sensible variations of other important nutrients.

You can see from this just how few calories, and consequently how little food, a dog really needs if he is to lose weight at a satisfactory rate. Scale 1 will cause reduction in body weight at a fairly slow rate, and even with ordinary foodstuffs the dog should not be too drastically hungry. Scale 2 is necessary when a more rapid reduction in weight is called for. It is still not a drastic diet regime.

As an example, if you wished to reduce your dog's weight to 20 kg (44 lb), using the slower scale you would need to feed not more than 600 calories a day. Without resorting to a special diet, this could be achieved by a total daily feed of 115 g (about 4 oz) of meat and 130 g (4½ oz) of biscuit mixer. This is not a lot of food on a large dog's plate, and it explains why special reducing diets, which give bulk and fill the dog's stomach, are popular.

◆ RIGHT
Obesity is best controlled by careful attention to diet before the dog's weight gets out of hand.

Grooming

Grooming your dog performs two functions. The obvious one is to keep him looking, and smelling, acceptable to you and to other people. The second one is just as important. Grooming, of a very different sort, between dogs establishes and maintains the relative status of each dog. By daily grooming you are telling the dog, in the most gentle terms, that you are in charge. The whole ritual of insisting that your dog stands while you brush and comb him emphasizes that when push comes to shove, what you say goes. There is no more important lesson in dog training.

◆ FACING PAGE
Grooming should
be an enjoyable
interaction between
dog and owner.

◆ LEFT
Some dogs, such as
this beautiful Afghan,
require more work
than others!

EQUIPMENT & HOME GROOMING

♦ BELOW
Wire-toothed grooming combs are essential for some breeds, but use with care to avoid injury to the dog's skin.

Many owners of long-coated breeds positively enjoy grooming their dogs, often achieving and maintaining near professional results. It demands a great deal of dedication, and time – the show trim of a poodle, for instance, is the result of several days hard work in total, possibly spread over a week or more. Owners of short-coated breeds are likely to be less dedicated to such perfection, although regular grooming is still necessary to maintain the dog's skin and coat in good condition.

Whatever the intention, you will need the proper equipment. For trimmed breeds, clippers are essential. Electric clippers are probably the most expensive item of actual grooming equipment, although grooming stands or tables can cost any price, depending on their construction and how firmly you feel it is necessary to restrain the

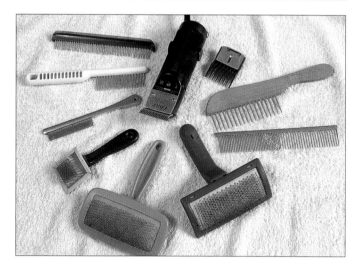

♦ BELOW
Professional grooming is a considerable skill and demands a detailed knowledge of every breed on which work is undertaken.

dog. Professional clippers do the best job and last longest, but a compromise on price and effectiveness can usually be reached. Whatever the make or cost of the clippers, they must be regularly sharpened. This is a job for the expert, and there are several companies in every country that specialize in a prompt and inexpensive service. Do not be tempted to economize. The dog won't like it, and you won't be happy with the result.

Most breeders of long-coated dogs do their own grooming. They will be happy to advise on the equipment that is suitable for your level of skill, and they usually will help the novice to get started. But don't expect show-winning results immediately, even with the best tools.

In addition to clippers, you will need a suitable brush and comb. There are many types. Again, take advice from breeders. The hard brush that is suitable for a mixture of massage and loose hair removal for a Boxer, say, may be death to the silky coat of an Afghan, and, conversely, a comb will do very little for the short coat of an untrimmed breed.

Many people give up on some of the long-coated breeds. They love the dog, but hate the regular chore of trimming and grooming and the coat-matting that is the inevitable result of failure to do both. Taking the scissors to such dogs is not an option. If you were tempted by a beautifully shaggy dog but find the reality all too overwhelming, there may be no alternative to taking most of the coat off. But please let a professional do it. Both you and the dog will feel less embarrassed at the result.

1 This Shih Tzu takes every bit as long to groom as an Afghan many times its size.

2 The first stage is to gently brush out the knots that always occur.

3 *(right)* Thoroughly brush the dog's entire coat, including the legs and tail.

4 A final grooming brings up the coat.

5 *(right)* The resplendent result – but for how long?

GROOMING FOR DIFFERENT COATS

Short-coated dogs may need less attention than other types and usually require no professional care at all. The downside to owning a short-coated dog is that they moult all the time, sometimes more than others. Dedicated owners of the short-coated breeds, especially breeds with white coats like Bull Terriers, will tell you that there is no colour or type of clothing that you can wear that does not get covered in dog hairs.

Daily grooming helps. A brush with stiff but not harsh bristles is all that is required, and it takes about ten minutes. Be careful to avoid the eyes, but otherwise brush the entire body.

Rough-coated dogs may need more attention. Some rough coats do not moult in the way that short coats do, but they "cast", which is a more substantial moult, every six months or so. When they cast, hair is lost in mats, especially if the dog has not been regularly groomed throughout the rest of the year.

Regular, daily brushing and combing will prevent the coat matting. Again, a stiff brush is the main piece of equipment, but a comb is also useful. It is essential to brush or comb right through the thickness of the coat. Just skimming over the top is of very little use.

Some rough-coated breeds need occasional attention from a professional groomer, particularly if you are intending to try your hand in the show-ring. All those artfully dishevelled creatures you see at major shows are the result of hours of attention by their dedicated owners.

The **silky coated breeds** – such as Cocker Spaniels and Irish Setters – need exactly the same attention as

SHORT COAT

1 A short-bristled brush is being used to clean the coat of this Brittany.

2 A wire-bristled glove makes easy work for short-haired breeds that need minimal attention.

ROUGH COAT

1 Rough-coated terriers need more attention to their coats than is realized.

2 Regular, daily brushing out is essential. This dog looks about ready for a professional trim.

SILKY COAT

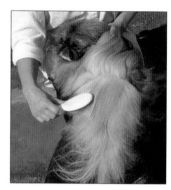

1 Dogs with long, silky coats demand much grooming. The coat should never be clipped.

2 Careful grooming right through the coat with a not-too-stiff brush must be a daily task.

◆ BELOW
No breed is more difficult to keep in perfect trim than the Old English Sheepdog.

TRIMMING THE POODLE

The Poodle is generally thought of as a trimmed dog, and the prospective owner usually realizes what is likely to be required. Daily attention is still necessary, but the monthly visit to the dog parlour may become a welcome ritual.

The exaggerated trim, derived from a working cut of long ago (the Poodle was originally a gundog), is not essential to these breeds and a version of the puppy trim can be carried on throughout the dog's life. This is simply a closer trim all over without the topiary of the show dog. Many owners feel it still keeps the essential nature of the breed. It takes less grooming than a show trim, but nevertheless needs daily attention. It also still needs regular attention from the professional to keep it in shape. The coats of ungroomed Poodles quickly get into an appalling state.

and the family all cry, "That is the dog we want." But none of them has the time or the inclination to spend time every day, brushing and combing and cleaning up their new dog; and still less when the novelty has worn off.

So if you must have a dog that needs a lot of daily work, be sure you are going to be happy to spend the time on it. Before you make up your mind, go and see the breeder to find out just what is involved.

Expert owners and breeders will usually trim their own dogs, but if you are getting one of the trimmed breeds as a family pet, it is sensible to contact your local grooming parlour with your puppy as soon as it is allowed out. The groomer will give you advice on daily care of the puppy's coat, and discuss with you when to start trimming, and what you can best do to keep the dog's coat in good shape between seasonal visits to the professional.

rough-coated dogs. Some tend to grow rather heavy coats and need to be trimmed regularly.

The breeds that demand really skilled attention are, of course, the **long-coated** ones – Poodles of all sizes, Old English Sheepdogs, the trimmed terriers.

The first question, therefore, is, "do you want the expense and the trouble of professional grooming for your dog every four weeks?" This is the question that many prospective dog owners fail to ask themselves. Sadly, the typical result is the Old English Sheepdog that has its coat trimmed to the skin to keep it socially acceptable. A beautifully groomed dog is seen on television advertisements

◆ BELOW
The coat of the Afghan is long and very fine-textured. Gentle but thorough grooming is necessary to maintain its condition.

BATHING A DOG

Dog owners in temperate climates are generally reluctant to bathe their dogs, remembering all sorts of old wives' tales regarding the adverse effects of doing so. These are probably the same arguments that people used in the Middle Ages about their own personal hygiene.

Some dogs may not need to be bathed, especially the short-coated breeds that tend to shrug off dirt; but the smell may remain.

There are, in fact, very few breeds of dog in which regular bathing causes any ill effects, although it is sometimes cited by breeders whose dogs' coats are less than ideal for the breed. "The new owner must have over-bathed or over-groomed the puppy" can be a convenient excuse. Some breeds should never, according to the

WHERE TO BATH THE DOG

1 Early training makes the task of bathing a dog easier, but few of them actually enjoy it.

2 A double-drainer sink is suitable for small breeds, while the family bath can be pressed into service for larger dogs.

♦ BELOW
Nail clipping is a regular necessity for many dogs. If you are not confident of your skill, ask a professional to do it – if you clip into the quick of the nail you will never be able to persuade the dog to submit to the task again.

breeders, be bathed. These are the dogs that veterinary surgeons can smell through the door when the dog is brought to the surgery!

In many tropical or sub-tropical countries dogs must be bathed weekly, without fail, if certain tick-borne diseases are to be avoided. There is no evidence of poor coats in show dogs in these countries.

There are three types of dog shampoo: the straightforward medicated shampoo, the anti-parasitic shampoo, and specialized, veterinary shampoos, which may be prescribed for particular skin conditions. If a dog is prone to allergies, any of these may precipitate one, but rarely. Shampoos from a reputable source will minimize such problems.

BATHING TIPS

1 A very small dog may fit into a basin, but wear waterproofs for the moment when it tips and spills everywhere.

2 Rubbing the dog semi-dry will prevent some of the water splashing all around the room when he shakes himself – which he will do shortly.

3 A good shake should be followed by some vigorous exercise to complete the drying out process.

4 Avoid getting water into the eyes during bathing, and wipe around them once the dog is out of the bath.

5 Grooming while the coat is still slightly damp, but not wet, will help make the job of removing tangles much easier.

6 (right) Clean and sweet smelling until some more horse manure to roll in is found.

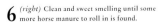

SHOWING

Dog shows are not reserved for the breeders of top-class pedigree animals. Classes are often available for ordinary household dogs, and if you are keen to enter your pet, all you need to do is find a suitable show.

THE REWARDS OF SHOWING

Showing your dog can be great fun, but it can also be very demanding. Competition, even in informal classes for pet dogs, is often intense and can create great rivalry between competing owners. Time as well as money needs to be spent on everyday maintenance, and on the preparation and training needed for the particular show class you are planning to enter. On top of that, you need to consider time spent travelling to and from the venue, and entry fees for the show. Even if your dog proves to be a winner, the rewards are far more likely to be a rosette or a silver cup than money.

That said, the show scene can become highly addictive. Not only will you be able to gain valuable advice from expert breeders and judges on all aspects of care for your particular breed, but you will also have an opportunity to join in the social circuit that comes with involvement in the breeder's network. You can gain enormous satisfaction just from taking part and, best of all, your dog is likely to enjoy the experience just as much as you.

EARLY DOG SHOWS

Man has always enjoyed proving that his possessions are better than his neighbour's. Past generations wanted to prove that their dogs could run faster or hunt more effectively than anyone else's. In time, dog owners

◆ ABOVE
These dalmatians are lining up to meet the show's judges. Each dog will be assessed in turn, and awarded points for how close it comes to the fixed standard for the dalmatian breed. Note the discipline of the dogs, as they keep their eyes fixed on their owners.

wanted to demonstrate that their dogs were more attractive than others. The first organized dog shows developed in the 1830s and 1840s. These tended to be small, local events, often held in public houses. Landowners and the gentry would pit their spaniels and pointers against each other, or miners would bring out their favourite whippets; after bull-baiting and dog fighting had been made illegal, bulldogs were bred for display.

There were no breed standards for these early shows, and this resulted in much controversy, with dogs being judged according to different rules at different shows. It was even possible for dogs of different breeds to compete against each other. Gradually, though, local breed clubs and societies were set up to officiate at the shows, and local breeders began to collaborate to produce dogs that conformed to specific standards of size and shape and temperament.

The Kennel Club was founded in the United Kingdom in 1873 to register breed standards and oversee dog shows. It was the first of its kind

anywhere in the world, but similar organizations followed on in other countries. The founders drew up rules to bring order to the early dog shows and these have lasted – with much alteration and expansion – to the modern era. The licensing of judges and the drawing-up of breed standards for every recognized breed has become the norm by which these "beauty" competitions are controlled.

MODERN COMPETITIONS

There are various levels of dog-show. Members' Limit shows limit entry to the dogs of members of the society organizing the event, while Open shows allow competition by members and non-members alike; Championship shows have as their top honours the Kennel Club's Challenge Certificates.

Shows which focus on the innate qualities of a particular breed are also popular. These include sheepdog trials, in which working sheepdogs compete against each other to herd a flock of sheep into a pen in the fastest time; field trials, in which gun dogs compete under shooting conditions to scent, locate and retrieve dummies on land or in water; agility competitions, open to all breeds, in which dogs negotiate an obstacle course to show their fitness, speed and training; and obedience contests, open to pedigree and non-pedigree dogs, in which the dogs are commanded to perform basic or advanced obedience tests, ranging from sitting, lying down and coming when called, to tracking and retrieving, sometimes commanded by hand signals alone. Other competitions may offer more lighthearted classes, open to purebreds, crossbreds and mongrels alike, such as ball-catching or frisbee championships, even "the dog with the waggiest tail" and "the dog with the most appealing eyes".

Dog shows may be run by either a General Secretary (for all breeds) or by a Breed Club (for dogs of a single breed); entries are taken for these type of events in advance, and a catalogue of entries is printed and available on the day. In contrast, there are Exemption Shows run in aid of any charity that the organizers wish to support. Entries are made on the day, and there are usually four classes open to pedigree dogs only, plus ten or 12 "fun" classes open to any type of dog.

WHAT THE JUDGES LOOK FOR

The judges check each pedigreed dog not against the other dogs entered for the class on that day, but against the standard for the breed. The breed

standard is defined by a list of points that have been set by the kennel club of that particular country. The points describe the perfect dog of each breed. No dog is likely to meet all the points and attain full marks, but the judges will look for the dogs that come as close as possible to the breed standard.

A maximum mark will be set for different characteristics of the dog – body shape, general appearance, coat colour, temperament, and the way it stands and moves in the show ring. Marks are deducted for failing to meet the breed standard.

HOW TO ENTER

If the idea of exhibiting your dog appeals to you, try making inquiries at your veterinary practice, which should be able to put you in touch with the secretary of the nearest all-breed show society. You can also check newspapers and dog magazines for news of upcoming events.

✦ ABOVE
This Maltese is a very stylish little dog. The all-white coat and round dark eyes are something breeders have striven to maintain in the breed for many centuries.

✦ BELOW
A golden retriever is put through its paces at an English country show. As the dog is led around the ring, the judges will be looking at its gait.

Breeding

There are tens of thousands of four-legged reasons for not breeding from your dog. They occupy hundreds of welfare and rescue kennels. So consider very carefully indeed whether you are at risk of adding to the large number of unwanted dogs. If you decide to go ahead, it is a most rewarding experience. Never decide to breed in the expectation that you will make money. It is almost certainly not true – the appetites of eight unsold twelve-week-old puppies are devastating – and you would be breeding for all the wrong reasons.

◆ FACING PAGE
Breeding from your dog
can be very satisfying.
However, it does entail
a lot of hard work and
should not be entered
into lightly.

◆ LEFT
Puppies are a joy to
watch and to play with,
but they are demanding
little creatures and
caring for them is a
full-time responsibility.

TO BREED OR NOT TO BREED?

The first thing to consider is that you cannot expect a crossbred dog or bitch to produce puppies in his or her own image. If you own a crossbred, and your reason for breeding is that friends have said that they want one "just like her", remember that the chances of a litter producing even one puppy that is just like its mother are small to very small.

Crossbred dogs, by reason of their own breeding, have a wider genetic pool than purebred animals. Any selection of the characteristics of either parent is a matter of chance, and the greater the variety of characteristics for nature to select from, the greater will be the differences between puppies in the litter, and the greater the difference between the puppies and their parents.

If you breed from parents of mixed ancestry, you will produce puppies that may not even remotely resemble the dog or bitch that your friends were looking for. Potential buyers may well melt away.

♦ LEFT
The standard Schnauzer, the middle size of the Schnauzer breeds, is not very common in English-speaking countries but is a delightful dog.

♦ BELOW LEFT
Looking after a litter of puppies is very demanding work for bitch and owner alike. For both it may easily involve many twenty-four hour days.

But it is not only with crossbred dogs that the phenomenon of the melting buyer exists. Many litters of purebred dogs are bred on the apparent promise that several friends are anxious to have a puppy of that breed, just like yours. From the time of your bitch coming into season there will be about two weeks before she is mated, nine weeks before the litter arrives, and another eight weeks before the puppies are ready to go to their new homes. That's a total of 19 weeks since the friends made their remarks – over four months for the enthusiasm to wane, for their circumstances to change, or for them to become really keen and buy a puppy from elsewhere. If you think this is a cynical attitude, try asking for a small deposit.

There are, however, good and sensible reasons for breeding.

The dog or bitch should be purebred. One or other should either be of a good working strain – and have shown itself to be a good working dog in the field – or be a sufficiently good show dog for the breeder or an expert to recommend that you should breed from it. The most straightforward way to determine the animal's show quality is to exhibit at shows with success.

The reason for restricting breeding to these two groups of animals is that

◆ LEFT
To many people the Airedale Terrier is an
old-fashioned breed. It is less spoiled than most,
but does have the typical terrier temperament.

◆ BELOW
In every healthy litter the puppies are looking
for mischief as soon as they are able to run
around.

there is much less likelihood of your
being left with puppies on your hands,
or worse, running the risk of sending
them to unsuitable homes. No
reputable breeder would ever do this.

Remember that buyers of purebred
puppies want the best, which means that
both parents have shown their quality.

A litter of puppies is great fun. But
after seven or eight weeks the fun may

become an expensive and exhausting
chore. Being left with six or more
14-week old crossbred puppies that
are starting to show that they had
Great Dane somewhere in their
ancestry is not as amusing as it sounds.

The same applies whether you own the
dog or bitch. There may not be
the same imperatives if you own the
dog and the bitch belongs to the lady
down the road, but you both have the
same responsibility for the outcome.

There is no truth in the commonly
held belief that siring a litter will in
any way settle a dog down. Neither
is there any truth in the belief that
a bitch needs to have a litter. There
is no medical reason for either belief.
The reverse may very well be true
as far as the male is concerned.

◆ LEFT
The pregnant bitch
needs special care
and feeding but
should continue
to exercise regularly
until the day she
whelps.

◆ BELOW
Cleanliness in the
litter box is, as
they say, "next
to dogliness".

CHOOSING MATING PARTNERS

THE STUD DOG

Stud dogs are always selected from the best. This may mean nothing more than being currently the most fashionable, but to be among the fashionable always means that the dog has sufficient merit, either as a working dog or as a show dog, to have attracted widespread attention.

It would be unusual for someone's pet dog to become a stud dog, but if a number of fellow enthusiasts ask if they can use your dog, take advice from someone you trust in the breed. Handling matings is a skilled job. If you want to learn, become an apprentice to an expert.

The better, or more fashionable, the stud dog, the higher will be the fee payable for his services. As a guide, the stud fee is likely to be somewhat lower than the price you might expect to get for a puppy. Special arrangements such as "pick of litter" are by no means

◆ LEFT
This outstanding Rough Collie may be the ideal stud dog.

uncommon. This means the stud dog owner has the right to pick whichever he or she regards as the best puppy from the litter, either in lieu of the fee, or as a consideration for a reduced fee.

However, it is not necessary or even desirable to go to the most fashionable stud dog for your bitch's mating. An experienced breeder will advise on which dog to choose, using

the physical appearance and pedigree of your bitch and the available dogs as a guide. Some breeders take more notice of pedigree, others of conformation. Learn about the breed, and decide how close to your ideal each breeder's stock is.

PEDIGREES AND CHAMPIONS

The Kennel Club has sole responsibility for registration of pedigree dogs in the United Kingdom. National clubs have the same responsibility in their own countries throughout the world. The American Kennel Club, although not the only registration authority in the United States, reciprocates its registrations with the Kennel Club and the Fédération Cynologique Internationale (FCI), to which the Australian Kennel Control is federated.

Most Kennel Clubs have reciprocal arrangements, and dogs registered in one country can be re-registered in another if the dog is imported. Official pedigrees are derived from the registration particulars of all purebred dogs that are themselves registered with the Kennel Club. Unless a dog is itself registered, its offspring cannot in turn be registered, except in certain special circumstances. Pedigree records are held for at least four generations, although some breeders will be able to show you much longer ones than that.

Different countries have different criteria for awarding the title of Champion. In the United Kingdom the title is awarded to show dogs and working dogs. Some aspire to, and some achieve, both titles.

To become a Champion in the United Kingdom, a show dog must have been awarded three Challenge

◆ BELOW
The Boxer is a very popular breed. There should be no difficulty in finding a suitable dog to breed with your bitch.

◆ LEFT
Careful noting of pedigree and breeding records is essential if you are serious about your breeding programme.

◆ BELOW
The Cairn Terrier, another popular breed.

◆ RIGHT
All breeding programmes start from small beginnings but may end with a Champion like this Yorkshire Terrier.

Certificates under different judges, with at least one certificate being awarded after the dog has reached one year old. Challenge Certificates are awarded to the best dog and bitch in each breed at specified Championship Shows. The name Challenge Certificate derives from the fact that the judge may invite unbeaten dogs from earlier classes to challenge the winner of the open class for the certificate.

The Australian system is identical to that of the United Kingdom but, in the United States, championships are gained under a points system, with points awarded in different fields: breed, obedience, field and herding.

The qualifications for Champions in working dogs take account of the dog's success in the working trials.

FINDING HOMES FOR THE PUPPIES

There is no point in breeding from a bitch unless you can expect to sell the puppies. Your best bet is to produce a litter that will be acceptable to enthusiasts, unless you have firm orders that ensure the sale of your puppies. The breeder of your bitch may be able to help. In many breeds, good puppies are at a premium. Reputable breeders will be asked regularly when or where there is a litter due. Your bitch's breeder may be happy to pass on applicants to you, and to explain to them about the breeding of your bitch.

◆ ABOVE
At three weeks old all puppies are delightful, but this pair are likely to get into mischief next week.

◆ LEFT
A rough and tumble is a vital part of the puppies' learning process.

MATING

◆ BOTTOM
Dogs will be interested in the bitch from day
one of her season, but she will usually refuse to
mate until she is in full oestrus.

THE BREEDING CYCLE

Male dogs become sexually mature at
about six months of age. From that
time their sexual behaviour is not
cyclical, and they are capable of mating
at any time and almost any place!

The bitch usually comes into season
for the first time when she is aged
about nine months, and fairly
regularly every six months thereafter.
It is not unusual, nor is it in any way
abnormal, for the first season to be
earlier, even as young as six months,
or for it to be postponed until the
bitch is over a year old. Neither is it
unusual or abnormal for the interval
between seasons to be longer than six
months. If the interval between one

season and another is very much less
than six months, and particularly if it
has become irregular in this respect,
there may be some abnormality, and
advice should be sought from your
veterinary surgeon.

A bitch's season lasts for about
three weeks. She will show some
swelling of her vulva shortly before
presenting a blood-stained discharge.
The discharge is usually very bloody
at the start of her season, becoming
paler after about ten days.

Although no risks should be taken
from the first signs of season, the
bitch will normally not accept a dog
until about halfway through the
season, at which time she will become

fertile (i.e. capable of conceiving).
There is normally no odour detectable
to a human from a bitch in season, but
there is a very powerful one detectable
by dogs a considerable distance away.
Do not assume that because you live
a mile from the nearest male dog, your
bitch will not be mated.

Do not assume, either, that a dog
that lives together with a bitch, though
they may be brother and sister, will
not be interested.

MATING AND CONCEPTION

True oestrus begins at about twelve
days from the first signs of the bitch
coming into season. From that time
she will accept the male's attempts to

Mating takes place when the bitch has ovulated. Ejaculation occurs quickly, and the tie is not necessary for conception.

Although not essential, the tie has a physiological function in helping the sperm to move up the genital tract.

mate her, and will be fertile, for about five to seven days. Ovulation, the release of eggs into the uterus, takes place during this period. The timing is variable, and the dog and bitch are the best practical arbiters of the bitch's fertile period, although laboratory tests are available to help timing if the bitch fails to conceive.

The mating act may be prolonged. Once the dog has ejaculated, the bitch continues to grip his penis in her vagina, by means of a ring muscle, for up to about 20 minutes. The dog may climb off the bitch's back, and turn to face the other way, but both stand "tied". The tie is not actually essential for a successful mating, although all breeders prefer to see it.

Pregnancy lasts for about 63 days from mating. The normal variation is from about 60 days to as many as 67. Outside this range, veterinary attention should be sought, although it does not necessarily indicate a problem and may simply be an extension of normal variation.

Bitches should not be bred from until they are physically mature. The ideal age for a first litter is about two years old.

Bitches should continue with normal exercise throughout pregnancy, although they are likely to become increasingly placid for its duration.

The bitch should be introduced to her whelping box at least a week before whelping is due in order to give her time to become comfortable with her surroundings.

WHELPING

Whelping is a natural event. In nine cases out of ten there is no need for human interference; in ninety-nine cases out of a hundred, interference takes place before it is necessary.

Be prepared. Let your veterinary surgeon know well in advance. He or she may have confirmed that the bitch is in whelp, but ask the vet to note the expected date on the calendar.

Make sure that you have decided where the bitch is to whelp, and that

Most breeders will show you a suitable box with a rail around the edge to prevent the bitch lying on her puppies and squashing them (some bitches are very clumsy). Bedding for the box needs to be disposable – whelpings are accompanied by a great deal of mess. Almost universally the basic bedding for a whelping box is newspaper, so start saving it up in advance. You can always do the crossword while you are waiting for the puppies to arrive.

Most bitches give warning of imminent whelping by going off their food. If you have a thermometer you may use it at this stage. A dog's normal temperature is approximately 101.5°F (38.5°C). A drop in temperature of two or three degrees nearly always indicates that the bitch will start to whelp within 24 hours.

For several days before whelping many bitches will start to make a nest somewhere – and usually somewhere

1 Bitches do not normally need human assistance to produce their puppies, although whelping may be a prolonged business.

2 The bitch breaks the puppy out of the foetal membranes and often eats the membranes. It is not usually necessary to tie off the cord.

she has agreed with you. If it is to be in a special place, and in a special bed, introduce her to it a week or two in advance, and teach her that it is now her bed. The ideal place is a quiet corner without passing traffic, and away from where the children play. Bear in mind that you, or the vet, may have to attend to her at some stage. Under the stairs may not be perfect for this reason.

She should have a whelping box. It needs to be large to accommodate the bitch and a litter, which may number as many as twelve puppies.

3 The puppy needs plenty of stimulation by licking from the bitch or, if necessary, by rubbing in a towel, to be sure that it is breathing satisfactorily.

highly inappropriate. Most bitches will become restless a few hours before they start to whelp, which is probably the most obvious sign that action is imminent.

Right up to the point of producing her first puppy, a family pet that in the nature of things is used to human company will probably want the comfort of human attention, but once she starts to strain for the first puppy, the great majority of bitches will become uninterested in the people around them and just get on with the business of producing a litter.

◆ BELOW
New-born puppies spend virtually all their
time drinking or sleeping. If the litter is
restless, urgent attention should be sought.

◆ BELOW RIGHT
With a large litter it would be wise to make sure
all the puppies get their share.

It may take several hours from the time the bitch starts to strain until the first puppy is delivered. Provided she is continuing to strain, there is no panic. If, after serious effort for an hour or more, she stops trying, ask your veterinary surgeon for advice.

The first sign that a puppy is due is the appearance of the water bag. This is an apt description for the foetal membranes; they look just like a small bag of water, which appears through the vagina. Do not attempt to remove it; it has the function of enlarging the birth canal to permit the following puppy to pass through.

The puppy may be born either head or tail first. Each is as common as the other, and the appearance of the tail first does not indicate a breech birth.

The first puppy may take some time to be born after you get first sight of it, and it may often seem to disappear back up the canal. The time for concern is when the puppy is obviously stuck fast with no movement up or down, despite continued straining, or when the bitch appears to have given up straining and is lying exhausted. The vet's attention is needed urgently.

CAESARIAN OPERATIONS

Veterinary assistance at a whelping is as likely to involve a caesarian operation as not. The bitch is too small to allow very much manipulation if she has problems producing puppies. In earlier times assisted whelping involved the use of instruments inserted into her vagina, but this has largely been discontinued in favour of surgery. Caesarians are now more popular, partly for humane reasons, but mainly because of the

◆ LEFT
Puppies are able to
eat solid food from
about two weeks on.

existence of low-risk anaesthetics
coupled with surgical techniques,
which have improved so much over
the years that a successful outcome
of the operation can usually be
anticipated.

To produce live puppies and
a healthily recovering bitch, the
operation must be carried out earlier
rather than later. The subject should
be discussed with the veterinary
surgeon well before the whelping is
due, so that both parties know the
other's feeling about the operation.
The veterinary surgeon must be called
in before the bitch has become
exhausted from straining unsuccess-
fully to produce her puppies.

Sadly, some breeds have such a
poor reputation for natural whelping
that caesarian operations are carried
out routinely. Breeders in these breeds
must reconsider their whole outlook
on dog breeding if their breeds are
to continue to be popular.

Other than in these particular
circumstances, caesarian operations
are usually carried out as a matter of
emergency. Most veterinary surgeons
will ask you to bring the bitch to
the surgery if there are whelping
difficulties, rather than visit the house,
so that operating facilities are at hand.

The otherwise healthy bitch and
her puppies will thrive best back in her
home environment, and the veterinary
surgeon will release them as soon as
possible. Once home, the bitch may
need a little coaxing to accept and feed
the puppies; as far as she is concerned,
they just appeared while she was
asleep. Careful introductions almost
always work, but she may need some
help initially to attach the puppies
to the teats. Once the pups are

sucking normally, the bitch will realize
what she is supposed to do.

After the first day or two, a bitch
who has had a caesarian may be treated
the same as a bitch who has produced
the puppies naturally.

AFTER WHELPING

The puppies must be cleaned behind
every time they feed. This stimulates
the passage of urine and faeces;
without the stimulation they will not
pass excreta and may become fatally
constipated. This is one of the bitch's
jobs, but if she has been under
anaesthetic, she may not realize this.
Holding the puppy tail to her will
quickly teach her the routine.

Normally, the bitch remains with
her puppies constantly for at least the
first couple of weeks. There may be
difficulty in persuading her to leave
them even for her own natural
functions. If this is the case, don't
worry, she will go eventually. Let her
do it in her own time.

A healthy bitch with puppies
quickly develops a large appetite. For
the first few days it may be necessary
to feed her in or very close to her bed,
but make sure there is plenty of food
available, and particularly plenty of
fluids. She may prefer milk. Forget
the once-a-day feeding routine, let her
have food whenever she wants it. She
has an enormous task ahead of her.

◆ BELOW
Any puppies that do
not get their share
may be bottle fed
successfully with a
suitable bitch-milk
substitute.

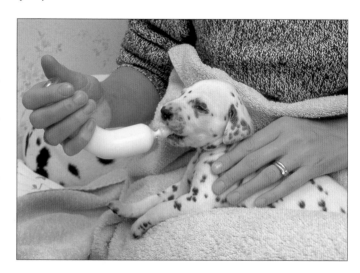

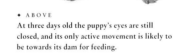

REARING PUPPIES

The first two weeks are the easiest. The puppies are relatively inert. They will wriggle around the bed a great deal but are incapable of recovering the nest if they accidentally fall out. Most whelping boxes have high fronts for this reason.

At this stage the puppies need no supplementary feeding, just their dam's milk, and should spend most of their time sleeping quietly. If they do not, seek help urgently.

Puppies open their eyes at about ten days old, though some breeds are notoriously lazy about this.

◆ ABOVE
At three days old the puppy's eyes are still closed, and its only active movement is likely to be towards its dam for feeding.

◆ ABOVE
By three weeks old the puppy will be trying to get out of the nest box.

◆ RIGHT
Five-week-old puppies are active and alert and already learning lessons about the world.

By about three weeks old the puppies are moving around much more; they will mostly have fallen out of the box several times, indicating that it is time to add another layer to the barrier at the front. It may also be the time to start to supplement their diet. This is done by hand-feeding.

Although most people think of the puppies' first hand-feeding as an occasion for something delicate, milky perhaps, just try scraping a little raw beef from the joint on to your fingers. You will be lucky to have a finger left!

The main reason for starting to wean puppies at three weeks is to spare the

bitch. With a large litter there is a tremendous physical demand on her, and she will certainly lose a lot of weight during the course of rearing a litter. By starting to wean the puppies relatively early she will be spared some of this load. Puppies do, in any case, start to look for more solid food at this age if given the opportunity.

At three weeks of age the litter must have its first worming dose. Take advice on this. Modern wormers cause no side effects.

From three weeks to about five weeks a gradually increasing proportion of the puppies' diet should be supplied from sources other than their dam. By six weeks they should be completely weaned, although the dam may take some convincing of this, and may keep trying to feed the pups. The action of sucking by the puppies prolongs the production of milk by the dam, and after six weeks this should be discouraged.

At six weeks the puppies should be feeding on a puppy food of your choice. It is also time for a second worming dose to be given.

◆ BELOW
By eight weeks it is time for the puppies to leave home, usually to the relief of their dam and often to the relief of their owner.

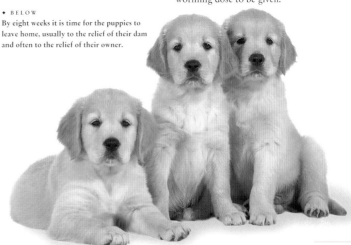

Training

Every dog is capable of learning a great deal more than is generally
recognized. Although it may take a special type of dog and a special type of
owner to create a canine film star, home helper or agility champion, there is no
reason why every dog should not achieve the essential basics of obedience and
well-socialized behaviour. A well-trained dog is less likely to develop
unwanted behaviour patterns, partly because dogs often adopt bad habits
when they are bored. Dogs enjoy the stimulation of training and most
love to please their owners too.

◆ FACING PAGE
There are many ways
that a trained dog is
capable of helping
its owner.

◆ LEFT
A well-trained pet dog
should be able to live
in the home without
causing problems for
other family members.

SOCIALIZING YOUR PUPPY

◆ BELOW LEFT
It is never too early to start to learn!

◆ BELOW
Socializing begins with human contact.

All puppies need to meet as many other dogs and as many people as possible. This is the essence of socialization and, when done effectively, most of the behaviour problems that may occur later will be avoided.

From the day you acquire him, your new puppy should start to meet other people. The puppy must not be overwhelmed but, within reason, the more people he meets the better. The visitors should be asked to hold the puppy, handling and cuddling him gently, so that he learns that people are friends. However, until the puppy has had his vaccinations some caution is necessary to avoid second-hand contact with other owners' dogs. Ask dog owners to delay their visit until your puppy has had his second round of injections.

Apart from other dogs in the household, to which the puppy should be introduced at the earliest possible moment, meeting dogs must be delayed until the new puppy has had his two sets of injections and the "all clear" from the veterinary surgeon, at about 12 weeks old.

In the United Kingdom, one of the most useful, as well as entertaining, developments in puppy training in recent years has been the creation of puppy parties. These are exactly what they sound like. Once or twice a week a group of puppy owners with their puppies meet for an hour or so in the village hall or somewhere similar. Puppies from 12 weeks of age up to six or seven months, and of all sizes, are allowed to play with each other with only the minimum restraint from their owners. The smaller ones are rarely overwhelmed by the larger, and all learn that their fellow canines can

be approached without fear. It is an object lesson for their owners.

The puppy party has revolutionized dog training in the United Kingdom. Most puppy groups have experienced trainers in charge, and the transition from pure play into early obedience training can be seamless. Lead training is nearly always part of it, perhaps simply walking at heel without tugging, and the foundations to more advanced work may be laid.

Puppy playgroups introduce all shapes and sizes of dogs to each other and help to overcome alarm at strange animals.

Basic training classes are held in village halls, or similar places, all over the world. Attendance at a weekly class is usually sufficient.

EARLY LEARNING

◆ BELOW
Bribery is all-important in encouraging a puppy
to come when called.

Teaching your dog good habits is best achieved by rewarding success, although it is nonsense to suggest that scolding is never necessary. From the earliest age, puppies learn to understand the word, or the action implying, "No". Their mother teaches them some discipline from a very early age, and their new mother – you – needs to carry that on.

Take the common game of chewing your shoelaces. A tap on the nose while saying "No" firmly, soon teaches a puppy that there are some things in life to avoid, and that "No" means just what it says.

Similarly, most puppies start the dominance game very early in life. Nipping whomever they see as being one down from them on the totem pole quickly develops into a bite to establish their rank. Immediate remedial action – another firm "No" – will save a great deal of trauma later.

In all training there is no substitute for persistence and patience.

HOUSE TRAINING

This is the number one priority. Many puppies will not have had any house training before they arrive at their new home. They will have lived in their kennel or box with their litter mates, but even there the sleeping area is usually taboo for toileting once the puppies are old enough to move

◆ RIGHT
By eight weeks puppies should be confident and have started their house training and lead training.

around. This can be used during the course of house training.

There are two methods of teaching a puppy to use an appropriate site for its toilet, and they can both be used simultaneously.

The first method involves eternal vigilance. Puppies squat to urinate and use a slightly more humped squat to defecate. As soon as the puppy postures to do either you must scoop him up and put him on the designated spot. If you miss the signs, do not scold the puppy. He doesn't yet know what he's supposed to do; he hasn't done anything wrong.

The second method is to use newspaper to cover the entire floor area on which the puppy runs. He will learn that newspaper is a suitable medium for his natural functions, and a gradual reduction in the size of the available newspaper will result in the puppy using a smaller and smaller area of floor. The theory is that you can then move the paper outside, and the puppy will continue to use it, until he learns that only outside the house is

◆ LEFT
It is important to learn the signs and to encourage the puppy by putting him outside as soon as he wakes up, and after every meal.

appropriate. Both methods work, one will suit one puppy better than another. A combination of the two by using the paper at night and extreme vigilance during the day, will usually produce the best results. Not uncommonly, older puppies may

"unlearn" about toilet training. Some trigger will cause them to break their newly formed habit. Again, please don't punish them.

This is where a dog's instinct can be useful. A healthy dog will not soil its own bed. It can be extremely helpful, for all sorts of reasons, to teach a dog to use a cage as a bed, and this is one of them. If you make it comfortable, the dog will very quickly learn to regard it as his own place to retreat to when the world gets too complicated. If the puppy does "unlearn" his house training, let him sleep in the cage, and put him out into the garden in the required place immediately after you open the cage door.

The cage mustn't be a prison for the puppy, rather a refuge, but it is useful for him to learn that sometimes the door must be shut. Suitable treats, something extra tasty, will usually persuade him to accept it.

◆ LEFT
If you are using the newspaper system for house training, it may be necessary initially to cover the entire floor.

EARLY LEAD TRAINING

1 Soft collars are more easily tolerated than new stiff leather ones.

2 Once the dog is at the stage of having a lead attached, a treat will encourage him to associate the lead with pleasure.

COMING WHEN CALLED

Your puppy will normally have an instinct to come to you from the word go. Encourage this with treats. Call the puppy by his name and, when he responds, give him a treat. It takes a very short time indeed for the puppy to associate his name with a doggy treat. But if the puppy doesn't come immediately, do not get cross and scold him. It takes an even shorter time for the puppy to learn when to run away.

GETTING USED TO A LEAD

This really must be regarded as fun by the puppy.

Step one is always to put on the collar. This will feel very strange, and his immediate reaction will be to try to scratch it off. But delicious treats will distract him and overcome the itchiness of the collar.

Step two, but not until the collar is tolerated happily, is to attach a light lead. Don't hold the lead at this stage – let the puppy become accustomed to it by dragging it around. Finally, hold the lead, and gradually wind it in loosely, calling the puppy for still more treats.

3 Bribery, yet again, will take the dog's mind off the new restraint.

TRAVEL SICKNESS

Overcoming travel sickness is, or should be, a matter of early learning.

Some puppies are never travel sick, but unlike some children, those that are can nearly always be taught to overcome the problem. You must act immediately when the problem arises, otherwise the puppy starts to associate cars with vomiting, and will salivate as a premonitory symptom as soon as you put him into the car. If travel sickness is allowed to persist, the puppy will learn to hate and fear car travel.

Simply taking the puppy on plenty of short journeys may be sufficient. If the puppy learns that he can go for a ride without being sick, especially if there is a walk or a game at the end of it, he may overcome his early nervous reaction.

If the short journey cure doesn't work, there is no substitute for travel sickness pills and a much longer trip. Bear in mind that travel sickness pills take some time to be absorbed and to work. They need to be given about an hour before the journey. To a considerable extent, the longer the journey, the more effective the treatment. Bear in mind also that most travel sickness treatments induce sleepiness, so giving the pills before going off for the family holidays can be doubly useful.

Most dogs will learn to overcome their travel sickness after a few training trips, but the longer the problem is allowed to persist before attempting a cure, the slower will be the response.

PUPPY BEHAVIOUR

Dogs are pack animals, which explains many behavioural characteristics. When you are having problems think "pack leader" and act accordingly.

One of the pack-behaviour features that all dogs bring to their relationships with human beings is hierarchy and, consequently, dominance. Puppies spend a great deal of their time trying instinctively to establish where their position is in the hierarchy, and they can only do this by attempting to establish their own dominance.

Some breeds are more dominant than others. The terriers, for instance, tend to be so; generally the gundogs do not try so hard. Being in the dominant role is not necessarily comfortable for a dog, particularly when the signals from their human companions are mixed and confusing. Most dogs settle happily in the submissive role once they are clearly placed there and learn that they do not have to attempt to keep everyone under control.

The dog's place must be established as soon as he arrives in his permanent home. He must learn that all the humans in his home are above him in the pecking order. This is not a matter of punishment for the dog. There are simple keys to make it plain.

FEEDING
The leader eats first. It is often convenient to feed the dog before you eat, but if the dog observes this, you are sending one of those confusing signals. If the family and the dog are going to eat at more or less the same time and in the same place, let the puppy wait. Puppy-feeding times are best arranged well away from your own meal times, which will avoid sending this signal.

From the start, it is useful to make

Early grooming is simply a progression from handling the dog.

the puppy come to you for his food and wait until you are ready, perhaps by teaching him to sit before you put the bowl down.

GROOMING
Touching and handling are potent signals to a dog. Daily grooming under proper control will indicate who is in charge. Some puppies will resent the handling involved – dominance again – they may react as though they are being hurt. Ignore it and insist. All puppies are capable of learning very quickly whether you really mean it.

NIPPING AND BITING
Most puppies will "mouth" things, including your fingers, when they are very young. This will progress to a nip. Mouthing is normal behaviour in the young as they learn with their mouth and nose. Nipping is the first step in learning dominance. It is not amusing; stop it immediately, by a sharp reaction – the "No" it has already learned – and a tap if necessary. Remember your pack leader role!

Introduce the brush as soon as the puppy has become used to sitting quietly on the table.

GAMES AND FIGHTING
All puppies like to play games; they are part of the puppy's education, and in the light of that you should think carefully about them.

Avoid contest games with your puppy. Tug-of-war is fun, but can easily develop into a contest of dominance, with the puppy either winning the tug, or growling or snarling while hanging on. If you must play tug-of-war keep it on the very lowest key and stop immediately if the puppy starts to become too excited. Simply to stop and go away after retrieving the tug is probably as good a lesson as any.

Running after a suitably large ball (not a stick, please, or a ball small enough for the puppy to choke on) can be fun for the dog. But teach your puppy to bring the toy back to you by not running after the dog to get the ball. Show indifference if the puppy runs away with the ball, and reward him with praise and pats if he brings it back to you. You have started obedience training, congratulations!

EARLY FEEDING

1 Show the puppy his food as a preliminary to persuading him to sit.

2 The puppy has sat down, so bring him his food bowl.

3 Make the puppy wait a moment or two before allowing him to put his head into the bowl.

4 Finally the puppy gets the reward.

BASIC OBEDIENCE TRAINING

The world is a crowded place. Every dog must be able to fit into the social system around it without causing problems. Dogs may have all sorts of functions and duties, but the first, and often the only, basic necessity is that they are sufficiently trained and biddable not to cause problems for their owners. To achieve this the dog must learn basic obedience to his owner's commands.

This does not mean that the dog should be beaten into submission by a dominant owner. Apart from the cruelty of such a regime, it doesn't achieve its objective: the dog will be cowed rather than obedient, he will run away rather than respond to his owner's commands.

Basic training and obedience should be a happy experience for dog and owner. Dogs are happy to work for rewards, from a tidbit to a pat on the head in praise, but they must know what you are seeking from them. Rule one is **do not confuse your dog.**

Dogs react to the immediate, not to something that happened ten minutes ago. Several other things will have happened since. Let's take as an example recalling a dog that is running free. You call him. He doesn't come back. You get cross and call him again in an angry voice, and he still doesn't come back. So you chase after him, catch him and give him a slap, or even a beating with his lead.

What does the dog learn from this? If I hear my owner calling me, I run away because if he catches me he will beat me. If I see him with the lead, I also run away because if he has the lead in his hand he uses it to beat me.

The dog shows impeccable logic in his reactions, rather than the reasoning

WALKING TO HEEL

1 Standing by his owner with a loose lead, the puppy is smelling the chance of a reward.

2 Still with a loose lead, the puppy's interest is held by the owner.

3 Moving out, the puppy stays close to his owner still with hopes of a treat.

4 Finally, the puppy has learnt that the treats will come later if he keeps by his owner's side.

that you might wish him to use. Rule two is **think like a dog**, not like a sophisticated human being.

WALKING TO HEEL

In the early learning section we explained how to accustom your young puppy to a collar and lead.

The next stage, the first in obedience, is to teach your puppy to walk on the lead without pulling. From the sight of the average dog on its lead, this is a lesson that is commonly never learned.

First steps are best taught in your own back garden or somewhere equally quiet. The puppy is already aware that a lead is attached to his collar but not that this is intended to restrain him. Pick up the lead and walk the puppy round the garden, telling him to "heel". As soon as the puppy starts to pull, simply stop and encourage him to come to you – bribes work. Do not have a tugging battle. Start moving around again, with the promise of more bribes, donkey-and-carrot style. The puppy will soon overcome his fear of the restraint. Remember, you are thinking like a dog. Trading a little restriction on freedom of movement for a choc drop (dog treat) is fair exchange.

These first steps need to be repeated for as long as it takes, but in sessions of only a few minutes. You will get bored but the puppy will not think "training session", it will think "choc-drop time".

Professional trainers often declare that bribes like treats are not to be encouraged, because they teach the dog to expect a treat whenever it does the right thing. This is true, but remember that dogs of different breeds vary in the ease with which they can be trained. A Border Collie may be so anxious to please that a pat on the head is sufficient reward for any obedience success. But a terrier is a very different matter. Pats are all very well, but they don't taste as good as choc drops.

Once the puppy has overcome his fear of the restraint of the lead, some discipline does have to be introduced. Every puppy will decide that being on a lead should be challenged, and he will try an experimental pull to see what happens. This seems to be where everything goes wrong. The owner merely pulls against the dog's pull, and the dog quickly learns that the normal thing is to lean into the lead and pull the owner around behind him. Many puppies on leads will reach this stage.

Do not allow the pull to become established. Call the dog back to you immediately and stop walking. Praise him, yes even bribe him, when he comes back. Start again and keep the puppy on a very short lead so that he is not moving out ahead of you. Remember also that the top dog walks ahead. Who is top dog in your family?

◆ ABOVE
The flexi lead is a useful training aid. All leads must be strong enough to restrain the dog in an emergency.

There is something to be said for remedial training immediately if loose lead walking seems to elude you and your dog. The simplest device is the "Coke can". This is exactly what it sounds like – an empty soft drink can that has been filled with small pebbles to make a rattle. If the dog persists in pulling ahead, throw the pebble can just ahead of the dog. The surprise will often help to break the habit. Repeat as often as necessary to convince the dog that if he pulls on the lead a startling noise will occur, which has nothing to do with the ineffectual human hanging on to the lead.

A little more expensive, but a useful investment, is to buy an extending flexi lead. These are nylon leads that extend to a considerable length, unwinding from a spring-loaded handle. Many owners use them to give their dog room to roam on a walk, without losing control of the dog.

The lead can also be used to cure a pulling dog. Allow the dog to run out on the lead – do not pull against it – and when the dog feels that he is running free, put the brake on the lead. It pulls the dog up suddenly.

SIT

Use of the flexi lead with a normal buckled collar avoids the risk of injuring the dog. The sudden stopping action teaches the dog that his lead is there as a restraint rather than to pull against. The lesson is usually learned very quickly if accompanied by a suitable command that the dog will associate with the sudden stop to its run. Clever owners learn to use the clicking noise that the lock makes as the signal that will tell the dog to stop right there in his tracks.

The choke chain has not been mentioned as a training aid for teaching walking to heel, mainly because it doesn't work until it is used so fiercely that there is danger of injury to the dog.

The choke chain and the slip lead are sometimes confused. They are two different things. The slip lead, which is usually a leather or nylon lead with a ring in one end threaded to form a noose, is a useful piece of equipment if there is a risk of the dog slipping its collar and lead. It is easily loosened, and does not have the harsh restraining action of the choke chain.

Once your dog walks to heel on a loose lead, and responds to your command to heel with reasonable alacrity, you are on your way to having an obedient dog.

SIT AND DOWN
Teaching the puppy to sit on command, and to "down", are the next practical steps for the dog owner.

As a matter of observation, if you restrain a dog in the standing position on a lead that is sufficiently short to prevent him from jumping to reach an offering, and move the offering from in front of the dog to just behind his head, the dog will sit and tip his head

1 Teaching a dog to sit starts with him standing, under control.

2 The dog has been encouraged to sit by light pressure on his haunches.

3 At a more advanced stage, hand signals may be used to instruct the dog to sit or go down.

back to try to reach the offering. Give him the sweet, and you have taught him to sit! Repeat the exercise, telling him to sit as you do so, and keep doing it until the dog has learned that "sit" means "sit for a sweet".

The "down" is an extension of the same exercise. Once your dog has learned the sit, and while keeping him under the same restraint, offer the sweet on the floor between his front paws; push the dog down at the same time telling him to "down".

All other obedience training is based on exactly these same principles, with patience and praise as the twin essentials for a happy partnership.

OBEDIENCE CLASSES
Elementary obedience lessons do not need skilled assistance, but even these can contain pitfalls for the new owner. There is an obedience class in practically every town, and it is well worthwhile for anyone with a new puppy to enquire about them. Most local obedience classes are run by experienced dog people who are only too happy to pass on their knowledge to newcomers. These obedience groups all have classes for beginners, dogs and owners, and certainly do not expect you to turn into an enthusiast for competitive dog obedience competitions. A well-trained house pet is the objective. If you get the bug and decide to join in the more advanced work, you will have started on a demanding but fascinating hobby.

An offshoot of the conventional obedience class is the ring-training class. This has much the same basis, but is intended specifically to produce well-trained show dogs. The emphasis is on good behaviour on the lead in the

DOWN

1 Teaching the dog to lie follows the sit. As before the dog is encouraged to lie down by the reward of a treat.

2 Once the dog has lowered his head, his front legs may be moved gently forward into the down position.

3 The dog is gently restrained in the down position and once again encouraged to remain there by bribery.

presence of other dogs and a crowd of people, training the dog to allow strangers to examine it, and, one particular quirk, to stand while on the lead rather than to sit, which is the practice in obedience classes.

AGILITY AND FLYBALL COMPETITIONS

Two sports that have achieved great popularity in the United Kingdom derive directly from advanced obedience training: agility and flyball.

The **agility** competitors run an obstacle course that includes a seesaw, a tunnel, jumps, a stay on a table and weaving in-and-out obstacles. The dogs are timed, with points deducted for failure to negotiate each obstacle correctly. The requirements are strict; if the dog jumps off the seesaw before he reaches the bottom, for instance, he will lose points.

Flyball appeals to owners who want some excitement with their dogs, and if the noise coming from the flyball competition ring at Crufts dog show, in England, is anything to go by, they certainly get it. The flyball course is a short straight strip at the end of which is a box with a trap and foot lever. On a signal, the dog is released by his owner, races to the box and leaps on the foot lever, which causes a ball to fly into the air. The dog leaps to catch the ball and rushes back to his owner to give it to him or her. The whole event is timed to the millisecond. Flyball competitions are usually run as a relay, with four teams of six or so dogs each.

Both these activities engender great enthusiasm among their supporters and demand great dedication from the trainers and competitors.

♦ BELOW
Working dogs are trained using very similar principles.

FIELD TRIALS AND GUNDOG (SPORTING) WORKING TESTS

Field trials and gundog trials have received the status of competitions in their own right, and championships are awarded in both.

The essential difference between the two is that field trials are conducted as similarly as possible to an ordinary day's shooting of live game birds, whereas gundog trials assess the working ability of gundogs without game being shot.

Both types of trial vary in their content, depending on the breed of dog undergoing the trial. Retrievers are expected to pick up and retrieve game or the dummy; spaniels, whose job on the shooting field is to find and flush out game, are expected to quarter the ground and mark the same. Pointing is considered difficult to assess, and trials for that purpose alone are rarely held. The Springer Spaniel, which is considered the general workhorse of the shooting field, performs "hunt, point and retrieve" tests.

WORKING DOGS

From the earliest days, humans have
considered their dogs to be not just
companions but working allies. The
dog probably came into the camps of
early humans for scraps of food, the
comfort of association and warmth.
But it soon became apparent to the
dog's host that here was a guard,
warning against strangers, and on
occasion, actually attacking intruders
with whom it was unfamiliar.

Dogs have worked ever since. Their
trainability has led to them being used
over the centuries in roles varying
from the simple barking burglar alarm
– a role that is today recognized by
some insurance companies – to out-
and-out attack dogs, epitomized by
the mastiff breeds, which functioned
as war dogs in the Middle Ages.

Roles have been refined over the
centuries, and the most important
function of the majority of dogs
nowadays is that of household

The Springer Spaniel, a versatile
gundog, has lately come into its
own as a working dog in another
field, that of "sniffer". The Customs
department and many police forces
maintain teams of sniffer dogs to
ferret out drugs being smuggled
into the country, and to perform
various other tasks where a keen
ability to scent a suspicious
substance is required. Several
breeds are used, but the Springer
is unsurpassed for this work.

companion, a role that should never
be underestimated.

Modern guard dogs are expected to
be highly trained and totally responsive
to their handler's control. The police,
the prison service and the armed forces
all maintain teams of dogs whose
function is to guard and, if necessary,
to corner an intruder or attack and
bring down an assailant. It is rare for
such a dog to go out of control.

There is a regular demand for
young dogs to train with the services.
They are looking for dogs that are
bold and, in civilian owners' hands,
often difficult to train. The majority
of these dogs are German Shepherds,
dogs that are a delight in the right
hands but that may be dangerous
without proper control.

Two of the oldest roles for working
dogs are as livestock guards and
herders, a distinction that is often
misunderstood.

The Collies and various British
sheepdogs have historically had a
herding role. Their function is to keep
the sheep flock under control at the
behest of the shepherd. They circle,
help move the sheep and bring strays
back into the flock. Their response is
to the shepherd, not the sheep.

This type of herding work depends
on a carefully controlled "attack" by
the dog, which runs in almost to nip
the heels of the sheep, pushing it away
in the direction that the shepherd calls
for. Despite the shepherd's handling,
the dogs learn more from their parents
than from any other source.

Many of the European sheepdogs
have a completely different function,
acting as guards to the flock against
predators. Some of the working dogs
of these breeds may actually be reared

Manwork should only ever be undertaken under
carefully controlled, professional supervision.

This police dog has been carefully trained to
show aggression on demand when his handler
requires it.

◆ LEFT
There are legal restraints to keeping guard dogs, intended to avoid risks to law-abiding citizens.

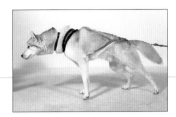

◆ ABOVE RIGHT
The Siberian Husky, bred for the specific purpose of pulling sleds, makes a delightful house pet, given the right environment.

◆ RIGHT
Police and Customs dogs are widely used for the detection of illicit drugs.

with the sheep from an early age, growing up as one of the flock, but better equipped to ward off intruders.

These dogs, when moved out of their own working environment and into the human's, become guards of property. As with almost any breed, however, when given the right upbringing, they can make wonderful house pets for their owners.

For many years, perhaps centuries, dogs have been used as guides for blind people. The work is highly organized, by the National Guide Dogs for the Blind Association in the United Kingdom and Guiding Eyes in the United States. Guide dogs are Golden or Labrador Retrievers, but less conventional breeds can also be trained. At least one standard Poodle has been trained to the necessary level and allocated to an applicant. The training is carried out at one of the organization's centres, and the individual dog tailored to the individual person, although sometimes applicants think it's the other way around after they have been on the introduction course!

The success of the scheme for guide dogs for the blind has encouraged enthusiasts to set up various other programmes for dogs to aid disabled people. Hearing Dogs for the Deaf is now well established in the United Kingdom, with dogs that have learnt to alert their deaf companions when, for instance, the front door bell rings.

One of the most successful schemes is Pat Dogs or Pet Partners. These are companion dogs whose owners take them to hospitals and hospices to visit the patients. Many people miss their own dog, or find comfort just from having a dog to talk to and stroke while they are in hospital. The therapeutic effect on the patients is demonstrable. Any breed is suitable, though not every dog; they must be dogs that enjoy human company but don't demonstrate their enjoyment too effusively.

The Harrier, one of the oldest breeds of hunting dog, has never been included in the Kennel Club registers.

Tracking, sometimes to search for criminals but often to seek out people or objects that may be lost, is another specialist duty of the ubiquitous German Shepherd.

BEHAVIOURAL PROBLEMS

Behaviour problems develop because the dog has received signals that the type of behaviour now regarded as a problem has been acceptable, up to now. This nearly always arises because we give conflicting signs to the dog.

Take sitting on the sofa. If you allow a sweet little puppy up on to your lap, how is he to know that when he gets bigger he can't do it? Until one

◆ ABOVE
Chewing of household objects may arise simply from boredom or separation anxiety.

◆ LEFT
Jumping up is probably the commonest objectionable behaviour by dogs. It is far better prevented than cured.

day you attempt to push him off, and there is a confrontation between you.

Curing behaviour problems is much more difficult than preventing them. Obedience training has a considerable role in overcoming potential behavioural problems, and many enthusiasts have developed their interest through the need to create a reasonably well-behaved pet.

DOMINANCE

The development of dominance is by far the most common cause of real problems. Dominant behaviour will lead to biting. Often enough, the dog will have learned that one or more of the family is in the pack leader's position, but that some, often the children, appear to be below the dog in the pecking order.

Dominance cannot always be cured, but it can usually be controlled, provided the whole family co-operates. The method is to re-establish the order of dominance in the pack.

Rule one is never to confront the dog unless you know you can win. A dominant dog becomes aggressive in order to protect his position. His bite is often worse than your bark.

Start by totally ignoring the dog, and that must include all the members of your family. Almost always the dog

◆ BELOW
Apparent over-sexed behaviour, often by small dogs, is frequently an expression of frustrated dominance.

◆ BELOW
If muzzles are to be used they must be effective and humane, permitting the dog to wear them comfortably and to breathe without difficulty.

will very soon approach you for attention. Make sure he doesn't get it. Put a long lead on as soon as you can do so safely, and leave it to trail. Use the lead to make the dog do what you want him to.

If the problem has been that he won't get off the sofa without growling at you, pull him off from a distance. You are beginning to re-assert your authority.

Re-establish the feeding regime – make the dog wait, and then make him approach you for his food rather than taking the food to him. Then ignore him again.

Stop greeting the dog. If he wants attention, he must come to you, and then be rebuffed until you have decided that he has behaved well enough to relax your attitude a little. He must be given no opportunity to reassert his own dominance – don't allow him into your bedroom, for instance. Keep him strictly off chairs and that sofa. Physical height, achieved by getting on to chairs, is a dominance signal, and sitting on a chair may be sufficient to indicate to your dog that he has made himself tops.

You don't need to be in any hurry to take the trailing lead away. This gives you a lot of control without risk to yourself. Games must be entirely in your control. You start them and you stop them, and above all avoid confrontational games that the dog can feel he has won. At the same time

◆ LEFT
All dogs enjoy foraging in dustbins. If you don't want the dog to get at the dustbin, put it out of reach.

Aggression needs professional attention. It may have several causes.

AGGRESSION TOWARDS GUESTS

1 Aggression towards guests is often a defensive or fear reaction.

2 Letting the dog realize that guests are not intruders may often be accomplished with a suitable treat.

as you are asserting the new regime, it is essential that the rest of the family behave in exactly the same way.

Most dogs never exhibit dominance problems; if they did they wouldn't be such popular companions for humans, but when a dog does start to show signs of dominant behaviour he must be controlled totally, or it will lead to trouble, and trouble means biting, humans or other dogs.

If you do not seem to be able to control incipient dominance, or aggression, quickly by these simple rules, take professional advice before the problem becomes serious.

FEAR BITING

A high proportion of unacceptable behaviour involves the dog biting someone. Aggression that arises from dominance accounts for much of this, but fear biting occurs regularly in less dominant dogs. The only way a dog has of protecting himself is to bite his perceived attacker or to run away. Fear biting will occur if the dog cannot run away.

Fear of the unknown is usually the problem. If a dog does not meet many

3 Overcoming this type of aggression is easier with a well-trained dog that can be kept under restraint.

people as a puppy, he may, depending on his natural disposition, regard people as a whole as the unknown and react accordingly. Early training will nearly always prevent this reaction. If early contacts are insufficient and the

dog is nervous of people he does not know, there is no substitute for slow and careful broadening of the dog's circle of acquaintances, until he has met so many people that nobody seems to be a stranger. The same approach must

◆ BELOW
A dog which doesn't come when called means
back to square one.

be taken if a puppy takes fright at cars, for instance. Non-confrontational acquaintance with his particular fear object will cure the problem.

BARKING FOR ATTENTION

It is not unknown for a dog to use a fear reaction as an attention-getter.

contrariness in our dogs. Nobody's perfect, and it's part of their charm.

There are other, more bizarre, behavioural problems that usually do not involve actual risk to the owner. One of the commoner of these problems is the dog that tears the house to pieces when the owner goes

◆ LEFT
It is natural for dogs to howl like their cousin the wolf. In domestic circumstances howling is usually a sign of distress.

◆ BELOW
Decide early what is tolerable in the way of begging for tidbits, and stick to it.

out. It doesn't help just to say that this is another anxiety manifestation. Sometimes the reasons are complex, and the cure always demands considerable commitment on the part of the owner. It should always be undertaken with the supervision of an expert animal behaviourist.

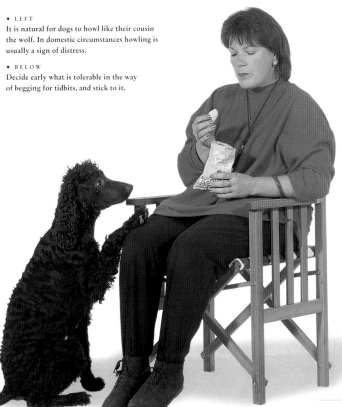

If a puppy learns that barking at an object – and it can be any object – will result in his owner giving him all sorts of comforting attention, he will also realize that if he wants attention, he should bark, preferably in an alarmed fashion, for an instant response.

ODD PROBLEMS

You may think you cannot win, but we all tolerate a certain amount of

Health Care and First Aid

In order to recognize when a dog is ill, you must know
the signs of good health. A healthy dog is alert and lively, and takes a great
interest in its environment, although young puppies will be, quite normally,
rushing about one minute and sound asleep the next. There should be no
discharges from the eyes or nose. The nose is usually moist and shiny, but this
will depend on what the dog has been doing – people are often concerned that
their dog's nose is dry, when all that has happened is that he has been digging
for his favourite bone! The ears should be clean and free of visible wax. The
coat should be free of dandruff and, depending on the coat type, more or less
shiny. The skin should be free from sores or spots. The dog should move
soundly, that is to say without favouring one leg over another, and he should
move freely. A healthy dog should have a healthy appetite. He should be ready
for his food, and eat it with relish.

◆ FACING PAGE
Vets' surgeries are
usually relaxed places
and visiting one
should not cause your
dog any stress.

◆ LEFT
This Basset Hound
is happy and healthy,
but, like many pure-bred
dogs, he is susceptible to
inherited problems – in
his case, the ears – which
are typical of the breed.

INTRODUCING YOUR DOG TO THE VETERINARY SURGEON

Ideally, if you have not previously owned an animal, you should make the acquaintance of your local veterinary surgeon before you acquire the dog. How you choose a vet is a matter of personal preference. You may be guided by friends, or the convenience of the surgery, but there is no substitute for a personal interview to get an idea of how the practice runs, its surgery times and facilities, all of which the veterinary surgeon will be pleased to discuss with you.

Within 24 hours you and your family are going to have grown very attached to your puppy. That is just the way it happens. It is important

that, if the veterinary examination discovers anything that indicates the puppy should be returned to the seller, you should know immediately before this bonding has taken place. So you must arrange for the puppy's examination to take place on the day you collect him.

The veterinary surgeon will repeat the superficial health checks that you will already have carried out before buying the dog, but will go into greater detail, with a check on the puppy's heart and lungs, his ears and skin, his legs and feet and his genito-urinary system as far as possible.

This examination should not alarm the puppy. The veterinary surgeon will spend time getting to know your new dog with a little friendly fussing to give him confidence, before making the more detailed examination.

Almost certainly, unless he has already received his first inoculation, he will be given it now. Again, this should not alarm the puppy, and many don't even notice the injection. At worst there may be a squeak, followed by some more comforting. The whole event should be very low key.

The veterinary surgeon will also probably advise on worming and anti-flea regimes, and tell you how long it must be before the puppy meets other dogs in order to give the vaccine a chance to develop the dog's immunity to infections.

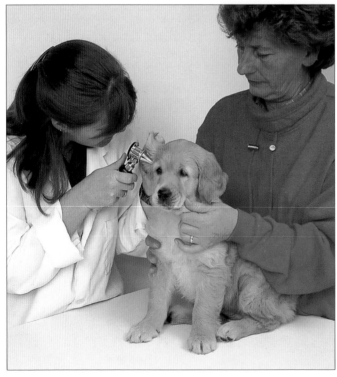

◆ ABOVE
Minimum restraint is important in encouraging your dog to relax at the surgery.

◆ LEFT
Most dogs, if handled with confidence, will not require heavy restraint during veterinary procedures.

THE INOCULATION REGIME

♦ BELOW
Inoculations are not usually painful to dogs, particularly if the dog is relaxed.

The dog's inoculations cover a core of four major diseases: distemper, which includes hardpad; leptospirosis, a liver and kidney infection; hepatitis, caused by a liver virus; and parvovirus. Kennel cough vaccine may also be included at a puppy's primary vaccination stage.

The first component of the vaccination course is usually given at seven to eight weeks old, although in circumstances where there has been a perceived risk in the breeder's kennels, much earlier protection may be given against certain diseases. Such early vaccinations are usually disregarded for the purposes of routine protection, and the pup is given a repeat injection at eight weeks.

The second injection is given at around 12 weeks of age. The interval between vaccinations is necessary to allow the puppy's immune system to react properly to the first dose of vaccine; the second dose then boosts the level of immunity so that the dog is protected for a prolonged period.

The vaccines are repeated annually, a process known as "boosters". Owners are inclined to be lax in their response to booster reminders as the dog gets older. Don't! Although some elements of the dog vaccination programme may confer a solid immunity for life, this cannot be relied upon, and other elements definitely need boosting annually.

LIFELONG IMMUNIZATION

Some infections in dogs are unlikely to strike the dog more than once in its lifetime. Vaccination against these diseases may confer a lifelong immunity. The virus hepatitis of the dog is one of these diseases.

BOOSTER INOCULATIONS

Unfortunately other infections, although again unlikely to affect the dog more than once, do not confer such a solid immunity for life, although the immunity that they do confer is excellent for as long as it lasts. Typical of this group is distemper and hardpad (which is caused by the same virus). Distemper vaccinations must be boosted about every second year to maintain a high level of immunity.

There is a third group of infections that may recur and to which the immunity offered by vaccination is relatively short-lived. It is still worthwhile to use the vaccine because of the dangerous nature of the illness. Such a disease is leptospirosis, transmitted usually by foxes or other dogs, but occasionally, in the case of one type of the disease, by rats.

Not all diseases to which dogs are susceptible can be avoided by vaccination, but the commonest killers certainly can.

KENNEL COUGH

A particular problem for which there is no total preventive control is kennel cough, an infectious inflammation of the larynx and trachea. Kennel cough may be an unfair description. The disease is transmitted by droplets coughed into the air by dogs actively suffering from the illness. Fairly close contact between dogs is necessary for its transmission, such as a nose-to-nose greeting through the wire by dogs in kennels. At least as common a cause is dogs meeting at shows, competitions or training classes.

Kennel cough is caused by a mixture of infectious agents. The most effective vaccine, although it still does not include every possible component of the infection, is given as a nasal spray. Most kennels advise owners to make sure their dogs have had a kennel cough vaccination shortly before going into kennels. Some insist before accepting the dog. The advice is sensible.

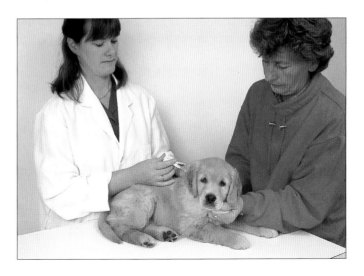

WORM CONTROL

Any tablet needs to be given right to the back of the dog's mouth. Wrap it in something pleasant to distract him from spitting it out.

A dog will eat grass when his stomach is upset, but many dogs simply enjoy a little grazing.

Dogs are prone to both internal and external parasitic infestations. There are two common worms in dogs: the tapeworm and the roundworm.

TAPEWORMS

Tapeworms may affect dogs at any age, although they are less common in young puppies than in older dogs. The tapeworm has a life cycle that depends on two different host species, in the case of the most frequently seen worm, the dog and the dog's fleas, although in another species they are transmitted through sheep.

Tapeworms may be recognizable as "rice grains" in the faeces, but the dog may give you an indication by undue attention to its anal region.

Control of the tapeworm in the dog is simple; modern treatments are straightforward, requiring no fasting before dosing, and highly effective, with very little in the way of side-effects (occasional vomiting).

It is a good idea to treat your dog routinely against tapeworms every six months. However, prevention of re-infection depends on control of the flea population in your house.

ROUNDWORMS

Roundworms are practically universal in puppies. They may be transmitted directly from dog to dog by faecal contamination, which is almost impossible to avoid. A high proportion of puppies are actually born infected with roundworms, transmitted via the uterus of the mother. Worms that had lain dormant in the tissues of the dam are activated by the hormones produced during pregnancy, circulate in the mother's bloodstream and pass into the unborn pups. There are control regimes that depend on using a safe anthelmintic early in pregnancy to destroy the maternal worm load, but this treatment is by no means universal.

A proper rearing regime will include dosing the litter when it is three or four weeks old, and perhaps again before leaving the kennels. Once in your home the puppy should be treated regularly, according to your veterinary surgeon's advice, every three to four weeks until it is six months old.

Adult dogs build up a level of immunity to the effects of roundworm infestations, and after six months do not need such regular treatment. Keep a constant look-out, although roundworms are not always easy to detect in a dog's faeces.

WORM TREATMENTS

There are drug treatments that are effective against tapeworms and roundworms in one dose. One possibility is to give older dogs this type of treatment once every six months. The ascarid roundworm may be the cause of a very rare eye condition in children. If the dog is regularly wormed, the risk, already remote, is eliminated. With this exception, the worms of dogs and of humans are not transmissible.

Other species of worms, including the hookworm, may occur in dogs. Treatment is not difficult, but diagnosis may not be straightforward. Consult your veterinary surgeon. In the United States, heartworm is a common problem. A preventive medicine is given orally; treatment can be costly, and dangerous for the dog.

♦ RIGHT
All dogs will lick and clean their anal region, but frequent licking is a sign that veterinary attention is needed.

EXTERNAL PARASITES

◆ BELOW
Dogs will lick and occasionally chew their paws, but if your dog does this persistently, examine his feet. Grass seeds are a common irritant.

FLEAS

Start by assuming that your dog has fleas. They are by far the commonest external parasite of the dog. A high proportion of skin problems may be caused, directly or indirectly, by their presence.

Fleas thrive in the warm and cosy environment of a centrally heated house, and there is no longer a flea season in summer followed by a flea-free winter. Treatment should be continued all through the year.

Fleas are often difficult to diagnose. They are small, move rapidly and are able to hop considerable distances. They are not very easy to see on the dog, but they never live alone. If you see one flea it is safe to assume that there are plenty more. If you see none at all, they are probably still somewhere around.

A useful home test is to scrape hair detritus on to newspaper, and then to dampen the paper. If red smears appear it is a certain indication that the dog does have fleas. The detritus may look like coal dust, but it is flea excreta.

Once you have convinced yourself that even your dog may have fleas, treatment is straightforward, although control is anything but. There are several effective sprays and washes available that will kill fleas safely (but some for which care is necessary), and most have some residual effect. But re-infestation is very difficult to prevent. If protection is, say, for three months, in practice the effectiveness is likely to decline well within that time. So some fleas come back.

Recent advances have been made with non-toxic preparations to be given to the dog monthly in tablet form. These do not kill adult fleas but act by breaking the flea's breeding cycle. All flea treatments are demanding in that they must be given regularly if they are to work.

The important thing to remember is that fleas leave the host to

◆ RIGHT
Scratching is normal, but persistent scratching demands attention. In nine out of ten cases it will be something as simple as fleas.

reproduce, and that for every flea you find on the dog, there are literally thousands in your dog's bed, in the nooks and crannies in the floor, in the carpets, between the cushions on the sofa, all breeding away like mad.

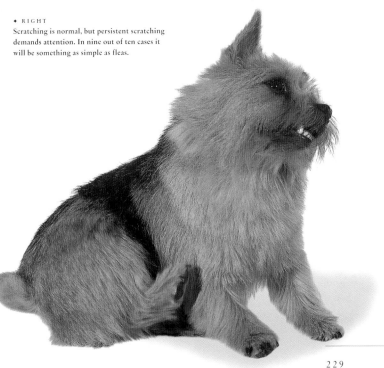

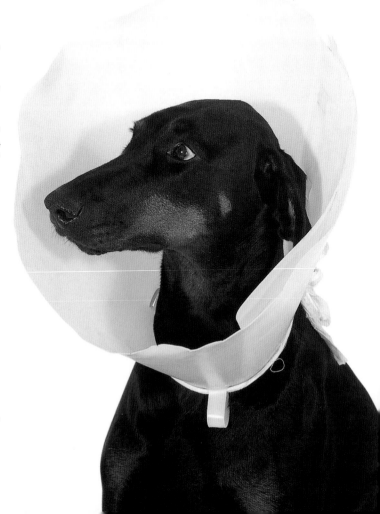

◆ BELOW
The Elizabethan collar is extremely useful to
prevent self-mutilation around the head. The
cause of the inflammation must be determined.

There are a number of preparations
on the market that provide effective
protection around the house.
Thorough vacuuming of the carpets
helps but will not overcome the
problem. Flea eggs, laid in their
thousands, are able to survive for
long periods in a warm environment.
Disturbance causes the eggs to hatch,
in itself a reason for regular vacuum
cleaning, as the eggs in their shells are
resistant to insecticides.

TICKS
These unplesant parasites tend to be
a country dog problem. Their usual
host is the sheep. In the United States,
Australia, South Africa and the
tropics, ticks transmit certain rapidly
fatal diseases to dogs, and the dogs are
routinely dipped or sprayed against
infestation, often on a weekly basis.
This is not necessary in Europe, where
tick-borne dog diseases are uncommon.

Ticks engorge on the blood of their
host; the engorged tick is sometimes
mistaken for a wart on the dog's skin.

Dogs will occasionally pick up a
solitary tick, but may sometimes be
seen to have several. Adult female
ticks lay groups of eggs, which hatch
at more or less the same time to form
a colony of young ticks attached to
grass stems waiting to find a host. If a
dog comes by, several of the "seed
ticks" may attach themselves to him.

The ticks are usually removed
individually. Do not try to pick them
off. That's rarely successful, and there
are various substances that will kill
them. Ear drops that are intended to
destroy parasites are useful as is
methylated spirit, or even gin! The
tick will not fall off immediately but it
should have disappeared twelve hours

after application. Most anti-flea
preparations will also kill them.

In the United States, Lyme disease
is transmitted by ticks that live on
deer and mice, and is a serious threat to
dogs. Fortunately, a vaccine is available.

LICE
Fortunately lice are now uncommon
parasites of the dog. Lice are
detectable by the presence of just

visible groups of eggs attached to the
hair, often of the ears or head of the
dog. Lice are small and are not mobile.
They tend to occur in large numbers,
but do not seem to be as itchy to the
dog as fleas.

Lice are transmitted directly from
dog to dog by contact. They are not
transmitted to humans or to other
animals. They may be controlled by
the use of insecticidal shampoos.

SIGNS OF ILLNESS

One of the first signs that a dog is ill is if he refuses his food. Most fussy dogs will at least smell the food on offer, but a sick dog may have no appetite and simply not approach his food.

The dog will tend to become duller than usual, although many sick dogs will still respond to their owner's enthusiasm for a game or a walk.

ACUTE ILLNESS

The term "acute" does not necessarily mean a serious illness. When your

The ear is an extremely sensitive organ. Any inflammation demands immediate attention from the veterinary surgeon.

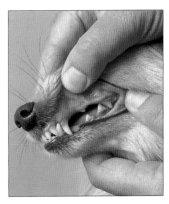

Dogs on modern diets are inclined to acquire tartar on their teeth, which needs attention if it is not to lead on to more serious problems.

SIGNS OF ACUTE ILLNESS

Tense, swollen stomach. A drum-like swelling of the abdomen an hour or two after feeding, accompanied by obvious distress with panting and salivation, may indicate that the dog has bloat. This is an emergency.

Vomiting several times, particularly if it persists for more than twelve hours. Vomiting once or twice is common, and a normal reaction to eating something unsuitable. Some dogs eat grass, appearing to do it to make themselves sick. If this happens occasionally, there is probably nothing to worry about. Persistent vomiting after eating grass may suggest an acute problem.

Diarrhoea persisting for twenty-four hours or longer. Diarrhoea will often accompany vomiting. If the faeces are bloodstained, treatment may be needed urgently.

Difficulty breathing, gasping, choking.

Collapse, loss of consciousness, fits.

Each of these conditions needs immediate attention from your veterinary surgeon.

veterinary surgeon refers to an acute illness he simply means one that has come on rapidly, whereas a "chronic" illness is one that is long lasting and has appeared gradually.

Young puppies are occasionally subject to fits, from which they usually recover quickly. Observe the fit carefully so that you can describe it when you get to the vet's. Did the dog just collapse silently, did it squeal or howl, did it paddle its legs, did it urinate or defaecate during the fit? Once a dog has recovered from a fit it may be very difficult for the veterinary surgeon to be precise about the cause; there may be nothing for him to see.

Other signs of acute illness include serious bleeding, or bleeding from any orifice (see First Aid); obvious pain, indicated by noise (squealing, crying, yelping on movement), lameness, or tenderness to touch; straining to pass faeces, or inability to pass urine; any obvious severe injury, or swelling on the body; a closed eye, or inflammation with excessive tears; violent

scratching or rubbing, particularly around the ears or head.

CHRONIC ILLNESS

The signs of chronic illness appear gradually and are likely to be more subtle and difficult to recognize.

Loss of weight, persisting over a period of weeks, is a common indicator of chronic disease. This may be accompanied by a normal or reduced appetite.

Gradually developing swellings may indicate the growth of superficial tumours, often not cancerous but usually needing attention.

Other signs include hair loss, with or without sore skin or itching and scratching; slowly developing lameness; excessive drinking, with or without an unpleasant odour from the mouth or body. Occasional vomiting may indicate an internal problem, although many healthy dogs may also vomit. In the normal course of events, bitches may frequently regurgitate food for their puppies.

FIRST AID FOR YOUR DOG

◆ BELOW
Sores and rashes may develop beneath a long coat for some time before they become obvious.

First-aid treatments may be divided into problems that you can deal with yourself, and treatments to carry out to keep the problem to a minimum before you take the dog to the veterinary surgeon.

SORES AND RASHES

A dog may get a sore place or a rash through chewing itself. Many dogs will chew their skin raw if there is an itch. The dog may get a rash from insect bites – typically flea bites, from skin contact with irritants such as nettles, or as an allergic response to an external or internal substance. It is often difficult to tell to what extent the sore area is caused by

the irritant or is self-inflicted as a result of the irritation.

The object of treatment, whether your own first aid or your veterinary surgeon's, is to eliminate the cause before attempting to cure the effect.

If a dog has been scratching itself a little more than usual, the most common cause is the presence of fleas. Fleas never come singly. If you see a flea, there will definitely be others. One or two may be sufficient to start the itch cycle off, and once started it will need intervention to stop it. The answer is to treat the fleas, and the problem will usually disappear. If it doesn't, a soothing cream, such as rescue cream, will be sufficient.

FIRST-AID KIT

The most important item in your first-aid kit should be your veterinary surgeon's name and telephone number. Even though you may have it else-where, it does no harm to duplicate it.

Absorbent cotton wool

Adhesive and gauze bandages, 5 cm (2 in) and 10 cm (4 in)

Gauze swabs, sterile wraps

Cotton buds

Scissors, sharp-pointed

Thermometer

Forceps, medium-sized, blunt points

Plastic syringe, 20 ml (½ fl oz)

Eye drops

Cleansing ear drops

Antiseptic or antibiotic ointment

Antiseptic powder and wash

Rescue cream

Medicinal liquid paraffin

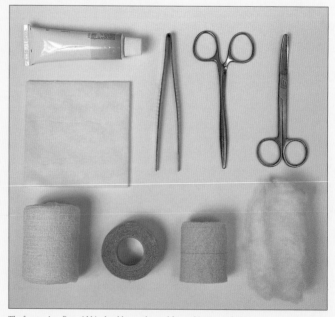

The forceps in a first-aid kit should never be used for probing around. You must always be able to see whatever it is you are attempting to remove.

TAKING TEMPERATURE

1 First, shake the thermometer so that the level of mercury is well below the expected temperature of the dog.

2 Slide the lubricated thermometer carefully into the dog's anus and press lightly against the side of the rectum.

3 The thermometer should be held in place for at least sixty seconds before reading.

BANDAGING A PAW

1 First, pad the leg with cotton-wool strips between the toes.

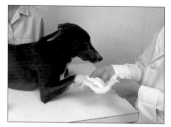

2 Place a generous amount of further padding over the end of the foot to cushion it before starting to bandage.

3 The bandage must always include the foot and be extended above the wound.

4 Bandage the leg firmly, but take care that the bandage is not so tight that circulation is restricted.

5 Tie the bandage off well above the site of the wound.

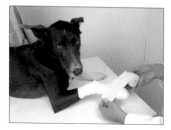

6 Cover the whole of the bandage in an adhesive dressing, firmly but not tightly, and secure it at the back of the dog's leg.

CUTS AND SCRATCHES

Treatment depends on how large and how deep the cut or scratch is. The dog's skin does not usually bleed profusely, and it is easy to miss even quite a large cut because there may be very little bleeding and the dog's fur covers the site.

If there is any sign of blood on the dog, look carefully and once you have located the cut, clip sufficient hair around it to expose the wound. If the

cut looks deep, or longer than about 1 cm (½ in), it will need attention and, probably, a stitch or two at the veterinary surgery.

If you decide to take the dog to the vet, do nothing with the wound, unless it is bleeding profusely. The nurse is likely to take longer cleaning your dressing off the wound than the stitching itself will take.

A minor cut, or a scratch that does not penetrate the skin, will usually

need very little treatment. Soothing cream will be sufficient, and even that may do more to prolong healing than to help, by bringing the attention of the dog to the wound.

Similarly, a small cut needs no particular attention once you have trimmed the hair away, other than to keep the wound clean with a mild antiseptic solution, and to keep an eye open for any swelling. Swelling may indicate that an infection has set in.

BITES

Dog bites will often become infected. This is particularly the case when the bite causes a puncture wound. Unless the wounds are multiple, or large enough obviously to require veterinary attention, there is no emergency, but the dog should be taken to the veterinary surgery within 24 hours to allow the vet to assess whether antibiotic injections are needed. Prior to that, the wound may be cleansed with antiseptic lotion.

BLEEDING

Treatment will depend on how heavily the wound is bleeding. Skin wounds may only need cleansing, followed by the application of a little antiseptic cream and a careful eye on the progress of the wound. It will probably stop bleeding in a short time.

Profuse bleeding is an emergency, usually indicating a wound that is sufficiently deep to need urgent veterinary attention. Steps to control the bleeding while on the way to the surgery are worthwhile, and may be life-saving. Tourniquets are no longer used, do not attempt to make one. Use a pressure bandage over the wound.

The rare need for a pressure bandage is one reason for the cotton wool and bandages in your first-aid kit. When needed, take a large wad of cotton wool, as large as is available in your kit. Place it directly over the wound, and bandage firmly. If the wound is on a limb, bandage right down to the foot and include the entire leg below the wound in your bandage. Make sure the site over the wound is firmly bandaged, and take the dog to the surgery.

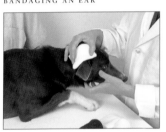

1 First signs of heat stroke are obvious distress and incessant panting.

HEAT EXHAUSTION

Some breeds of dog are more prone to heat exhaustion than others – Chow Chows and Bulldogs come to mind, but several other short-nosed breeds can also be affected.

The most common reason for heat exhaustion is human error. Dogs are too often left inside cars in summer

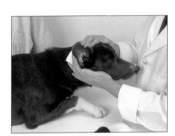

2 The dog should be cooled immediately by sponging or hosing down with cold water. Ensure that the head is drenched.

without adequate ventilation. The owner is usually just thoughtless, or caught out by a change in the weather during a longer-than-expected shopping trip. The temperature inside a closed car in summer in even a temperate climate can kill a dog. Many have died in this way. The signs of heat stress are obvious distress, heavy

BANDAGING AN EAR

1 Ears are often damaged in dog fights and can bleed profusely. Clean the wound, then place an absorbent pad behind the dog's affected ear.

2 Carefully fold the ear back on to the pad.

BANDAGING A TAIL

1 Successful tail bandaging is fraught with difficulty. First enclose the tail lengthways in a bandage.

2 Lay strips of bandage along the length of the tail.

3 A wet towel, frequently changed, will help to cool the dog down and in a hot environment may help to prevent heat stroke.

panting, and an inability to breathe deeply enough indicated by a half strangled noise coming from the dog's throat. The dog's tongue will look swollen and blue.

Treat any dog with these symptoms as an immediate emergency case, and do not attempt to take the dog for veterinary treatment, or move him, until you have started resuscitation.

Plenty of cold water is the first-aid treatment. Ideally, immerse the whole dog in a bath – use a cattle trough if there is one nearby. Bathe the dog all over with cold water, but especially drench its head; and keep doing it until the dog shows signs of easier breathing. Then take it to the vet. The vet will possibly put the dog on to an oxygen air flow, and will probably give it an injection to reduce the swelling in its throat, but unless the vet happens to be at hand, as he may be at a dog show, the life-saving treatment will have been given before the dog gets to the surgery.

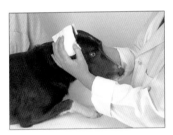

3 Place the pad over the folded back ear.

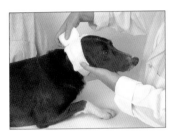

4 Start bandaging around the neck from behind the ear and work forward, enclosing the affected ear, not too tightly.

5 The unaffected ear should not be included in the bandaging.

3 Bandage the tail around its length, whenever possible including some of the dog's tail hair within the turns of the bandage.

4 Cover the bandage with an adhesive dressing.

5 Take the adhesive dressing well above the end of the bandage and include strands of hair within each turn.

EXAMINING AND BRUSHING TEETH

1 Regular brushing will slow up the formation of plaque and tartar.

2 Some dogs will resent the use of a brush, but toothpaste on the end of a finger can be almost as effective.

3 Specially made dog toothbrushes are often well tolerated.

EXAMINING EYES

1 Take great care when administering eye drops or ointment. It is important to hold the dog's eyelids open so that the medication actually goes into the eyes.

2 After the drops have been put in, the eyelids must be gently massaged over the surface of the eye to encourage the spread of the medication.

Sick dogs must be kept warm, dry and comfortable. They may be encouraged to eat but never force fed. The dog should always have easy access to water.

SNAKE BITES, AND STINGS FROM OTHER VENOMOUS CREATURES

These are often difficult to recognize unless the bite is witnessed. The degree of urgency depends on the type of venomous creature, where on its body the dog was bitten, and the age of the dog. Small puppies are obviously more at risk than older, larger animals.

The only venomous British snake is the adder. The risk is greater in areas with certain types of soil – sandy downs seem to harbour more adders than most other areas. In the United States, Australia and Africa the most common snake bites in dogs are from the viperine snakes. Poisonous North American snakes include rattlesnakes and coral snakes.

Snakes are often more likely to bite when they come out to sun themselves on a warm spring day, and the dog goes to investigate. So the dog is most likely to be bitten on the face, head or neck.

If the dog's face starts to swell up while you are out on a walk, the chance of a snake bite must be considered. Unless the swelling starts to cause obvious breathing distress, treatment is urgent, but this is not a life-threatening emergency. You can afford to walk back to the car, no need to run, but make sure the dog walks quietly – exercise should be minimal. Carry a small dog. Take the dog straight to the

◆ RIGHT
Disturb an injured dog as little as possible,
although be prepared to lift it carefully and
take it to a veterinary surgeon immediately.

surgery. Very few dogs in Britain
die from the effects of adder venom,
but many each year have distressing
abscesses caused by a combination of
the venom and infection.

Bites from non-venomous snakes
should be thoroughly cleaned as the
snake's teeth may be carrying bacteria,
which could cause infection.

The only reason to include snake
bites in the first aid section is that
there is a belief that the venom of a
snake should be "sucked out" of the
wound. Do not attempt to do so.

Bee and wasp stings carry a similar
risk of death to snake bites – generally,
they are only likely to be lethal if the
swelling from the bite blocks the dog's
airway. The exception to this is the
case of multiple stings, the shock of
which can cause the death of the dog.
Such events are rare.

Venomous spiders are unknown in
the United Kingdom and uncommon
in the United States, although they
do occur there. The Australian funnel
spider, however, is an extremely
venomous arachnid.

A single swelling from a bee or
wasp sting does not usually require
veterinary treatment, but home
attention with a soothing cream will
speed the dog's recovery, and possibly
stop the "sore scratch" cycle.

CHOKING

Some dogs are inveterate pickers up of
sticks and stones, or ball chasers. All
carry the risk of getting an object
stuck in the mouth or throat. A half
swallowed ball may be an emergency
by reason of a blocked airway. First
aid may be a two-handed job. You
could get bitten. If the dog seems to
be choking, look in his mouth with

care. A block of wood to prevent
him closing his teeth over your
fingers can help, with one person
holding the dog's head while the
other looks into his mouth. If there is
a ball in the dog's throat, try to lever
it out with a fine rod rather than with
your hand.

A frequent occurrence is that a
piece of wood becomes wedged across
the teeth, or between the back teeth.
Treat removal with similar caution,
using some sort of lever to remove it.
This type of incident not infrequently
requires a trip to the vet and sedation
to remove the object.

WHAT TO DO IN A ROAD
ACCIDENT INVOLVING A DOG

It is virtually certain that a dog
involved in a road accident will not be
under control. The first step, even
before looking to see what may be
wrong, is to leash the dog with
whatever comes to hand. But you
must do it without risk to yourself.

A noose needs to be made and
slipped over the dog's head without
actually touching the dog. The noose
may be easily made from your own

dog's lead or any other line, such as
a belt, or even a piece of string.

The next step, unless the dog
is obviously unconscious, is to
muzzle the dog. Any dog that has
been involved in a road accident is
likely to be in shock, and even the
most friendly can bite whoever is

Many road accidents and injuries to dogs may
be avoided if the owner exercises the dog
sensibly by restraining it with a lead.

Large injured dogs may be carried with one arm at the front of their chest, under the neck, and the other looped through to allow the back legs to hang. A muzzle may be necessary.

attending it, through a combination of pain and fear. You are unlikely to be carrying a proper muzzle with you. Once again, a dog lead or a bandage can be used. Only once the dog's mouth is secure, should you attempt to examine the dog.

If the dog is not conscious, do not try to resuscitate it – get it to the veterinary surgery as quickly as possible. If other people are there, ask someone to phone ahead to the surgery to warn them that you are coming.

A coat or blankets may be used as a makeshift stretcher, but only a dog that is unconscious or is so badly injured that it is unaware of its surroundings is likely to tolerate being carried in this way.

If the dog is bleeding heavily, use whatever materials are available to make a pressure pad. Bind the wound and take the dog to the surgery immediately.

If the dog is carrying a leg, or is limping, there may be a fracture. Despite the first-aid warning about not

moving an injured person, you are better to take the dog straightaway to the veterinary surgery than to wait while someone phones around to find a vet who can leave the surgery to attend the accident. There is as yet no organized emergency ambulance service for animals.

Once the dog's mouth is bound and it cannot bite, it is almost always safe to carry the dog. If possible, let the affected leg hang free – you will avoid further damage, and pain.

Dogs in road accidents will often run away, despite serious injury. If you see this happen warn the police, who will at least be able to inform anyone who enquires about their missing dog.

Sometimes the police will accept immediate responsibility for the care of dogs involved in road accidents. If they are informed of an accident and are able to attend the scene, they will usually know the local veterinary surgeons and be able to advise on the vets' phone numbers.

MUZZLING AN INJURED DOG

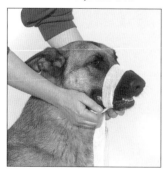

1 An improvized muzzle may be made with a bandage or almost any material. Make a loop, pass it over the dog's muzzle and under its chin.

2 Take the ends of the material up behind the dog's ears.

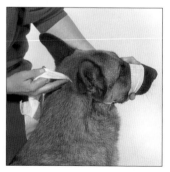

3 Tie the muzzle firmly behind the dog's head. An improvized muzzle must be tied tightly. It will not choke the dog.

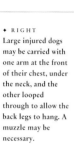

◆ BELOW
If poisoning is suspected, take the container
and, if possible, some of its contents to the
veterinary surgeon with the dog.

◆ BELOW
Cigarettes are toxic to dogs and may cause
nicotine poisoning. Fortunately, few dogs will
eat cigarettes.

POISONING AND COMMON POISONS

The poisons likely to be encountered by a dog are almost always those found around the house and garden. They include tablets and medicines intended for human consumption, or not for internal use at all, household chemicals such as bleach or detergents, and garden chemicals.

Puppies will try anything. You must keep all potentially dangerous materials out of their reach, preferably in a locked cupboard.

If an accident does occur, and you think your dog has eaten something that could be poisonous, there are two things to do.

1 Make the dog sick. If this is to be of any help, it must be done before the poisonous substance has had a chance to be absorbed from the stomach, so do it before contacting your veterinary surgeon. But if you know your vet is immediately available for advice, and you are certain what it is the dog has

eaten, do not make the dog sick until you have spoken to the vet.

The most effective substance to use to make the dog sick is washing soda. Put two small crystals on to the back of the dog's tongue, and make him swallow them by holding his mouth shut and stroking his throat. Vomiting

will take place within minutes so be prepared with old newspapers at hand.

2 Contact your veterinary surgeon. Retain some of the poisonous substance, or at least its wrapping, to show him or her. There may be no ill effect, or immediate further treatment may be necessary.

Do not make the dog vomit if the toxic substance is already being absorbed, which occurs within thirty or so minutes of ingestion.

SOME COMMON POISONS

Rat poisons – all rat poisons are coloured to indicate the active substance. They are of low toxicity to dogs when used properly, but dogs may get hold of bulk quantities.
Blue: Anticoagulants
Brown: Calciferol
Green: Alphachloralose
Pink or Grey: Gamma-HCH (Lindane)
  If rat poisoning is suspected, the package or some of the suspect material must be retained for examination by the veterinary surgeon.

Barbiturates – human sleeping pills.

Sodium Chlorate – weed killer.

Detergents – usually safe, but if concentrated may cause external lesions, or vomiting if swallowed.

Antifreeze – Ethylene glycol.

Lead – old paint chewed by dogs.

Slug bait – metaldehyde, attractive to dogs, now has anti-dog component.

Cigar and cigarette ends – nicotine.

Organochlorine, Organophosphorus compounds – flea and lice killers.

Paraquat – herbicide.

Aspirin – taken in large quantity.

Strychnine – vermin killer, dogs may get at carcasses.

Toad – from mouthing the toad. Exotic toads are more venomous.

Tranquillisers.

239

INHERITED DISEASES

An inherited disease is one that may be passed from generation to generation through affected genes of the sire or the dam, or sometimes through a combination of both. Genetics, the study of inheritance, is a highly complicated science, and it becomes increasingly so the more we learn of the subject.

There are two main problems in the control of inherited diseases in dogs. Some diseases are partly inherited, and partly occur as a result of some environmental influence, which is often difficult to determine precisely. The inherited element may depend on several inherited factors rather than a single gene. Typical of this type of disease is hip dysplasia, probably the most widely known of all inherited diseases of the dog. It is a hind-leg lameness, caused by severe erosion and damage to the hip joint.

It is generally considered that inheritance accounts for about 50 per cent of the clinical signs of hip

◆ BELOW
This Irish Setter is free from the distressing condition of Progressive Retinal Atrophy (PRA), which responsible breeders are doing a great deal to eliminate in the breed.

◆ LEFT
Dalmatian puppies may now be tested scientifically for deafness before they are six weeks old.

dysplasia, and that the remainder is caused by one or more environmental circumstance – such as the dog's weight, exercise and diet – but precisely what is not known. In these circumstances, attempts at control are slow at best, depending on diagnosis of the disease and the avoidance of affected dogs in breeding. This may sound simple but is not.

The condition affects many breeds, mostly the larger ones, including the German Shepherd. Largely due to the efforts of German Shepherd breeders, control schemes have been operating in several countries for many years now. Progress has been real but is slow, and sometimes heartbreaking for breeders, who may have used a dog and a bitch that both have excellent "hip scores", only to find that the offspring are seriously affected.

The second problem is that the disease may not show itself until the affected animal is mature. The dog

or bitch may well have been used in a breeding programme before any signs that it has the condition are seen. To some extent this may be overcome by control schemes that do not give certificates of freedom from the disease until the dogs in the scheme are old enough for the particular disease to have shown itself. Hip dysplasia is again an example: hip scoring is by an expert panel who examine X-rays of submitted dogs. These X-rays may not be taken until the dog is 12 months old.

There are several diseases that are known to be inherited in a straightforward way and are present at birth. These diseases can be controlled, depending for the success of the control scheme on the co-operation of the breeders, and their recognition that animals that show signs of the disease are actually afflicted, rather than the subject of accidents that mimic the condition.

Until a specific gene test becomes practicable,
it is important that not only this pregnant
bitch, but the sire, have been certified healthy.

ears. There is evidence that partially
deaf dogs can pass on partial or
complete deafness to their offspring,
and the numbers of dogs being tested
are increasing rapidly in several
countries. The test for dogs originated
in the United States, which is probably
leading the world in this area.

Almost certainly, present studies
of the "genome", the genetic make-up,
of all species will result in a revolution
in the study and control of genetic
diseases. Once the precise positions
of inherited diseases on the DNA
molecule are known, specific action
may be taken to eliminate the
problem. This approach is no longer
pie in the sky. Within a very few years
DNA testing will become routine.

The outstanding example of breeder
co-operation in control of inherited
disease must be the experience of
Progressive Retinal Atrophy, night
blindness, in Irish Setters. By the
involvement of nearly all the breeders,
and with recognition that the disease
had a straightforward inheritance
pattern, the condition has been
virtually eliminated from the breed.

Up-and-coming schemes include
one to control deafness in Dalmatians.
For many years, a proportion of
Dalmatian puppies have been born
deaf or partially deaf; but breeders
were generally only able to recognize
stone-deaf puppies, which were put
to sleep soon after birth.

Scientific testing, developed for use
in people, has now enabled breeders
to have their puppies examined before
sale, not only for total deafness, but
for partial deafness in one or both

◆ BELOW
The breeder carries a heavy burden
of responsibility to produce a
healthy, keen-to-please dog such
as this German Shepherd.

NEUTERING

The advantages of neutering (altering) both male and female dogs far outweigh the possible disadvantages, and overcome the specific problems associated with either sex. Neutered males do not wander, and neutered females do not come into season.

Fewer owners in Britain neuter their dogs than in America, where the operation is as routine as neutering cats in Britain. It is noticeable also that fewer male dogs than females are neutered. Females, of course, are at risk of having a litter.

Both dogs and bitches may be neutered at the age of about six months, and it is not necessary to wait until a bitch has had a first season before having her spayed. To a considerable extent, the earlier the dog is neutered, the less complicated the operation. Early neutering does not result in failure of the dog to mature

mentally; all the dogs bred by the Guide Dogs For The Blind Association are neutered before they reach the age of six months. There are several disadvantages to neutering. After dogs of some breeds have been neutered their coats become heavier and fluffy. This happens to breeds such as the Irish Setter and the Cocker Spaniel, both of whom have naturally silky coats. The extent of the problem varies. In some dogs it may be necessary to trim the coat.

A problem that may be associated with spaying the bitch is the development of urinary incontinence

in later life. This problem is easily cured by hormone replacement therapy, but it would still be sensible to discuss this possible problem with your veterinary surgeon before the operation. A research project currently underway may provide an answer. The problem does not occur after castration of the male.

Dogs and bitches often put on weight after being neutered. This need not happen. Dietary investigations suggest that neutered dogs have a lower nutritional requirement than entire (un-neutered) animals, possibly by as much as 15 per cent. To avoid a dog putting on weight after it has been neutered, simply reduce its daily food ration. As with any weight-control regime, it is much easier to prevent the weight going on than to take it off once it's there. Weigh the dog regularly for a time after the neutering operation, until you have established that its weight is steady.

If you intend to keep more than one dog in your house, the situation is somewhat different. Two animals of opposite sexes will tend to live more easily together than two of the same, other than when the bitch comes into season. Two dogs kept together will tend to sort out their dominance once and for all, but two entire bitches are quite likely never to sort out their arguments, with problems tending to arise whenever one of them is coming into season.

Once you start to keep larger numbers you are likely to come across dominance problems that will have to be sorted out. Neutering has some effect on the control of dominance problems but should not be looked upon as the complete answer.

♦ RIGHT
One of the few genuine disadvantages of neutering is that it could cause the beautiful glossy coat of this Cocker Spaniel to become coarse and fluffy.

DOGS AND HUMAN HEALTH

There are some diseases that may affect both dogs and humans. The technical term for such a disease is "zoonosis".

The most feared of these diseases is undoubtedly **rabies**. When travelling in an area that is not rabies-free, it is essential that you consult a doctor immediately if you are bitten by a dog or any other animal.

Fleas, common on dogs – most frequently actually the cat flea – will bite humans. It is unlikely that dog or cat fleas can survive on humans, so a few intensely itchy bites are the only likely problem. The presence of flea bites on you or your children is a timely reminder that flea control on your dog has, perhaps, not been as effective as you thought.

Rabbit mites can cause a skin rash in dogs. They are capable of biting humans, and may cause an itchy rash from contact with the affected dog. The rash is unlikely to spread.

Ringworm is not a common disease in dogs but, when it does occur, precautions should be taken to avoid its spread to human members of the family. It is a true zoonosis and can establish itself on the human skin. Affected areas will be those of contact – the hands and forearms.

Toxocara, the most frequently encountered roundworm in puppies, and indeed almost universal in very young puppies, has been implicated in a rare specific type of eye disease in children. Roundworms that are ingested by a species other than their normal host may encyst and settle in almost any part of the body, but are known to invade the eye. These cysts have been known to cause blindness. Such an accident is extremely rare but, of course, a tragedy for the child and his or her parents if it happens.

Good hygiene should prevent any child from coming in contact with dog faeces. Puppies must be wormed every three weeks until they are six months old. Their faeces must be collected, and the puppy should be taught to defecate in a prescribed spot in the garden, not in a public place.

Simple hygiene for children must be practised: they should wash their hands after playing with the dog. But children should not be discouraged – there is so much to be gained from a happy association between child and dog that, provided risks are minimized, their close companionship should be encouraged. Remember, the dog is our oldest friend.

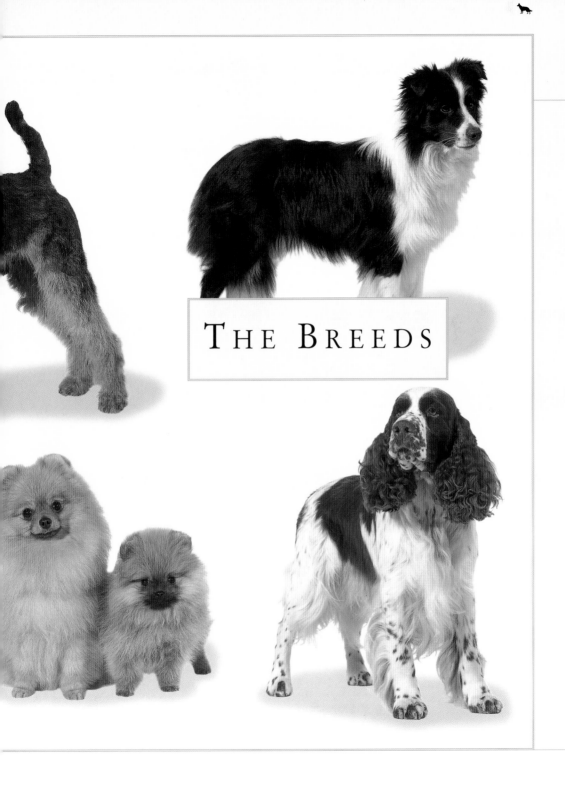

THE BREEDS

AFGHAN HOUND

The Afghan, one of the most glamorous breeds, has a superbly elegant silky coat on an athletic frame, as befits a hunting creature originating in the mountains of Afghanistan.

The Afghan's expression is one of dignity and superiority, but he can have moments of hectic eccentricity, racing across garden or field.

Not inclined to heed the wishes of an exasperated owner unless handled with firmness as he grows up, this is a dog that is not for the uncommitted. Treating one casually will not lead to a happy relationship in the household.

More than capable of acting as a watchdog, the Afghan may use his powerful teeth on intruders if his warnings are not heeded.

In spite of standing over 70 cm (27½ in) at the withers, he is not a greedy feeder; in fact he may be a little finicky if allowed to have his own way. He is an athlete and needs a lot of exercise to cope with his restless energy.

BREED BOX

Size	medium-large
	dog: 70–74 cm
	(27½–29 in), 27 kg
	(60 lb)
	bitch: 63–69 cm
	(25–27 in), 22.5 kg
	(50 lb)
Grooming	frequent and thorough
Exercise	essential
Feeding	medium
Temperament	wary of strangers

The Afghan's silky coat will not look its best without constant care. It needs regular and thorough grooming, and any knots must be removed every day. The breeder from whom he is purchased will show the new owner how this is best done.

The Afghan is a dog for the true enthusiast who has the time and the patience to get the best out of a canine glamour star.

◆ ABOVE
A shining silhouette that characterizes one of the most dignified of all the breeds.

◆ ABOVE
The Afghan's eyes look straight through you, one of the truly glamorous expressions of dogdom; they seem to defy you to resist them.

BEAGLE

As a breed, Beagles produce their puppies easily in reasonable numbers and seem to accept a life in kennels in philosophical fashion. As a result they have been bred extensively for use in medical/veterinary research laboratories, making them victims of their own super-friendly temperaments.

From the point of view of life as a member of a human household, they are similarly accommodating. They enjoy being part of a gang in much the same way as they make good team-members of a pack hunting hares. They are tidy creatures, although they are not always easy to housetrain. Their short waterproof coat makes them drip-dry in the foulest of weathers. Even after a day running across clay, a quick sponge-down soon makes them acceptable in the kitchen.

The Beagle is not greedy, though life in hunt kennels tends to make him swallow his daily ration fast. He is not prone to veterinary problems and lives to a reasonably ripe old age.

It is unusual to see a Beagle winning an obedience competition, as the breed has a tendency not to stay around for the recall once off the lead.

This is a breed that pleases families who lead active lives.

♦ LEFT
Beagles are hunters with handsome muzzles designed to make a thorough job of sniffing out their quarry.

BREED BOX

Size	small 33–40 cm (13–16 in), 9 kg (20 lb)
Grooming	easy
Exercise	considerable
Feeding	reasonable
Temperament	genially stubborn

♦ RIGHT
Tough forelegs and tight feet make the Beagle able to last all day whatever the activity, in the field, the park or the garden, as long as there's human company.

DEERHOUND

◆ RIGHT
The Deerhound has been used to hunt
red deer for a thousand years.

The Deerhound (Scottish Deerhound) hails from Scotland and is in fact a Greyhound with a harsh and shaggy overcoat. It is said that he has hunted deer for a thousand years, and ancient depictions of him suggest that he has altered little over the centuries. He appears to capture the heart of all who fall under his spell, but in return he demands great loyalty.

He stands 76 cm (30 in) and weighs around 45 kg (100 lb), so he is not a lightweight, but he has a surprising ability to curl up in a corner and not get in the way, even in a small house. He is not a big eater and gives the impression that ordinary oatmeal would be welcome along with the venison.

Grooming should be regular but is not a chore as the harshness of his shaggy coat renders him relatively easy to keep tidy.

As far as his temperament is concerned he is a friendly, faithful creature with a dignified attitude to strangers. One of the most venerated among his breeders travels with a team of Deerhounds from the outer regions of mid-west Scotland to shows all over Britain and does so by train, which must say something about the breed's charm and adaptability.

BREED BOX	
Size	medium–large dog: 76 cm (30 in), 45.5 kg (100 lb) bitch: 71 cm (28 in), 36.5 kg (80½ lb)
Grooming	moderate
Exercise	moderate
Feeding	medium
Temperament	highly companionable

◆ ABOVE
The shaggy coat comes in mainly pastel shades, from grey through brindle to fawn.

◆ ABOVE
A narrowish front shows the depth of chest displayed by all sight hounds.

POINTER

The Pointer is instantly recognizable. The clean-cut lines of his lean frame covered by a short, shining coat make a beautiful silhouette on grouse moor and in city parks alike, although his whole purpose in life suits him better for the countryside.

At 69 cm (27 in) he is quite a tall dog. He does not carry much surplus flesh so gives the impression of being bony. His movements are fluent and athletic. He is not a big eater; he is very easy to clean up after a day's work, and he is

◆ RIGHT
The Pointer is built for speed and endurance.

◆ ABOVE
He uses his aristocratic nose to cover a great deal of moor or pasture remarkably rapidly.

relatively easy to teach reasonable manners, though he is unlikely to win a top-standard obedience competition.

While most paintings depict him as white with a number of liver or black patches, he also comes in lemon and orange patterns. A kindly, gentle dog, he should appeal to the active owner.

BREED BOX	
Size	large
	dog: 63–69 cm
	(25–27 in),
	29.5 kg (65 lb)
	bitch: 61–66 cm
	(24–26 in),
	26 kg (57½ lb)
Grooming	minimal
Exercise	medium
Feeding	demanding
Temperament	kind and reasonably
	biddable

◆ RIGHT
The **Pointer** was developed in Britain in the seventeenth century to find and point hares for Greyhounds to chase. Dogs of a similar type are thought to have been bred in Spain around the same time.

IRISH SETTER

The Irish Setter is known to his friends as the Mad Irishman, with a devil-may-care way about him. He is certainly beautiful, but to keep that long, silky coat of deep chestnut gleaming requires thorough and regular grooming.

He stands around 65 cm (25½ in), but the official breed standard does not contain a height clause because, according to those who have bred him all their lives, a good Irish Setter cannot be a bad height. He is actually allowed to have a small amount of white on the front of his brisket, but nowhere else.

He does not carry a great deal of flesh, but his musculature has to be powerful because he is expected to work at top speed in the shooting field. He is not expensive to feed, although he can burn up a lot of calories, and he expects to be well exercised. He can be trained to curb his wildness by those who set out to be firm, and his attitude to one and all is of sheer friendship and *joie de vivre*. The recall exercise is not easily mastered by him.

The bitches of the breed tend to have very big litters of up to sixteen puppies at a time.

◆ RIGHT
The Irish Setter first appeared in recognizable form in the early eighteenth century.

◆ RIGHT
Almond-shaped eyes with a soft, kindly expression characterize the Irish Setter.

◆ RIGHT
The sheen on the deep chestnut coat is the reason why this is among the best known and most popular breeds in the world.

BREED BOX	
Size	large
	dog: 65 cm (25½ in),
	30.5 kg (67 lb)
	bitch: 26 kg
	(57½ lb)
Grooming	demanding
Exercise	demanding
Feeding	reasonable
Temperament	affectionate and racy

GOLDEN RETRIEVER

The Golden Retriever is a canine all-rounder. He can turn his talents to anything, from his natural retrieving to acting as a guide dog for the blind, a detector of drugs or explosives, a reasonably laid-back obedience worker or just being a most attractive member of a household.

He stands 61 cm (24 in) at his tallest but gives the impression of being a solid comfortable dog; he is inclined to get his snout into the trough as often as possible, and owners need to watch his waistline. There is often quite a difference in appearance between those retrievers used in the shooting field and the type that are bred for showing and the home.

The Golden Retriever has a dense undercoat with a flat wavy top-coat; the colour varies from cream to a rich golden, which is sometimes very deep.

He is easy to train, but needs to be kept interested, because he is easily bored. His ability as a guide dog for the blind demonstrates his temperament, as the work involves a great deal of steady, thoughtful walking.

♦ LEFT
The Golden Retriever, one of the most popular dogs, is a wonderful all-purpose breed, although guarding is not his forte.

He is one of the most popular household dogs because of his generous loving nature. Such popularity is often a curse because dogs are bred by people who are not always conscientious in their dedication to producing truly healthy stock. As is true of any breed of pedigree dog, the best source of supply is direct from a reputable breeder who has the welfare of the dogs he or she produces at heart.

BREED BOX

Size	medium dog: 56–61 cm (22–24 in), 34 kg (75 lb) bitch: 51–56 cm (20–22 in), 29.5 kg (65 lb)
Grooming	fairly demanding
Exercise	demanding
Feeding	demanding
Temperament	intelligent and biddable

♦ RIGHT
The Golden Retriever was developed in Britain in the late nineteenth century.

♦ ABOVE CENTRE
These dogs have generous soft muzzles that are able to carry shot birds, hares or even the newspaper without leaving a mark.

LABRADOR RETRIEVER

The Labrador Retriever is instantly recognizable. Thought to have originated in Greenland, he is a stockily built dog; his coat is short and hard to the touch; it is entirely weatherproof and basically drip-dry. At one time the black coat was the best known, but yellow (not golden) became more widely seen fifty years or more ago. Today there is quite a trend for chocolate, which is also called liver.

The Labrador stands as high as 57 cm (22½ in), which is not very tall, but he is extremely solid. Another characteristic is his relatively short, thick-coated tail, which is known as an "otter" tail. Like the Golden Retriever he is a multi-talented dog, being much favoured as a guide dog for the blind. (In fact these two breeds are regularly cross-bred to utilize their combined skills.) He is also useful in drug-searching and has been used by the army as a canine mine-detector.

♦ LEFT
Labradors were brought into Britain in the nineteenth century by the Earl of Malmesbury to work the water meadows of his estate.

♦ ABOVE
Wisdom in a canine expression is difficult to define, but the true Labrador seems to get as near as any.

BREED BOX

Size	large
	dog: 56–57 cm
	(22–22½ in),
	30.5 kg (67 lb)
	bitch: 54–56 cm
	(21–22 in),
	28.5 kg (63 lb)
Grooming	easy
Exercise	demanding
Feeding	reasonable
Temperament	friendly and
	intelligent

Undoubtedly his greatest skill is as a retriever from water.

The Labrador seems capable of taking all the knocks of a rough-and-tumble family, which is why he rates so highly as a household member. His temperament is such that he does not seem to take offence at any insult.

He can consume any quantity of food so needs rationing if he is not to put on too much weight. He must have exercise and, although he can live in town surroundings, he should not be deprived of regular, long walks.

♦ RIGHT
With a frame like this, it is easy to see why the breed is famous for its stamina.

ENGLISH COCKER SPANIEL

The English Cocker Spaniel is the original of the American breed. He stands around the same height at 41 cm (16 in), but his coat is shorter and therefore nowhere near such hard work to keep well groomed, provided adequate attention is paid to his fairly hairy feet and his longish ears. He can

◆ RIGHT
The orange-roan colour is one of a huge range that this neat dog comes in. The breed is the basis of several of the land spaniels.

◆ LEFT
Low-slung ears with long hair make regular grooming a must.

be found in whole colours such as red (gold) and black, also in black and white, and in multicolours.

A thoroughly busy dog, he is always searching and bustling around

BREED BOX

Size	small
	12.5–14.5 kg
	(27½–32 lb)
	dog: 39–41 cm
	(15–16 in)
	bitch: 38–39 cm
	(15–15½ in)
Grooming	regular
Exercise	medium
Feeding	small
Temperament	merry, exuberant

in the grass and bushes. His name comes from his ability to flush out game, particularly the woodcock. He also delights in carrying things about whether on command or purely voluntarily. He is often portrayed as the original slipper-fetching dog by his master's fireside, tail wagging furiously.

◆ ABOVE
This dog shows a differently shaped eye, but still the gentle, relaxed expression.

◆ LEFT
The Cocker's job is to flush ground game for his handler; the tight body is essential for his bustling way of moving.

253

ENGLISH SPRINGER SPANIEL

The English Springer Spaniel gets his name from his ability to flush birds rapidly into the air or "spring" them. A handsome dog, relatively tall for a spaniel at 51 cm (20 in), he covers much ground at a galloping pace. His coat is close and weather-resistant, and he is either liver and white or black and white. It is not hard to groom him as long as the hair round his ears is kept fairly trim.

He enjoys his food but is not greedy. He is a compulsive worker, apparently absolutely tireless. As a household companion he is similarly minded, expecting walks in either town or country, and he reckons that those walks should not be a mere stroll down to the shops. He is capable of learning all manner of games, preferably those requiring him to retrieve a ball – endlessly!

BREED BOX

Size	small-medium 51 cm (20 in) dog: 21.5 kg (47½ lb) bitch: 19 kg (42 lb)
Grooming	reasonable
Exercise	demanding
Feeding	medium
Temperament	friendly and biddable

◆ LEFT
The thoroughly balanced shape of the Springer means he moves rapidly and easily.

◆ LEFT
The Springer has a charm that he is quite capable of using to his own ends.

FIELD SPANIEL

The Field Spaniel from England is easy to mistake for a Cocker with an over-long back. He stands around 46 cm (18 in) at the withers, and although he does come in black, liver or roan, the majority are a very definite liver colour. His coat is long, glossy and needs regular attention, especially around the ears.

He is a noble-looking dog, described as having rather grave eyes in his official Standard, and that is a reasonable description. He is active and biddable, making a worthy companion as a country dog, whether working or simply as a member of a household. He does not demand unreasonable quantities of food and deserves greater popularity.

◆ BELOW
Several breeds of dog are liver coloured – this one shows that gleaming colour at its best.

◆ LEFT
The Field Spaniel is a dog for the country-dwelling family – steady and trainable.

BREED BOX

Size	small 46 cm (18 in), 18–25 kg (39½–55 lb)
Grooming	reasonable
Exercise	medium
Feeding	small
Temperament	active and independent

WEIMARANER

◆ LEFT
The rare long-haired
Weimaraner: note
the undocked tail.

The Weimaraner is an outstanding dog. He stands tall in the gundog group at 69 cm (27 in). A highly unusual colour, the Weimaraner is nicknamed the Grey Ghost though the grey can be slightly mousy rather than the silver-grey that experts crave. Possibly his most outstanding feature are his eyes, which can be either amber or blue in colour.

This is another HPR breed originating on the European mainland. His coat is short, smooth and sleek, although there is a rare version which sports a longer coat. In the more unusual coat he is no problem to groom – it is more a matter of polishing! Even when he spends a long day in the shooting field or on a country stroll through winter mud, he does not bring the outside world into his home.

The Weimaraner is not a big feeder, although he appreciates and needs a generously filled bowl on a cold winter's day. He does need exercise, because he has a temperament that requires plenty to occupy his very active mind. He can be trained fairly easily but does not suffer fools gladly.

He has a friendly attitude to people but will act as an impressive guard if his home or his family are threatened. He is not a fawning, easy-going type of dog, even if he comes from a group that appears generally placid.

◆ BELOW
The truly stylish Grey Ghost is built on racy lines, but with the stamina and turn of speed which emulates the thoroughbred stayer of the horse world.

◆ LEFT
The Weimaraner's piercing eyes are a distinctive feature. Normally shades of amber or blue-grey, they may appear black when dilated with excitement.

BREED BOX	
Size	medium-large dog: 61–69 cm (24–27 in), 27 kg (59½ lb) bitch: 56–64 cm (22–25 in), 22.5 kg (49½ lb)
Grooming	easy
Exercise	demanding
Feeding	medium
Temperament	fearless and friendly

SHIH TZU

The Shih Tzu (Toy Group) originated in China. He has a host of admirers who greatly appreciate his wide-eyed expression and his distinctly cavalier attitude to the world about him. He views that world from a fairly small frame which is only some 26.5 cm (10½ in) high, but he gives the

◆ BELOW
Shih Tzus are sturdy, bouncy extroverts that make delightful family companions.

◆ ABOVE
The golden head typifies a breed that is totally convinced of its superiority.

impression of mental superiority in no uncertain terms.

He has a long, dense coat, which rewards hard work and gets distinctly ragged if neglected. He comes in a

glorious variety of colours, often with a white blaze to his forehead, and he carries his high-set tail like a banner over his back. He definitely enjoys being part of the family, but does not suggest that he is anxious to partake in long, muddy tramps across the fields. He takes a fair deal of cleaning up if he does feel an urge towards outdoor forays in mid-winter.

BREED BOX	
Size	small
	dog: 26.5 cm (10½ in)
	bitch: 23 cm (9 in)
	4.5–7.5 kg
	(10–16½ lb)
Grooming	demanding
Exercise	reasonable
Feeding	reasonable
Temperament	friendly and
	independent

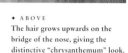

◆ ABOVE
The hair grows upwards on the bridge of the nose, giving the distinctive "chrysanthemum" look.

◆ LEFT
This beautiful coat gives a very good idea of the work involved in grooming a Shih Tzu to show standard.

DALMATIAN

The Dalmatian is as distinctive a breed as any. With his white base colour and plethora of spots, either black or liver, all over his head, body and limbs, he is the original "spotted dog". He has been known in Britain for well over a century and was originally used as a carriage dog; he has a penchant for

running between the wheels, quite undaunted by the close proximity of flashing hooves. In the US he was used to control the horses that pulled fire appliances and is still a well-known fire house mascot.

The Dalmatian is a handsome dog up to 61 cm (24 in) in Britain, 58.5 cm (23 in) in the US. He could

not be more friendly to people. He lives to a ripe old age and never seems to slow down. He loves running and needs plenty of exercise, so owners need to be fit. His coat, being short, is no problem to groom, and in spite of his size he does not overeat.

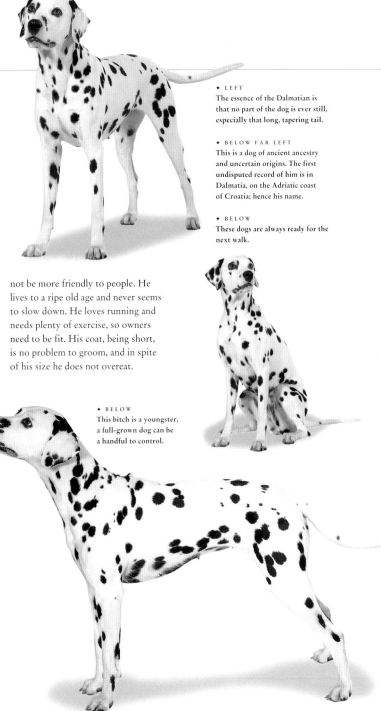

♦ LEFT
The essence of the Dalmatian is that no part of the dog is ever still, especially that long, tapering tail.

♦ BELOW FAR LEFT
This is a dog of ancient ancestry and uncertain origins. The first undisputed record of him is in Dalmatia, on the Adriatic coast of Croatia; hence his name.

♦ BELOW
These dogs are always ready for the next walk.

♦ BELOW
This bitch is a youngster, a full-grown dog can be a handful to control.

BREED BOX	
Size	large
	dog: 58.5–61 cm
	(23–24 in),
	27 kg (60 lb)
	bitch: 56–58.5 cm
	(22–23 in),
	25 kg (55 lb)
Grooming	easy
Exercise	demanding
Feeding	medium
Temperament	outgoing and
	friendly

AIREDALE TERRIER

The Airedale, from northern England, is the largest, by some degree, of the terriers. He is a splendid fellow, with a genuine style about him that entitles him to his nickname, King of the Terriers. He stands as tall as 61 cm (24 in) and has a head with an expression suggesting total command of any situation.

The Airedale is somewhat less aggressive towards other dogs than some breeds in the group, but will not companion and not a show-dog.

He makes a very good guard dog as he considers that his owner's property is his to look after. He has a loud voice that can be very convincing to any intruder. He is not a greedy feeder, but at the same time he is a well-built dog and naturally needs an adequate supply of nutrition.

BREED BOX	
Size	medium
	21.5 kg (47½ lb)
	dog: 58–61 cm
	(23–24 in)
	bitch: 56–59cm
	(22–23 in)
Grooming	medium
Exercise	reasonable
Feeding	medium
Temperament	friendly and
	courageous

back down if challenged. Few would dare! He is reputed to be intelligent but can be stubborn unless handled in a firm manner.

He has a black saddle and the rest of him is mostly tan; the tan can be a gloriously rich colour. His coat is harsh and dense and grows impressively but can be kept tidy with regular brushing. He sheds his coat twice a year, and at such times it is good for him to be trimmed or stripped by a professional. The experts will frown on the use of clippers, but it can be an alternative if he is destined to be a household

◆ ABOVE LEFT
The Airedale greets
friends with a
laughing expression
on an impressively
bearded face.

◆ LEFT
This splendidly
elegant mature dog is
ready to stand up to
monster rat or
human intruder
alike. Although
unable to go to
ground, the Airedale
displays all other
terrier characteristics
in abundance.

WEST HIGHLAND WHITE TERRIER

The West Highland White Terrier, or
"Westie", has pushed his way steadily up
the popularity charts, and this is no
wonder; he is a handy size to pick up and
carry when necessity requires it; he has an
outgoing manner; he loves people and,
though he will not buckle under when
challenged, he does not go out of his way
to pick a quarrel with other dogs.

He stands a mere 28 cm (11 in) at the
withers, but he packs a great deal of spirit
into his small frame. He is not as stocky as
the Scottish Terrier. As his name implies,
the Westie's coat is white and can get dirty
very easily; he therefore needs a regular
bath or a form of dry-cleaning with the
use of chalk. The coat is also harsh and
recovers its quality surprisingly quickly
after a shampoo, but Westies do need a
trim every now and then to keep them
looking neat.

He will use his sharp voice to warn off
strangers and so is a good guard. He
makes a great family friend or a
companion *par excellence* for someone
living on their own.

BREED BOX

Size	small
	28 cm (11 in)
	dog: 8.5 kg (19 lb)
	bitch: 7.5 kg
	(16½ lb)
Grooming	medium
Exercise	undemanding
Feeding	easy
Temperament	active and friendly

+ ABOVE
The Westie shares common ancestry with the
Cairn. They were selectively bred to the white
by the Malcolm family of Poltalloch in
Argyleshire, Scotland.

+ BELOW
The Westie has a merry expression and loves
company and attention. A devoted family
member, his small size will not prevent him
from protecting hearth and home.

+ LEFT
The various
predecessors of today's
Westies were known as
Poltalloch, Roseneath,
White Scottish and
Little Skye. These were
merged under one
name, the West
Highland White
Terrier, in 1904.

STAFFORDSHIRE BULL TERRIER

◆ RIGHT
This solid boned and well-muscled dog was originally bred for fighting and ratting.

The Staffordshire Bull Terrier is not just a breed; it is a cult. The devotees of this smooth shiny-coated dog from central England often appear to be blind to the existence of any other sort. The breed is renowned for its courage, and certainly if any dog would be willing to defend owner and house to the death, this is the one. All he asks in return is adequate rations and a lot of love.

Officially the Staffie measures up to 41 cm (16 in) tall, but many bigger dogs are seen. His head is fairly big without being exaggerated. He views life as if it is entirely for his benefit. His body is built on the lines of a muscled midget, and he walks with a swagger – for prodigious distances

if invited. He can be groomed in a minute, not only because he is short-coated but brimming with vitality into the bargain. He comes in red, fawn, black or brindle with varying amounts of white. The colours can be predominantly in patches, sometimes over his eyes.

◆ FAR LEFT
The power of the Staffie should never be underestimated. In the company of other dogs or animals, the Staffordshire Bull Terrier may need to be carefully controlled.

◆ BELOW
The Staffordshire Bull Terrier is a loyal and affectionate breed, with an ever-increasing following.

BREED BOX

Size	small–medium dog: 35.5–41 cm (14–16 in), 12.5–17 kg (27½–37½ lb) bitch: 35.5 cm (14 in), 11–15.5 kg (24–34 lb)
Grooming	easy
Exercise	medium
Feeding	medium
Temperament	fearless, dependable

GERMAN SHEPHERD DOG (ALSATIAN)

The German Shepherd Dog (Herding Group) must be the best known breed of them all. His breeding and training have led to his renown as a herding sheepdog, a leader of the blind and as a police dog. Police forces, the armed services, prison officers, drug officers and private protection agencies all over the world employ the GSD.

There are considerable variations in what is regarded as the ideal shape for this multi-purpose dog. Traditionally, the dog is a proud, powerful creature, standing an average 63 cm (25 in), with a body length slightly greater than its height. Coat lengths vary; some enthusiasts state that a medium length coat is the only acceptable version, while others accept a long-haired type. Colours include black, black and tan, and sable. White and cream dogs do occur, but raise loud, horrified protests from many aficionados, something to bear in mind if the ultimate intention is to show the dog. All such matters of taste aside, the fact remains that, at his best, the GSD is an intelligent, trainable dog with a pleasant, loyal disposition and makes a first-class household member. He needs exercise and, on occasion, may need to be stimulated in that direction as he can be wilfully idle. On the other hand, most need to have their energies directed into useful pursuits as the GSD, in common with so many breeds in the Working Group, originated as a shepherd dog.

BREED BOX	
Size	large
	dog: 60–66 cm
	(24–26 in), 36.5 kg
	(80½ lb)
	bitch: 55–60 cm
	(22–24 in),
	29.5 kg (65 lb)
Grooming	medium
Exercise	demanding
Feeding	medium
Temperament	steady, highly
	trainable

◆ TOP RIGHT
The eyes show the breed's intelligence – the GSD does not miss a trick.

◆ RIGHT
A handsome all-purpose dog that enjoys walking.

DOBERMANN

◆ LEFT
Well controlled, the Dobermann is as good
a guard dog as any.

The Dobermann (still known in
the US as the Doberman Pinscher)
originates from Germany and is
a tough, fast-moving guard dog.
He was bred selectively by Herr
Louis Dobermann as an all-purpose
tracking/police dog. He is built on
clean, powerful lines and reaches
ideally 69 cm (27 in) at the withers.

His short, close-lying coat responds
to polishing with a true gleam. He
is most commonly seen as black,
with tan colouring on the muzzle,
forechest, legs and feet; but the black
can be replaced by red or blue, or
even, more rarely, with fawn.

He is energy personified, and at
one time had a reputation for being
bad-tempered. Careful, sensible
selection and training has altered this
to a very large extent, but he is still a
dog that needs to know who is going
to be the boss in any family or work-
place. As a house-dog, he ranks with
any breed for faithful performance. He
demands exercise as a right and needs
a sizeable amount of food as a result.

◆ RIGHT
A soft expression is the result of leaving
the ears uncropped, as in the UK.

◆ RIGHT
This elegant and powerful breed has an
enormous following throughout the world
but frightens some people.

BREED BOX

Size	large
	dog: 69 cm (27½ in), 37.5 kg (83 lb)
	bitch: 65 cm (25½ in), 33 kg (73 lb)
Grooming	simple
Exercise	demanding
Feeding	medium–demanding
Temperament	alert and biddable

BORDER COLLIE

The Border Collie (Herding Group) is the classic farm dog. He is neat; he is agile; he thinks on his feet, and if his owner does not occupy his mind with useful training he will get into mischief, because his brain is always active.

Ideally he stands some 53 cm (21 in) at his withers, though he may look lower to ground as he travels at speed in a form of permanent crouch. His eyes show keen

intelligence and his type is the favourite for those who wish to compete at top level in obedience competitions.

His coat is usually moderately long but is relatively easy to groom as long as the tangles are dealt with on a regular basis. He comes in all kinds of colours with white, but the commonest base colour is black. He demands exercise for his muscles just as much as for his brain. He makes an ideal family dog for the grown family, but he is not best suited to be a nursemaid to the very young, though no doubt such heresy will raise a few protests.

To put it bluntly, he does not suffer fools gladly, and he is not averse to taking a swift nip at those who do not get his point, in the same way that he will liven the reactions of the sheep or cattle which are his natural flock.

✦ LEFT
This is the sharp expression of what is, by common consent, the most trainable breed of them all.

✦ BELOW
Working dogs from the Scottish borders, this is a breed that needs to be constantly occupied if destructive behaviour is to be avoided.

✦ LEFT
The low-slung body of the Border Collie is essential for his super-agile performance at work.

BREED BOX

Size	small–medium dog: 53 cm (21 in), 23.5 kg (52 lb) bitch: 51 cm (20 in), 19 kg (42 lb)
Grooming	medium
Exercise	demanding
Feeding	medium
Temperament	very alert and trainable

CAVALIER KING CHARLES SPANIEL

◆ LEFT
A neat breed, ideal for anyone who wants an active and cheerful companion.

The Cavalier King Charles Spaniel (the Cavalier) is a popular Toy dog with everyone. Built on the lines of a small gundog, he has a charm for the elderly as well as the young family. He seems to love people and he does not find fault with other dogs.

His weight range is 5.5–8 kg (12–18 lb), which is a wide enough range, but as a breed they do tend to get even heavier. The Cavalier's placid nature and friendliness often induces people to give him injudicious titbits that encourage obesity!

He has a good-looking head and a well-balanced body. He can appear in a series of colours, from ruby (red), black and tan, and tricolour (black and white with tan markings) to Blenheim, which is a mix of rich chestnut and white, often with a lozenge of chestnut in the centre of a white patch down the middle of his head.

He enjoys exercise and is built on elegant, athletic lines; indeed, he needs it in view of his hearty appetite. He is not difficult to groom as his coat can be kept tidy with normal brush-and-comb techniques; a true favourite.

◆ BELOW
The charm of the Cavalier's expression is beautifully caught in this head-study.

BREED BOX

Size	small
	32 cm (13 in),
	5.5–8 kg (12–18 lb)
Grooming	medium
Exercise	medium
Feeding	medium
Temperament	very friendly

◆ BELOW
The Cavalier is in fact a miniature spaniel, combining all the qualities of a Toy and a Gundog.

YORKSHIRE TERRIER

The Yorkshire Terrier is a breed of
two distinct types. The tiny dog, seen
immaculately groomed in the show-ring,
weighs up to 3.1 kg (7 lb). The jaunty
dog seen on a lead in the street or racing
joyfully around the park is the same dog,
but often twice the size. The fact is that
the long steel blue and bright tan hair that
bedecks the glamour star of the shows
would break off short if he ran loose.
But the spirit of the true Yorkshire tyke
is the same inside whatever the outward
appearance.

♦ ABOVE
This Yorkie is groomed to perfection as befits
a top dog.

Grooming the household
companion, a dog that is immensely
popular throughout the world, is
easily accomplished with ordinary
skills. As a home-loving animal, the
Yorkie is tough, ready to play with the
children or dispatch any rat unwise
enough to invade his owner's dwelling.

♦ ABOVE
Companion Yorkies wear their coats
shorter than these show dogs and do not
require the same amount of artistry.

BREED BOX	
Size	very small maximum 3.1 kg (7 lb) dog: 20.5 cm (8 in) bitch: 18 cm (7 in)
Grooming	demanding
Exercise	medium
Feeding	undemanding
Temperament	alert and intelligent

♦ RIGHT
This elegant display shows canine
grooming at its most spectacular.

SMALL MAMMALS

The vast majority of small mammals that are popular as pets belong to the rodent family. The word "rodent" comes from the Latin word *rodere*, meaning "to gnaw", and describes the very sharp pair of chisel-shaped incisor teeth found in each jaw right at the front of the mouth. The shape and strength of these teeth is crucial to the survival of rodents as they enable them to crack seeds and nuts easily. Unlike our teeth, they continue growing throughout the rodent's life. This is essential to stop them from wearing down, which would prevent the rodent from eating.

Rabbits are not actually rodents, but are grouped instead with hares and pikas in a separate family known as lagomorphs. However, the structure of their teeth is very similar to that of rodents, except that they have a further tiny set of incisors each side of the main teeth at the front of the mouth.

Most rodents are relatively small in size, which makes them vulnerable to larger predators. As a result, they have keen senses to help them avoid detection. Their hearing is very acute, and they often communicate with each other using ultrasonic calls, which we are unable to hear because the frequencies are too high for our ears. They also have a very keen sense of smell. However, rodents generally have poor vision, since they spend much of their time hidden away in burrows during the day, emerging to forage for food at night.

♦ OPPOSITE
Guinea pigs are friendly rodents and they make excellent pets. They are suitable for housing either in outdoor accommodation or indoors in the home.

♦ LEFT
Rabbits come in a wide variety of sizes and colours. They are easy to care for, and an increasing number of owners are now keeping rabbits as indoor companions.

RABBITS

The rabbit is the most popular of all the small mammals kept as pets, thanks in part to its friendly nature. An ever-increasing range of breeds and colour varieties, many of which are likely to be on view at shows, has served to enhance their appeal both to breeders and pet-seekers. Rabbits have also proved to be very adaptable pets, with individuals settling well either in an outdoor hutch or as house-rabbits in the home.

INTRODUCTION

There are 25 different species of wild rabbit found around the world, but the ancestor of all today's domestic breeds is the Old World rabbit (*Oryctolagus cuniculus*), which was originally found in the Mediterranean region. At first, rabbits were kept as a source of food, in large outdoor enclosures. It is unclear when they were first brought to northern Europe; they may have been originally introduced by the invading Roman armies, but there is no evidence of an established wild population until after 1066.

Rabbits were originally valued for their fur and as a source of meat, and it was not until the late 1800s that they became popular with breeders as pets. By this stage, a number of the distinctive varieties were already established and, as a legacy from this era, the breeds today are often classified on the basis of fur or fancy, with the former group featuring those

which were originally kept for food. The advent of the killer viral disease myxomatosis in the 1950s altered the public's attitude to rabbit meat,

however, as the sight of sick and dying rabbits in the wild was very distressing.

As a result of changing perceptions, the rabbit has evolved into the most popular of all small animal pets, due to its friendly nature and attractive appearance. There are now more than 200 breeds in existence, some of which are very rare, while others are still being developed. One of the latest to be added to this list is the lionhead, a relatively small rabbit with a lion-like mane on its head. Unfortunately, some breeds have also become extinct, such as the angevin, which was the largest breed of rabbit ever known. Individuals were said to have a leg span of nearly 1.2 m (4 ft), and could weigh as much as 15 kg (33 lb).

Most breeds are short-coated, although the angora, which has been kept for centuries for its wool, is long-coated and needs special care to prevent its coat from becoming matted. Any rabbit that has an angora breed in its ancestry, such as the cashmere lop, must be groomed on a daily basis. Most other rabbits, however, do not need much grooming.

RABBITS AS PETS

All breeds of rabbit make appealing pets, although it is not a good idea to buy an adult rabbit without knowing its age. Start out with a youngster that is approximately nine or ten weeks old. At this age, the rabbit is fully

♦ ABOVE AND LEFT
The European wild rabbit, from which all of today's domestic breeds and varieties have been created. Domestication of the rabbit began thousands of years ago.

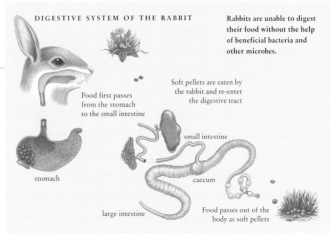

DIGESTIVE SYSTEM OF THE RABBIT

Rabbits are unable to digest their food without the help of beneficial bacteria and other microbes.

Food first passes from the stomach to the small intestine

Soft pellets are eaten by the rabbit and re-enter the digestive tract

small intestine

stomach

caecum

large intestine

Food passes out of the body as soft pellets

independent, but is still young enough to be tamed readily. Older rabbits that are not used to being handled are likely to be nervous and may never settle as pets. A rabbit will usually live for between six and eight years.

If, however, you are hoping to breed from your rabbit for show purposes, you will need to acquire older rabbits, although it may be better to start out with youngsters and wait for them to mature. It is generally better to start out with a doe (female) if you intend to breed rabbits for shows because, if necessary, you can arrange for her to be mated with

someone else's buck (male). However, most breeders are not keen to part with their best does.

Before buying any rabbit, always check its condition. The ears should be clean and clear of scabs, which can indicate an ear mite infestation. The eyes should be free from discharge, as should the nose. It is also important to part the lips so you can check the incisor teeth. If these are misaligned, you will have to have them trimmed back regularly throughout the rabbit's life. Check that the claws are not overgrown and that there are no sore patches on the underside of the hind legs. It is important to make sure that there is no sign of staining on the fur surrounding the vent, as this can indicate a digestive upset, which can be serious.

♦ ABOVE LEFT
Rabbits in the wild are very alert, since they face many dangers. The position of their eyes helps them to see well, while their tall ears detect and pinpoint the source of sounds accurately.

♦ BELOW
It is vital to consider size when choosing a rabbit. The larger breeds, such as the British giant, shown here with a Netherland dwarf, may be too big for younger children to handle easily.

♦ ABOVE
The sharp incisor teeth allow the rabbit to nibble plant matter, which is then ground up by molar teeth further back in the mouth.

A SELECTION OF SMALLER BREEDS

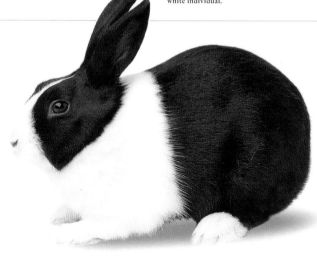

Rabbits today vary in size from the Flemish giant, which can tip the scales at 10 kg (22 lb), down to the tiny Netherland dwarf, which typically weighs about 900 g (2 lb). It is not just a matter of size, however, because breeds do differ significantly in temperament, and it is important to bear this in mind, especially if you are choosing a pet for a child. While the bigger breeds are generally placid, their size can make them difficult for a child to handle safely, and since rabbits are very susceptible to injury through falls, it is a better idea to choose a smaller breed for younger owners.

THE DUTCH

Although not as small as today's dwarf breeds, the Dutch, which weighs up to 2.5 kg (5½ lb), has long been a popular choice with rabbit enthusiasts. While pet owners enjoy its friendly nature, exhibitors are challenged by its highly distinctive coat markings.

The Dutch has a broad white area of fur encircling the front of the body, a half-coloured rear and white feet. The head and ears are coloured, with a distinctive white blaze extending down over the nose to the jaws. Dutch rabbits are currently bred in eight

◆ BELOW
The English rabbit is also known as the English butterfly because the dark fur around its nose resembles a butterfly's wings.

colours. The dark shades, such as black or blue, are generally preferred to lighter shades, such as yellow. Rabbits with good fur markings can be identified while still hairless newborns, as the white areas can be recognized by their lighter pink skin coloration.

THE ENGLISH

The ever-popular English is the oldest of the fancy breeds, dating back as far as the early 1800s. It has a dark stripe running down its back to the base of the tail, with a variable pattern of spots on its sides, particularly on the hindquarters. There are several varieties, including black, blue and chocolate, plus a tortoiseshell. The ears are dark, as is the muzzle, with an area of dark fur usually encircling the eyes. The English is friendly, and the does usually make good mothers.

THE NETHERLAND DWARF

The breed known as the Netherland dwarf, which evolved from the Polish breed during the late 1800s, did not

THE REX

The smooth, soft, sleek coat of the rex rabbit meant that it was originally very popular with furriers, but today, the rex has become a common sight at rabbit shows, and is now bred in a large range of colours and markings. The mini rex is a smaller version of the rex itself and, at only half its weight, tips the scales at up to 1.8 kg (4 lb). The rex's thin coat means that it needs snug winter quarters in temperate climates. Make sure that these rabbits have sufficient bedding on the floor of their hutch; the fur below the hocks on the hind legs may otherwise become thin, and this can be the cause of recurring soreness, which can prove troublesome to both you and your rabbit over the course of its lifetime.

♦ LEFT
When deciding to buy a Netherland dwarf, inspect the teeth very carefully; these rabbits are vulnerable to malocclusion, and this will be a lifelong problem.

♦ BELOW
A fawn dwarf lop. Unlike some of the bigger lops, its ears are relatively short. The breed's friendly nature has made it very popular.

♦ BOTTOM
The fur of rex rabbits is short with a velvety feel as these rabbits lack the longer, coarse guard hairs seen in other breeds.

become well known until the 1950s. In some parts of Europe it is known as the dwarf Polish.

The Netherland dwarf is the smallest of today's breeds. Now available in a huge range of colours, this breed has a characteristic compact nose and short ears. The breed is perhaps not always as friendly as others of a similar size.

DWARF LOP

This breed has grown in popularity over recent years, thanks to its gentle disposition. The appeal of the dwarf lop has been enhanced by its floppy ears, which hang down the sides of its head but do not touch the ground. The dwarf lop is a scaled-down version of the larger French lop, and was created during the 1950s in the Netherlands. Young dwarf lops are born with upright ears that start to trail down as they grow older. In turn, they have been bred to create the even smaller mini lop, which was first recognized for show purposes in 1994.

A SELECTION OF LARGER BREEDS

With the growing interest in keeping rabbits in the home, larger breeds have become very popular, and they can be given plenty of space to roam. Some of these rabbits are larger and heavier in size that a small dog. As an example, the British giant, closely-related to the Flemish giant, weighs up to 6.1 kg (15 lb). The breed originated from stock kept as long ago as the 1500s around the city of Ghent in Belgium.

FLEMISH GIANT
The traditional colour of the Flemish giant is steel grey, and it was the refusal of the British show authorities

♦ ABOVE
Large breeds of rabbit like this British giant are back in fashion, thanks to growing interest in keeping house-rabbits. The British giant is ideal for this purpose, but can be rather large for a small child to handle.

♦ LEFT
A white New Zealand rabbit. This breed is characterized partly by its relatively coarse, shaggy coat as well as its pink eyes. These rabbits have a steady temperament and make good pets.

to recognize this breed in other colours that originally triggered the development of the British giant strain in the 1930s. The Flemish giant is still better known internationally, and is also slightly heavier, averaging 7–8 kg (15½–17½ lb). These large rabbits are known to be friendly, with calm temperaments. As house-rabbits they will settle quickly into a domestic lifestyle, and can be trained to use a litter tray from an early age. Although the typical agouti-patterned form, resembling that of the wild rabbit, is commonly seen, a range of colours from pure white through to blue and black is available as well.

NEW ZEALAND VARIETIES
Several varieties of rabbit have their origins in New Zealand. The original white variety was created as a meat breed. It has a well-muscled body and relatively short ears, typically weighing up to 5.4 kg (12 lb). These rabbits grow very quickly and are capable of reaching almost half their adult weight by just ten weeks of age. They are

◆ BELOW
The similarity to a true hare can be seen in this
Belgian hare, although it is a pure rabbit breed.
These rabbits became immensely popular in the
United States in the early 20th century.

an attractive silky texture, with
individual hairs that are over 2.5 cm
(1 in) long. The traditional colour is a
pale shade of lavender. The black form
was developed in 1919, followed by
albinos and dark-eyed whites, and then
the brown. One of the most recent
additions to this group of friendly
rabbits is the lilac, created during the
1980s. Recognizable by its white body
and dark markings on the extremities,
it is now becoming more common.

◆ BELOW
The Beveren has now been developed in a range
of colours, but the attractive lavender variety,
seen here, is the traditional form of the breed.

pure white in colour, with the pink
eyes that confirm they are true
albinos. Since the 1960s, two more
colour forms have been developed –
a black and a blue variety, both of
which resemble the New Zealand in all
respects apart from their coloration.
Like the white New Zealand, the blue
and black varieties are docile and
placid. There is also a smaller breed
called the New Zealand red, which
has been developed in America. It is
thought to be descended from crosses
between Flemish giants and Belgian
hares carried out in the early 1900s.

BELGIAN HARE
This slim, athletic, long-legged
Belgian breed resembles a hare, but
is nevertheless a rabbit. Its highly
distinctive appearance caused a stir
when it was first developed at the end
of the 19th century. Early attempts at
cross-breeding rabbits with hares

always proved futile, which
confirms that the Belgian hare
is in fact a pure rabbit.
The coat is a deep
chestnut colour
with black
shading. The
long body means
that it requires a
tall hutch, to enable
it to sit up on its
hindquarters. It is active by
nature, and this, coupled
with its sleek appearance,
makes it an attractive choice
for a pet.

BEVEREN
The rabbit known as the Beveren
also originates from Belgium, and was
developed during the 1890s. Today, the
breed is large, typically weighing up
to 4.5 kg (10 lb), and has a distinctive
mandolin-shaped body. The coat has

HOUSING IN THE GARDEN

◆ BELOW
Mount the hutch on legs to ensure the base remains dry and to keep wild rabbits away from your pet. Secure door fastenings are essential to protect against foxes and other predators.

Rabbits can be kept outdoors throughout the year, although they must have a snug, draught-proof area to retreat to when the weather is bad. As rabbits need to feel secure, the hutch should be divided into two connecting sections, one with a solid door, the other with a front made of wire mesh. Many pet shops sell hutches, or alternatively you can build one yourself. When choosing a hutch, make sure that it is high enough for the rabbit to be able to sit up to its full height and stand without difficulty. Ideally, the hutch is connected directly to a run, which allows your rabbit to run around and exercise freely without the need for supervision.

Position the rabbit hutch in a sheltered spot, out of the direction of prevailing winds. Avoid an area beneath trees, as branches may break off and damage the hutch. The run may extend off one of the sides or from the back of the hutch, with a broad, gently sloping ladder giving easy access in to and out of it. A door, which can be securely closed (and preferably locked), should always be incorporated into the hutch design.

If you decide to make your own hutch, choose good materials. Thick plywood should be used for the covered part, with good quality roofing felt providing a barrier on top to keep the interior dry. Place sliding trays inside to make cleaning easier. Put these in the rabbit's sleeping quarters and cover them with a layer of coarse shavings, with hay on top.

The run needs to have wire on its underside, unless it is placed on concrete slabs, such as a patio. This will prevent your rabbit from tunnelling out, or a predator, such as a fox, from getting in. Especially if the run is not connected to the hutch, place it in the shade: rabbits exposed to hot sun can die rapidly from heat stroke. Incorporate a sheltered area in the run to be safe.

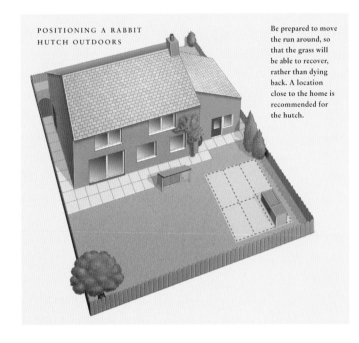

POSITIONING A RABBIT HUTCH OUTDOORS

Be prepared to move the run around, so that the grass will be able to recover, rather than dying back. A location close to the home is recommended for the hutch.

CONSTRUCTING A RABBIT RUN

1 Building your own run for your rabbit can be cheaper than buying one, yet you will get a run of better quality. Start by preparing all the different components.

2 Power tools have greatly simplified the construction process, making it an easy task to prepare holes for the scews used to hold the run together.

3 A different fitment on the power tool will enable you to use it as a screwdriver, having drilled the holes first. Use stainless steel screws, which will not rust.

4 For some parts of the run, the timber will be better fixed together with nails. Always provide good support when nailing lengths of timber together.

5 When fixing the mesh on to the framework, use special netting staples for the purpose. Trim back any sharp ends of mesh, which could otherwise injure your rabbit.

6 Weatherproofing is essential, but it is safer to treat only the outer surfaces, where your rabbit will not gnaw the woodwork, to avoid any risk of poisoning.

7 Position the sides together carefully before drilling fixing holes, because any mistakes at this stage will be hard to rectify. You may want to use a clamp.

8 The run is now partially assembled, with just the other side section to fit into place. This will then anchor the structure together firmly.

9 Easy access to the run, so you can catch the rabbit without it being able to slip past you, is vital. Provide access by constructing doors in one of the sides.

10 If the run is to sit on grass rather than a solid base, cover the floor with mesh. Attach this along one edge and keep it taut.

11 Finally, fix bolts on to the doors. These should be well oiled to prevent them sticking and rusting up in the future.

12 *(right)* The completed run. This design provides sufficient height so that the rabbit can sit up on its hindquarters, and incorporates a dry retreat if the weather turns bad.

HOUSING IN THE HOME

◆ BELOW
It is possible to keep more than one house-rabbit together. Neutering for behavioural reasons is usually recommended in any event, and this will also prevent unwanted offspring.

House-rabbits have become very fashionable pets in recent years. One reason may be that, unlike cats and dogs, they do not require exercise outside and so they are ideal for city-dwellers. They can also be trained to use a litter tray. Most house-rabbit owners keep their pet in its hutch when they are out, and then allow it to run around the house when they are at home. This will help to prevent accidents, although some adjustments in the home will still be necessary.

PREPARING YOUR HOME

If you decide to keep a house-rabbit, you will need to follow a few practical safety measures in the home. A stair guard will be essential to protect the rabbit from accidents. You will also need to hide any exposed electrical cables, as a rabbit is more than likely to gnaw them. If you see your rabbit with a live cable in its mouth, switch off the power supply at the wall and disconnect the cable immediately. If the cable shows signs of damage, it will need to be replaced. Discourage the rabbit from nibbling at furniture and carpet by providing special rabbit chews. Ingested carpet fibres can cause a fatal intestinal obstruction if they are swallowed by the rabbit.

INDOOR HOUSING

Specially designed hutches are now available for rabbits living indoors. It is a good idea to fit a pen around the hutch for extra safety, and to keep your rabbit in its hutch or pen when you are out. Although it may seem appropriate to place the hutch and run

◆ ABOVE
A house-rabbit can prove to be as affectionate as a dog or cat in the home, and may be trained with surprising ease. The main problem is likely to be the rabbit's enthusiasm for nibbling.

◆ LEFT
Special indoor housing systems are available for house-rabbits, with this type of design giving your pet a clear view of its surroundings. An indoor hutch is another possibility.

in a conservatory or porch, bear in mind that the temperature here can rapidly rise to a fatal level for your rabbit on a hot day. Prepare the hutch in just the same way as outdoor accommodation. Do not forget to provide hay as this is an essential source of fibre in the rabbit's diet, and will lessen its inclination to chew at the carpets.

For house-training, choose a low-sided cat litter tray that gives the rabbit easy access, and use a lightweight litter. Scoop up some of the rabbit's droppings on to the litter, and then put the rabbit on the tray. It is often helpful to have a pen at this early stage as you can keep your pet confined here until it is trained in using the litter tray, and this will avoid any soiling around the home.

INDOOR SAFETY HAZARDS

Don't leave the doors to your home open, or your rabbit may run out.

Household plants can be dangerous for rabbits. Place them safely out of reach.

Rabbits like the warmth of the fire, but be sure they cannot singe their coats.

A kitchen is a very dangerous room for a rabbit, especially when you are cooking.

Keep electrical cables out of your rabbit's reach, disconnecting them if possible.

A washing machine can attract a rabbit, so keep the door firmly closed.

Furniture may be gnawed by your rabbit. Provide chews as a safe alternative.

FEEDING

Rabbits have an unusual digestive system, which means that they are susceptible to digestive upsets. This makes feeding your rabbit one of the most important aspects of its care.

DIGESTION

The rabbit's food will pass from the stomach to the small intestine and on to the caecum, a sac at the junction with the large intestine. Here, the rabbit does not have the enzymes needed to break down the cellulose present in plant cell walls, even though the bacteria in the caecum will break down the food. The absorption of nutrients takes place in the small intestine, and so in order to absorb cellulose the rabbit will pass the food out of its body, usually at night, in the form of soft pellets, and then consume them. This allows the nutrients to re-enter the digestive tract, passing to the small intestine, where they can be absorbed into the body.

Rabbit pellets

The most common digestive upset in rabbits is caused by a sudden change in diet. This means that the bacteria that play such a vital part in the rabbit's digestive process cannot adapt in time. Treatment with antibiotics is difficult because these drugs interfere with the functioning of the bacteria.

For this reason, it is essential to be aware of what food your new rabbit has been eating, and to keep to it for the first two or three weeks. Changes should be made gradually, with the new brand being introduced at the end

of the second week after the rabbit is rehomed. Mix the new food with the old, and increase the percentage of the new food over the next couple of weeks, to allow the rabbit's digestive system time to adjust to the change.

RABBIT FOODS

There are many different types of rabbit food on the market. Most mixes contain a variety of ingredients, such as cereals and pellets. Recent concerns over locust beans, which have been blamed for the death of some rabbits, have led to these being removed by some manufacturers. Check the labelling for the precise ingredients, and make a note of the "use-by" date for the vitamin and mineral content of the mix.

If your rabbit has not been used to fresh foods, introduce this carefully in small amounts. You can feed a rabbit a wide range of fresh foods, including dandelion, grass, carrots and cabbage.

◆ BELOW
A selection of food dishes and a water bottle. Food dishes chosen for rabbits must not be easy to tip over, or light enough to allow your pet to throw them around.

Rabbit mix

Bran mash

Vitamin supplement and mineral blocks

Always wash the food beforehand and make sure it is fresh. Many rabbits develop serious diarrhoea when they are first put in an outdoor run, because they are not used to eating grass. The consequences can be fatal, so it is important to acclimatize the rabbit to grass before it goes outside.

A rabbit that is fed a commercial formulated food is unlikely to need any supplements to its diet. Treats available from pet stores can be offered occasionally, but watch out for signs that your rabbit is overweight: pet rabbits can become obese, especially if they are fed a diet that is too concentrated. Aim to provide a balanced diet, matched to your pet's energy requirements. Rabbits kept outside need more food than those kept indoors. A neutered rabbit will also need less food.

Pet rabbits can be tamed to eat from the hand. Children need to be taught not to hold on to the food item for too long, however, because the rabbit will carry on nibbling and may then take a bite at their fingers.

✦ BELOW
A rabbit diet should consist of both fresh and dry foods. Make any dietary changes gradually to avoid digestive upsets.

Seed sticks

Rabbit biscuits

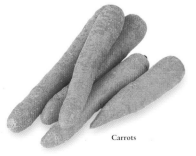

Carrots

Cabbage

Apples

GENERAL CARE

Rabbits can be nervous when they are first rehomed and it is important to get into the routine of picking up a young rabbit regularly so that it becomes accustomed to it. Always supervise a child attempting to pick up their pet for the first few weeks. Make sure that the child does not have bare arms as rabbits have sharp claws, which can cause painful scratches if they struggle. This applies especially in the case of young rabbits, whose claws are often especially needle-like. Although rabbits must never be picked up by their ears, holding these gently while supporting the body can quieten a rabbit that is proving difficult to restrain. Support the underside of the rabbit's body with one hand and use the other hand to hold its body, so that it will not leap

PICKING UP
A RABBIT
PROPERLY

1 *(left)* Gently restrain your rabbit by placing one hand on the side of its body and another under its hindquarters. Never pick a rabbit up by its ears.

2 *(left)* Then slide your hands under the body, providing support especially for the hindquarters.

◆ ABOVE
It helps to have a secure carrier so that you can move your rabbit safely from its hutch to the run.

out of your grasp. Once settled, rabbits rarely try to wriggle free, nor will they attempt to bite.

HYGIENE AND MAINTENANCE

You will need a suitable carrying container for your rabbit, particularly when you want to move it from its run back to its cage. Although you can use a strong cardboard box, a cat carrier will be more secure for longer journeys, such as trips to the vet.

Change the bedding in the rabbit's hutch at least once a week, and occasionally scrub out the hutch. Try to do this on a warm day, when the rabbit is in its run, which will allow the interior to dry quickly. You can use a special disinfectant recommended for this purpose. Check regularly on the back and undersides of the roof of the outdoor hutch for any leaks. A hole

◆ RIGHT
A large door forming part of the side of the run means that you will also be able to catch your rabbit easily when the time comes to return your pet to its hutch. The carrier itself will also be useful if you have to go to the vet.

in the roofing felt is the most likely reason, and this will need to be repaired before it becomes more serious. Do not treat the exterior woodwork of the hutch with a weather-proofing agent when the

rabbit is inside, as chemical fumes can be harmful. You should expect a well-maintained hutch to last for the rabbit's lifetime.

Gnawing of furniture and carpets can often be a problem inside the

house. Providing wooden blocks for your rabbit to gnaw on will help, or you can prepare dry crusts of wholemeal bread by roasting them in the oven. Allow the crusts to cool before offering them to your pet.

CLEANING OUT A RABBIT HUTCH

1 The hutch must be cleaned thoroughly at least once and possibly twice each week. A plastic dustpan and brush will be useful for this task, helping to remove the soiled bedding.

2 Having removed much of the soiled bedding, pull out the tray and tip the rest of the contents into a sack. This discarded material is ideal for composting.

3 When you decide to scrub out the interior, choose a sunny day when the rabbit is in its run, allowing the hutch to dry thoroughly before returning the rabbit here.

BREEDING

◆ BELOW
Young rabbits at three days of age. Note the
dark patches of skin which indicate that these
areas will have dark fur in due course. Avoid
any disturbance to the nest.

Rabbits have a justified reputation
for being prolific breeders, and it is
important not to let them breed
without having planned what you
are going to do with the offspring.

It is relatively straightforward to
sex rabbits once they are mature, from
about five months of age, when the
testes of the buck have descended into
the scrotum. Before this, a clear sign
will be that the gap between the anal
and genital openings will be longer in
the case of the buck, compared to the
doe. One of the reasons that rabbits
breed freely is that does do not have
a regular reproductive cycle resulting
in ovulation. They are unusual among
mammals, being "induced ovulators",
which means that it is the stimulus of

◆ BELOW
A Dutch rabbit with her young. In the case of
this pure-bred breed, the pattern of markings
is highly distinctive, with the white area on the
face being called a blaze.

mating which triggers the release of
eggs from the ovary. As a result, the
likelihood of fertilization occurring
is greatly increased.

It is not recommended to keep
bucks together as they can fight
viciously. Does are more likely to live
in harmony in spacious surroundings,
but it is not uncommon for bullying
to occur, with a doe proving to be
spiteful towards her companion.

MATING AND PREGNANCY

The larger breeds of rabbit can be
much slower to mature than their
smaller relatives. It may take up to
nine months for giant breeds to
become mature, which is twice as long
as it takes in the Dutch, dwarf or rex
breeds. The doe will be ready to mate
when the skin around her genitals
takes on a deep reddish hue, rather
than pink. At this stage, she can be
introduced to the buck, and mating is
likely to occur soon afterwards. It may
be better to leave the pair together for
a couple of days to be sure, and then
the doe can be transferred back to
her quarters.

Assuming that she is pregnant,
the doe will start to build a nest as
the time for giving birth approaches,
although in the first two weeks or
so, she will not appear to put on any
weight. This tends to occur towards
the end of pregnancy, and her mobility
is not unduly restricted in the early
stages. The doe will benefit from being
supplied with a kindling box, lined
with clean hay, where she can give
birth. Just beforehand, she will start
to pluck her fur to form a nest for her
offspring. Pregnancy in the rabbit lasts
approximately 31 days. Although as
many as 12 offspring may be born, a

typical litter comprises six to nine young, which are known as kittens. At birth, they have no hair, although dark fur markings, such as spots, will appear as blotches on the skin, which is otherwise pink. The kittens' ears are short in relation to their body size.

Development is rapid, with fur appearing after four days. The eyes open just over a week after birth. It is vital not to intrude into the nest, because your scent may cause the doe to abandon or even attack her offspring. A problem is most likely to be drawn to your attention by repeated calls from the young if they are not receiving enough food. The doe may be suffering inflammation of the mammary glands, known as mastitis, which will require urgent veterinary treatment.

HANDREARING

If you should have to handrear a litter of young rabbits, you will need to feed them on warm goat's milk, which is the nearest natural substitute to that of the doe. Use an eye dropper or a small syringe as a feeding tool, but always disinfect this between feeds. Unfortunately, the task of hand-rearing is made difficult by the fact that the doe transfers immunity to her offspring via her milk, and if this is denied to them, they are likely to succumb to minor infections. Young rabbits will normally be fully weaned at nine weeks.

◆ LEFT
A group of Dutch rabbits at 12 days old. Their ears are still quite short at this stage, compared with their bodies, which is a feature of all young rabbits.

◆ BELOW
By 30 days old, the young rabbits are starting to eat independently, and will soon be ready to be weaned. They can be tamed easily at this stage by being handled.

◆ ABOVE
Exhibition stock is usually rung in order to identify the rabbits individually. The ring on this rabbit cannot be removed without being cut off, as the leg will have grown too large.

◆ LEFT
The patterning of rabbits such as the Dutch does not vary as they grow older. These particular individuals are now 60 days old.

283

GROOMING AND SHOWING

Most rabbits need very little by way of coat care, but the angora, with its soft, long coat, needs daily grooming to prevent the coat from becoming tangled and matted. If left, mats will need be to cut out of the fur. Breeds derived from the angora require similar care. Use special grooming combs, which are sold for cats and dogs. These have rotating teeth that help to tease the fur apart, rather than pulling on the strands of hair.

During the summer months, it is vital to examine the underparts of a rabbit regularly for fur soiled through a digestive upset. If bluebottle flies lay eggs in or near the soiled fur, the maggots will bore into the body through the skin, releasing potentially fatal toxic compounds into the blood. A rabbit with fly strike, as this condition is known, will need urgent veterinary treatment to remove all the maggots and treat the infected area; otherwise, the rabbit will die. It may be necessary to keep the rabbit indoors until the infection has healed, to reduce the chance of it recurring.

◆ LEFT
The grooming requirements of individual breeds differ significantly, and this is a factor that you need to consider when choosing a rabbit. The angora, seen here, is a particularly demanding breed in terms of its grooming needs.

◆ LEFT
Considerable care has to be given to show rabbits like this angora, so that they look at their best when being judged. Competition at rabbit show events is invariably fierce.

◆ BELOW LEFT
The result of all that hard work – an immaculate angora rabbit. If it is not groomed, the fur quickly becomes matted.

CLAW CLIPPING

A pet rabbit's claws can become overgrown quite easily. This is especially dangerous for a rabbit that lives in the home as it can become caught up by its claws in upholstery or floor coverings. You can clip the claws back yourself, although a steady hand is needed, and this is not a job for young children. If in any doubt, your vet will be able to do it for you. You will need a proper pair of claw clippers, rather than ordinary scissors, which are likely to cause the nail to fray and split instead of cutting it cleanly off.

If clipping the claws yourself, first locate the blood supply to the claw, visible as a reddish streak. This may be difficult to detect in rabbits with dark claws, and if this is the case, you will need veterinary experience to prevent the claw from being cut too short and starting to bleed as a consequence. Should you see blood when you are clipping the claws at home, press a damp piece of clean cotton wool (cotton ball) to the wound.

SHOWING RABBITS

Rabbit shows at local and regional level are listed in newspapers and specialist publications and, if you are interested in one particular variety of rabbits, there may be a breed club that you can join as well. Rabbits are rung for exhibition purposes at about two months of age, before the ankle joint becomes too big for the ring to pass over it. Rings are produced in various sizes for different breeds and it may be necessary to band the smaller breeds at a slightly younger age. The breeder's details and the year of the rabbit's birth are encoded on the ring, which will normally remain in place throughout its life. Check the ring occasionally, however, to check that it moves freely on the leg and is not causing the rabbit any discomfort. If the ring needs to be removed for any reason, ask your vet do this for you. Ringing is not the only way to mark rabbits for identification, however. In many countries, tattooing is preferred.

◆ ABOVE LEFT
At a show, it can appear as if the rabbits are being compared with each other to find the winner. However, in reality, they are being judged against the breed standard.

◆ ABOVE RIGHT
It is vital that show rabbits are used to being handled, so that when being judged, as here, they will not struggle but remain relaxed.

◆ RIGHT
Rabbits are kept in pens before and after judging. Vaccination, especially against the rabbit disease VHD, is very important for show rabbits.

GUINEA PIGS

Guinea pigs are unusual among rodents in that they lack a tail. It is possible that, in evolutionary terms, the tail was deemed unnecessary because of the guinea pig's reluctance to climb. Taming is straightforward, especially if they are obtained when young, as guinea pigs will not attempt to bite when being picked up, making them an ideal choice of pet for children. Guinea pigs are also highly popular as exhibition subjects.

INTRODUCTION

◆ BELOW
The agouti colour form approximates most closely to that of the wild guinea pig.

Guinea pigs are members of the rodent family, forming part of a group known as the caviomorphs. They originate from the Andean region of South America, and were probably first domesticated by the Incas over 750 years ago. The wild ancestors of the guinea pig look very different to the colourful varieties kept today. Their coats show greyish agouti patterning, not unlike that of a wild rabbit, and provide them with a good level of camouflage.

It was not until the 1700s that guinea pigs were first brought to Europe. There are a number of different explanations for their unusual name. It could be that they were brought from the area of Guianas, which became corrupted to "Guinea", or it may have been because the first ships that carried them across the Atlantic ocean visited Guinea, on the west coast of Africa, before sailing north to Europe. Alternatively, there could be a financial explanation – these rodents soon became immensely sought-after as pets, and it could be a reflection of the high value initially placed upon them in England, where they could fetch the princely sum of one guinea. It is easier to see why they became known as pigs. This is not just a reflection of

◆ LEFT
Camouflage is very important for the survival of guinea pigs in the wild, as they are surrounded by many potential predators.

◆ RIGHT
Young wild guinea pigs. Unlike many rodents, they are developed enough when born to move around freely.

◆ BELOW
A wide range of colours now exists in the case
of the domestic guinea pig. Specific judging
standards have been established for all of
today's popular varieties.

◆ BELOW
A tortie and white Abyssinian guinea pig,
revealing the characteristic fur pattern made up
of ridges and rosettes, with a longer mane of
hair on the head.

While it is possible to keep
pet rabbits and guinea pigs housed
together, the rabbit may bully its
smaller rodent companion. If you
choose to have these pets sharing
accommodation, make sure that the
hutch is spacious, and select a smaller
breed of rabbit, which is less likely to
hurt the guinea pig if it accidentally
jumps on top of it. Separate them at
once if you notice signs of bullying.

Unlike some of the other rodent
species, there is no unpleasant odour
associated with guinea pigs.

their corpulent body shape, but also of
their "oinking" calls. Not surprisingly,
therefore, males are known as boars
while females are called sows.

Rather confusingly, guinea pigs
are also sometimes known as cavies,
which is a reflection of the name of
the group to which they belong –
the caviomorphs. This group is
characterized by the arrangement of
the muscles of their jaws, and also
their long gestation period, compared
with that of other rodents. As a result,
although they have fewer young, their
offspring are born in a relatively
advanced state of development.

GUINEA PIGS AS PETS
Guinea pigs make ideal pets for
children, particularly as they are small,
easy to handle and will not attempt
to bite when picked up. They can be
housed either in the home or outside
in a hutch throughout the year, even
in temperate areas. Even so, as with
rabbits, it is certainly not advisable
to buy a guinea pig that has been
kept in the relative warmth of a pet
store, and then transfer it immediately
to an outdoor hutch during the winter.

As household pets,
however, guinea pigs are
far shyer than rabbits.
They can be handled
easily since they do
not bite, but they are
likely to scurry away
under furniture for
long periods rather than
being content to remain
alongside you like a
rabbit. Under normal
circumstances, guinea pigs
will live for about six years.

◆ BELOW
A typical guinea pig hutch. This can be lower in
height than a rabbit hutch, but must still have a
spacious interior.

SMOOTH-COATED BREEDS

◆ BELOW
A self black guinea pig. This individual is
showing reddish hairs in its coat, which would
spoil its exhibition potential; however, this will
not make it any less attractive to keep as a pet.

The smooth-coated guinea pigs are
nearer in appearance to their wild
ancestors than other varieties.
They are now sub-divided into two
categories – the self (single colour)
varieties, such as cream, chocolate
or black, and the patterned varieties,
such as the tortoiseshell.

SELF VARIETIES

The black is one of the most popular
members of the self group, thanks
to its glossy, sleek coat. For showing
purposes, it should be entirely black
in colour. Breeders regard any odd
white or even red hairs in its coat as a
serious show flaw. Even as they grow
older, these guinea pigs do not fade
in colour. The self chocolate is
another dark variety, the colour of
plain (semisweet) chocolate, with
similarly coloured dark eyes and ears.
Depth of coloration in the coat is
essential, as it is with all self-coloured
guinea pigs.

   As new colours have been
developed, some of the older varieties
have declined in numbers. One of
these is the self red, which is an
attractive shade of rich mahogany
with ruby-red eyes. The coloration of
the self golden can sometimes almost

◆ ABOVE
Agouti coloration arises from the
fact that there is a series of dark
and light bands running down the
hairs. Some forms of the agouti
have red eyes.

◆ LEFT
Light shades within the self
category are very popular. This is a
self beige, a dilute form of the self
chocolate. The depth of coloration
should be seen over its entire body.

♦ LEFT
The coat texture
of the rex is very
distinctive, giving
these guinea pigs
a rather woolly
appearance. This
feature can be
combined with the
smooth, short coat
type, as here, or with
longer hair.

verge on red, although the preferred shade is ginger. The eyes in this case are usually pink, although there is also a rarer dark-eyed form.

Lighter shades in the self-coloured group include the cream, and a darker form that has a much yellower appearance, known as the self buff. The cream is sometimes known as the "champagne cavy" to describe the shade of colour required for show stock, with paler coloration being preferred. Self white guinea pigs are often slightly smaller than other colours, especially the true albino, which is recognizable by its red rather than dark eyes. The stipulation here is for the coat colour to be pure white, with no trace of a yellowish hue. These white guinea pigs should not be confused with the Himalayan form, which is also pure white, but is distinguishable by the darker chocolate or black areas on the nose and ears. The chocolate is the lighter form of the two Himalayan varieties.

New self colours are still being evolved as the demand for novelty shades grows. The self blue – a bluey shade of grey – which has been developed in the United States, marks a significant departure from existing solid guinea pig colours.

PATTERNED VARIETIES

The tortoiseshell and white is a striking example of a short-coated, patterned guinea pig, with black, white and red patches in its coat. The Dutch form of the guinea pig bears a strong resemblance in its patterning to the rabbit of the same name; the coloured and white areas must be clearly defined for showing. Darker colours, such as red or black, are preferred, because these create a more evident contrast in the coat,

but other colours are seen, even agouti Dutch combinations. Agouti markings result from light and dark banding running down each individual hair.

The more recently developed varieties include the Dalmatian, so-called because its black and white spotted patterning is reminiscent of the dog breed, while roans are distinguished by an even distribution of coloured and white areas throughout their coats. Roans can be bred in various colours.

♦ BELOW
Coat patterning is an important feature of certain guinea pig varieties. The three tortoiseshell and white, short-coated individuals shown here are siblings.

LONG-HAIRED AND REX COATS

ABYSSINIAN

For many years the Abyssinian and Peruvian breeds were the only long-haired guinea pigs recognized. The Abyssinian has a coat comprising a series of rosettes and ridges. The rosettes do not overlap but, where the hair extends out around the edge of the rosette to meet another rosette, a ridge is formed. There should ideally be four symmetrical rosettes running down the sides of the body, and a similar number along the back. In fact, the coat of the Abyssinian should not lie flat at any point over its entire body. The individual hairs themselves are quite short, measuring no more than 4 cm (1½ in) long.

As the wiry-haired coat of the Abyssinian is genetically dominant over short-coated cavies, if these are paired together, the offspring will have rosettes, but these are usually not as well defined as the rosettes seen in a true Abyssinian lineage. In this way, however, new self colours can be introduced to the Abyssinian breed. Even so, self reds and self blacks, as well as brindles, tortoiseshells and roans, are the most common colour forms of the Abyssinian because their

◆ TOP
A self red Abyssinian. This breed is characterized by the lie of its coat. In this particular case, the fur must be entirely red, displaying no trace of white hairs.

◆ ABOVE
Bi-colours exist in the case of the Abyssinian, as shown by this gold and white individual.

◆ BELOW
The rex mutation gives a coarser texture to the fur. This is a silver agouti example.

hair texture is often better. It can take up to 18 months for their coats to develop to their full extent.

PERUVIAN

Because of the Peruvian's demanding grooming requirements, it is not recommended as a pet, except for the most dedicated owner. The young are born with a short coat, but by adulthood it can reach 50 cm (20 in) or more in length. As the coat mats very easily, the Peruvian is not kept on hay, which can become entangled in the coat. Instead, the hay should be supplied in a hayrack.

SHELTIE

The sheltie is the long-haired form of the smooth-coated guinea pigs, and is instantly distinguishable from the Peruvian by its fur, which lies flat and is not swept forwards over its head, and the absence of a parting extending

◆ LEFT
Grey agouti and cream Abyssinian. The agouti
characteristic is shown by the dark and light
banding extending down the individual hairs,
creating a sparkling appearance.

CRESTED MUTATION

Another characteristic, linked with a wide range of colours, is the crested mutation. The crest itself should be even in size and circular in shape, being located just in front of the ears. In the case of the English crested mutation, the crest matches that of the surrounding fur, but it is always white in the case of the American crested. When combined with the texel, the crested has given rise to the form known as the alpaca.

down the back. The satin characteristic has been introduced to these long-haired guinea pigs, and this has ensured that their coats do not lose their lustre as they grow older. In other cases, the satin characteristic highlights the natural gloss of the coat.

REX MUTATIONS

The rex mutation is a relatively new variant, but has become very popular both in Europe and North America, where it is often described as a teddy. The rex's fur is slightly curly and very coarse to the touch. It is a recessive mutation, so rex guinea pigs must be paired together to produce rex offspring. The rex has now been bred in a very wide range of colours. It has also been possible to combine it with the sheltie to create the texel, which has a curly but shorter coat than the true sheltie. The merino is the result of crosses between the rex and the Peruvian guinea pigs.

◆ BELOW
The crested characteristic can be combined with any colour. In the American form, seen here, it is always white.

◆ BELOW
A family of tortoiseshell and white rex guinea pigs. Note the favoured white blaze extending down the nose between the eyes. Individual markings are variable.

HOUSING IN HOME AND GARDEN

Guinea pigs are less destructive than some of the other rodent species, but it is to be expected that they will gnaw at woodwork within their hutch, often concentrating on one particular spot.

OUTDOOR HOUSING

Hutches outdoors should be divided into two sections – an outer area with a mesh front, and secure, snug sleeping quarters. Guinea pigs do not sit up like rabbits, so the hutch does not need to be especially tall. When you buy a hutch check that the doors are secure, and add combination locks to latches to deter dexterous foxes. It is also a good idea to oil the hinges every couple of months, enabling them to open smoothly and helping to prolong their lifespan.

Regularly check the roofing felt to ensure that the interior remains dry. A dense layer of hay will help to provide warm sleeping quarters, and will supplement the guinea pig's diet. If you are planning to construct the hutch yourself, you should give it

◆ RIGHT
An indoor enclosure for a guinea pig, complete with a water bottle. The base prevents bedding from being scattered in the room. Note the removable mesh lid, protecting the guinea pig from any dogs and cats also sharing your home.

secure legs, made of 5 cm (2 in) square timber, that stand at least 30 cm (1 ft) off the ground. The sides of the hutch can be constructed using tongue-and-groove timber, although thick marine plywood often proves to be more durable. The roof should slope from front to back, with an overhang at the back so that rainwater runs off readily, rather than down the back of the hutch where it would rot the wood.

Outdoor runs for guinea pigs are similar to rabbit runs, although, like hutches, they do not need to be as tall.

Pet stores usually stock a variety of runs, including ark-shaped designs, which have a dry section at one end where the guinea pig can retreat in bad weather, and rectangular runs, which also have a covered area. Check that you can reach right into the run to pick up the guinea pig, since guinea pigs can be very difficult to catch.

Position the run in a shady spot and remember to move it every week or so, to ensure that the area of grass beneath the sides of the run does not die back. Avoid using lawn that has recently been treated with weedkillers or potentially harmful chemicals. Place the run on level ground as a guinea pig may otherwise escape beneath one of the sides; you may not be aware of this danger if the grass is long. Fresh drinking water should always be available in the run.

INDOOR HOUSING

An indoor hutch should combine a cage with a plastic base and a wire mesh surround that prevents the guinea pig from clambering out. The base will ensure that bedding is not scattered out into the room. Wire mesh lids, which clip on to the hutch, prevent attacks from dogs and cats.

◆ LEFT
Outdoor guinea pig hutches need to be well constructed from durable materials, with a covering of heavy-duty roofing felt to keep the interior dry. You may need to reinforce the door fitments to keep your pet safe.

MAKING A GUINEA PIG HUTCH

1 Start by cutting all of the components to size. These may then be glued in place, using a non-toxic adhesive. Leave to dry.

2 Clamps will help to hold the glued surface to the adjacent area until it has dried. Holes can then be drilled as necessary.

3 Power tools will often simplify the assembly process. The screws themselves should fit snugly into the holes.

4 Here the sections are being assembled. The wooden supports are on the outside of the hutch, out of the guinea pig's reach.

5 The door hinges are an important part of the hutch. Do not economize here, as they may otherwise start rusting prematurely.

6 The assembled hutch, apart from the roof unit. Trim off any sharp edges of mesh on the door frame, so that they cannot injure your pet.

7 Apply the roofing felt. Note how the roof of the hutch is broader than the interior to ensure a better fit.

8 Fold over the roof felt at each of the corners, once the required length has been cut off the roll. Take care not to damage it at this stage.

9 Broad-headed clout nails are needed to attach the roofing felt. Check that this is taut as otherwise it may be ripped off in a strong wind.

10 The roof section can then be fitted on top of the hutch. Screws fitted through the sides into the inner supports provide anchorage.

11 Bolts to keep the hutch door securely closed can be fitted next. These will make it difficult for a predator to reach the guinea pig.

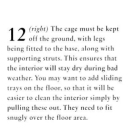

12 *(right)* The cage must be kept off the ground, with legs being fitted to the base, along with supporting struts. This ensures that the interior will stay dry during bad weather. You may want to add sliding trays on the floor, so that it will be easier to clean the interior simply by pulling these out. They need to fit snugly over the floor area.

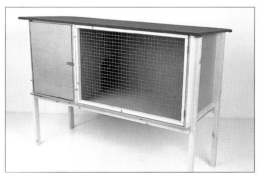

13 Treat the exterior sides, legs and underside of the hutch with a non-toxic wood preservative, and allow this to dry before placing the guinea pig into its new home.

FEEDING

◆ BELOW
A bottle brush will be required to clean the guinea pig's drinker at least once a week, preventing it becoming green on the sides as the result of algal growth.

Guinea pigs have an unusual metabolic quirk, shared with humans beings and marmosets but no other mammals. They are unable to manufacture Vitamin C from their food, and it must therefore be present in their diet if a deficiency is not to occur. As a result, complete foods for guinea pigs are supplemented with appropriate levels of this vital vitamin. Even if you are housing a rabbit and guinea pig together, it is very important to feed your guinea pig formulated food. A deficiency of Vitamin C causes a condition known as scurvy, resulting in dry, crusty skin and hair loss. Since

scurvy can be confused with mite infestations, you should seek veterinary advice if the guinea pig shows these symptoms.

In addition to a prepared food, a guinea pig will readily eat a wide variety of greenstuff and vegetables. Broccoli and other brassicas, and spinach all contain relatively high levels of Vitamin C. Spinach is especially useful in the winter, when other sources of greenfood, such as dandelion leaves, are hard to find. Root vegetables, such as carrots, can also be offered regularly, particularly during the winter months.

Like rabbits, guinea pigs rely heavily on bacteria and protozoa in their large intestine to break down plant material, consuming their

◆ BELOW
Guinea pigs need to be fed each day, with their dry food being provided in a heavy container that they cannot tip over easily. Change the drinking water at the same time.

own droppings to obtain maximum nutritional benefit from their food. This means that you should not change your guinea pig's diet suddenly, but should make changes gradually, over a couple of weeks. It will not matter if you do not offer the same type of greenstuff each day, but it is harmful not to offer such foods for a period and then allow the guinea pig into a run where it will gorge itself on grass.

Always feed your guinea pig every day, and provide fresh water as well. It may help to provide the fresh food in a feeding bowl, rather than simply dropping it in the bedding where it can be harder to clear up and can possibly turn mouldy.

A range of treats is available for guinea pigs, but one addition to the diet traditionally favoured by guinea pig keepers is a bran mash. This is made by mixing bran with a little warm water and is especially valued during the winter months. Mix just enough to be eaten in a day, removing the food container when your pet has eaten and washing it out thoroughly.

There are a number of plants that are potentially poisonous for guinea pigs, and these should never be fed to your pet. Avoid bulbous plants, bracken and ragwort (*Senecio*). Among the more common garden weeds, both buttercups (*Ranunculus*) and convolvulus (*Convolvulus*) are toxic. The dangers posed by garden plants are usually listed in horticultural catalogues. Foxgloves (*Digitalis*) and lily-of-the-valley (*Convallaria*), as well as rhododendron (*Rhododendron*), should also be avoided.

Guinea pig mix

Bran mash

Broccoli

GENERAL CARE

It can be rather unnerving to hold a guinea pig for the first time as it may squeal as if in pain, and this can be especially alarming for a child. However, this shouldn't happen if you are gentle, and once your guinea pig is used to being handled regularly it will usually stop making this noise. Since guinea pigs do not bite instinctively, they can be picked up easily, although they will often try to avoid capture.

◆ LEFT
Starting out with a young guinea pig means that it will soon become used to being handled. Guinea pigs will not attempt to bite when picked up, but they will usually attempt to burrow deep into their bedding to avoid being caught.

HANDLING

To pick up your guinea pig, place your left hand in front of it as it runs around its hutch, with your right hand behind it. Use your right hand to restrain the guinea pig by placing your fingers around its body. If you are left-handed, it may be easier to reverse your grip. Having caught the rodent, slide your hand under its hindquarters, and lift it up out of its hutch. Once it is held in this way, the guinea pig will generally not struggle, but take care not to loosen your grip at this stage because if you do drop it accidentally it is likely to be seriously injured in the fall.

TRANSPORTING YOUR PET

Use a sturdy cardboard box or pet carrier for transporting your guinea pig. Check the flaps on the base of the box to ensure that it is strong enough. Reinforce the base with packaging tape, and, as a further precaution, support the box from

◆ LEFT
Transferring a guinea pig from its hutch to a carrier. Always support your pet's hindquarters from beneath, holding it gently but securely.

PICKING UP A GUINEA PIG

1 By scooping your hand under the guinea pig's body, you will stop your pet from being able to run away. Do not be alarmed if the guinea pig squeaks – this is its warning call to others.

2 As you start to lift the guinea pig off the ground, slide your other hand beneath its abdomen to provide support for its hindquarters. Take particular care if the guinea pig is pregnant.

beneath with your hands. If you place some hay in the box, the guinea pig will burrow comfortably and will not panic. It is not likely to gnaw its way out of the box if housed here only for a short time, but never leave it where cats or dogs could gain access to it.

GUINEA PIG HYGIENE

The hutch should be cleaned out thoroughly at least once a week, with the bedding making ideal compost.

◆ ABOVE
Once it realizes that it will not be hurt when picked up, a guinea pig will lie comfortably in this position. This is a male, known as a boar.

Always keep a close watch on your guinea pig's droppings because these give a vital insight into its state of health, and they can be particularly significant in the case of older boars. In later life, boars are especially susceptible to a condition known as rectal impaction, when the muscular contractions necessary to force the faeces out of the anus become weak, causing the droppings to accumulate. This results in a painful swelling at the end of the digestive tract.

The problem will be apparent if the guinea pig is examined from beneath. Although it is a highly unpleasant task for both parties, the only solution will be to pour olive oil carefully into the anus and then gently massage the obstruction out wearing disposable gloves (your vet will do this for you if you prefer). A general purpose dietary supplement may be needed to prevent further deterioration.

WINTER CARE OUTDOORS

During the colder winter months, it is a good idea to bring the hutch into a sheltered, well lit outbuilding. If you leave the guinea pig outside, be sure that it has enough bedding to stay warm and check it daily. Check also that there is an adequate supply of drinking water available. It is not

recommended to use an earthenware bowl for this purpose, because it will quickly become fouled with bedding. A better option is to use a bottle that can be attached to the outside of the cage. Take precautions with this system if the temperature is set to drop below freezing point: do not fill the bottle to the top or when the water expands, as it changes into ice, it may crack the bottle. Check also that the stainless steel spout is free from ice, as this will stop the flow of water. Squeezing the bottle when it is full is the best way of checking for a blockage.

◆ BELOW
Take care when carrying guinea pigs in this way that they do not become scared, wriggle free and fall to the ground.

BREEDING

◆ BELOW
It is relatively easy to identify the sex of guinea pigs. This is a female, known as a sow. There is a membrane which may be visible over the opening, apart from when she is ready to mate.

◆ BELOW
A male guinea pig or boar. Gentle extrusion of the penis, as shown here, identifies the male, even in the case of immature individuals where the testes are less visible.

◆ BELOW
It is relatively easy to identify the sex of guinea pigs. This is a female, known as a sow. There is a membrane which may be visible over the opening, apart from when she is ready to mate.

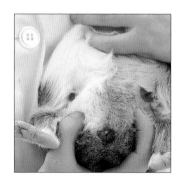

It is potentially dangerous to wait until a guinea pig sow is a year old before allowing her to have a litter. As the sow grows older, her pelvic bones will fuse together, and they will not expand easily to allow for the passage of young through the birth canal. This means that the risk of the young being trapped and having to be born by a Caesarean section is greatly increased. The ideal time for a sow to be mated for the first time is between five and six months of age. The stretching of the bones and muscles that takes place within the pelvis is then permanent, so that future litters born later in life are unlikely to result in a sow experiencing a difficult birth, which is known as dystocia.

◆ BELOW
It is preferable to restrict the breeding period to the warmer months of the year. The young of long-coated varieties, such as the sheltie, have shorter coats when newly born.

Males mature even earlier and are able to mate successfully at only one month old. It is necessary, therefore, to separate males from females at an early stage, although it is usual to wait until the age of four months or so before using males for stud purposes.

Sexing of guinea pigs is reasonably straightforward. With a boar, gentle pressure either side of the genital opening will bring the penis into view. In the case of sows, there is usually a membrane over this orifice. Breeding is straightforward, with the female being placed in the male's quarters. More than one sow can be housed successfully with a boar, provided that the hutch is sufficiently large. Sows come into season approximately every 16 days, so that leaving a pair together for about five weeks should give adequate time for mating to take place.

The sow should then be transferred back to separate quarters to give birth. You can usually tell if a female is pregnant about six weeks after mating occurred, as the movements of the foetuses will be clearly discernible from this stage onwards. Do not squeeze her body to detect the offspring though, as this could inflict serious damage on them. A dietary supplement of Vitamin C may be useful during pregnancy, when the sow will double her requirement for this important vitamin.

The young are born – very often during the night – after a gestation period of approximately 63 days. Around this period, you may not know with any certainty if the young have been born. Take particular care when opening the hutch door to the sleeping quarters for an inspection, to prevent any newborn babies tumbling down on to the floor.

CARING FOR THE YOUNG

Baby guinea pigs are miniature adults, fully developed at birth, with their eyes already open. They may be somewhat darker in colour, however, and, in the case of long-haired breeds, they will have much shorter fur. A typical litter is made up of three or four offspring, but if the litter is much larger, keep a close watch on the female for signs of a serious

condition known as pregnancy toxaemia. Typical signs include loss of appetite and twitching, followed by convulsions. Obese sows are the most at risk. Rapid veterinary treatment will be needed if the sow is to recover.

Young guinea pigs are born in an advanced state of development, which means that they can eat solid food almost immediately, although they still benefit greatly from their mother's milk. If a litter is orphaned, supplementary feeding is not so critical to their survival. They can be handreared on evaporated milk, diluted with two parts of cooled boiled water, and mixed with a cereal baby food and a vitamin supplement.

◆ LEFT
Young Himalayan guinea pigs are predominantly white in colour at birth. The darker markings on their bodies will develop with age.

◆ BELOW
A female tortoiseshell and white Abyssinian with her litter. Note the variability in their markings.

299

GROOMING AND SHOWING

The grooming requirements of guinea pigs vary greatly from minimal to fairly heavy, depending on whether your pet is long- or short-haired. To keep a pet guinea pig tidy and clean, you will need to make sure there is no food or bedding material lodged in its fur. If you have a long-haired guinea pig, you will also need to give the coat a regular brush to keep it free of tangles and mats.

SHOW PREPARATION

If you want to show your guinea pig, you will need to make some finishing touches before the show to make sure it looks its best.

With a Peruvian guinea pig, you will need to train its hair, using brown paper strips and small blocks of balsa wood, from the age of three months. This helps to encourage the sweep of the hair, which, for the purpose of the show, extends over all parts of the guinea pig's body, including the head. The wrappers, which are like hair curlers, are folded in a concertina shape with the balsa block held inside and kept in place with rubber bands. Each wrapper measures 15 cm (6 in) in width, with the balsa block being 5 cm (2 in) wide and 2.5 cm (1 in) across. In the case of young Peruvian guinea pigs, wrappers are placed first on the sweep at the tail end and on each side of the body, with further wrappers being added as the guinea pig grows older and its coat develops.

Preparing an Abyssinian guinea pig for a show will involve brushing the animal with a toothbrush, using a brush with natural bristles, to avoid introducing static to the animal's coat. Brushing in this way will emphasize the rosettes and ridges that are so characteristic of the Abyssinian's coat.

AT THE SHOW

When it comes to judging, Peruvian guinea pigs are placed on a special judging stand – a hessian- (burlap-) covered platform measuring 45 cm (18 in) square and standing 15 cm (6 in) off the ground – to display their magnificent coats in all their finery. With any exhibition guinea pig, it will be necessary to train it to stand still while being judged. Guinea pig shows are held often, although they are rarely advertised outside the pages

◆ LEFT
A Peruvian guinea pig being prepared for a show. It is standing on the typical hessian-covered show stand.

◆ BELOW
Guinea pigs in their show pens. Advertisements
of such events can be found in the specialist
press, as well as club newsletters, usually giving
the address of the show secretary.

of specialist publications. Even if you
are not exhibiting, it is interesting to
visit a show and see the many varieties
of gunea pig that now exist. This is
also a good place to meet breeders,
who will often have stock for sale.

If you are interested in exhibiting
your guinea pig, attending shows
provides an opportunity to see what

the judges are looking for. This will
give you a much clearer idea than
trying to visualize what is required by
reading show standards and pouring
over pictures in books. At both local
and national shows, there may not
be only guinea pigs on view, but also
other small mammals, such as rabbits,
rats and other rodents.

If you are wanting to see the rarer
colour varieties of guinea pig, you
will need to visit the bigger national
events. If you are interested in
exhibiting your own pet, however,
it will be better to start out at local
level, by joining a club in your area,
before progressing to larger events
with stronger competition.

◆ RIGHT
A group of smooth-
coated guinea pigs
being judged. The
temporary spots on
their ears correspond
to their pen
numbers, enabling
individuals to be
identified easily.

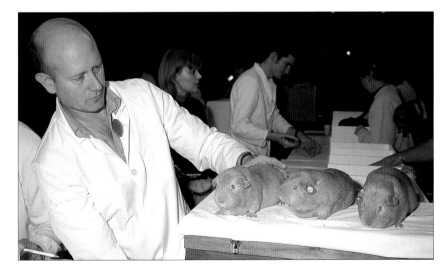

HAMSTERS

These small rodents are very popular throughout the world. They are bred in a range of colours and coat types, yet they still retain the rather nocturnal instincts of their ancestors, sleeping through most of the day. Bear in mind that hamsters are anti-social by nature, especially the Syrian or golden hamster, and they must be housed on their own. Hamsters make good children's pets, and they can be handled, although they may bite occasionally.

INTRODUCTION

Hamsters are a group of mainly small rodents with a wide distribution throughout the Old World. The common hamster (*Cricetus cricetus*) is the biggest member of the group, measuring 33 cm (13 in) in length and weighing approximately 475 g (17 oz). It is found in parts of Europe, where its numbers have declined significantly over recent years.

The appeal of hamsters as pets is relatively recent, and dates back to the capture of a female Syrian hamster (*Mesocricetus auratus*) and her young, in a field on a mountainside near Aleppo in Syria, in 1930. It was hoped that they could shed some light on a parasitic blood disease

♦ LEFT
Only when they are young can Syrian hamsters be housed together safely. They are otherwise likely to fight severely, even when introduced for mating, which needs to be closely supervised as a result.

♦ LEFT
The coat of the dwarf Russian hamster becomes white in the winter.

but, before they could be taken to the University of Jerusalem, a number of the family had escaped and could not be recaptured.

The group that remained proved to be quite prolific, however, and before long these hamsters were sent to both the United States and the United Kingdom. Again, they bred well, and ultimately stock from London Zoo was passed to private breeders. This marked the start of the hamster's rise to popularity as a pet, and the first hamster club was formed in the United Kingdom in 1945. However, this was not the first time that Syrian

Dwarf Russian hamsters have become very popular over recent years, with an increasing range of colour forms being developed. They are smaller than Syrian hamsters.

hamsters had been kept in Britain. In the late 1880s, the former British Consul in Syria had returned to the United Kingdom with a breeding colony, but this ultimately died out during the 1920s.

When they were first introduced to the public, these hamsters were described as golden hamsters because of the golden colour of their coat. Today, this name has become less appropriate as a wide range of colour varieties has been developed. Now they are better known as Syrian hamsters, which also helps to distinguish them from the Russian and Chinese hamsters. The Russian forms in particular have grown greatly in popularity over recent years, partly as a result of their more sociable natures. They, too, are now being bred in different colours and coat types.

The dwarf Russian hamster (*Phodopus sungoris*) occurs in the eastern part of that country, and in two different forms. The most striking feature of the dwarf winter white (*P. s. sungoris*) is its coat, which changes colour, as its name suggests, before the onset of winter, losing its colour pigment and turning white. This form originates from Siberia and northern Kazakhstan, whereas the dwarf Campbell's Russian hamster (*P. s. campbelli*) ranges as far east as northern China. This hamster, which was not discovered until 1905, is closely related to the winter white. Both forms are also known as Djungarian hamsters.

The third dwarf hamster from this part of the world is Roborovski's hamster *(P. roborovskii)*, whose home is the desert area of Mongolia. It can be distinguished easily by the lack of a dark stripe down its back. All three forms of dwarf hamster have only been widely available to pet-seekers since the 1980s.

The Chinese hamster (*Cricetulus griseus)* is less commonly kept than the other breeds, and is therefore less widely available. This hamster is distinguishable from other breeds by the length of its tail, which measures about 2 cm (¾ in). These hamsters originate from northern China, and have a dark stripe down their back. The coat itself is shorter and sleeker than that of the Russian dwarf.

On average, a pet hamster can be expected to live for between two and three years.

◆ LEFT
In spite of their size, dwarf Russian hamsters are very active by nature, and will appreciate having a special hamster wheel in their quarters for exercise purposes.

SPECIES AND BREEDS

A wide range of colours have now been developed for the Syrian hamster, and an increasing number are emerging in the Russian species in particular. The wide choice of colours has helped to increase the hamsters' popularity with fanciers.

SYRIAN FORMS

The original golden form of the Syrian has a golden coat with black ticking on the individual hairs. The underparts are a contrasting shade of ivory white, and the ears are dark grey. There is also a darker golden form, with more extensive ticking and black ears, as well as a dilute form known as the light golden. The latter has no ticking on the coat and pure white underparts.

Among the other colours that have now been created is an attractive cream form, available in red-, ruby- and black-eyed variants. The yellow resembles the black-eyed cream, but can be distinguished by its darker coloration, which produces tipping on the guard hairs. The honey is very similar to the yellow, but can be easily distinguished by its paler ears and red eyes. The most colourful form of hamster is the cinnamon, which has orange-coloured fur.

♦ LEFT
For many years, the Syrian hamster was known as the golden hamster, thanks to its attractive flaxen coloration. As more colour varieties became established, so its name changed.

♦ LEFT
The Syrian hamster will sit up sometimes when it is eating or, as here, when it is looking around its environment.

♦ BELOW LEFT
Hamsters will use their forepaws like hands for eating and grooming purposes. This adds to their appeal as cute pets.

♦ BELOW RIGHT
It is not just the coloration of the Syrian hamster that has changed as a result of domestication. This is the long-coated or teddy form.

The three different forms of white Syrian hamster are distinguished by the pigmentation of their eyes and ears. The albino is a pure red-eyed white with no colour pigment present, in contrast to the dark-eared form.

The third form is the black-eyed white, recognizable by its black eyes and pink ears. All three forms have a pure snow white coat. Several grey forms of the Syrian hamster are also now established, as well as the dove,

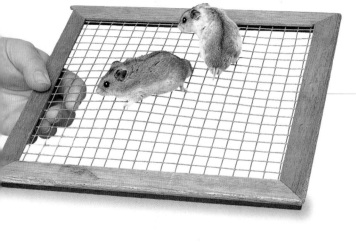

♦ LEFT
Smaller in size than their Syrian relative,
Russian hamsters, too, have become popular
in recent years. Colour and coat varieties of
these hamsters are now becoming established.

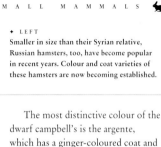

The most distinctive colour of the dwarf campbell's is the argente, which has a ginger-coloured coat and a chocolate-coloured stripe down its back. There is also a true albino form, which is entirely white in colour, with the characteristic pink eyes. A satin-coated mutation has also been developed in recent years, and, as the name suggests, this variety boasts a noticeably sleek coat.

which has a lilac tinge to its colour. Among other darker shades are the chocolate, which is brown in colour, and a new pure black variety.

In addition, there are a range of marked colour varieties. These include the banded, which has a white area encircling the body, in combination with any solid colour. Less rigorously defined in terms of markings is the variegated, with white and coloured areas in its coat. The spotted is similar, but in this case the markings are circular. There is also a tortoiseshell form, with yellow or black and brown markings, which can also be combined with white.

The potential for different hamster varieties is enhanced by the various coat types, which have been developed to supplement the standard short-haired form. The satin mutation can be combined with this to make the coat more shiny than normal. There

♦ BELOW
Syrian hamsters are being bred with specific markings. The tortoiseshell and white, seen here, has variable colour markings.

are also long-haired Syrian hamsters, often known as teddies, and rexes, distinguished by their curly coats.

RUSSIAN COLOUR FORMS

Of the dwarf Russian, one of the first colours to be created was the sapphire. This is bluish-grey with a stripe along its back and blue markings. The pearl, which is greyish in colour, has become popular in recent years.

CHINESE HAMSTER

The best-known colour variant of the Chinese hamster is the dominant spot, which displays one or more white spots on its body. A white patch on the head is also favoured as a requirement for exhibition stock. Still rare is the white form of the Chinese hamster, which is recognized by the dark stripe running down the length of its back.

♦ LEFT
The colour of dwarf Russian hamsters may change through the year. Their dark fur will be replaced by white at the start of the winter.

♦ RIGHT
In spite of their large eyes, hamsters do not have good vision. They rely very heavily on their sense of smell.

HOUSING AND FEEDING

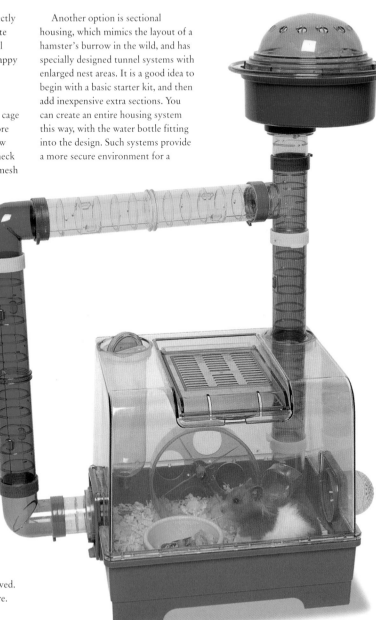

Looking after your hamster correctly
involves providing it with adequate
food and shelter. These basics will
ensure that it stays healthy and happy
throughout its life.

HAMSTER CAGES

Although the traditional hamster cage
is still a popular option, other more
inventive housing systems are now
available. If you opt for a cage, check
that the base fits securely to the mesh
roof area. Should there be any
weakness here, the hamster
is likely to find a gap and
escape into the room.
This applies especially in
the case of young Russian
hamsters, since cages on
the market are generally
intended for the larger
Syrian species.

Another important
aspect of cage design to
consider is the strength
of the door. It will be
easier to take your hamster
out of its quarters if the
door is on the side of the
cage, rather than in the
roof. Door hinges have a
tendency to become weaker
over time, so it is a good
idea to invest in a small
combination padlock as an
extra security precaution.

A cage should have a
sleeping area. Make sure
the bedding is safe hamster
bedding, which will not cause a
potentially fatal blockage in the
rodent's intestinal tract if swallowed.
You can buy bedding at a pet store.
Tease it out by hand, so that the
hamster can burrow into it easily.

Another option is sectional
housing, which mimics the layout of a
hamster's burrow in the wild, and has
specially designed tunnel systems with
enlarged nest areas. It is a good idea to
begin with a basic starter kit, and then
add inexpensive extra sections. You
can create an entire housing system
this way, with the water bottle fitting
into the design. Such systems provide
a more secure environment for a

♦ LEFT
A typical hamster
cage. Always check
the door fastening
is secure, because if
a hamster escapes
into the room,
recapturing it is
likely to prove
very difficult.

hamster than a cage, but you should still check regularly to see that the rodent is not nibbling at the plastic at any one point, through which it might attempt to escape.

HAMSTER FOODS

Hamster mixes are readily available from pet stores. These will usually contain a variety of cereal seeds, as well as sunflower seeds and peanuts. These oil seeds should be offered in small quantities because of their high fat content, which can lead to obesity if they form the bulk of the hamster's diet. Commercial pelleted diets are

also available, although these tend to be the more expensive option. Use a small, heavyweight earthenware pot as a food bowl and provide fresh drinking water in a bottle, attached to the side of the hamster's quarters.

Do not forget to offer a little fresh food, such as a piece of sweet apple or greenstuff, on a daily basis as well. This can occasionally be sprinkled with a special small-animal vitamin and mineral supplement as an additional tonic. It is very important to match the amount of food offered to the hamster to the quantity being eaten because, otherwise, a hamster is likely

to waste food, carrying it back to its nest in its cheek pouches. Hamsters instinctively hoard food in this way, building up large supplies in their burrows when food is scarce above ground. Take particular care with fresh food, because this is likely to rot if left in the bedding material for a couple of days. It's a good idea to check the bedding regularly as this is likely to be harmful to your pet's health.

There are also a number of commercial treats now available to supplement your hamster's diet. These are useful for taming purposes, and can be offered directly by hand.

Feeding bowl

Mineral block

Hamster mix

GENERAL CARE AND BREEDING

It is important to provide a range of other items apart from food and water to ensure your hamster's well-being. Chews of various types will help to keep your hamster's incisor teeth in trim, although short branches cut from apple trees – which have not been sprayed with chemicals – can serve the same purpose. Crusts of bread, roasted in the oven, can be a valuable addition to the diet as well.

EXERCISE

It is vital to keep your hamster fit. In the wild, hamsters emerge from their burrows under cover of darkness, and may travel several miles in search of food or a mate. An exercise wheel will give your pet hamster a substitute for this night-time activity. Modern closed-wheel designs are the safest option, as a hamster could slip and injure itself in an open-weave wheel. Check regularly that the wheel is firmly in position and will not collapse on the hamster. Oil the wheel from time to time; it may be noisy when in use and, if the cage is in a child's bedroom, the wheel can disturb a sleeping child. Pregnant females seem to use a wheel most, and it may be that this helps to tone up their muscles in preparation for the birth of their pups.

◆ ABOVE
Syrian hamsters especially will benefit from having an exercise wheel. A closed wheel as shown is the safest option. Oil the wheel occasionally so that it moves freely.

◆ BELOW
A wide range of other toys are now available for hamsters. Being burrowing creatures by nature, they need adequate retreats of various types in their quarters.

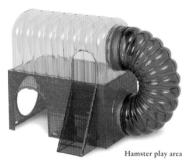

Hamster play area

Sectional unit

Hamster nest

◆ BELOW
A male Syrian hamster. Note the scrotal
swellings. Males can also be recognized by the
relatively longer gap between their anal and
genital openings.

◆ BELOW
A female, showing a much shorter ano-genital
gap. In addition, females have a smoother rear
profile when viewed from the side, compared
with that of the males.

MATING AND PREGNANCY

Pairings of Syrian hamsters need to be
carried out very cautiously to prevent
injuries caused by fighting. Once
mature, the female can be recognized
by the rounded, rather than step-like,
profile of her hindquarters when
viewed from the side, and she will be
larger in size than the male. Never
be tempted to introduce him to her
quarters, because she will almost
inevitably attack her intended partner.
Aggression is less likely if she is placed
in alongside the male, because in the
wild, it is the female who journeys
in search of a mate. The other
alternative is to introduce the pair
on neutral ground in a container with
a removable partition. If the female
is receptive to her intended partner,
then mating will normally occur
within an hour, after which the pair
should be separated again.

It is usually possible to tell when
the female is ready to mate by stroking
her back. If she stands still with her
tail raised, this is a sign that she is
ready. Female hamsters come into heat

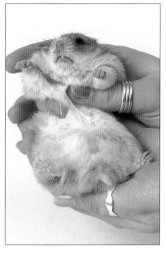

roughly every four days, so you will
not have long to wait in any event.
In pregnancy, the gestation period for
hamsters is among the shortest of all
mammals. A female Syrian hamster
will produce her offspring just 16 days
after mating, and the five to seven
young pups will be totally helpless at
birth. The normal gestation period for

Russian and Chinese hamsters will
last about 19 days in both cases.

Avoid disturbing the nest as this
can cause cannibalism. The young
grow quickly and will start to emerge
from their nest at about two weeks
old. Within a further fortnight, they
will be independent and should be
moved to separate accommodation.

◆ RIGHT
A young Syrian
hamster with
its mother. Hamsters
are not social by
nature, and now
that this youngster
is feeding itself,
it will need to be
transferred to
separate quarters to
avoid fights breaking
out between the pair.

GROOMING AND SHOWING

When it comes to grooming, or indeed showing, it is important that your hamster is tame and used to being handled. Hamsters have poor eyesight as, like many rodents, they spend much of their time underground in the dark. As a result, their sense of smell is significant. If you pick up a hamster too quickly, you are likely to be bitten. Instead, you need to accustom your pet to your scent. Place your hand on the floor of the cage and encourage the hamster to step on to it. You can then lift out the hamster by scooping it up, using your other hand like a cup. Avoid gripping your pet tightly, as it will then panic, struggle and bite. Occasionally, you may have to tempt your hamster into a container in order to take it out of its quarters without a struggle.

Ease of handling is another reason for starting out with a young hamster, as at this stage hamsters are far more responsive to being tamed. Taming will be virtually impossible with an older individual.

To restrain the hamster in an emergency – if it is out of its cage and is escaping under furniture, for example – hold the skin at the back of its neck. This will secure the hamster's head, so it will not be able to turn round and bite. You can then pick it up as normal to return it to its cage.

◆ LEFT
When it comes to exhibiting hamsters, not all individuals will meet the show standard. You will need some luck when breeding colour varieties with markings.

KEEPING CLEAN

Short-coated hamsters need very little grooming, although wiping them with a chamois leather, in the direction of the lie of the fur, is recommended before a show, to improve the appearance of the coat. Short-coated rexes have curly coats that do not lie flat. However, their coat care is quite straightforward as their hair is far less likely to mat. Hamsters are actually very fastidious about grooming and will usually keep themselves looking immaculate and sleek – if your pet does appear to be fluffed up with an unkempt look about it, it may indicate an illness.

Hamsters with long coats need combing once or twice a week, to prevent the hair from becoming matted and to remove bedding or pieces of food, which can get caught up here. Use a small comb with rotating teeth or a soft toothbrush. The former is a better option as it helps to break down any tangles that are forming, rather than pulling at the coat. If there is a bad knot in the coat you may have to cut it out. If you have to do this, you won't be able to show your hamster until the hair regrows to its original length.

HAMSTER SHOWS

If you are interested in showing your hamster, it is a good idea to join one of the many specialist societies, which are generally a good source of information and equipment (such as show cages).

At the show, the judges will assess the hamsters' colouring and form, and it is vital that you are aware of the show standard for the type of hamster that you are exhibiting. As well as the overall appearance or "type" of the hamster, the judges will also consider individual requirements for the different colours and coat types. Do not despair if your initial attempts at

exhibiting do not result in any wins. This is partly because hamsters are only likely to win when they are in top condition. When being judged, the condition of each entry is significant, and a hamster may win at one show and fail to be placed at the next. Always make sure you turn out your entry in immaculate condition.

♦ ABOVE
The pairing of hamsters needs to be carried out with regard to their physical appearance or type, as well as coloration, if you hope to breed exhibition winners.

♦ BELOW LEFT
Grooming a long-haired hamster is a more involved task, which needs to be carried out a couple of times a week; otherwise, the coat will become matted.

♦ BELOW
Be careful which foods you offer your hamster before a show. Avoid carrot as the juice is likely to stain the fur on the face, and this will affect the coloration, albeit temporarily.

GERBILS AND JIRDS

This group of rodents is found in arid parts of the world. Like hamsters, they burrow to escape danger and the heat of the midday sun, but they are also far more agile. Their hind legs are especially well developed, and this enables them to jump long distances. In a home setting, you will need to handle them carefully to prevent them from escaping. The Mongolian gerbil has a social nature, and should be kept in pairs or trios rather than on its own.

INTRODUCTION

The Mongolian gerbil (*Meriones unguiculatus*) is the best-known member of this group – it is the most friendly of the pet gerbils – and has built up a strong following since first becoming available to pet-seekers during the 1960s. The first specimens were collected on an expedition to Mongolia by a Japanese scientist in 1954, and were bred in Japan before some stock was sent on to the United States, and then to Europe. These gerbils were actually discovered during the mid-1800s by the missionary Pere David, who travelled widely in this part of the Orient.

Mongolian gerbils are well adapted to living in desert areas, with the sandy colour of their coats and black tipping providing excellent camouflage when they are seen from above. Their underparts are white, to reflect the heat of the sand beneath them, while their long tail is also covered in fur. The tail serves as a stabilizer when the rodent is running, with its long hind legs helping to support its weight so

◆ LEFT
The natural colour of the Mongolian gerbil is called the agouti, and this helps to provide camouflage when the gerbil is viewed from above. The underparts are paler in colour.

that it can sit up and look around, jumping away if danger threatens, in a similar way to a kangaroo. Mongolian gerbils can leap 45 cm (1½ ft) to elude a would-be predator, and then quickly disappear down their burrow.

Internally, their bodies are well equipped to withstand the rigours of life in the desert. Their kidneys are incredibly efficient, allowing them

◆ LEFT
An ever-increasing range of colour mutations and varieties has been created in the case of the Mongolian gerbil, and this has led to a growing interest in exhibiting them.

to produce a very concentrated urine. This in turn means that, unlike rats and mice, gerbils have no pungent odour associated with them.

Jirds are very similar to gerbils in their habits, and the descriptions of the two species are sometimes synonymous, as in the case of the Shaw's jird which is another member of the *Meriones* genus. Like gerbils, jirds are found in arid areas. Both gerbils and jirds are found in an area ranging from North Africa through the Middle East into Asia. Only in the case of the Mongolian gerbil, however, have colour variants become widely known at present, and you may well need to track down specialist gerbil breeders in order to obtain stock of other species.

◆ BELOW
Gerbils use their long hind legs to stand up and explore their environment. You must ensure their housing is covered, to prevent any escapes.

GERBILS AS PETS

The most important thing to bear in mind with gerbils is that they are highly social by nature, to the extent that they must be housed in groups, rather than singly. If you do not want them to breed, then you should keep them in single-sex groups. Their natural curiosity means that they are easily tamed and can be encouraged to feed quite easily from the hand.

As children's pets, gerbils have the advantage over hamsters in that they are not primarily nocturnal. Even so, they are not really pets that like to be handled or cuddled for any length of time, since they have very active natures and prefer to have the freedom to scamper about.

Although gerbils are not easy to recapture in a room because they are so agile, they are less likely to disappear in these surroundings than a hamster, for example, which may well choose to slip down under a gap in the floorboards, or disappear out of sight. Gerbils often remain on the surface and, with care and patience, it is possible to net them, or persuade them into a large cardboard box placed on its side, if food has already been placed there as a bait.

Gerbils and jirds can be expected to live for up to three years.

◆ RIGHT
When it is standing up, the gerbil relies on its tail to help to support its body. In this position, it is not just looking around but also sniffing the air, to pick up scents.

◆ ABOVE
While balancing on its strong back legs, a gerbil may pick up and eat food using its shorter front legs, which serve rather like hands.

SPECIES AND BREEDS

MONGOLIAN GERBIL

A number of different colour varieties of the Mongolian gerbil have been developed. The first originated in Canada and is known as the Canadian white spot. It has a white spot on the coloured area of the body, and often has white legs and white on the tail.

A pure albino form is identified by its reddish eyes and pink ears. Up until the age of about three months or so, when the dark fur develops along the tail, it is difficult to distinguish between the albino and the dark-tailed white. At the other extreme is the pure black gerbil, known for its glossy coat. Another popular variety is the lilac, which has a bluish-grey coat (with a rosy hue) and pink eyes. Although similar, the dove grey's coat is lighter and more silvery in colour. It also has pink eyes.

A very popular variety is the predominantly gold-coloured argente, which has a white abdomen and feet, and pinkish claw and ears. The dark-eyed honey is a more unusual colour; the young, in this case, undergo a colour change at about two months old. Up until this stage, they have a yellow coat with black fur on the extremities of the body, such as the

◆ LEFT
The lilac form of the Mongolian gerbil. This colour was originally developed from crossings between the black and argente varieties. Occasional white patches do sometimes crop up on their coats.

◆ RIGHT
The argente has been described under various names, including cinnamon, golden and, perhaps most accurately, as the white-bellied golden, with a very clear delineation between white and golden areas.

◆ LEFT
The black mutation was first recorded in laboratory stock housed at the USAF School of Aerospace Medicine in Texas. Ideally, these gerbils should be pure black, with no odd white patches at all.

legs, tail and nose, giving them an appearance rather reminiscent of a Siamese cat. When they moult for the first time, these dark areas disappear from the extremities, and then ticking appears on the yellow hair of the body. As the gerbil grows older, so its white belly patch becomes more obvious. The eyes in this case are dark, as are the nails and ears.

In the silver agouti or chinchilla form, the beige and black of the normal agouti has been modified to silvery white and black, with the belly

◆ LEFT
The Mongolian gerbil has a natural agouti coloration, with dark and light banding running down each hair, making it hard to spot from above.

◆ RIGHT
Always check on
compatibility when
considering the
purchase of other
types of gerbil or
jird. Some, such as
the relatively large
Jerusalem jird shown
here, may need to be
housed on their own.

◆ RIGHT
A pallid gerbil.
Note the relatively
large eyes, indicating
that it becomes more
active as darkness
falls. Like other
gerbils, the pallid is
very active by nature,
and jumps well, with
its tail serving as
a counterbalance.

JERUSALEM JIRD

One breed that you may occasionally encounter among the other varieties of gerbils and jirds is the Jerusalem jird (*Meriones crassus*). This variety differs significantly from its smaller Mongolian cousin in its requirements, and is very solitary by nature – to the extent that it will need to be housed on its own. The coat of the Jerusalem jird has a more reddish hue, while in terms of temperament, it tends to be less friendly than the Mongolian.

OTHER SPECIES

The attractive Egyptian gerbil (*Gerbillus gerbillus*) is sandy brown in colour. It lives on a colony basis and can become very tame. Shaw's jird (*Meriones shawi*) is found in parts of Egypt but, unfortunately, these rodents are not social by nature. Perhaps the most bizarre species of all is the fat-tailed or Duprasi's gerbil (*Pachyuromys duprasi*), which occurs in northern parts of the Sahara desert in Africa. These gerbils have a rounded body shape, and a broad, pink tail, which acts as a store for their body fat, keeping it aside to be metabolized when food rations are in short supply. The fat-tailed gerbil is nocturnal in its habits. Again, these rodents are not social by nature, and they should always be housed on their own to avoid fights.

being white. The eyes and claws are black. It has also proved possible to combine the chinchilla and dark-eyed honey mutations to create a variety known as the polar fox. This gerbil's silvery-white coloration replaces the honey coloration, although the characteristic change in markings, associated with the dark-eyed honey, is seen in this case as well. The unusual name of these gerbils stems from the similarity in appearance to the fox found in the Arctic region.

Gerbils are now being bred that display the Himalayan gene, which is responsible for the appearance of the Siamese and related cat breeds. The points of these gerbils – their legs and feet, ears, nose and tail – are dark in colour,

whereas the body is a lighter shade. Tonkinese and Burmese forms of gerbil, which show less contrast thanks to their darker overall body coloration, have also been bred; again, their names derive from breeds that exist in the cat fancy. Other new varieties of Mongolian gerbil are also being developed at present, including creams and sepia forms. These may not always be widely available.

◆ RIGHT
A number of other gerbils and jirds are available from specialist breeders. This is Shaw's jird, which, like its Mongolian relative, displays a dark tip on the upper surface of the tail.

HOUSING AND FEEDING

As gerbils are natural burrowers, it is best to house them in converted aquaria, as these allow more depth than wire-mesh cages.

GERBIL HOUSING

A lightweight acrylic tank is preferable to a glass tank because it is easier and safer to move. Equip the tank with a secure, ventilated hood to prevent the gerbils from using their jumping abilities to leap out, and to stop cats from reaching in. You should be able to acquire a special housing set-up for gerbils, which includes not only a hood but also a colour co-ordinated drinking bottle, which fits into the enclosure as part of the hood and can be removed easily from the outside.

One of the major advantages of keeping gerbils, compared with rats and mice in particular, is that they produce very little urine and so have virtually no odour associated with them. This makes caring for them more straightforward, as the lining

Gerbil mix

✦ BELOW RIGHT
Young gerbils born in a colony can be left with their parents, but you will need to check that their quarters do not become overcrowded.

✦ BELOW LEFT
Gerbils of different colours can be housed together without problems, but avoid adding newcomers to an existing colony, as this can result in fighting.

in their quarters does not need to be changed as frequently. Coarse shavings, sold as small-animal bedding, should be used to line the cage. It is important not to use sawdust, as the gerbils' burrowing activities mean that their eyes can be irritated by flakes of sawdust. You can bury lengths of tubing in the substrate to allow the gerbils to explore these areas, as their own tunnels, built from shavings, could collapse. Do not forget to provide bedding material, which the gerbils can use to line their nesting chambers.

Clean out the gerbil's cage on a weekly basis, discarding the soiled shavings and replacing them with fresh ones. You will need to transfer the gerbils into a secure carrier while you clean out their quarters. A simple acrylic enclosure with a hood will suffice for this purpose, and can also serve as a suitable carrier should you need to take your gerbil to the vet. This type of carrier is much safer than a cardboard box, which gerbils will often gnaw their way out of.

SUITABLE FOODS

Feeding gerbils is straightforward, and the procedure is the same as for other small rodents. Gerbils feed mainly on a diet of seeds, greenstuff and vegetables, and they may also eat a few invertebrates, such as mealworms. However, do not feed them large quantities of oil-based seeds, such as sunflower, as these can cause obesity, which can prove fatal. A small amount of hay is important, not just as bedding but also to add fibre to their diet. An earthenware food pot, which they will be unable to tip over, makes an ideal feeding bowl.

CONVERTED AQUARIUM SET-UP

1 It is relatively easy to set up a home for a colony of Mongolian gerbils by converting an aquarium into what is sometimes described as a gerbilarium. Ensure the tank is clean and dry before tipping in coarse wood shavings.

2 Gerbils will want to have areas where they can retreat in their enclosure, and you can help by including cardboard tubing in the substrate. Food, water and a selection of toys should also be provided.

3 A secure covering over the enclosure is important, both to stop the gerbils jumping out and to protect them from cats or dogs. A secure covering can be made using wire mesh attached to a wooden framework. Make sure the covering can be securely fixed in place.

4 As a further precaution, weigh down the roof with blocks placed at each end, which will stop any cat from being able to dislodge the lid. Note how the water bottle is suspended from the roof, allowing the gerbils to drink without difficulty.

Although gerbils do not drink large volumes of water, it is important to provide them with a supply of fresh drinking water on a daily basis. The bottle should be fixed securely in place so that it will not leak – originating from an arid area, gerbils are very susceptible to damp surroundings, and can suffer from respiratory problems.

Before you obtain a gerbil, find out what it has been feeding on, and do not change this diet for the first two weeks after rehoming. Sudden changes made during this period can lead to a fatal digestive upset. Provide your gerbil with something to gnaw to stop its teeth from overgrowing, which would prevent it from eating properly.

GENERAL CARE AND BREEDING

Gerbils are surprisingly agile creatures, able to escape encircling fingers by using their powerful hind legs to jump out of your grasp. They are not pets that enjoy being handled, although they will often feed from the hand.

HANDLING

When you need to restrain a gerbil, start by allowing it to sniff at your fingers, and then gently coax it on to your hand. Place your other hand on top, so that the gerbil can see out but will still feel reasonably secure. Since it is not being held tightly, it will also be unlikely to bite under these circumstances.

Handling a gerbil can sometimes be rather alarming because, acting on instinct, it will often faint in the same way that it would if caught by a predator. Some strains of gerbils are more prone to this behaviour than others. If a gerbil does react in this way, the best thing to do is to place it in a quiet spot and it will soon recover.

Although you can restrain a gerbil by gently holding the base of its tail close to the body, never grasp it by the tip of its tail. The skin here is very loose and sheds rapidly, resulting in bleeding and even partial loss of the tail. Again, this is a defensive mechanism that helps the gerbil to escape from a predator. Careful handling should prevent this from being a problem.

MATING AND PREGNANCY

It is important to sex gerbils correctly at the outset as they will need to be kept in single-sex groups; if not, you will almost certainly end up with unexpected litters. Male gerbils can be identified easily by comparing the length of their ano-genital gap with that of the females, since this space is significantly longer. Once mature, male gerbils are also significantly larger than females and are nearly twice as heavy.

When breeding Mongolian gerbils, introduce the male and female carefully. Initially, place them both in neutral territory. Some acrylic containers have a divider, so, after a couple of days, the two gerbils can be allowed direct contact by removing the partition. Even so, watch for any signs of aggression, although normally there are no problems under these circumstances, and mating soon takes place. The pair should be left together for about a week, after which they can be separated.

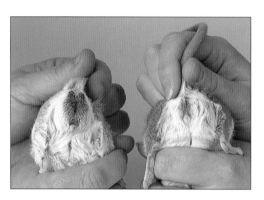

◆ LEFT
Sexing gerbils is straightforward, with the male shown on the left here. The swellings caused by the testicles will be less evident in younger males.

◆ RIGHT
When picking up a gerbil, do not hold it tightly in your hand but cup it gently, as shown here.

♦ BELOW
The long tail of the gerbil acts as a
counterbalance, helping to ensure that
when the gerbil jumps, using its powerful
limbs, it will usually land safely.

♦ BOTTOM
Young Mongolian gerbils can remain within an
established colony, provided that the group will
not be overcrowded.

It is not a good idea to leave
the male with the female because she
can mate again very soon after giving
birth, and this will mean that the
gerbils are likely to produce an
unexpected second litter. About
24 days after mating, a female will
typically give birth to five cubs,
which are without fur and totally
helpless at this early stage, usually
measuring about 2.5 cm (1 in) in
length. The young gerbils will grow
rapidly, and can be weaned once they
are about five or six weeks of age.
They are likely to be mature after
a similar period of time, and will
continue to breed well until the age
of about 14 months old.

♦ LEFT
Young gerbils can
be weaned at five
or six weeks. They
will be mature about
6 weeks later, and
will breed well up
to 14 months.

GROOMING AND SHOWING

Gerbils need very little grooming
in order to look immaculate, partly
because no long-coated mutation has
yet been developed, and their coats
are not prone to becoming tangled.
In addition, gerbils frequently clean
themselves. However, for exhibition
purposes, a degree of tidying-up will
usually be necessary to ensure that
your gerbils are looking their best.

SHOW PREPARATION

The most common problem is that the
coat may have become stained by juice
from greenstuff, particularly the area
around the face. It is a good idea to
leave items such as carrot and cabbage
out of the gerbil's diet for a week
beforehand as it may be difficult to
remove these stains, especially as it is
not advisable to wash the coat. Aside

from the stress involved, there is a risk
that the gerbil could develop a chill.
Serious exhibitors often resort to
using corn flour to mask stained areas,
carefully moistening the area and
rubbing in the corn flour. Once it has
dried, the area needs to be brushed
very gently to remove all trace of the
powder. If you place the gerbil in a
hay-lined box, it will burrow in and

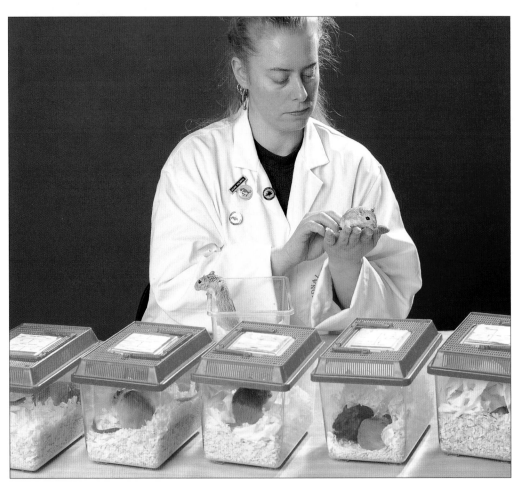

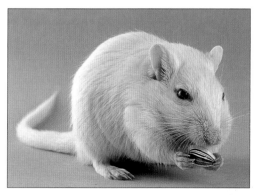

◆ RIGHT
Gerbils are shown
individually, so
you will have to
wait until a female
has given birth
and her litter are
independent before
showing her again.

◆ BOTTOM
You will need to
be familiar with the
show standard for
particular varieties,
in terms of coloration
and patterning.

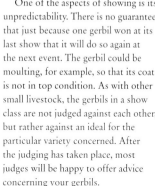

◆ BELOW
Always ensure that your gerbil is in perfect
condition prior to entering a show. Any loss of
hair or damage to the tip of the tail will almost
always count against it.

this will have the effect of grooming
the coat. Finally, stroking the gerbil
with a silk cloth helps to impart a
good gloss to its fur.

GERBIL SHOWS

Standard show cages for gerbils are
essential for serious exhibitors. For
pet classes, however, the gerbils'
regular home can be used, although
you should cut down on the
bedding for the show, so
that the judge will be
able to see your entry

easily. It is also very important that
the judge will be able to handle your
gerbil without difficulty. If you hope
to show your pet gerbil, you will need
to train it when it is young
to get it used to handling.
In addition to the
condition of the
gerbil and

its tameness, the judges will
also look at its surroundings. An
otherwise excellent entry will be
penalized if exhibited in a dirty or
chipped show cage. It is important
to maintain show cages or pens in
top condition by washing them out
after each show. After they have dried,
keep them dust free by storing them
in plastic bags until required again.

One of the aspects of showing is its
unpredictability. There is no guarantee
that just because one gerbil won at its
last show that it will do so again at
the next event. The gerbil could be
moulting, for example, so that its coat
is not in top condition. As with other
small livestock, the gerbils in a show
class are not judged against each other,
but rather against an ideal for the
particular variety concerned. After
the judging has taken place, most
judges will be happy to offer advice
concerning your gerbils.

RATS AND MICE

While these rodents may not top the list of everyone's favourite pet, they can turn out to be truly excellent companions, with rats in particular proving to be highly intelligent. Although rats and mice are very similar in appearance, rats are distinguished by their larger size. They must not be housed together, since rats will often instinctively attack mice. The choice of colours available in the case of rats is far less varied than it is with mice.

INTRODUCTION

Although rats and mice have a justified reputation for spreading various unpleasant diseases, the simple fact is that today's domesticated, or "fancy", rats and mice are far removed from their wild relatives, and are unlikely to present any significant health risks to people keeping them.

The process of domestication began well over a century ago, when rats were a major cause of disease in densely populated cities. The high death toll from rat-induced infections led to the employment of rat-catchers to keep a check on their numbers.

On occasion, the rat-catchers would catch rats that were different in colour to the normal type. These oddities were often kept on display at public houses, whereas their less fortunate relatives were killed by dogs in rat pits for customer entertainment.

◆ ABOVE
The brown rat is the original ancestor of all of today's fancy rats, although the black rat was also kept and bred for a period.

◆ LEFT
The wild form of the house mouse, with its typical brownish coloration – far removed from today's colourful domesticated mouse varieties.

By this stage in history, the brown rat (*Rattus norvegicus*) had become far more numerous than the black rat (*Rattus rattus*), and all of today's fancy rats are of brown rat descent, although different-coloured strains of black rat were kept during the 1920s.

The keeping of fancy rats lost favour for a period after this era until the 1970s. Since then, however, there has been much interest in keeping these intelligent rodents as pets and for exhibition purposes, and more colour varieties have been established.

The domestication of the fancy mouse from its wild ancestor, the house mouse (*Mus musculus*), first began in the United Kingdom in the latter part of the 19th century. As in the case of rats, mice were widely used for medical experiments at this time, although their show potential was quickly recognized. The National Mouse Club in the United Kingdom was established in 1895 and is the oldest body of its kind in the world. Its creation led to the development of a vast colour range of fancy mice.

◆ BELOW
Rats can become very tame if handled regularly, and they will soon learn to identify their owners by their scent. They rarely bite, unless frightened or badly handled.

RATS AND MICE AS PETS

When it comes to choosing between a mouse or a rat as a pet, it is worth bearing in mind that rats are significantly larger, averaging at least 25 cm (10 in) in length, and will consequently need more spacious accommodation. Mice typically measure around 15 cm (6 in) overall, including their tail. Rats have a significantly longer lifespan than mice, living on average for five years or more, while mice have a lifespan of around three years. Rats are also more likely to become tamer and are more amenable to handling. The strong odour of both rats and mice can be a

problem in the home environment, although females tend to produce a less pungent urine than males and may make a more suitable pet. While rats are typically kept on their own, mice can be housed comfortably in single-sex pairs or even trios.

It is important to buy pet mice and rats when they are young so that they accept being handled. They are then far less likely to inflict a painful bite when picked up.

Rats and mice are nocturnal by instinct, but they will usually be active during the day as well. Ensure that the fur looks sleek when you buy – if it is not, it could be a sign of ill-health, particularly if the rodent also appears to be hunched up.

COLOUR VARIETIES

While there are now over 700 different varieties of mice, the number of fancy rat mutations is much lower, totalling less than 30. In most cases, the choice of colours available in most pet stores is small, so if you are seeking out some of the more unusual colours, you will usually need to contact a breeder. Look through the advertisement columns of specialist magazines or contact clubs. Details can usually be obtained through local libraries or via the Internet.

RATS

Breeds of rat that are furthest removed from the natural agouti form are the most popular. The most widely kept variety of rat is the albino form, sometimes called the white, which is distinguished by its pink eyes. Its lack of colour pigment also accounts for its pink ears and tail. Most of the new rat varieties have direct counterparts in

♦ ABOVE
The silvered mink is just one of a growing number of exotic colour varieties of the domestic rat. All are descended from the brown rather than the black rat.

♦ BELOW
A Himalayan rat, so-called because of the darker areas of fur present on the extremities of the body. These will be far less apparent in newly born pups.

the mouse fancy, with the exception of the mink. This rat is coffee coloured, with a bluish sheen to its coat.

Darker colours include the chocolate, which should be an even dark shade, as well as the black, which must also be pure in colour with no odd white hairs visible in its coat. In addition, there are other self (solid colour) varieties with pink eyes and a rosy hue – including the champagne, which is beige. The patterned colour variants include the hooded, which has a coloured area over its head and shoulders, extending down the back to the base of the tail. In the case of the capped form, there is no darker streak running back down the spine, and the remainder of the fur is white. There is no long-coated form, although there is a rex mutation, which has distinctive curled fur and whiskers.

♦ ABOVE
An agouti and white rat. The agouti colouring corresponds to that of the wild brown rat, which explains why these varieties are not the most popular choice as domestic pets.

♦ LEFT
A silvered black rat. At shows, it is not just the coloration of these rodents that is judged, but also their physical appearance, or "type".

MICE

There are both self and patterned varieties of fancy mice. One of the most striking is the self red, which is a rich shade of chestnut. Its coloration is improved by the addition of a satin mutation, which gives a glossy sheen to the coat. The eyes are black, but some varieties, such as white and cream, exist in both pink-eyed and black-eyed forms. Evenness of colour through the coat is an essential attribute for self-coloured mice of all varieties.

Tan varieties are instantly recognizable by their appearance. Their underparts are tan-coloured, while the remainder of the body is a contrasting shade. The feet should match the body colour on the outside and be tan-coloured on the inside. Nor is it just dark shades such as black and tan that are regularly seen. Lighter variants, too, such as silver and tan, are quite commonly bred.

Mice showing various other markings are also widely kept today. These include Himalayans, with dark points, and the Dutch, which has a similar pattern to that of the corresponding guinea pig or rabbit breeds.

The features of the long-coated and rex variants can be combined with any colour form or patterning. The scope here is truly enormous, and some fascinating specimens can be seen at the larger mice shows.

◆ BELOW
Even coloration is an important feature of the silver-grey variety. Sometimes, the body extremities may lack adequate silvering. This individual is a buck (male).

◆ ABOVE
The chinchilla mouse is so-called because it resembles the wild chinchilla in colour. The individual hairs are tipped with black, and the undercoat is slate blue.

◆ BELOW
The black form of the mouse must be jet black, with a glossy coat. Mice of this colour were first recorded as far back as 1640. Any white markings are a serious flaw.

◆ ABOVE
A black and tan mouse. The tan underparts are most obvious when these mice sit up on their haunches. There must be clear delineation between the colours, as in this individual.

HOUSING AND FEEDING

Caring for rats and mice in the home does not present problems, providing the housing is roomy and secure and the diet is suitably nutritious.

ACCOMMODATION

The range of housing options for rats and mice has grown significantly over recent years. Special cages are now available that provide plenty of climbing space and are essentially escape proof – a highly important consideration when keeping these rodents in the home as, once free, they can be difficult to recapture. To be extra safe, it is worthwhile adding a small combination lock to the door.

If you prefer not to use a mesh cage – which can be a magnet to a cat – an acrylic container with a ventilated roof is a suitable alternative. This lightweight option is easy to move around but, as with any housing for pets in the home, be sure not to position the cage resting on furniture in front of a window. In hot weather, your pet may be affected by heat stress, with the glass magnifying the

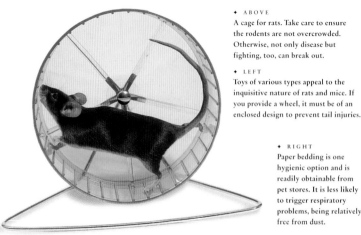

sun's rays. Rats and mice are also nocturnal creatures and bright daylight can upset their sleep patterns. Position cages in a draught-free place because, in spite of the hardiness of their wild relatives, domestic rats and mice are susceptible to chilling.

♦ ABOVE
A cage for rats. Take care to ensure the rodents are not overcrowded. Otherwise, not only disease but fighting, too, can break out.

♦ LEFT
Toys of various types appeal to the inquisitive nature of rats and mice. If you provide a wheel, it must be of an enclosed design to prevent tail injuries.

♦ RIGHT
Paper bedding is one hygienic option and is readily obtainable from pet stores. It is less likely to trigger respiratory problems, being relatively free from dust.

Most cages for rats are equipped with a detachable metal tray where the droppings collect. It is a good idea to line the tray with shavings but do not use this as a lining material in the rats' quarters, where they can burrow directly into it. A better option for this purpose is to use dust-free bedding also sold in pet stores.

Both mice and rats are shy creatures so it is essential to provide them with a thick layer of bedding in a corner of their quarters where they can retreat

Rat mix

Sunflower seeds

Peanuts

Dog biscuits

and curl up to sleep. A wooden box surrounding this area will give them greater security. Special paper bedding is a better option than hay as both rats and mice are susceptible to respiratory diseases, and these can be triggered by the dust and fungal spores in hay.

SUITABLE FOODS

You can feed your rodent a seed-based diet, which contains cereals such as wheat and flaked maize (corn), or, preferably, a pelleted diet, which contains all the necessary ingredients to keep rats and mice in good health.

✦ ABOVE, BELOW LEFT AND BELOW RIGHT
Retreats are very important, allowing rats and mice to feel secure in their quarters; the natural instinct of small mammals is to stay hidden, out of sight of possible predators.

If you are not feeding your rodent a pre-formulated diet you may need to use a supplement to compensate for any nutritional deficiencies. Sprinkle the supplement over the rodent's favourite tidbits. When it comes to fresh food, it is best to offer it in small amounts on a regular basis. Although it will not contribute greatly to the protein intake, it will provide valuable vitamins and minerals. Large amounts of fresh food eaten at one time can trigger digestive upsets.

Avoid using mixes that contain significant proportions of oil seeds, such as sunflower or peanuts. These are not recommended for rats and mice on a long-term basis as they are likely to provoke skin irritations. There is no harm in offering other treats occasionally, such as small cubes of cheddar cheese and raisins.

The occasional sunflower seed or nut can be used when taming your rodent to feed from the hand. Otherwise, attempts to hand-feed could lead to bitten fingers.

A water bottle that attaches to the rodent's quarters and an earthenware food container are both essential.

GENERAL CARE AND BREEDING

You can purchase accessories of various kinds for the enclosure, but bear in mind that mice and especially rats can inflict damage on plastic items, and these may need to be replaced in due course. It is actually much better to provide them with wooden blocks for chewing purposes or dried crusts of bread, on which they can wear down their incisor teeth. Avoid exercise wheels which have an open-weave design, as the rodent's long tail may become trapped.

Some household items can also be used to amuse your rodent, such as the lining tubes out of paper towelling, which make excellent tunnels. Rats are very playful by nature, and glass marbles that can be rolled along with their paws are another item that often appeals to them; glass marbles will also prove indestructible.

HANDLING
The handling of rodents requires particular care, as rats and mice have poor eyesight and rely more on their

sense of smell for information about the world around them. If you attempt to pick one up too suddenly, you are likely to be bitten. Instead, allow the rodent to sniff at your fingers, and then gently scoop it up from beneath. Your new pet will quickly come to recognize your distinctive scent and

will become much more amenable to regular handling. Even so, take care not to clench your pet tightly – this will make it panic and it could then bite – but allow it to rest in your hand. If necessary, mice can be restrained from scampering off by gently grasping the base of their tails.

◆ ABOVE
Handling a mouse. Do not try to grip your pet tightly in order to restrain it. Instead, encourage the rodent to step on to your hand and hold it gently by the base of the tail.

◆ LEFT
Rats are slightly more difficult to hold than mice because of their larger size, but they will rest in the hand for short periods, being cupped in this way, without attempting to bite or struggle.

◆ ABOVE
Rats will step readily from one hand to another, usually sniffing cautiously before they do so. Many will also perch on your shoulder.

NEWBORN RATS

Young rats are helpless and blind at birth. Do not disturb them at this stage because it could cause the doe to abandon them. Dark markings indicate black fur.

One of the features of rodents is the speed at which their young develop. This litter of rat pups is 12 days old and their coloration is already apparent. They sleep together for warmth.

A three weeks old, these young rats are moving and exploring their environment. It will be a further two weeks, however, before they are fully weaned and able to go to a new home.

◆ RIGHT
The rapid growth of young rodents can be seen by comparing the size of the younger four-week-old rat here with its larger companion, which is just a fortnight older.

MATING AND PREGNANCY

This is a relatively straightforward procedure. Male rats and mice, known as bucks, have the typical longer ano-genital gap and a visible scrotal sac. Females (does) in general are smaller in size. If you want to encourage mating, introduce the pair to neutral territory and leave them together for up to a fortnight, by which time mating will have taken place. The doe should then be housed on her own in preparation for the birth. Pregnancy lasts about 23 days in the case of rats, and a couple of days less in the case of mice. Rats may have slightly larger litters on average, comprising ten or more pups, which can be separated from their mother at five to six weeks old. Young mice pups should be weaned at three weeks old. Mice will often reach maturity at three months of age.

NEWBORN MICE

The breeding cycle of mice is faster than that of rats, but otherwise similar. No special foods are required for rearing purposes.

Young mice aged ten days old with their mother. The pup on the far right is smaller than its nest mates and is the runt of the litter.

Mice at 25 days, which have been weaned. The genetics surrounding the breeding of different colours have been intensively studied.

GROOMING AND SHOWING

Coat care for rodents is generally minimal, although long-coated mice do require grooming to prevent the hair becoming matted or soiled by bedding underneath. Exhibitors often have their own particular ways of conditioning their stock prior to a major show but, in many cases, it is possible simply to take rats or mice from their regular cages, transfer them to show cages and go on to win without any further preparation.

SHOW PREPARATION

To improve the sheen on your pet's coat, gently groom it with a piece of silk in the direction of the lie. As condition is very important in the judging process, do not expect your rodent to win if it is moulting. There is nothing that can be done here other than allowing the new fur to grow. It is worth noting, too, that a mouse or rat that is out of condition could be vulnerable to illness.

✦ ABOVE
Rats need little in the way of grooming, and keeping the fur free of food or bedding material is usually the most that will be required.

✦ BELOW
The condition of the mice is very important for show purposes, and those that are moulting are unlikely to excel. The Maxey show cage is typically used for exhibiting mice.

AT THE SHOW

It is well worth visiting shows, even if you are not entering any rats or mice yourself. This will give you the opportunity to study the entries and build up an image in your mind's eye of the ideal for your particular variety.

To gain even greater insight into the exhibition side of the hobby, you could volunteer to steward at show events. Stewarding itself entails taking the entries and facilitating the judging process by removing the hay, for example, from the Maxey show cages, allowing the judge to remove the mice more easily so that they can be examined individually. As a steward, you will be able to see how judges assess the entries at close quarters, and, after judging has occurred, you can ask the judge about the points that have influenced the placings.

Judging standards are laid down for the different varieties. These relate firstly to the overall appearance of the rats and mice in general terms, specifying what is considered to be desirable, such as the shape of the head

A wide variety of different retreats can be
purchased for mice, although plastic designs
are preferable to wood, because they will not
become stained by urine.

It is not a good idea to allow your pet mouse
to exercise in the garden, as these rodents are
very nimble and can quickly run off and
disappear from view.

and ears. They also highlight serious
flaws, such as kinked tails, which
would merit penalties – including
possible disqualification – although
it is unlikely that rodents with these
weaknesses would have been entered
in the first place.

Then there are the more specific
requirements – depending on the
variety concerned – that specify the
pattern of markings or the desired
depth of coloration. Condition is not
overlooked either, with obese entries
being penalized, while ease of handling
is another important factor that can
help to influence a judge's decision.
Those varieties that are not yet
standardized because there are too
few examples in existence, are usually
grouped together. Assuming that the
popularity of these varieties continues
to grow among fanciers, and no major
weaknesses crop up in the bloodlines,
then these are likely to be recognized
with specific official standards in due
course and will be transferred into
classes of their own.

Red-eyed white mice are popular pets. This
may be linked to the fact that they appear
very clean, thanks to the colour of their fur.

CHINCHILLAS

The requirements of these rodents are rather different from other members of the group. Chinchillas are also more costly to purchase, although this is balanced to some extent by their relatively long lifespan. As quite new entrants on the show scene, chinchillas are not widely exhibited as yet. However, there are signs that this state of affairs is changing, particularly as new colour varieties are becoming more commonly available.

INTRODUCTION

Chinchillas belong to the caviomorph sub-group in the rodent family and, as such, are closely related to guinea pigs. Like guinea pigs, chinchillas originate from the Andean region of South America, on the western side of this continent, and are found at relatively high altitudes where the temperature can become very cold, particularly at night. They are well equipped to survive in this type of terrain, however, thanks to their very dense coat. In fact, the coat is so dense (there can be 70 or more hairs growing from a single hair follicle) that parasites cannot become established in it.

Unfortunately, this very dense, soft fur proved ideal for clothing and accessories, and this led to the Spanish explorers of South America taking chinchillas back to Europe in the early 1500s. The growing European and North American demand during the 1800s led to the determined hunting

◆ LEFT
The mountain viscacha, which lives in the Andean region of South America, is closely related to the chinchilla. It has similarly dense fur but much larger ears.

◆ BELOW LEFT
A young viscacha in the wild. All members of the family Chinchillidae produce fewer offspring than other rodents and after a longer gestation period.

of these rodents for the fur trade. By the early 1900s the chinchilla was becoming an endangered species.

The first efforts to farm chinchillas for their fur proved unsuccessful, and by the time a mining engineer called M. F. Chapman tried to obtain chinchillas for a further attempt, during the 1920s, they were on the verge of extinction. It took 23 men three years to obtain just 11 live examples for him. Fortunately, this was sufficient to establish the first chinchilla fur farm and, also, ultimately, to safeguard the future of these unique rodents.

After careful acclimatization from the Andean mountains to sea level, the chinchillas were taken by ship to California, where they started

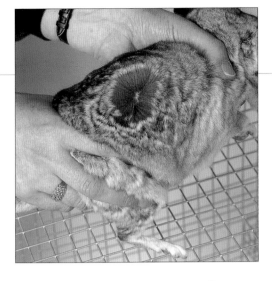

♦ RIGHT
The soft, dense coat of the chinchilla proved so popular with furriers that it nearly brought about the extinction of the species.

♦ BELOW
The coloration of both the chinchilla and the mountain viscacha, seen here, help them to blend into the background in the wild.

breeding rapidly. Stock initially changed hands at high prices, but by the 1960s the appeal of chinchillas started to grow. They started to be sold as pets for the first time, and the market for their fur began to decline.

CHINCHILLAS AS PETS

Chinchillas are now highly popular around the world as companion animals. They are still more expensive than other pet rodents but their exclusivity and clean image has helped them to become favourite pets. As chinchillas tend to be more active at dusk, they are a good choice of companion for people who are out at work all day, and they can become very tame, especially if handled regularly from an early age. Unlike the guinea pig, the chinchilla is very much a household pet and it will require special care and grooming. Chinchillas have sharp incisor teeth, which can inflict serious damage on plastic food containers and play equipment in their cages; these will need to be checked and replaced on a regular basis.

Unlike many rodents, chinchillas have an unusually long lifespan, and can live for over a decade. Some have been known to live for over 20 years.

COLOUR VARIETIES

The typical wild form of the chinchilla, known as the standard, is variable in colour, with light and dark bands encircling the individual hairs, creating a slightly mottled impression over the body. The depth of colouring differs between individuals, ranging from shades of grey through to black, with the hairs darkest at the tips. In contrast, the fur on the underside of the body is pure white. The eyes are always black and the ears, too, are dark in colour.

WHITE FORMS

The palest varieties now available are the white forms. The true white is pure white in colour, sometimes displaying odd darker patches. It is not a true albino, as it may have some black hairs on the body and has black ears and eyes. This is in contrast to the

♦ BELOW
The alert nature of the chinchilla is clearly displayed by this standard individual, with its large ears helping to pinpoint the direction of sounds with great accuracy.

pink white where the presence of any pigment is restricted to traces of beige colouring. The ears and paws are both pink, and the eyes may vary in colour from pink to red, emphasizing the lack of dark melanin pigment in the white chinchilla form.

BEIGE FORMS

There are two forms of beige chinchillas, and these differ in their genetic make-up and thus, their coloration. The pure homozygous beige is paler in colour than its heterozygous counterpart, and is a very pale shade of cream with a slight pink suffusion. The eyes in this case are also a pale shade of pink, with a whitish ring surrounding the pupil at the centre of each eye. Heterozygous beige chinchillas vary in colour from cream through to shades of dark beige, with significantly paler underparts, as in the standard variety. The eye coloration of the heterozygous is often more clearly defined, ranging from pink through to red.

◆ BELOW
A young standard chinchilla. As with related members of the caviomorph group of rodents, including the guinea pig, they are born in an advanced state of development.

◆ BELOW
The standard varies in its depth of coloration. This is a dark individual, but note that the whiter underparts are retained. Fresh tidbits can be offered regularly to these rodents.

BROWN EBONY FORMS

The brown ebony can be distinguished by its even brown fur over its body, and contrasting pink ears and eyes. The ebony is entirely black in colour, while the charcoal mutation is grey, including the underparts and the paws.

VIOLET FORMS

One of the more recent varieties to capture the imagination of chinchilla breeders is the violet. Here, the body colour is a softer shade of grey, and it is distinguished from the charcoal chinchilla form by white underparts. As with some of the other recent colour varieties, the violet form will doubtless become more widely available as its popularity grows.

COLOUR BREEDING

Chinchilla breeding, as far as colours is concerned, is still rather a hobby in its infancy, and it offers plenty of scope for the future. Not all pairing can be carried out safely for genetic reasons. White chinchillas, for example, must

not be paired together. Outcrossing, as this is known, is also recommended for the black velvet mutation, where the depth of colour can vary from a matt shade of black on the body to a more glossy colour across the back.

◆ RIGHT
The fawn mutation of the chinchilla is markedly different in terms of coloration, compared with the usual form, with its coat displaying a decidedly brownish tone.

The underparts are much paler than the body in this case. Brown velvets can be distinguished from their black counterparts by their coloration, but again, these chinchillas should not be paired together for breeding purposes.

HOUSING AND FEEDING

Chinchillas require spacious indoor
quarters, and it is now easy to find
cages for them from pet suppliers.
It is also possible to convert sectional
cat pens into suitable accommodation,
bearing in mind that chinchillas like
to spend time off the ground.

CAGE DESIGN

A pair of chinchillas can be housed in
a cage measuring about 50 cm (20 in)
square by approximately 1 m (1 yd)
high. The mesh spacing should not
exceed 5 x 2.5 cm (2 x 1 in) in the case
of adult chinchillas, and half this size
for young animals. If you are making
an enclosure yourself, it is important
to use mesh which is at least 16 gauge
or thicker, to resist their sharp teeth.
All timber should be placed on the
outside of the cage for this reason.

◆ BELOW
Providing a floor
covering on the tray
of the chinchilla
cage. Shavings are
ideal for this purpose
but, as always, only
use those sold as
animal bedding.

A metal base, on which the
enclosure can stand, is a much more
durable option than a plastic tray,
which your pet could destroy, but it
is important to ensure that there are
no sharp edges where the chinchillas
might cut themselves. They need to be
provided with thick branches to climb
up and gnaw. These should not be cut
from trees that have recently been
sprayed with chemicals, or which

might prove to be poisonous, such as
yew, laburnum or fresh pine. Sycamore
or manzanita are good choices; they
provide straight wood and are resistant
to the chinchillas' teeth. Branches
from apple trees are another hard-
wearing alternative, and these are
quite commonly available.

Ensure that these lengths of wood
are held securely in place, however,
because if they do fall down they
could seriously or even fatally injure
the occupants. Large netting staples,
fixed across the mesh from outside the
cage, will serve to hold the branches
in place; take care to ensure they
do not become exposed as
the timber is gnawed away.
It is also a good idea
to include a nest box for
the chinchillas, where they
can sleep. It should measure 50 cm
(20 in) in length and 25 cm (10 in) in
width and height, and should be placed

◆ BELOW
Items needed for a chinchilla cage. Some of
these can be purchased from pet stores but the
special dust for bathing, and the pellets, may
need to be ordered from a specialist supplier.

◆ BOTTOM
A well-equipped chinchilla cage. Note the way
in which the hay is placed on a rack, which
helps to prevent it becoming soiled. The dust
bath should not be left in the cage permanently.

Hay

Shavings

Log

Pellets

Water
bottle

Dust bath

Nest box
lined with hay

on the floor. There should also be a
climbing shelf where they can rest,
but this must be made of mesh that is
no larger than 1 cm (½ in) square, to
protect the rodent's legs and feet from
any injury.

To wear their teeth down, a special
pumice block should be provided in
the quarters. Never offer them
ordinary rodent foods containing
seeds, and restrict treats to a small
piece of fresh-cut apple or a couple of

raisins each day. Fresh drinking water
should be provided in a drinking
bottle attached to the outside of the
cage; provide a metal screen to protect
the water bottle from the risk of being
punctured by sharp chinchilla teeth.

CHINCHILLA FOODS

As the dietary needs of chinchillas
are highly specific, you need to feed
them with special chinchilla pellets
which may have to be bought by mail
order. Even a change of brand needs
to be carried out gradually, over a few
weeks, to avoid the risk of diarrhoea,
which may prove to be fatal. On
average, an adult chinchilla will eat
about 35 g (1¼ oz) of pellets each day.
Special feeders that dispense pellets
from outside the cage will prevent
any soiling of the food.

Chinchillas are adapted to a high
fibre diet, and the only other food
required to meet their nutritional
needs is a constant supply of good
quality meadow hay. Alfalfa cubes are
an alternative to increase the fibre in
the diet and can be provided alongside
a reduced quantity of hay.

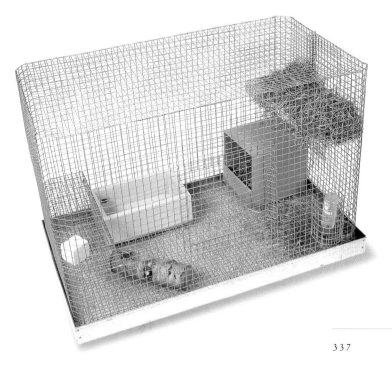

GENERAL CARE AND GROOMING

Handling chinchillas is not difficult, especially when they are tame. Simply encircle the body with your hand and lift up the chinchilla, providing adequate support for its underparts. Restrain a less friendly animal by holding the base of the tail gently and using your other hand to pick it up.

◆ LEFT
In spite of their active natures, chinchillas can be handled quite easily, especially if picked up regularly from an early age. Adequate support stops them struggling.

SAFETY IN THE HOME

Chinchillas appreciate exercise outside their cage but you must adapt your room to ensure your pet's safety. Check that there are no trailing electrical cables leading up to power sockets, which could be gnawed, and move valuable furniture out of reach. Never leave your chinchilla alone in a room as it might start chewing on wooden furniture and may ingest harmful paints or wood preservatives.

Most chinchillas develop a routine when they are out of their quarters and will return to their cages by themselves in due course. While free they may soil the room, although they can be trained to use a litter tray. Chinchillas are clean animals, with no unpleasant odour, but the cage will need to be cleaned out once a week. Keep the chinchillas away from their floor covering as much as possible – it can be harmful if ingested – and do not allow them to gnaw on cedarwood or cardboard. Since chinchillas will usually soil the same part of their cage, it is a good idea to add baking soda to the lining on the floor here, which will serve as a non-toxic deodorizer.

COAT CARE

The unique coat of a chinchilla needs attention to maintain condition. This is achieved with regular dust baths.

Using a formulated dusting powder made from volcanic ash or activated clay (other materials can be harmful), pour a layer of 5 cm (2 in) in a shallow box or on a tray. Place this on the floor of the cage. By rolling about in the dust, the chinchilla will remove excess grease from its coat. After five minutes the bath can be removed. Chinchillas require a dust bath two or three times a week, although heavily pregnant chinchillas should not dust bathe until their kits are about a week old. You can also comb their distinctive coats using a chinchilla comb: the hair will stand upright away from the body.

Damage and hair loss do occur on occasion, with fur nibbling often being a sign of stress. It may be that the chinchilla does not feel secure in its quarters, possibly because it does not have a nest box for sleeping purposes. Overcrowding can also lead to fur damage – an affected individual may be being bullied. Hair loss around the nipples is normal in the case of females that are suckling offspring; this will regrow once her kits are weaned.

◆ LEFT
Preparing a dust bath. This is an essential part of the chinchilla grooming process.

◆ RIGHT
A dust bath helps to keep the coat free from grease. It should only be offered for a few minutes, and should be withheld from pregnant females who are about to give birth.

BREEDING AND SHOWING

Although they mature between three and five months of age, it is not recommended to breed from chinchillas for the first time until they reach seven months old.

MATING AND PREGNANCY

Female chinchillas have a shorter gap between their anal and genital openings than males, and are smaller in size when adult. The female has a relatively long breeding cycle and only comes into heat once a month. Pairings need to be made carefully to avoid genetic incompatibility and to minimize any risk of fighting when the pair are introduced. Place them in adjoining cages and then, after a few days, if they are showing an interest in each other, transfer the male into the female's quarters. Assuming all goes well, he can be left in there with her until after the young are born and are independent.

One of the most reliable signs of pregnancy is the presence of a white plug of mucus, called a stopper, on the floor of the cage. This is produced by the female. She may also adopt an unusual sleeping posture, although the impending arrival of a litter is not the

only cause of this. Pregnancy lasts for 16 weeks. Three young will be born in an advanced state of development, as miniature adults, with their eyes open. At this stage, they weigh up to 55 g (2 oz), less than a tenth of the weight of an adult. The young chinchillas, known as kits, will be suckled by their mother for six to eight weeks before they are fully independent.

EXHIBITIONS

Chinchillas are not commonly exhibited at present but as the number of colour varieties

♦ BELOW
An older fawn chinchilla. The coat by this stage is much more developed, and the brush of longer fur on the tail is clearly apparent, compared with the youngster.

♦ ABOVE LEFT AND ABOVE RIGHT
The sexing of chinchillas is done by examining their underparts. The female is seen here on the right. Note the swelling of the male's scrotal sac.

♦ LEFT
A fawn chinchilla baby at two days of age with its mother. The difference in size is very obvious, and it will be at least six weeks before the youngster is independent.

♦ BELOW LEFT
A young chinchilla. Note the relatively short tail, and the covering of short fur here. It has a long potential lifespan, often living for ten years or more.

continues to increase this situation is changing. Chinchillas may be seen at larger small-animal shows, as well as at events organized by chinchilla clubs. Standardization of the chinchilla's type is underway because of pressure on coat quality, following selective breeding for fur over the generations.

When travelling with chinchillas it is vital to remember that they are highly susceptible to heat stroke in temperatures above 25°C (77°F). This applies even in the home, where they may need to be transferred to a cooler location on particularly hot days.

OTHER SMALL MAMMALS

Several other different types of rodents and other small mammals are becoming popular with enthusiasts, although their requirements tend to be more specialist than in the case of the more regular pet rodents. These mammals make original and charming pets, but they can be expensive to buy and you will often need to spend more time tracking down appropriate food and equipment suppliers.

SPECIALITY PETS

Always aim to find out as much as you can about the needs of your pet before you take it home. The breeder from whom you buy the animal will be able to advise on most aspects of its care.

CHIPMUNK

One of the most widely kept members of this group is the Siberian chipmunk (*Eutamias sibiricus*). This is an attractive shade of brown with darker stripes running down its back and white underparts. These rodents measure about 10 cm (4 in) long, with a slightly shorter tail. They can be housed either indoors or out, in an aviary-like structure. Provide plenty of branches for climbing purposes.

The wooden supports of the cage should be built on the outside, out of reach of the chipmunk's strong teeth. The mesh for the frames should be 16 gauge in thickness, with a strand size no bigger than 2.5 x 1 cm (1 x ½ in). The base must be solid to prevent escapes and to ensure that other rodents cannot tunnel their way in.

♦ RIGHT
A Korean chipmunk housed in a large indoor bird cage. These rodents are very lively and agile by nature. Note the nest box provided as a retreat, and the wooden branch for climbing purposes – this may also be gnawed on occasion.

♦ BELOW LEFT
The spikey appearance of the fur is one of the characteristic features of spiny mice. These rodents need to be handled with particular care, since their tails are easily injured.

While chipmunks are naturally active you should not expect to handle them as you would a conventional pet rodent, although they can often be tamed enough to feed from the hand. A seed mixture makes a good basic diet, with added nuts, vegetables, apple chunks and mealworms.

Provide a nest box for roosting and breeding. Between four and eight young will be born after a gestation period of 31 days. The young leave the nest at seven weeks and will become independent shortly afterwards. If housed outdoors, the chipmunk will be less active in cold spells of weather.

SPINY MICE

Several different species of mouse are being bred by enthusiasts, of which the best known are probably spiny mice (*Acomys* species). Originating from parts of North Africa and the Middle East, these mice have unusual spiky fur, as their name suggests. Ideal housing for a spiny mouse would be a converted aquarium with a ventilated hood. Because of their small size, they may find a cage too spacious to make them feel secure. Care needs to be taken when handling these mice as their tails are easily injured. Damage to the tail can also result if the mice are housed in overcrowded accommodation, even if it is only for a relatively short time.

The breeding habits of spiny mice are unusual for small mammals. They have a long pregnancy, lasting around 38 days, and usually only give birth to two or three pups in one litter. The young are active almost from birth and are covered in grey fur at this stage. In addition to seeds and greenstuff, spiny mice will also eat mealworms.

SUGAR GLIDER

The small marsupial known as the sugar glider (*Petaurus breviceps*) originates from Australia and New Guinea. Its main diet should be a nectar solution mixed fresh each day. Fresh fruit and vegetables can also be provided, along with nuts and seeds, a few mealworms and other sources of protein, such as commercial dog or cat food.

Sugar gliders need indoor aviary-type housing, and it is a good idea to make sure this is easy to clean: the sticky nature of their droppings means that the gliders' quarters must be cleaned out on a daily basis.

A nest box for sleeping purposes should be included in their enclosure, and add tree branches, such as apple, to simulate their natural habitat and provide them with an opportunity for regular exercise.

As marsupials, the newborn young move after birth to their mother's pouch, where they will remain for the next ten weeks. Weaning occurs about five weeks later. Young sugar gliders mature at around ten months old and may go on to live for a decade or more.

♦ ABOVE
A pair of sugar gliders. They require an aviary-like structure, equipped with branches to allow them to climb freely. Their quarters need to be designed so that they can be cleaned easily.

♦ LEFT
Sugar gliders reproduce in a different way to the small mammals more usually kept as pets. They are marsupials, forming part of the group that includes kangaroos.

341

HEALTH CARE

Once established in their quarters, small animals usually prove to be very healthy. One of the more common causes of serious health problems in small mammals is a sudden change in their diet, which is likely to lead to digestive upsets. Treatment of these animals is not always straightforward because, in many cases, they will react adversely to certain antibiotics. Seeking veterinary advice early offers the best hope of recovery from illness.

SMALL MAMMAL HEALTH

Once they are settled in their housing, small animals are usually healthy, and need very little in the way of routine health care. Sometimes though, you may need to clip back their claws if these become overgrown. If you prefer, you can ask your vet to do this for you. However, clipping claws is straightforward, provided that you have a suitable pair of clippers for the purpose.

Guillotine-type clippers with a sliding blade are to be recommended. This makes it easier to control the amount of the nail which you will be trimming off, as the claw is placed within the ring of the blade. It is helpful to have someone else to restrain your pet, so that you can concentrate on clipping the claw

◆ BELOW
Rabbits often need to have their claws trimmed back. If overgrown, walking will be difficult.

safely. If left, the claws can otherwise curl back into the pad, causing great discomfort to the animal. Guinea pigs are most susceptible to overgrown claws, but rabbits can also suffer from this problem.

Carry out claw clipping in a good light, so that you can detect the quick, visible as a pink streak running down the claw from the base. You then need to cut at a point where this disappears towards the tip of the nail, so as to avoid bleeding. In the case of individuals with black claws, however, it may be impossible to spot the end of the quick, and particular care needs to be taken in these cases. If you do nick a claw too short, or it is injured and starts bleeding, pressing on the tip for a few moments should help to stem the blood flow. A styptic pencil, as sold in chemists (drug stores) for shaving nicks, may also help.

◆ BELOW LEFT
If the incisor teeth do not meet correctly in jaws, it will soon be impossible for the rabbit to continue eating.

◆ BELOW RIGHT
Hair loss is a relatively common condition in many of the smaller mammal breeds.

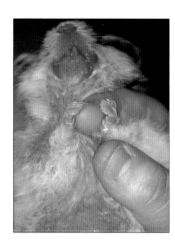

◆ BELOW
Vitamin C deficiency can arise quite easily in
guinea pigs. It results in scurvy, reflected here
by the dry, scaly skin. This is a dietary problem
which can be treated fairly routinely.

◆ BELOW
Rabbits are especially at risk from being
attacked by dogs and even cats on occasions.
The resulting shock may prove fatal although,
thankfully, not in this case.

Overgrown teeth, caused by
malocclusion, when the top and
bottom incisors do not meet properly,
are a more serious proposition to deal
with, and these are best attended to
by your vet. The teeth are likely to
need trimming back every eight weeks
or so, to allow your pet to continue
eating without difficulty.

Nutritional problems are rare in
small animals, particularly now that
specially formulated diets are widely
available. Even so, cases of Vitamin C
deficiency do occur occasionally in
guinea pigs which, unlike other small
animals, cannot manufacture this
vital vitamin in their bodies. It must
therefore be present in their diet. If
you are housing a rabbit and guinea
pig together and offering them rabbit
pellets, then a deficiency, giving rise
to the condition known as scurvy, is
likely to occur before long. Dry,
flaky skin which can bleed readily
is the commonest sign. Vitamin C
supplements and regular use of a
guinea pig food, which will contain
this vitamin, should lead to a cure.

Hair thinning in hamsters is a sign
of old age rather than a nutritional
deficiency, and there is really nothing
that can be done about it. Equally,
another quite common condition
which is difficult to deal with in
elderly male guinea pigs is a distended
rectum, which leads to swelling as the
result of a build-up of faecal matter

here. This appears to be the result of
the loss of muscular tone. Increasing
the fibre content of the diet may help
but, ultimately, the rectum will need to
be emptied manually, gently massaging
the affected area with a little olive oil
first to loosen the obstruction. This
can be done at home but your vet can
perform it for you, if you prefer.

◆ LEFT
Hair loss in hamsters
can be difficult to
resolve, with the
coat often becoming
noticeably thinner
in old age. Distinct
bald patches may
indicate parasites.

BACTERIAL ILLNESSES

It is not difficult to recognize signs of illness in a small animal as, when sick, an individual will usually be less active than normal and it may lose its appetite. It is likely to sit in a hunched-up fashion, with its fur held out from the body, creating a ruffled appearance. Even so, it can be very difficult to diagnose the cause of the illness accurately, because the symptoms of many infections are fairly similar.

As a result of their small size, pet rodents especially will lose heat rapidly from their bodies, which results in their condition deteriorating quickly. As a first step, therefore, it is important to provide some additional heat, while leaving a cooler area where your pet can retreat if it starts to feel too warm. A heat lamp will be useful for this purpose.

A small mammal that is sick needs urgent veterinary attention but, unfortunately, the choice of drugs which can be used to treat infections in this group of creatures is more restricted than in other pets because they react very badly to a number of antibiotics. Some antibiotics will have

a harmful effect on the beneficial bacteria in the digestive tract, and this can prove fatal. You should never be tempted to use remedies prescribed for other pets for treatment purposes.

Young, recently-weaned rodents are perhaps most prone to bacterial illnesses, particularly if their diet is changed suddenly, because this can allow harmful bacteria to colonize the digestive tract, and interferes with the digestion of food. The stress of rehoming can also be significant.

Tyzzer's disease for example can strike young mice, rats and gerbils in particular. It is caused by a bacterium

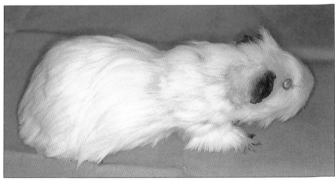

known as *Bacillus piliformis*, with symptoms typically including diarrhoea; sometimes in epidemics, a large number of young animals will die suddenly from this. Young hamsters can suffer from an infection known as wet tail, or proliferative ileitis, which again is often linked with a bacterial infection. Diarrhoea

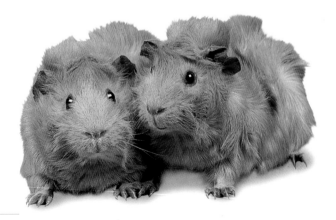

◆ BELOW
Health problems can be caused by unsuitable
bedding. Eye and associated nasal irritations
in gerbils can be triggered by allowing them
to burrow into fine sawdust.

◆ BELOW
There is now much more that veterinarians
can do to prevent and treat illnesses in small
mammals, but much depends on owners seeking
professional advice at an early stage.

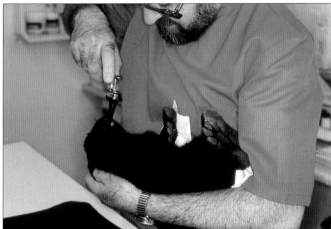

affecting the area under the tail
causes the fur here to appear wet,
while internally, the part of the small
intestine known as the ileum will be
badly inflamed. Again, treatment is
difficult, but it can be successful,
especially if carried out before the
hamster becomes badly dehydrated.

Other illnesses may be more
localized. Rats and mice are
particularly vulnerable to infections
of the upper respiratory tract, which
result in runny noses and noisy
breathing. Similar symptoms can be
triggered by dust from unsuitable
bedding, which will provoke an
allergic reaction. Rapid treatment
is vital before the infection spreads
further down into the respiratory
system, causing pneumonia. Rabbits
can suffer from a similar condition,
often referred to as snuffles.

Guinea pigs are especially prone
to pneumonia, which can be caused
by a range of different bacteria.
This is often linked to poor
ventilation in their quarters, or

damp surroundings, and there may be
few, if any, early-warning symptoms.
Only if the unfortunate guinea pig
is autopsied will the cause of death
become known. Laboured breathing

and loss of appetite are the most likely
indicators of this problem. Antibiotic
therapy may help a sick individual,
although pneumonia in any small
animal is a very serious condition.

◆ BELOW
You can prevent dental problems
in small mammals by providing
them with various chews, which
will help to keep their teeth in
good condition.

345

VIRAL AND FUNGAL ILLNESSES

◆ BELOW
Myxomatosis is a killer viral disease which relatively few rabbits will survive, and there is no treatment available. All pet rabbits should be protected by vaccination.

The most significant viral illnesses for owners of small animals occur in rabbits, and both have been developed with a view to controlling wild rabbit populations by biological means.

MYXOMATOSIS

This is a virus which can be spread to domestic rabbits by wild rabbits visiting their hutches; for this reason it is recommended to stand hutches at least 60 cm (2 ft) off the ground in areas where wild rabbits are prevalent, and to double-wire runs on both faces of the timber around the perimeter. Outbreaks of myxomatosis tend to occur in the summer in more temperate areas because biting insects, such as mosquitoes, are also capable of spreading the infection, and these are most numerous at this time of year.

The earliest signs of infection are inflammation of the eyes, quickly accompanied by a whitish discharge. By this stage, the rabbit will be seriously ill and will have lost its appetite. Sadly, there is no treatment for myxomatosis, and most affected

individuals will die within a couple of days. Those which survive beyond this stage develop scabs around their eyes, and their ears become badly swollen and start to droop. With virtually no hope of survival, therefore, it will be kindest to have a rabbit which has contracted myxomatosis painlessly

◆ BELOW LEFT
A guinea pig that is housed with a rabbit does not need to be vaccinated against myxomatosis or VHD, which only affect rabbits.

◆ BELOW
Ringworm on a rabbit's face. This fungal ailment is usually characterized by its circular pattern of spread, with accompanying hair loss.

◆ BELOW
A vaccine to protect against VHD being administered. The vaccine is essential, especially in exhibition stock, to guard against this relatively common killer rabbit disease.

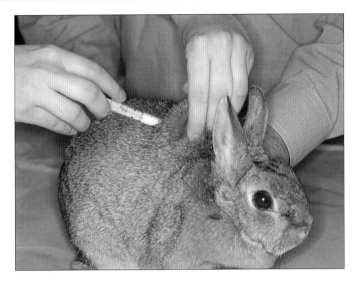

euthanased after diagnosis. In areas where this infection crops up regularly, it is vital to have pet rabbits protected by vaccination, since they are more vulnerable to the disease than wild rabbits, which may have some immunity to this illness. In areas where a vaccine is not available, then, keeping domestic rabbits isolated from wild rabbits, and screening their quarters from insects, should offer some protection against myxomatosis.

VHD

Viral haemorrhagic disease (VHD) has only been recognized in rabbits since the 1980s, but has spread through the wild population and infected domestic stock as well. There are very few symptoms, and an affected rabbit will usually die suddenly. One tell-tale sign is a slight haemorrhaging of blood from the nose. There is no treatment, and vaccination against this disease is important, particularly for show stock because the virus survives well in the environment. It is spread by contaminated food and water bowls, housing pens and even clothing, as well as directly from one rabbit to another.

Because rabbits are prone to digestive upsets, viruses may have a role in some cases of digestive illness, although the role is not yet clearly understood. The hope of recovery stems from preventing dehydration, which accompanies severe diarrhoea, from becoming life-threatening. This should enable the body's own defence mechanisms to overcome the illness.

RINGWORM

Viruses are less important to small mammals such as hamsters, which are usually housed on their own in the home, and are therefore at a much reduced risk of acquiring this type of infection. But, very occasionally, small mammals may be afflicted by the fungal disease called ringworm. This causes a loss of the coat in circular patches. The risk is that this condition can be spread to human beings, where it will show up as red blotches, in the shape of circles, on the arm where the infected area of fur was in contact with the skin. Fortunately, it can be treated.

Ringworm is transmitted very easily by fungal spores on grooming equipment. If you suspect ringworm, avoid using this on any other animal in your collection. The spores will linger in hutches and elsewhere for years, so thorough disinfection is essential after an outbreak, using a hexetidine preparation to kill the fungus. Wear gloves when cleaning out the quarters and burn the bedding, which is likely to be contaminated with spores.

◆ RIGHT
Hamsters rarely suffer from viral illnesses. However, the hamster plague virus will cause fits, and an affected hamster will die within 24 hours.

PARASITIC ILLNESSES

Rabbits and guinea pigs in particular are both prone to external parasites living on their bodies. Rabbits can often suffer from ear mites, which cause the condition sometimes described as canker. The mites cause irritation within the ear canal, resulting in the formation of brown scabs here, with the resulting discomfort causing the rabbit to scratch its ears more frequently than normal. If left, the mites are likely to spread into the inner part of the ear, permanently damaging the rabbit's sense of balance.

Do not attempt to pick off the scabs but, instead, dust the ears with flower of sulphur, a yellow powder available from pharmacies, which will kill off the mites effectively. Disinfect the hutch thoroughly once the rabbit has recovered fully, to eliminate any risk of reinfection as far as possible, although there is a risk that the mites could be reintroduced on dusty bedding material such as hay.

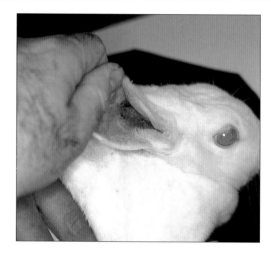

✦ LEFT
Ear mites attack the inside of the ear, creating brownish, crusty deposits here. These parasites can spread easily from rabbit to rabbit but can be treated easily.

Guinea pigs are vulnerable to skin mites, which again may lurk in contaminated bedding. You may miss the initial stages of infection, when the mites cause tiny white spots under the fur. Skin shedding, in the form of pronounced dandruff, then follows along with hair loss. At this stage, a

mite infestation may sometimes appear like ringworm, and skin scrapings from an affected area will be necessary to identify the mites under a microscope.

Treatment by injection, using the drug ivermectin at the appropriate dilution, is now the simplest way to kill off these mites, although this treatment will be needed over a period of a month or so, with injections being given every fortnight. The cage must also be thoroughly disinfected, to kill off any surviving mites. Other guinea pigs sharing the hutch will probably need to be treated as well. The susceptibility of guinea pigs to skin problems means that a thorough examination will be necessary to determine the cause of the problem, which is not always infectious. Some sows, for example, lose patches of their fur when pregnant, but this should regrow in due course.

It is always very important, particularly if your rabbit or guinea pig has suffered recently from diarrhoea,

✦ BELOW
Rex breeds of rabbit may suffer fur loss because of their housing conditions, rather than as a result of illness.

♦ BELOW
Diarrhoea in rats or mice can be caused by parasites, but tests will need to be carried out by your vet to obtain a definitive diagnosis.

♦ BELOW
A severe case of mange in a guinea pig. Treatment by a series of injections will be required, but always seek advice at an early stage to minimize your pet's suffering.

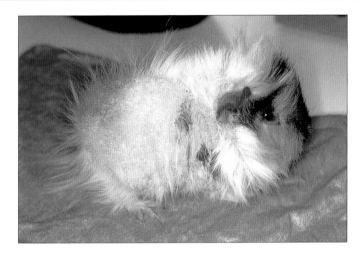

to check there is no soiling of the fur around the animal's rear end. Otherwise, your pet could become parasitized by the larvae of blowflies, responsible for the condition often described as fly strike. Bluebottles and similar flies will be attracted to the soiled fur, laying their eggs here which hatch rapidly into larvae. These literally bore into the flesh, releasing deadly toxins. This is why it is so important to remove the larvae without delay because, otherwise, they will kill the rabbit or guinea pig. Your vet will be able to remove them with special forceps; a wound powder may also be used to promote healing.

A wide range of microscopic, single-celled organisms, called protozoa, can be found in the intestinal tract of small mammals, often helping to digest the food here so that the nutrients can be absorbed into the body. Some of these protozoa are likely to be harmful, however, giving rise to the disease known as coccidiosis. They can cause diarrhoea, which may be blood-stained,

and permanent damage to the lining of the intestinal tract, so that a young rabbit will not grow properly.

In order to protect against this infection, drugs called coccidiostats are sometimes incorporated in the rabbit's food. Another form of the infection attacks the liver, causing what is described as hepatic coccidiosis, which can also be fatal.

Actual treatment of coccidiosis will be possible using specially formulated sulphur-based compounds available from your vet. Cleanliness is equally vital, however, because the infection is transmitted via the rabbit's droppings.

♦ BELOW
If you have a number of guinea pigs, use separate grooming tools for them. This will help to prevent the spread of skin mites.

PET BIRDS

Birds have been popular as pets for over 5,000 years. The ancient Greeks used to marvel at the ability of parrots to learn different languages. This ancient link is commemorated today by the Alexandrine parakeet (*Psittacula eupatria*), which was first taken back to Greece by soldiers in the army of Alexander the Great.

Overseas voyages of discovery brought European sailors into contact with a large number of previously unknown birds. When Christopher Columbus returned from his successful sailing to the New World in 1493, he brought back a pair of Cuban Amazon parrots (*Amazona leucocephala*).

Soon afterwards, small finches with an attractive song were brought from the Canary Islands, off the west coast of Africa, and these became immensely popular. These rather dull-looking green birds were the ancestors of today's amazing range of canary breeds. The pure yellow coloration of the birds of today did not emerge until domestication was well underway, around the early 1700s.

When it comes to coloration, of course, it is the budgerigar that now reigns supreme. These popular parakeets originate from Australia, and first started to become well known in Europe during the 1840s.

+ OPPOSITE
A pair of masked lovebirds. These small parrots make highly attractive aviary occupants. Males and females cannnot be distinguished visually from each other.

+ LEFT
Budgerigars have been bred in a huge range of colour varieties and this has enhanced their popularity. These birds are talented mimics and will breed readily.

CANARIES AND OTHER FINCHES

These attractive and often colourful small birds are very popular occupants of garden aviaries, as they are neither destructive nor noisy by nature. Some members of the group, especially canaries, are also highly prized by pet-owners on account of their singing prowess, while others, such as zebra finches, will nest readily, even when housed in a cage indoors, although they are unlikely to become as tame as some members of the parrot family.

INTRODUCTION

All of these birds are easy to cater for in terms of food and housing needs. They feed primarily on seed, although other foodstuffs, such as greenstuff and small invertebrates, are also significant in the diets of many species, particularly during the breeding season. At this stage, finches, such as waxbills, become highly insectivorous and their young are unlikely to be reared satisfactorily without a supply of livefoods such as hatchling crickets, which are available commercially, and aphids, which are found in parks and gardens.

The housing of canaries and finches is also straightforward, thanks in part to their small size. Most finches average between 10 and 15 cm (4–6 in) in length and, unlike most parrots, finches will not destroy their quarters. If they are housed in an outdoor aviary in temperate areas, they are likely to need additional heat and lighting to see them through the cooler and darker days of winter. This can add significantly to the expense of keeping them, and you should calculate this expenditure at the outset. As an alternative, you can bring the birds indoors and house them in a flight over the winter period. They can then be released back into the aviary in the spring when the risk of frost has passed. Few finches, with the notable exception of the canary and its close relatives such as the singing finches,

are talented songsters but many, such as the Gouldian finch (*Chloebia gouldiae*), are beautifully coloured.

As finches are often social birds, it is not uncommon for pairs of several species to be housed together in the same aviary. You need to ensure that they will be compatible in these surroundings, however, and are not overcrowded as outbreaks of fighting

may otherwise occur, particularly during the breeding period when the birds' territorial instincts will be at their strongest.

Most finches have a life expectancy of around seven years, although, on occasion, individuals have been known to live much longer – for more than 20 years in the case of some green singing finches.

◆ LEFT
The Gouldian finch
is one of the most
colourful finches
in the world today.

◆ BELOW
Cock singing
finches will display
their talents as
songsters, especially
during the breeding
period, although
their fluency of song
does not match that
of the canary.

SEXING

It is often possible to sex finches by differences in their plumage but, where this is not possible, you can start off with several individuals of the same species, which should ensure that you have at least one breeding pair in the group. It can be virtually impossible to distinguish between the sexes when canaries are moulting, as cock birds will not attempt to sing at this stage. At other times, patience is important so that you can watch the birds carefully, picking out which is likely to be a cock in the group.

BREEDING BEHAVIOUR

Certain finches, notably male weavers and whydahs, undergo a dramatic change in appearance during the breeding period when they become much more colourful. Their breeding requirements differ quite markedly from other finches as well, with male weavers building ornate nests and needing to be kept in harems comprising a single cock and perhaps three or four hens. Male whydahs have an elaborate display dance, while the hens will deposit their eggs in the nests of waxbills, rather than incubating them themselves.

The typical breeding behaviour of weavers and whydahs may represent a challenge, even for the experienced bird-keeper. However, other species of finch will breed readily, and will also make popular exhibition subjects as they have been developed in a wide range of attractive colours and feather types. The Bengalese finch, which is better known in the United States as the society finch, and the zebra finch are among the most widely kept finches for this reason.

SPECIES AND BREEDS

CANARIES

Since wild canaries (*Serinus canaria*) were first brought to Europe several centuries ago, a number of different breeds have been developed, and the process of evolution is still continuing today. Canaries are divided into three basic groups: singing breeds, type breeds and breeds developed for their coloration, known as new colours.

Of the singing breeds, the ancestral form, called the roller, is still the best known and most widely kept. Although all cock canaries have an attractive song, top rollers are unrivalled, both in terms of the quality of the song and their range, which can extend over almost three octaves.

The type breeds are characterized by their appearance, which must conform as closely as possible to the official standard laid down for judging purposes for the breed concerned. This is a large grouping, with some breeds, such as the attractive Gloster canary which occurs in both a crested and plainhead form, having established an international following, whereas others remain localized. The unusual frilled breeds are also included in this category, with the names of many such canary breeds traditionally reflecting their area of origin, as in the case of the Parisian frill.

The third category of canaries are the new colours, which have been bred primarily for their coloration. They include the stunning red factor birds, which were created in the 1920s as the result of an attempt to create pure red canaries by way of cross-breeding experiments involving a South American finch, the black-hooded red siskin (*Carduelis cucullata*).

+ LEFT
The crest of the Gloster corona should be even, and must not obscure the eyes. The neck should be relatively thick. This is a variegated bird, with both dark and light areas in its plumage.

+ BELOW
The green singing finch is a close relative of the canary, found over a wide area of mainland Africa, and has an attractive song. It needs similar care in aviary surroundings. The hens can be identified by the black spots across the throat. They have been known to live for 20 years or more.

+ LEFT
The hens originally bred from pairings between canaries and black-hooded red siskins were infertile until the third generation. Today, the fertility of red canaries, such as this intensive clear red, is normal.

GREEN SINGING FINCH

The green singing finch (*Serinus mozambicus*) is the closest wild relative of the canary that is widely

◆ LEFT
The markings of the cock bird, here on the left, can be clearly seen in this exhibition pair of chestnut-flanked white zebra finches.

◆ BELOW
In the fawn mutation of the zebra finch, it is easy to distinguish the sexes. The grey plumage has been replaced by a warmer shade of brown.

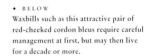

kept today. Smaller in size, averaging about 12.5 cm (5 in) in length, these finches can be sexed easily: cock birds display more yellow coloration on their heads and lack the black throat spots seen in hens. These finches need similar care to the domestic canary, and may breed successfully in a breeding cage, although success is more likely in a garden aviary. They build a cup-shaped nest and, as with canaries, two rounds of chicks may be reared in succession. Provide daily supplies of egg food for rearing.

WAXBILLS

These birds make ideal companions for singing finches in aviary surroundings, although they are often more difficult to breed. Sexing in most cases is straightforward. For example, the hens of the red-eared waxbill (*Estrilda troglodytes*) have paler plumage on their underparts. These finches may use a domed nesting basket or they may prefer to construct their own nest from vegetation found in the aviary – clumps of dried grass, sticks, moss and similar materials.

The blue waxbills can also be housed as part of a colony as they all require similar care but, since they can be aggressive towards others of their

own kind, only one pair should be kept in an aviary alongside other finches. The red-cheeked waxbill (*Uraeginthus bengalus*) is a good choice, not only because of its attractive appearance, but because pairs are easy to distinguish: only the cock bird displays the red cheek markings.

◆ BELOW
Waxbills such as this attractive pair of red-cheeked cordon bleus require careful management at first, but may then live for a decade or more.

ZEBRA FINCH

These birds (*Taeniopygia guttata*) rank among the most widely kept of all finches. Their name comes from the black and white striping usually seen on the chest of cock birds, although this feature may not be apparent in some of the colour forms that have since been developed. Hens can be identified by the more orangish rather than red coloration of their bills. Zebra finches are lively little birds, and they are highly social by nature, living well in groups or as single pairs. They can be housed with waxbills and other non-aggressive finches as part of a collection. Pairs are equally adaptable in breeding terms, using open-fronted finch nest boxes or nesting baskets for this purpose.

Among the popular colours are chestnut-flanked whites, which replace the grey coloration of the normal variety on the head, back and wings with white. Pieds with variable white and coloured areas are also popular, although it is not possible to predict the markings of chicks from those of their parents. Fawn, silver and cream varieties are equally well established, while among the newer variants is the black-breasted, with the barring on the chest of the cock replaced by solid black coloration. There is also a crested form.

BENGALESE FINCH

The origin of the Bengalese (*Lonchura domestica*) is mysterious – this finch does not occur in the wild, and is thought to be the result of cross-breeding with the striated mannikin (*L. striata*). Bengalese finches are thought to have been developed at least 500 years ago, probably in China. Their coloration is shades of brown. The fawn of the species is pale compared to the darker chestnut, while the chocolate colour is regarded as the original form. These colours also exist in combination with white, and the crested Bengalese, as they are known, are very popular. Visual sexing is impossible with these finches, and it is only the cock's song that distinguishes them.

GOULDIAN FINCH

The stunning Gouldian finch (*Chloebia gouldiae*) is unusual in that it occurs in the wild in three different head colours – red, black and yellow

◆ ABOVE
Red-eared waxbills are hard to sex outside the breeding season. Two birds preening each other does not signify they are a pair because they are social birds by nature.

◆ RIGHT
The Gouldian finch is often called Lady Gould's finch in the United States. It was named by the Victorian explorer John Gould after his wife, Elizabeth. This is the black-headed form.

◆ ABOVE
The self chocolate variety of the Bengalese or society finch, as seen here, is closest to the ancestral form of this domesticated finch.

(which is in reality a more orangish shade). With domestication there have been other changes in colour, including the introduction of white-breasted variants among others.

Gouldians are delicate birds and must be given heated accommodation, certainly through the winter. They can be bred either on a colony basis or, more commonly, in breeding cages. The bills of cock birds take on a cherry-coloured tip as they come into breeding condition.

ORANGE WEAVER

The orange weaver (*Euplectes orix*) is also highly coloured, as least in the case of cock birds during the breeding season, when you may see them advertized as "I. F. C." (in full colour). These birds can be rather bombastic, however, and they should not be housed with small companions such as waxbills. Once they have become properly established, both they and whydahs, such as the pin-tailed (*Vidua macroura*), will be quite hardy, and they can be comfortably housed through the cold months without artificial heat, provided that they have well lit, snug roosting quarters. It is not suitable to keep them in cages as the long tails of the cock whydahs in their breeding finery will soon be damaged.

◆ LEFT
The cock bird of this pair of orange weavers is in his breeding plumage. Colour feeding at the time of the moult can help to maintain the intensity of the orange feathering, although this is not always necessary.

HOUSING

A wide range of cages is available for pet canaries and other finches, but as a general rule it is best to choose as large a design as possible. You can also buy attractive flight cages, mounted on castors, or indoor aviaries that are sold in self-assembly form. To assemble, they simply require screwing together. For breeding purposes, however, your birds may appreciate a greater sense of security. This can be provided by a breeding cage, in the form of a box-type design with a finch- or canary-type front. These cages are used in birdrooms as well, where they are arranged in tiers supported off the ground. They are equipped with a sliding tray that can be lined with a sandsheet or sheets of old newspaper, weighed down with bird sand, as an absorbent floor covering.

Building an aviary for finches is quite straightforward, as there are a growing number of manufacturers

◆ BELOW
Cages with vertical bars are most suitable for finches and canaries, which do not climb around their quarters. The perches need to be placed near the raised food pots.

◆ BELOW
Additional lighting can be very valuable in a birdroom, particularly in temperate areas, allowing the birds' feeding period to be extended on dull days. Fluorescent strip lights give off a natural light but they cannot be operated with a conventional dimmer switch.

advertising in bird-keeping magazines who offer designs in sectional form to be delivered to your door. The panels should be covered with 19-gauge mesh, with strand dimensions that are ideally 1 cm (½ in) square and not exceeding 2.5 x 1 cm (1 x ½ in). These units simply need to be fixed together on secure footings.

In the case of finches, it may be better to choose a chalet-type design, which has mesh confined to the front of the flight only. This will give the birds better protection from wind and rain than an open flight. The siting of the aviary is also important. It should be located in a sheltered part of the garden, preferably not in the path of the prevailing wind. A location near the house, where the birds can be seen easily, is ideal because, if you intend to house them here throughout the year, running an electrical supply for heating and lighting purposes will be easier and less costly. The work of

◆ BELOW
Finches can be housed with other species of
birds, but take care with more aggressive species
such as pheasants. A planted aviary will provide
cover and will minimize the risk of aggression.

wiring the electrical cables to the
aviary will need to be undertaken
by a qualified electrician.

There are aviary designs available
that incorporate the shelter into a
larger birdroom area, and so provide
more flexibility. This additional space
can be useful for breeding cages and
the storage of seed and other items.
There may also be space for an indoor
flight as well. Supply heating in the
form of tubular convector heaters,
which can be operated under
thermostatic control. Fan heaters

are much more costly to operate,
and can become clogged with dust.
Lighting can be operated on the basis
of a time-switch. Birds should be given
no more than 12 hours of artificial
light every day, so as not to interfere
with the moulting cycle.

Within the flight, a variety of plants
can be grown for decoration and to
provide interest and perches for the
birds. The vegetation within the flight
can be watered from the outside with
a hose to avoid disturbing the birds
when they are breeding. The other

option is to set the plants in containers,
on a concrete or paving slab base; this
base will be easier to clean thoroughly
than an earth floor.

Plants that provide dense cover,
such as conifers and bamboos, are
often favoured for nest-building by
the birds. Climbing plants can help to
disguise artificial nesting sites, making
them more appealing to the birds. You
will need to provide supports for the
climbers, as the weight of the growing
branches may damage the mesh, and
seasonal pruning will be necessary.

FEEDING

The dietary needs of finches fall into two groups. There are the true finches, such as canaries and green singing finches, which require a diet consisting of a mixture of cereal and oil seeds, and all other finches, such as waxbills and zebra finches, which need to be fed primarily on cereal seeds. Suitable seed mixes are available from pet stores, or they can be ordered from specialist seed suppliers listed at the back of bird-keeping publications.

It is better to purchase seed either in packets or sacks, rather than loose seed in bins, which is more likely to have been contaminated by dust and dirt, and could be a cause of disease.

A canary seed mixture is made up mainly of plain canary seed, which is brown and oval in appearance, and red rape, a dark reddish, circular seed. Other ingredients may include hemp, which is a dark shade of brown and is significantly larger than the other seeds, as well as niger, which is long, thin and black. A typical finch mix comprises plain canary seed and a variety of millets, which may range in colour from shades of pale yellowish-white through to red. Millet sprays or seedheads are given separately. They are considered a valuable rearing food. Other seeds offered to canaries at the rearing stage include teasel, fed as soaked seed, and blue maw, which is valued for weaning purposes and is sprinkled directly on top of egg food.

SOAKED SEED

Soaking seed in water, prior to feeding it to the birds, triggers a variety of changes, including stimulating the germination process of the seed and improving its nutritional value.

Canary seed

Millet

Egg food

Red rape

Niger

for these shortcomings.
Some seed mixes
contain vitamin
and mineral
supplements
coated on to
dehulled seeds,
so that they will not be wasted
as there is no husk for the bird to
remove. Other mixes contain added
pellets of nutrients, although birds
will often avoid eating these nuggets,
choosing to eat only their regular
seeds, and it will be less easy for you
then to monitor their diet.

As an alternative, try a vitamin
and mineral powder, which will
stick well to damp greenstuff,
or a similar product added to
the drinking water. Feeding fresh
natural foods, such as chickweed,
dandelion and seeding grasses, can also
help to compensate for any deficiency.

To prepare soaked seed, start by
rinsing the required amount of seed in
a sieve under running water and then
immerse it in a container of hot water.
Leave the seed to stand overnight,
then rinse thoroughly, and offer to the
finches in a separate food tub. Soaked
seed will quickly turn mouldy, and any
left uneaten should be removed at the
end of the day and discarded.

FOOD SUPPLEMENTS

Bird seed is deficient in a number of
key ingredients, and you will need to
supplement the birds' diet to make up

Calcium is an essential mineral and
is particularly important for the hen
during the breeding season as it is
the main constituent of eggshells.
Cuttlefish bone is a valuable source of
calcium, and this will also help to keep
the birds' bills in trim as they peck at
the powdery surface. Scrape a little off
the surface at first to make it easier
for them to start nibbling.

Grit will supplement mineral
requirements and will assist in the
birds' digestive process. Oystershell
grit dissolves more readily than
mineralized grit in the acid of
the bird's gizzard, where seed is
broken down. Cuttlefish can be
held in place in the aviary with
a clip, while grit can be offered
in a small container, which will
need to be topped up regularly.

Tubular
drinker

◆ LEFT
A selection of food
and water containers
used for small birds.

Food container

Small seed
hopper

Small container
suitable for grit

GENERAL CARE AND BREEDING

◆ BELOW
Lift a bird very carefully out of the net. Most birds anchor their claws into the material, and these will need to be freed first.

Finches need to be given fresh drinking water each day and fed as necessary. Since canaries in particular can be very wasteful in their feeding habits, it is better to feed them on a daily basis, providing just the required amount for that day rather than leaving several days' supply at one time, which is likely to end up scattered around the flight or cage.

Always put food containers for aviary birds in the shelter rather than the aviary, to ensure the seed stays dry and to reduce the possibility of attracting rodents. Use heavyweight pots as food bowls, and brush off discarded seed husks with your hand before the pot is topped up. Perishable foods should be provided in separate pots, and any spillages cleaned up thoroughly before they can turn mouldy or attract wasps and insects.

HANDLING

Finches are very agile little birds and, although it can be relatively easy to catch them within the confines of a cage, it will be much harder doing so in aviary surroundings. Taking down the perches initially and then shutting the birds in the aviary shelter will simplify this task. You may want to use a special bird net to catch them, but do ensure this is well padded around its rim, to minimize the risk of injury to the birds, and only try to catch one bird at a time.

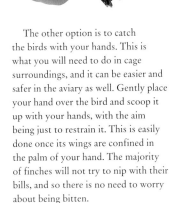

The other option is to catch the birds with your hands. This is what you will need to do in cage surroundings, and it can be easier and safer in the aviary as well. Gently place your hand over the bird and scoop it up with your hands, with the aim being just to restrain it. This is easily done once its wings are confined in the palm of your hand. The majority of finches will not try to nip with their bills, and so there is no need to worry about being bitten.

BREEDING

In the spring, as the breeding season approaches, position a choice of nesting sites around the aviary, in the form of nest boxes, baskets and canary nest pans. These can be screwed to the aviary framework or, in the case of baskets, held in place with netting. Take care to ensure they are positioned under cover, in a secluded part of the flight. Nesting materials such as moss, dried grass and coconut fibre should all be provided.

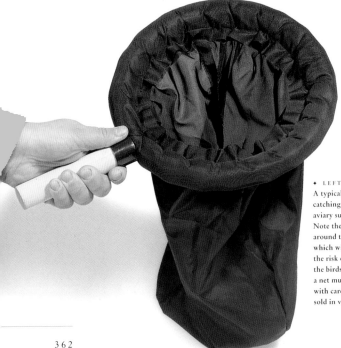

◆ LEFT
A typical net for catching birds in aviary surroundings. Note the padding around the rim, which will reduce the risk of injury to the birds. Even so, a net must be used with care. They are sold in various sizes.

♦ LEFT
Two designs of finch nest box, made out of
plywood. These should be suspended in a
secluded part of the aviary, at a relatively high
point under cover.

♦ BELOW FAR LEFT
A wide range of nesting material may be used
by finches. Canary nest pans are lined with
circular felts, with softer material added on top.
Longer lengths of coconut fibres are also used.

♦ BELOW, LEFT AND RIGHT
A woven nest site for finches (*left*) and a canary
nest pan (*below*). While canaries and singing
finches build a cup-shaped nest, other finches
build much more elaborate nests.

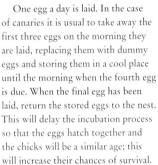

One egg a day is laid. In the case
of canaries it is usual to take away the
first three eggs on the morning they
are laid, replacing them with dummy
eggs and storing them in a cool place
until the morning when the fourth egg
is due. When the final egg has been
laid, return the stored eggs to the nest.
This will delay the incubation process
so that the eggs hatch together and
the chicks will be a similar age; this
will increase their chances of survival.

Egg food should be fed to parent
birds throughout the rearing period,
to provide the vital protein necessary
for the growth of their young.
Waxbills will require tiny livefoods,
such as micro-crickets, which can be
sprinkled with a nutritional balancer.
It helps if the live crickets are cooled
beforehand, as they will then be easier
for the birds to catch. Most pairs will
nest twice during the breeding season.
When the young have fledged, the
cock bird will take over feeding duties.

♦ BELOW
The wide gape of the chicks ensures that they swallow their food. Food passes to the crop at the base
of the neck, and the chicks cease begging when this is full.

BUDGERIGARS AND OTHER PARROTS

Members of this group of birds have been popular pets for centuries and, in recent years, even those species which had a reputation for being difficult to breed are now nesting quite regularly in aviary surroundings. Some are much better mimics than others, however, and if you are seeking a parrot as a pet, be sure to choose a young bird which has preferably been handreared, so that it will already be tame, with no instinctive fear of people.

INTRODUCTION

There are more than 330 different species of parrot found in tropical areas throughout the world, but only relatively few are popular as household companions. The talking abilities of the different species vary quite widely, but the budgerigar and the African grey parrot are considered to be the champion chatterboxes. Both can amass a vocabulary of more than 500 words, although individuals vary in their talking abilities and much depends on the skills of their teachers.

In contrast, other larger parrots, such as cockatoos, are limited in terms of their talking abilities and are rarely likely to master as many as 30 words; the harsh natural calls of these birds are more likely to lead to complaints from neighbours. Cockatoos can also be destructive, and accommodating them either in the home or outdoors in aviary surroundings can be costly. Handling, too, can be difficult.

BUDGIES AS PETS

Few birds are as versatile as the budgerigar, which makes an excellent pet and aviary occupant. It is also a popular bird for showing, and if you are interested in this, you should contact a breeder of exhibition budgerigars for sales stock.

♦ ABOVE
Light green and sky blue budgerigars. Both these birds are cocks, as shown by the blue ceres above the bill. Light green is the budgie's natural colour.

♦ LEFT
The broad crest feathers that help to distinguish the umbrella cockatoo, along with its white plumage, can be clearly seen here.

364

The cere itself is important in determining the budgerigar's gender, although sexing is more difficult in recently fledged chicks than in older individuals. The cere of a young cock is a deeper purple shade than that of a hen, whose cere turns brown as she reaches maturity.

There are many thousands of colour combinations of the budgerigar. Among the most popular are red-eyed lutinos, which have deep yellow plumage; snow white albinos; and rich violets, which can be bred with either white or yellow faces. Colourful pieds, with their variegated appearance, and rarer crested varieties are just some of the other options available from breeders. Budgerigars may live for ten years.

PARROTS AS PETS

In the case of parrots, a handreared chick is the best option if you are seeking a pet bird to house indoors. The chicks should be independent by approximately 16 weeks of age. Young grey parrots, for example, are distinguished from adults by their dark rather than straw yellow irises. Visual sexing is impossible so, if you want to know the sex of your pet, you will need to take a feather sample to a laboratory for DNA testing. Grey parrots, like many of the larger parrot species, have a life expectancy roughly equivalent to our own, and this adds to their appeal.

◆ ABOVE
The collar of the adult Indian ring-neck will identify the male, but it may take up to two years for this feature to become apparent in young birds.

If you are looking for a pet budgerigar, you need to choose one between six and nine weeks old as young birds will settle more easily in a new home. Solid-coloured eyes that have no white ring around them are the most reliable means of recognizing a budgerigar of this age. Other features that may be apparent, depending on the colour variety, include a dark tip to the upper bill, with the barred markings on the head extending down to the cere at the top of the beak. The throat spots are also likely to be smaller at this stage.

◆ RIGHT
A young grey parrot, as shown by its dark eye – adults have straw-yellow irises. Grey parrots are the best mimics of the parrot family, and are capable of building a vocabulary of hundreds of words.

SPECIES AND BREEDS

The choice of parrots suitable for housing outdoors in an aviary in urban areas needs to be made carefully, to avoid complaints about the noise from neighbours. As a general guide, the smaller species are quieter by nature, and also less destructive.

COCKATIELS

Aside from the budgerigar, one of the most popular and widely bred birds for aviaries is the cockatiel (*Nymphicus hollandicus*). You can house these gentle birds in a collection with finches. Cocks of the normal grey form have bright yellow facial feathering, with orange ear coverts. The faces of hens are a greyer shade with yellow markings on the underside of the tail feathers. Young birds, which can make superb companions, are similar to hens, but have shorter tail feathers and pinkish ceres.

The striking lemon-yellow lutino retains the orange cheek patches seen in the grey. Other popular colours include the cinnamon,

◆ ABOVE
Grey is the usual colour of cockatiels, as shown by this pair. Cockatiels breed well in outdoor aviaries, while the young birds can develop into excellent companions.

◆ BELOW
Peach-faced lovebirds are now being bred in a wide range of colours in addition to the normal green form, such as the popular cremino variety seen here on the right, and various yellow forms.

which has a brownish hue to its plumage, and the white faced; these are entirely white in colour in the case of the cock birds, while the faces of the hens are greyish. Pied variants are also common.

Cockatiels should be fed on budgerigar seed and sunflower seed, along with a suitable nutritional supplement, which can be sprinkled over greenstuff, sweet apple or carrot. They can live well into their teens, and have been known to live into their late twenties in some exceptional cases.

GRASS PARAKEETS
The needs of grass parakeets, such as the splendid (*Neophema splendida*), are very similar to those of cockatiels. Also known as scarlet-chested parakeets, the cock can be recognized by his red breast feathering. A greenish-blue variety, in which the breast colour has been modified to salmon-pink, has also been bred.

PEACH–FACED LOVEBIRDS
Although rather underestimated as pets, peach-faced lovebirds (*Agapornis roseicollis*) are full of character. You can recognize young fledglings by the dark markings on their upper bill. Pairs will breed readily in aviaries, but sexing can be difficult. Only when they are in breeding condition does the gap between the pelvic bones above the vent enlarge in the case of hens, to the extent that they can be distinguished from cocks; at other times DNA sexing can be used. When breeding, these lovebirds are unusual among parrots in requiring nesting material,

✦ ABOVE
The celestial is the most widely kept parrotlet. These birds can be very aggressive, however, in spite of their small size. Like most parrots, they need to be housed individually or in pairs.

which they will carry in their bills. A wide range of colours are now established, of which the most colourful is possibly the lutino, with its bright yellow, rather than green, plumage offset against the peach-coloured feathering on the face.

PARROTLETS
These rank among the smallest members of the parrot family, but they can be quite savage and should be housed on their own in pairs. Always cover both sides of an intervening partition between flights with mesh, to prevent neighbouring birds from biting each other's toes. Chicks must also be removed as soon as they are independent as the breeding pair are likely to want to nest again, and the cock in particular may then attack his older offspring. The celestial (*Forpus coelestis*) is one of the most widely kept species, with hens lacking the blue plumage seen on the cock birds.

✦ ABOVE
The pure blue form of the splendid grass parakeet is less common than the greenish variant. The cock is shown on the left. Note the white and slight salmon coloration.

CONURES

Originating from parts of Central and South America, conures are a group of parakeets whose common name derives from their older generic name, *Conurus*. They can be broadly divided into two groups. Members of the Pyrrhura group are significantly quieter and less destructive by nature than their Aratinga cousins. Pyrrhuras are also called scaly-breasted conures because of the characteristic scaly markings on their breast feathering. The rest of their plumage is predominantly green, with red markings on the wings and sometimes on the underparts. These birds are quiet by nature and can become very tame, even in aviary surroundings. Feeding is straightforward as their inquisitive natures mean they will eat a variety of foods.

A number of species are commonly bred, including the black-tailed (*Pyrrhura melanura*), red-bellied (*P. frontalis*) and green-cheeked (*P. molinae*). It is not

◆ ABOVE
When they fledge, sun conures have greenish backs and a greenish tone to their underparts. Their distinctive coloration takes two years to develop over successive moults.

◆ ABOVE
The plum-headed parakeet is an ideal choice for a garden aviary. Quiet, colourful and graceful in flight, these birds are justifiably popular.

possible to sex these conures by sight, and DNA sexing will be necessary. Breeding pairs are quite prolific. They are relatively hardy but will require a nest box, for roosting purposes, throughout the year.

HAHN'S MACAW

The Hahn's macaw (*Ara nobilis*) is rather like a conure in terms of its size and coloration, but the bare facial patches of skin on the face confirm that it is in fact a macaw. Although social by nature, even this smallest member of the macaw clan is relatively noisy. Young handreared birds do make good pets, however, although they are not talented talkers.

Pairs are likely to breed in the early summer and require a stout nest box for this purpose, which they will use for roosting for the rest of the year. It is best to feed them a complete diet although, if a parrot mix is used, then at least half of the food intake must consist of fruit and vegetables, ranging from pomegranates and peas to grapes and peeled carrots, sprinkled with a vitamin and mineral supplement.

◆ LEFT
The white-fronted Amazon is instantly recognizable by the white area above the cere and the adjoining area of red plumage, which forms a narrow band around the eye. These parrots are sometimes called spectacled Amazons.

PLUM–HEADED PARAKEET

In contrast, the plum-headed parakeet (*Psittacula cyanocephala*) is another species that is ideal for a typical suburban aviary as its calls are unlikely to cause offence. Hens and cocks are easily distinguished because only the cock bird has the distinctive plum-coloured feathering on the head. The immature cock birds resemble adult hens, however, so it is always better to obtain a proven pair rather than buying odd birds in the hope of obtaining a pair. The nest box must be located in a sheltered part of the aviary because these parakeets do not brood their chicks closely, and there is a real risk that they could become fatally chilled in cold weather. This is especially disastrous because plum heads usually only lay one clutch of eggs in a year.

AMAZON PARROTS

There are over 30 species of Amazon parrot, most of which are predominantly green in colour. The white-fronted (*Amazona albifrons*) is the smallest species, but its calls are almost as strident as those of its larger relatives. These parrots are very destructive by nature but can be housed in an aviary clad with 16-gauge mesh. Sexing, in the case of the white-fronted Amazon, is straightforward, with red feathering running down the edges of the cock bird's wing.

◆ ABOVE
Even smaller members of the parrot family, such as this Hahn's macaw, are likely to be destructive. They are relatively hardy once acclimatized, especially if provided with a nest box for roosting purposes.

HOUSING

Because of their generally destructive natures, parrots will require much stronger housing than finches. Even budgerigars can whittle away easily at wood, and it is especially important that aviaries for all these birds have mesh on their inner faces, when they are assembled, to cover and protect the timber frame. The wire gauge also needs to be correspondingly thicker to resist the bills of parrots.

♦ LEFT
A small parrot cage, suitable for a Senegal parrot, for example. The bird should be let out of the cage each day for a period of exercise.

OUTDOOR ACCOMMODATION

If you are buying an aviary flight, check the mesh is firmly attached to the timber framework by proper netting staples rather than ordinary staples, even if this means having to reinforce them yourself before assembling the aviary. The mesh should be anchored to a blockwork base by means of frame fixers, with the base itself extending at least 30 cm (12 in) below ground level to provide support and exclude rodents. The panels themselves, as before, can be held together with bolts, which should be well oiled and fitted with washers so that the flight can be moved easily – if you move home, for example.

Entry should be via a safety porch, located at the rear of the aviary, leading into the shelter. This will ensure that the birds do not escape when you enter the aviary. It is important that the safety porch door opens outwards, however, to give you easy access to the interior of the aviary; both the aviary door itself and the connecting door leading into the flight should open inwards.

Where parrots are housed in individual pairs, as is usual, then a deep layer of gravel can be used as a floor covering, and paving slabs can be placed under the perches where the

♦ LEFT
A block of raised aviaries intended for parrots. The birds are fed at the back of the structure, and the raised floor area will usually have a mesh base.

nearest the shelter, as well as guttering to carry away rain water. This will also be needed on the shelter itself.

INDOOR QUARTERS

Space is extremely important when selecting a cage for indoor birds; it should be as large as possible as cramped quarters can trigger feather plucking. Always replace the plastic or dowel perches supplied with most parrot cages with fresh cut branches, as these will help to prevent any sore patches developing on the bird's feet, which can easily become infected.

It is normal for a pet parrot to gnaw the perches away, and these should be replaced as necessary. Only use branches from trees that have not been sprayed recently with chemicals as perches. Most fruit trees, such as apple, elder and sycamore, are suitable but avoid poisonous trees, such as yew, lilac and laburnum.

majority of droppings will accumulate. The perches themselves should be positioned across the flight, to provide plenty of flying space, but not so close to the end that the birds will damage their tails when they turn around here.

The floor covering in an aviary of budgerigars should be concrete, which can be hosed down regularly and disinfected at intervals. The floor needs to be sloped away from the shelter so that cleaning and rain water can drain away through a hole bored into the floor at the opposite end.

Although parrots are hardy once acclimatized in their quarters, they still need protection from the elements. You can provide this by fixing corrugated plastic sheeting on to the roof and sides of the flight

✦ ABOVE
Cleanliness is important in a colony aviary, such as this, where a number of birds are housed. Establish a regular cleaning routine and keep to it.

✦ RIGHT
A view from inside an aviary showing a safety porch in use. The purpose of the porch is to stop birds escaping when you enter the aviary by means of a double-doored entry system.

FEEDING

Most larger parrots are traditionally fed a seed mixture mainly comprising sunflower seed and peanuts, and lesser amounts of foods such as flaked maize, and pumpkin and safflower seeds. In comparison, cockatiels and parakeets are offered a higher percentage of cereal seeds in their diet, such as canary seed and millets, including millet sprays, as well as groats, which are a particular favourite of Pyrrhura conures. Seed mixes for budgerigars consist exclusively of small seeds, notably millet and canary seed, which can be provided more easily in a seed hopper than in an open food container.

As with seed mixes for finches, however, even the best of these diets

◆ LEFT
A hopper used for budgerigars. Seed is tipped into the top section, with the husks collecting in the drawer located below the level of the perch.

will not meet all the nutritional needs of the birds. They are generally deficient in key dietary ingredients such as Vitamin A and calcium, which is why a comprehensive vitamin and mineral supplement will be required, along with daily portions of fresh, diced fruit and greenstuff.

In recent years, manufacturers have developed a range of complete diets

suitable for small parrotlets up to large macaws. It is not always so easy to persuade birds to sample them, in spite of the fact that they have a superior nutritional value to seed. Young parrots that have been hand-reared on complete diets in a liquid form will usually continue eating them, once they are weaned, but older individuals that have lived on

Large pine nuts

Small pine nuts

Groundnuts

Groats

Safflower seeds

White and striped sunflower seeds

◆ LEFT
Taming a budgerigar sufficiently to have it eat
from your hand will often be possible, especially
if you have had the bird since it was young.

◆ BELOW
Tame birds such as this blue and gold macaw
will often be keener to sample new foods,
compared with aviary birds. Seed alone does
not provide a balanced diet.

because these components are already
present at the required levels
within the formulated food.
Complete foods need to be
kept dry, as with seed, and
must be used before
their stated expiry date
in order for the birds to gain
maximum benefit from them.

Never try to switch the birds' diet
just prior to or during the breeding
season. If you want to change your
birds' diet, the simplest way is to mix
some of the new food into the old,
gradually increasing the quantity as
the birds start to take the unfamiliar
food, until it has entirely replaced the
familiar diet. The other option is
simply to remove the familiar food
and present the birds with the new
food, effectively forcing them to
eat it. However, this may give
rise to digestive problems
and can result in loss
of condition as well.

sunflower seed for years can be very
reluctant to sample something new.
Certain types of parrot are worse
in this respect than others, with
cockatoos being especially reluctant
to try unfamilar foods, including fresh
fruit and greenstuff.

Complete diets are more expensive
than seed on a weight-for-weight
basis but there is very little wastage
with them (providing the bird will
co-operate) whereas, with seed, the
husks will be discarded. There is an
additional saving with complete diets
in that there will be no expenditure
on vitamin and mineral supplements

Special drinking bottles are
normally supplied to larger parrots,
although tubular drinkers can be
given to budgerigars. In both cases,
these will keep the water clean. In
an outdoor aviary, check on cold
mornings that ice has not formed in
the spout, blocking off the flow
of water. Birds must
always have free
access to clean
drinking water,
particularly when
they are eating
a dry diet.

◆ LEFT
Clean drinking
water is essential
for all birds. This
bottle-style drinker
can be suspended in
an aviary or left
standing on the
floor. Keep it in a
shaded spot, out
of direct sunlight.

GENERAL CARE AND BREEDING

◆ BELOW
Greenstuff can be used to encourage a pet bird, such as this cockatiel, to feed from your hand. Always wash greenstuff and fruit thoroughly before offering it to birds.

Parrots are more difficult to handle than finches, thanks to their powerful bills, although they can usually be caught in a similar way. It is worthwhile wearing a pair of thin leather gloves when handling parrots as these will protect you against being bitten; take extra care when wearing gloves not to injure the bird by holding it too tightly. You can restrain the bird's head easily, between the first and second fingers of your left hand (assuming that you are right-handed), so that it will not be able to bite.

Gloves can also be useful when you are training a young parrot, whose claws are likely to be especially sharp: they will wear down once the bird is perching regularly. Most handreared birds will perch readily on the hand so it is always better to encourage them to do this rather than physically restraining them, partly because they may then grow fearful of the gloves.

Only allow your parrot out of its cage into the room when you are present, particularly because there are likely to be a number of dangers

lurking here. While some hazards, like dangerous plants such as cacti with their sharp spines, and potentially poisonous plants, such as winter cherry with its orange berries, and poinsettia, can be kept elsewhere in the home, window glass is an ever-present hazard. Net curtains or blinds indicate the presence of a barrier.

Always check that the windows are closed before letting your parrot out of its quarters. Any fires in the room should be adequately guarded to keep your pet away from the flames.

When first allowed out within the confines of a room, a young parrot is likely to fly around wildly, and may crash-land, knocking over ornaments.

TAMING A YOUNG PARROT

1 Start by encouraging the bird to take food from you by offering a tidbit, such as a piece of fruit, with one hand. In this way, persuade the bird first out of its quarters, then on to your hand.

2 As the parrot approaches, extend your other hand to encourage the parrot to step on to it. This will also make it easier for the bird to reach the fruit. Be patient.

3 In due course, your young pet parrot will step readily on to your outstretched hand, especially when food is being offered. If its claws are quite sharp, you may prefer to wear gloves.

In the case of aviary birds that will not talk, then either ringing or microchipping will be necessary. The microchip unit, about the size of a rice grain, is inserted by a vet into the bird's breast muscle. The chip is read by a special reader to identify the bird. It can prove vital in cases where birds have been stolen and then recovered.

BREEDING

Parrots housed outdoors should only be encouraged to breed during the warmer months of the year. In the case of budgerigars breeding on the colony system, their nest boxes must all be positioned at roughly the same height to prevent fighting. All nest boxes should be located under cover, preferably in the aviary shelter.

Birds will like to rest from time to time, and it helps if you provide perches in the form of stands around the room, which your pet will be able to use. Toys are also a good idea, and even a parrot play area that includes a play-gym, if you have the space.

TRAINING

If you place your finger alongside the perch your parrot should soon step on to it. When it comes to teaching a bird to talk, pick a word or short phrase and repeat this regularly. Training sessions should be kept short to maintain your pet's concentration, although you can reinforce these lessons with the use of a recorded audio cassette tape. One of the first things that a bird needs to learn is its address or telephone number, so that if it does escape and is found, there is at least some chance that you will be traced and reunited with your bird.

♦ ABOVE
In many cases, cock birds are more colourful than hens, but there are exceptions, as with Ruppell's parrot, which is an African species.

♦ RIGHT
Some birds prefer a deep, natural nesting site. This Levaillant's barbet has bored into an old log to create its nesting chamber.

HEALTH CARE

The care of sick birds has advanced considerably in recent years, but much still depends on the owner spotting that an individual bird is off-colour at an early stage. This will greatly increase the likelihood of a successful recovery.

Allow time each day to check your birds for signs of illness, especially when they are housed in aviary surroundings. It is critical that a sick bird is dealt with quickly, otherwise its condition will deteriorate rapidly.

BIRD HEALTH

Birds are very adept at concealing signs of illness. By the time the symptoms are clearly apparent, the bird is likely to be seriously ill, with its chances of recovery much reduced.

DETECTING ILLNESS

It is difficult even for an experienced avian vet to diagnose the cause of illness in some cases without tests, because the symptoms of many serious bird diseases are very similar. Sick birds will be less active than usual, with their feathers fluffed up

◆ LEFT
A commercially available hospital cage for smaller birds. The heat controller on the side of the unit makes it possible to reacclimatize the bird.

◆ LEFT AND INSET
An alternative system of providing warmth for a sick bird is to suspend a dull infrared lamp over the cage, to supply heat rather than light. Position food and water containers away from the perches to avoid the contents being contaminated by the bird's droppings.

and not preened. They lose interest in food and in their surroundings, will remain huddled up, and may become too weak to perch. Their droppings are likely to turn greenish in colour as a reflection of the fact that they have not eaten properly for some time.

CARE FOR SICK BIRDS

Sick birds must be kept warm because they lose body heat rapidly and, since they are unlikely to be eating properly, are vulnerable to hypothermia. A sick bird therefore needs special care – to be kept warm and helped to feed. For this, it is possible to buy hospital cages for smaller birds, or a better option may be to invest in an infra-red lamp with a reflector hood. This can be suspended over the cage,

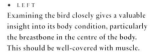

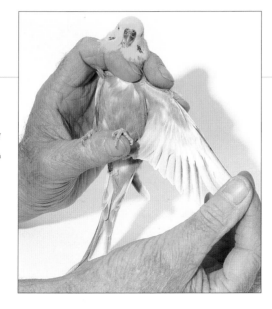

◆ BELOW LEFT
It may be necessary to give medication by means of a tube that has been passed down into the crop. Never attempt to do this without the advice of an avian vet.

◆ BELOW RIGHT
Accidents involving birds may result in fractures, as seen in this radiograph. It is often possible for a vet to repair such injuries successfully.

until the bird has recovered fully and is eating normally again. In the case of birds that fall ill outdoors over the winter months, it may be better to keep them in a birdroom or indoor aviary until the following spring.

ACCIDENTS

It is not just illness that may require emergency care. Birds can sometimes fracture their limbs and when this happens they will need veterinary attention immediately. A fracture of the skull may occur if a bird tries to fly through a window pane that has no curtains to clearly indicate a barrier. There is often little that can be done in these cases, however, particularly if internal haemorrhaging occurs.

Injuries to the feet or claws are fairly common and these may cause bleeding to varying degrees. If this happens, pressing on the affected area with a clean paper tissue for two minutes should stop the bleeding. If you have any worries about your bird's health, consult an avian vet.

ensuring also that there is a cooler area where the bird can go if it feels too warm. Reduce the heat output as the bird starts to show signs of recovery.

It is equally important to ensure that the bird can reach its food and water easily. If it is too weak to perch, place these containers on the floor of its quarters. You can often rekindle the appetite of a sick bird by providing soaked rather than hard seed; this is especially true in the case of finches, which can usually be persuaded to eat soaked millet sprays. Seek veterinary advice if you experience problems getting a larger parrot to feed.

As the bird recovers, so it will need to be gradually reacclimatized first to room temperature, and then to an outdoor existence. Never try to rush the bird back to its former way of life, and do not even start rehabilitation

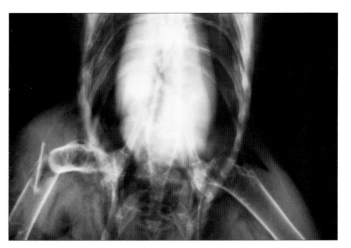

INFECTIOUS ILLNESSES

Infections are most likely to spread in aviary surroundings where a number of birds are housed together, rather than affecting a pet bird in the home. However, if dirty seed is used, then any bird is vulnerable. This is why it is important to ensure that only top quality foodstuffs are fed to the birds, and a good standard of hygiene is maintained in the preparation area.

ANTIBIOTICS

These can be very helpful in combating many of the common bacterial illnesses to which birds are susceptible. Always use antibiotics with care, particularly in countries where they can be bought over the counter without veterinary guidance. Never be tempted to stop treatment until the course has been completed. Stopping treatment too soon means that not only may the infection recur, but that the bacteria concerned may become resistant to the antibiotic. The only way to determine this is to carry out a series of tests, which will involve culturing the bacteria and testing for the most appropriate antibiotic for treatment purposes.

✦ ABOVE
Birds living in groups, such as canaries, are the most vulnerable to infections.

✦ BELOW
An antibiotic sensitivity test. The disks contain different antibiotics, while the cloudy areas show bacterial growth. The most effective drugs, on the left, have the largest clear areas around them, showing inhibition of bacterial growth.

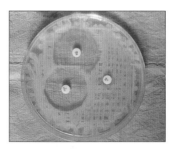

✦ LEFT
Small birds such as finches are especially at risk from hypothermia when they fall ill.

✦ BELOW
A cockatiel with a badly inflamed eye. This could be the result of an injury, or it might indicate an underlying infection, especially if both eyes are affected.

Antibiotic treatment often comes in the form of medicated seed or a powder that has to be added to the bird's drinking water. It can be difficult to ensure that a sick bird consumes sufficient amounts of the medication to reach a therapeutic level in its body, which is why your vet may start by giving an injection, to help the bird over the critical phase of its illness.

PRECAUTIONARY HYGIENE

Always remember to take sensible precautions yourself when handling a sick bird, because there is a slight possibility that the infection could in turn spread to you.

Clean out the sick bird's quarters thoroughly, particularly if it is being housed with a group of birds, to stop the infection spreading. Wash and disinfect food and water containers as a priority, as well as changing the floor covering in the shelter and scrubbing off the perches. If there is a bad outbreak of disease try to find the source. New birds should always be isolated for the first two weeks to ensure that they are healthy as, otherwise, they could introduce an infection into the aviary. Attend to the needs of sick birds after those of healthy stock, and do not wash their food containers in the same water.

◆ ABOVE
Enteric injections are relatively common in budgerigars but they can often be treated successfully with antibiotics. Green droppings are a typical sign of enteritis.

You also need to be vigilant to the possibility of rodents entering the aviary and soiling the food. Rodents can introduce unpleasant bacteria, such as *Salmonella* and *Yersinia*, both of which are hard to treat successfully, and will cause widespread mortality.

Some ailments can be treated topically, as in the case of minor eye infections. If you are using an ointment, hold the bird for a few minutes afterwards to allow the medication to start dissolving into the eye, because otherwise the bird may simply wipe the treatment straight off on to the perch. Drops may be easier to apply but, if the bird blinks, they may not reach their target. Recovery from eye ailments is usually very quick, but you must maintain the treatment to the end of the course to prevent the symptoms recurring. Eye treatments need to be given often, as the tear fluid will wash the medication out of the eyes.

FRENCH MOULT AND PBFD
Not all infectious diseases can be treated successfully, notably those of viral origins. These include French Moult, which affects young fledging budgerigars, causing them to drop

their flight and tail feathers, and Psittacine Beak and Feather Disease (PBFD), a chronic and invariably fatal disease, which affects cockatoos and other parrots. This causes feather loss and distortion of the bill and claws, which soften and become flaky. The emphasis in combating viral diseases is essentially on prompt diagnosis and vaccination to protect individuals that are at risk.

◆ ABOVE
Some groups of birds are more vulnerable to certain types of infections. Australian parakeets may develop infections of the upper respiratory tract, for example.

◆ LEFT
Sick birds have a dull, depressed demeanour and ruffled plumage. They lose interest in their surroundings and will be reluctant to fly.

PARASITIC ILLNESSES

Although parasitic illnesses are most likely to affect collections of aviary birds, they may sometimes occur in pet birds housed on their own, particularly budgerigars.

EXTERNAL PARASITES
Budgerigars are prone to the disease known as scaly face, and in most cases they will have been infected with the parasites that cause the illness while still in the nest. This is a relatively easy condition to identify. Symptoms include tiny white spots, which start

◆ LEFT
Scaly face mites result in crusty swellings on the bill and cere. Early treatment is important because, if left, not only does the bird represent a hazard to others, but it can also suffer permanent damage to the bill.

◆ LEFT AND INSET BELOW
Lice can be seen with the naked eye (*left*), lying close to feather vanes. Lice have strong mouthparts, as revealed under the microscope (*below*). Spraying the bird with an aerosol recommended for red mite will kill lice. The treatment will need to be repeated after about 14 days.

out on the bird's upper bill and spread to the sides of the face, causing coral-like encrustations here. Treatment is with a proprietary cream spread over the affected area.

You will need to continue treating the bird for a period after the obvious signs have disappeared, to be sure of eliminating any mites that may still exist in the skin. Otherwise, the infection can recur. It is important to replace the perches at this stage because the bird may have transferred mites, which could reinfect it in the future. Scaly mite can also affect the legs in some cases, resulting in the appearance of white scaly swellings on this part of the body.

Red mite is another common avian parasite and this is often spread during the breeding season. The mites lurk within breeding cages and nest boxes, and they emerge to suck the blood of the chicks, which gives them their characteristic coloration. Covering the cage with a white cloth overnight is likely to reveal the presence of red mites in the morning, with their coloration standing out against the cloth. A specific avian aerosol can be

◆ BELOW AND BELOW RIGHT
A roundworm expelled with the droppings
after treatment was given. Australian parakeets
and lovebirds (right) are especially at risk from
these internal parasites.

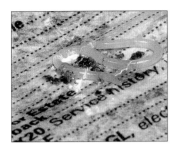

flare up, causing the budgerigar
to regurgitate its seed. On closer
examination, the crop, at the base
of the neck, will also be swollen
with air. It is usually possible to
treat trichomoniasis successfully,
but be aware that the condition
may recur again, should any of
the parasites have survived.

INTERNAL PARASITES

The most common internal parasites
in birds are roundworms. These are
a particular problem with Australian
parakeets because of their habit of
foraging on the ground, which makes
them far more likely to come into
contact with the microscopic worm
eggs. It is possible to determine
whether a parakeet is infected by
examining a sample of its droppings.
Direct treatment via a crop tube is
the most effective way of eliminating
the problem, and this should only be
carried out by an avian vet. Treatment
administered via the drinking water
can also be used.

used to kill these parasites, and the
birds' quarters should also be washed
thoroughly. The best of the products
now available commercially have a
residual action and will offer some
protection against reinfection. Aside
from resulting in anaemia, especially
in chicks, red mite can also cause the
condition known as feather plucking.

Mirrors can help to keep a pet
bird occupied but, on occasion, cock
budgerigars may end up feeding their
reflections repeatedly. This phase
will usually pass as the bird's desire
to breed subsides, but there may be
another, more sinister cause of the
behaviour. A crop parasite called
Trichomonas, often passed from adult
birds to their chicks in the nest, can

In order to minimize the likelihood
of reinfection, disinfect the aviary
thoroughly, as the roundworm eggs
can survive for well over a year outside
the bird's body. This must be done at
the same time as treatment is given.
Breeders often routinely de-worm
their birds twice a year, just prior
to and after the breeding season, to
prevent a build-up of the parasites.
Roundworms may cause relatively
few symptoms in adult birds but can
often be fatal in young, recently
fledged chicks, which acquired them
in the nest from their parents.

◆ LEFT
Finches, as well as
budgerigars, can be
very vulnerable to
the illness known
as trichomoniasis,
which causes
weight loss and is
often known as
"going light".

◆ RIGHT
Tapeworms, such
as this one trailing
out of a parrot's
vent, have a more
complex life-cycle
than roundworms.
They cannot usually
be spread directly
from bird to bird.

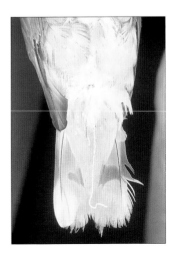

HERPTILES AND INVERTEBRATES

Interest in this group of creatures as pets has grown greatly over recent years, partly because of the ease with which they can be maintained in domestic surroundings. Yet, although most species are relatively easy to take care of, you need to bear in mind that some will grow quite large and can rapidly outgrow their accommodation. This is an important consideration when making your choice of pet. Another significant factor is that although a number of these creatures, such as the bearded dragon lizard (*Pogona vitticeps*), can become tame and will respond well to handling, many others, including the invertebrates, are very much to be admired from a distance rather than handled regularly.

Individual feeding needs may also affect your choice. Snakes, for example, are carnivores, whereas some lizards and a number of invertebrates are herbivores. Lifespan may be another consideration. Although tortoises are famed for their longevity there are some surprises as well, in that female tarantulas can potentially live for over half a century. Toads and some other amphibians can also have a lifespan measured in decades, whereas for snakes and lizards ten to 15 years is the average.

◆ OPPOSITE
Amphibians such as the stunning red-eyed treefrog are popular vivarium subjects. They require a rainforest-type set-up in order to thrive in these surroundings.

◆ LEFT
Tortoises are reptiles with very widespread appeal. Some species, typically those of Eurasian origin, can be housed outdoors in temperate areas for part of the year.

SNAKES

No group of reptiles is more misunderstood than snakes, but as people have been keeping and breeding them on an ever-increasing scale over recent years, this has helped to dispel many of the misconceptions. Snakes are interesting vivarium occupants, and there is a wide choice of species now being bred, including some attractive colour variants. The snakes featured here are chosen for their suitability as pets: are all non-poisonous and handling is relatively easy.

INTRODUCTION

♦ BELOW
Many of the most widely-kept snakes, such as ribbon or garter snakes, originate from North America.

Snakes evolved from lizard-like ancestors around 120 million years ago, and one of their most obvious features is an absence of limbs, although traces of limbs can be seen in certain snakes, such as boas. This loss of legs originally came about to help snakes burrow and today they are not noticeably handicapped by their absence. In fact, snakes can move very effectively; they are very able escape artists and can usually slip out through the smallest of gaps.

Snakes have adapted to live in a wide range of habitats, and a careful study of their body shapes can help to reveal the environment that they prefer. Those with raised nostrils, for example, tend to be aquatic by nature, while those with shiny scales and blunt-ended tails are burrowers.

♦ BELOW
A young Amazon tree boa. This tropical species undergoes a change in colour on maturity, becoming emerald green with white markings.

Colour can also be significant. Green coloration invariably indicates those snakes that spend most of their time off the ground, such as the green tree python (*Chondropython viridis*), in contrast with snakes that are predominantly brown and terrestrial in their habits. However, this is not an infallible guide: the boa constrictor is brownish with dark, irregular markings, which help to break up the outline of these large arboreal snakes.

Snakes have a wide distribution, and although the majority of species are found in tropical and sub-tropical areas, some, including the most commonly kept species, range into temperate areas. The type of vivarium and general management that these

◆ RIGHT
A snake shedding its skin. This process is often
described as "sloughing". The skin should come
off easily in one piece, as here, if the snake is in
good health.

snakes require differs quite widely
from that of their tropical cousins.

All snakes are predatory by nature.
In the wild they will hunt prey but it
is quite possible to persuade captive
snakes to eat artificial substitutes, in
a number of cases. This means that it
will not always be necessary to keep a
stock of dead rodents or chicks, which
many people find unpleasant. It helps,

more problematic, especially in the
case of young snakes. There are
techniques available to identify true
pairs: your vet should be able to advise
you on this. In most cases, it is not
a good idea to allow a pair of snakes
to live together; snakes are often
solitary hunters, and they can turn
cannibalistic when living in close
confinement with each other.

in this respect, if you obtain a young
snake that has been reared only on
artificial substitutes.

As they grow, snakes will shed their
skin. This is often an anxious time for
new owners who are not expecting
this to occur. The snake's eyes will
become a milky white colour and its
appetite will decline. Rather than
a sign of illness, this is normal; a
healthy snake will shed its entire skin,
including the eye covers. Incomplete,
patchy moulting is a sign that the
snake is not in good health and, if the
so-called "spectacles" covering the
eyes remain after the moult, they will
need to be removed by a vet. Not
surprisingly, young growing snakes
moult most frequently but the process
will continue throughout their lives.

Breeding snakes in vivarium
surroundings is not especially difficult,
but sexing in the first instance can be

◆ ABOVE
The frequency of shedding
depends on the age of the snake.
Young snakes which are growing
fast will slough more frequently
than adults.

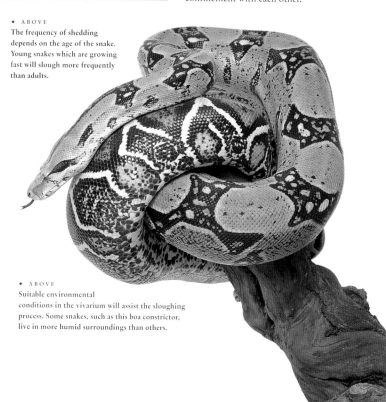

◆ ABOVE
Suitable environmental
conditions in the vivarium will assist the sloughing
process. Some snakes, such as this boa constrictor,
live in more humid surroundings than others.

SPECIES

It is no coincidence that some of the
smaller and more colourful snakes
are among the most popular, and for
this reason the most widely bred.

COMMON GARTER SNAKE

The snake known as the common
garter snake (*Thamnophis sirtalis*)
has the widest distribution of any
snake in North America, and takes its
name from its narrow girth. Its needs
are quite specific. It has to be housed
at a temperature of about 25°C (77°F)
in the summer, which can be allowed
to fall back to a maximum of 15°C
(59°F) in the winter, mimicking the
changes that occur naturally in
the snake's habitat. The
vivarium temperature
can then be raised
gradually.

◆ RIGHT
There are many
localized forms
of the milk snake,
which differ in terms
of their patterning.
They feed primarily
on mice, and will
grow up to about
130 cm (52 in) long.

◆ ABOVE
A chequered garter snake. These snakes give
birth to between six and 12 live young. Garter
snakes will grow to 70–100 cm (28–40 in) long.

◆ BELOW
The Sinaloan form of the milk snake. It used
to be thought that these snakes fed on cows'
milk, because they are often found in open
areas; however, they do not.

Although they are often
found in areas of water, it is
important that the substrate in
the garter snake's vivarium stays
dry. Provide a large water bowl in
which the reptile can immerse itself –
without flooding its surroundings, as
dampness can trigger skin infections.
It is also very important to feed the

correct diet to these snakes if they are
to remain in good health. There are
now specially prepared foods, available
from reptile stockists, which contain
a range of the important nutrients.

MILK SNAKE

Bright colours in nature usually
signify danger, and this fact has
been exploited by the milk snake
(*Lampropeltis triangulum*), whose
appearance closely resembles that
of the deadly coral snakes (*Micrurus*
species). The natural forms of the
milk snake are variable in appearance;
for example, the Central American
subspecies are far more brightly
coloured than those of North
American origin. They also produce

Corn snakes can grow up to 150 cm (5 ft) in length. Colour variants of the corn snake have helped to increase the popularity of these snakes as pets.

RAT SNAKE

Although the most commonly available rat snakes are from North America, Asiatic species are also occasionally available. There are often distinct colour differences between young and adult rat snakes. Colour mutants have also cropped up, as in the case of the black

The attractive snow form of the corn snake. Females lay clutches of between ten and 20 eggs in the springtime.

An amelanistic corn snake. The lack of dark melanin pigment is responsible for their attractive bright coloration.

larger hatchlings, and this makes the young easier to rear successfully on whole pinkies (dead day-old mice). The Central American milk snakes do need to be kept at a slightly higher temperature as they originate from nearer to the Equator.

CORN SNAKE

A large number of colour varieties of the corn snake (*Elaphe guttata*) have now been developed, including the "snow corns", which are white to reflect their native habitat. Usually, however, corn snakes have a red, orange or grey background colour and red or orange markings. Corn snakes are adaptable by nature, and will make a good introduction to snake-keeping as they reach maturity at around two years of age.

rat snake (*Elaphe o. obsoleta*). Young individuals, which display greyish markings, can be tamed quite readily and grow fast, but adults unused to handling are likely to remain wild. They are somewhat arboreal by nature, and will appreciate some opportunity to climb. Another popular subspecies is the yellow rat snake (*E. o. quadri-vittata*). It has dark stripes on a yellowish background when adult, and is closely related to the Everglades rat snake (*E. o. rossalleni*), which has an orange background colour.

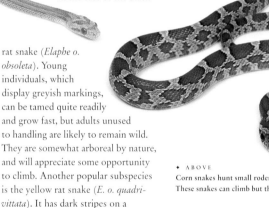

Corn snakes hunt small rodents such as mice. These snakes can climb but they rarely do so.

The colourful Everglades rat snake is also sometimes called the orange rat snake because of its coloration. It grows to 180 cm (72 in).

As their name suggests, rat snakes will prey on rodents such as rats. Their quarters should allow them the opportunity to climb.

COMMON KING SNAKE

There are many different forms of the common king snake (*Lampropeltis getulus*) but they all require similar conditions. These snakes are boldly marked in many cases and are a good choice if you are looking for a species that can be expected to breed well. An albino form of the Californian race (*L. g. californiae*) is also widely kept. King snakes are not keen climbers and their vivarium does not need to be tall, but it must have suitable retreats, such as cork bark, allowing the snakes to hide, as they are rather shy by nature. They can reach 180 cm (72 in).

♦ ABOVE
While some forms of the common king snake are banded, as here, others have longitudinal stripes. Speckled and spotted individuals are also known.

INDIGO SNAKE

Another popular species is the indigo snake (*Drymarchon corais*), which again displays considerable variation in its coloration and markings. Young snakes in this case are banded, whereas adults tend to be dark in colour. They will make a sound with their tails, rather like rattlesnakes, when threatened. Pairs need to be supervised when mating because male indigo snakes can become very aggressive.

♦ ABOVE, CLOCKWISE FROM TOP
A colour variant of the Queretouro king snake; a Sonoran Mountain king snake, one of the tri-coloured species originating from Arizona; the "Blair's form" of the grey-banded king snake, found in Texas.

SMOOTH GREEN SNAKE

A less widely available species is the brightly coloured smooth green snake (*Opheodrys vernalis*), along with the

♦ BELOW RIGHT
A rough green snake. Daily feeding is usually recommended for these insect-eating snakes. They are arboreal by nature, and will grow to about 50 cm (20 in) in length.

related rough form (*O. aestivus*), which has a reputation of being easier to keep. Green snakes require a vivarium with plenty of branches for climbing purposes, usually inhabiting the lower levels of bushes in the wild. In contrast to most snakes, they feed on insects. Crickets are a useful basis for their diet but supplementation is essential, since they are vulnerable to nutritional deficiencies. They also need to be fed more frequently than other snakes. Breeders have sought to maintain the distinctive regional differences that exist in many North and Central American snakes by careful pairings.

♦ RIGHT
The glossy black coloration of the indigo snake is impressive. These are quite large snakes, growing to a length of about 200 cm (80 in).

EMERALD TREE BOA

Reaching about 150 cm (60 in) long and needing thicker branches in its quarters is the beautiful emerald tree boa (*Corallus caninus*). These snakes originate from tropical parts of the world, where the climate is both hot and humid, and regular spraying is required, combined with good ventilation in the vivarium to prevent the development of moulds. These snakes may even drink the water that falls in their coils but do not spray them directly for this purpose – you should always provide a separate container of fresh water to supplement their fluid intake. Tree boas will hunt in the trees, spending most of their time there, and their food and water should be provided high up in the vivarium on a purpose-built shelf.

BOA CONSTRICTOR

The boa constrictor or common boa (*Boa constrictor*) is one of the most widely kept and bred of the large snakes. Occurring over such a vast

◆ LEFT
The coloration of the emerald tree boa helps it to blend in among vegetation. It is an arboreal predator, hunting birds and other creatures in the trees.

◆ BOTTOM
Boa constrictors range over Central and South America. They grow up to 3 m (10 ft), and can be difficult to handle at full size.

range, their coloration varies. For example, those found in southern parts, such as Argentina, are darker in colour, with the dark pigmentation helping them to absorb more heat in the cooler areas of their natural habitat. A red-tailed boa originates from northern South America.

Young boas, which measure about 50 cm (20 in) at birth, are quite easy to care for and can be reared without difficulty. However, they will need

much more spacious housing as they grow, and correspondingly larger quantities of food. Adult boas are quite capable of consuming dead rabbits and chickens, and will become more active at night, which is when they would hunt in the wild. Young boas will reach maturity when they are about three years old. A slight cooling in their quarters during the winter months, for up to eight weeks, will trigger breeding behaviour.

HOUSING

One of the most important basic features of vivarium design for snakes and other reptiles is the thermal gradient across the enclosure. In practical terms, this means that one end will be kept hotter than the other, allowing the snake to adjust its position in response to its body temperature. As the snake cools down it will move back to the warmer area. Since reptiles cannot regulate their body temperature independently of their surroundings – they are often described as cold-blooded – this is how they control their body temperature effectively.

Snakes are not especially active reptiles by nature and they do not need very large quarters, but their housing must reflect their needs. As a guide, allow between 30–45 sq cm (1–1.5 sq ft) per 30 cm (1 ft) length of the snake. Although there can be cases where snakes are housed together, this is not recommended, particularly as some species – such as king snakes – can be cannibalistic if housed with smaller companions. The height of the enclosure will be influenced by the size and habits of the species you are keeping. Generally, a height of 38–45 cm (15–18 in) is adequate in most cases, although taller designs are recommended for arboreal species.

Vivaria, in a range of suitable sizes, can be easily obtained from pet stores specializing in herptiles. Ease of cleanliness is a vital consideration, especially as snakes can be vulnerable to parasitic mites, which will establish themselves easily in the reptile's quarters. If you do not choose a seamless design of vivarium, and prefer a melamine design, seal the

◆ ABOVE
Lengths of wood may be useful in a vivarium to provide climbing opportunities for arboreal snakes.

◆ LEFT
Plastic plants can serve to create a impression of a natural environment in the vivarium, as well as providing cover.

◆ LEFT
Special fluorescent tubes will illuminate your snake, although the vivarium should never be brightly lit.

◆ BELOW LEFT
An infra-red heat lamp and surrounding reflector holder.

◆ BELOW
Screening of the heat source is vital to prevent burns.

joints inside with a special silicone sealant as used for fish tanks. Avoid sealants recommended for household use as they often contain harmful chemicals such as fungicides.

It is possible, especially with smaller snakes, to house them in a modified aquarium, but you will also need to invest in a special vivarium hood. These are manufactured in a

range of sizes and will fit snugly over the outside of the aquarium. Even so, it is important to secure the lid with a heavy weight because snakes can manage to force up the roof and slip out, escaping into the room where they can be very difficult to find.

There is usually a hole for an incandescent light bulb in vivarium lids; this is not necessarily the most

◆ FAR LEFT
Digital thermometers can be
relied upon to give accurate,
highly visible readings.

◆ LEFT
Temperature control is
important in helping to
encourage breeding activity.

suitable heating option, although it
is useful for snakes from temperate
areas. Infra-red heat lamps are a more
useful choice. All heating of this
type must be adequately shielded,
particularly in the case of snakes that
climb, because they can suffer serious,
if not fatal, burns if they come into
direct contact with a heat source.

Lighting is of less significance in
the case of snakes, compared with
other reptiles, simply because they
do not need to synthesize Vitamin D
in this way. However, lighting is
important to allow you to see the
snakes easily, and it may influence
their breeding behaviour. Even so,

as snakes are secretive creatures,
the lighting should be subdued. It
is equally important to provide them
with suitable retreats in their quarters,
such as cork bark or special hides, for
this reason. A range of substrates that

are appropriate to the needs of the
individual species can be used in
the snake's quarters. Some breeders
prefer to use ordinary newspaper as it
is cheaply available, absorbent and can
be easily changed.

◆ LEFT
A snake can
easily slip
through a
partially opened
vivarium door,
so be sure to fit
a special lock.

◆ LEFT
A typical glass-fronted
vivarium. The sliding
doors, set in runners,
provide easy access to
the interior.

◆ RIGHT
Choose attractive shapes
of driftwood to decorate
the vivarium, ensuring
that they are anchored
securely in place.

FEEDING

All snakes are predators and most feed on rodents (their natural prey in the wild) and chicks. Yet this emphatically does not mean that housed snakes need to be fed live food. In fact, not only is this illegal in many countries, it can also be harmful to the reptile itself – for example, a live rat may attack the snake. Dead rodents are often used, and they are sold in various sizes, from day-old dead mice, known as pinkies, to young and adult rodents. Large snakes may feed on chicks or adult chickens, but these are unsatisfactory from a nutritional standpoint and should not make up the bulk of the snake's diet.

SNAKE FOODS

Prepared foods are now available to meet the nutritional needs of many snakes. You can acquire suitable frozen

♦ LEFT
Most snakes need warm-blooded prey. Only a few species will feed on insects such as crickets. Check that these are of appropriate size, and dust them with a nutritional balancer, to improve their feeding value before placing them in the snake's vivarium.

food for snakes from specialist reptile suppliers and some larger pet stores. It is preferable to acquire foods that have been frozen individually, as you will then be able to defrost only the precise amount required at any one time, thereby avoiding wastage.

Some species, notably garter snakes and their close cousins, the ribbon snakes, are often fed on fish, but this needs to be prepared carefully to ensure that the snakes do not develop a serious deficiency of Vitamin B (thiamine). This can occur because of the presence of an enzyme called thiaminase in raw fish, which destroys the vitamin. Affected snakes will start twitching uncontrollably and will suffer more serious convulsions if the condition is not treated by a vet as a matter of urgency.

Prevention relies upon heating the fish to denature the enzyme and then allowing it to cool again before offering it to the snake. Sprinkling the fish with a multi-vitamin powder is also recommended, although the best solution is to use one of the specially formulated diets now available for this particular group of snakes. In the case of those snakes that feed on invertebrates, such as crickets, some supplementation of their food will also be necessary.

When buying a new snake, try to watch it being fed, if possible, prior to purchase, and always find out what

♦ ABOVE
Carefully formulated diets are available for garter and ribbon snakes, and special snake sausages (*right*) mean that dead chicks or rodents may not be required.

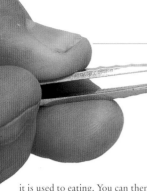

✦ ABOVE
Snakes will swallow their prey head first, so
offer food in this way. If using forceps, ensure
these are blunt ended rather than pointed, in
case your snake grabs them.

it is used to eating. You can then
obtain the necessary food before you
take it home. In the case of frozen
snake foods, these need to be thawed
thoroughly, preferably by being left
to stand at room temperature. You can
use a microwave to defrost foods, but
there is a risk of ice crystals being left
within the food, and these could prove
harmful to the snake.

GETTING YOUR SNAKE
TO FEED

For most snakes, especially when
they have been tamed, feeding is
straightforward and you need only
leave their food in the vivarium.

You may have to use forceps in the
case of more reluctant eaters; these
must be blunt ended to avoid any
injury to the snake when it strikes.
Slowly wave the food item in front
of the snake's head, encouraging it to
lunge at the item and not at your hand.

Prepared snake foods have a high
palatability, but you may still need to
carry out what is described as "odour
manipulation" when introducing new
food to the snake's diet. These reptiles
rely very heavily on scent to determine
what is edible. You will need to rub
the new item, such as the complete
food known as snake sausages – which
resemble sausages in appearance –

with a dead mouse or whatever the
snake has been eating previously. This
will transfer the familiar scent to the
new food, making it palatable to the
snake. Once the snake is eating the
new food readily, there will be no need
to carry out this procedure.

✦ BELOW LEFT
Not all snakes live and hunt on the ground. As
a result, particularly for a nervous individual,
food may have to be provided off the floor on
a raised feeding shelf.

✦ BELOW RIGHT
Make sure your snake's food is carefully
prepared, and that frozen food is thoroughly
defrosted before it is fed to the snake.

GENERAL CARE

Snakes are not difficult creatures
to care for in a home environment
but their needs do have to be met.
Ultimately, this will ensure that they
thrive without problems.

TRANSPORTING YOUR SNAKE
Take great care when travelling with
a snake. There is a real risk of chilling
and also of death from heat stroke
if the snake is left for even a few
minutes in a locked car during cold
or hot weather. In addition, if the
travelling container is not secure,
there is a risk that the snake could

◆ BELOW
While small snakes can be carried in
ventilated plastic containers, large
individuals must be carried in special
escape-proof canvas bags with the
top always firmly tied.

◆ ABOVE
All snakes should
be provided with a
container of fresh
water. Do not fill
this to the top,
however, as when
the snake enters the
bowl, the water will
overflow and soak
the bedding.

escape and become lost in the vehicle,
slithering under a seat, for example,
where it will be difficult to retrieve.
Special canvas bags, tightly tied at the
top, are the safest option. The bag
itself can then be conveniently carried
in a box. When you first arrive home
with a new snake, place the bag in the
vivarium (set up in advance to check
the equipment is working properly)
and untie the bag. The snake will
emerge on its own in due course.

HANDLING
When it comes to handling a snake,
you need to restrain its head
adequately, while placing a hand
around the middle of the body and
lifting the reptile up. Never grip a
snake tightly but allow it to curl
loosely around your hand and arm.
Otherwise you can inflict severe, if
not fatal, bruising on its body. It is
extremely dangerous to allow the large
and incredibly strong boas and pythons
to curl around your or anyone else's
neck: it is natural for these constrictor
snakes to suffocate their prey, and you
would be taking a real risk.

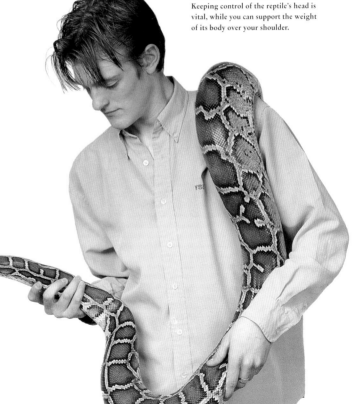

♦ LEFT
Snakes must not be gripped tightly when being handled. Instead, they should be encouraged to wrap around the hands. A Durango king snake is shown here.

Check the heating system in the vivarium using two thermometers, positioned one at either end, to show the temperature differential. The regulation of heat output is easy to control by adjusting the thermostat. Always keep a spare heating bulb, as there is a chance that these will stop working at a time when it is impossible to obtain a replacement.

If you there is a power cut (outage), switch off all the equipment at the mains, and cover the vivarium with a thick blanket, leaving a slight space for ventilation, as this will help to conserve the heat within. Once the power is restored, remove the cover and reconnect the power supply. Most reptiles will survive these situations without problems and will become more active as they warm up again.

♦ BELOW
Handling a large snake can be difficult. Keeping control of the reptile's head is vital, while you can support the weight of its body over your shoulder.

EVERYDAY CARE

Most snakes need feeding two or three times a week when fully grown, although young hatchlings are likely to require feeding more frequently. The water in their quarters must also be changed on a daily basis, and the substrate in the vivarium should be cleaned as required, with soiled areas being removed when necessary. A cat litter cleaning scoop can be useful for this type of spot cleaning.

Decor in the snake's quarters should also be washed as necessary, using one of the special vivarium disinfectants now available. It is not recommended to place living plants in a vivarium because they rarely thrive in these surroundings. If you choose to incorporate some of the realistic plastic substitutes now available, such as ivies and vines, then these also should be washed off at regular intervals. Perhaps most important, however, is the water container as this can very easily become a focus for infection, particularly if the snake is bathing here as well. Wash out the container on a weekly basis.

BREEDING

Snakes fall into two categories on the basis of their reproductive habits: many lay eggs; others, such as boas and garter snakes, give birth to live offspring, although they are not nourished in the body like mammals. Instead, the young snakes develop in eggs and these, in effect, hatch just at the moment of birth.

Unfortunately, one of the major difficulties when it comes to breeding snakes is that the sexes are usually very similar in appearance. On close examination, however, the tails of adult male snakes are often significantly longer, with a slight swelling in the vicinity of the external opening, called the cloaca. This is caused by the paired copulatory organs, known as the hemipenes. However, an internal examination performed by a vet is always required to confirm the gender of a snake.

◆ ABOVE
Snake eggs in an incubator box. Note the ventilation holes around the sides of the container. Snake eggs have leathery shells and will readily desiccate if kept too dry.

MATING

There are a number of factors that are involved in encouraging snakes to breed successfully in vivarium surroundings. Firstly, they must be

◆ ABOVE
The everted hemipenes of this Trans-Pecos rat snake can be clearly seen here. These reproductive organs are normally kept retracted within the body.

in good health and they must be mature. There are also significant external factors. In the case of the temperate species, the most important is the cooler "wintering period", which should last for two to three months. After this time the vivarium temperature should be raised again, and the level of light exposure should be increased to mimic the start of spring. After a further short interval, the snakes can be put together. Signs of courtship should soon be noted, with the male following the female around the vivarium and entwining himself around her.

SEXING A SNAKE WITH A PROBE

1 Probing a snake needs to be undertaken very carefully, to ensure that no injury results. In the first place, choose a probe of appropriate size and lubricate it well.

2 If you are uncertain about the procedure, seek expert advice. Never try to force the end of the probe into the snake's body, as this is likely to cause a fatal injury.

3 The inverted (withdrawn) hemipenes are located towards the tip of the tail, and so the probe will extend much further back in this direction in a male than a female.

◆ BELOW
A female python brooding her clutch of eggs. These snakes remain in this position throughout the incubation period, which can last over 60 days, without feeding.

◆ BELOW
Most snakes, such as this Pueblan milk snake, simply lay their eggs in a concealed locality, and then leave them to hatch on their own. These eggs need to be incubated.

◆ BELOW
Milk snake eggs hatching. An incubator set-up for snakes does not need to be sophisticated but the eggs themselves will need to be kept on a moist substrate.

REARING YOUNG SNAKES

Those species that give birth to live young require relatively little additional care, although the pregnant females are likely to spend longer basking under the heat source in their quarters. Egg-laying snakes, however, will be keen to find a suitable area in the vivarium where they can produce their eggs. An area of damp sphagnum moss is suitable for this purpose. The eggs of snakes are all semi-permeable; the shell is leathery in texture rather than hard. They need to be transferred to a reasonably sterile surface, such as damp (not sodden) vermiculite. This medium is kept within a plastic container, which serves as a simple incubator. The vermiculite must not be allowed to dry out, and the eggs must remain in direct contact with it so that they can absorb water.

Keeping the container covered slows the rate of evaporation, and this will lessen the likelihood of eggs drying out during the incubation period. This can be fatal.

Hatching will normally take place within two or three months, if the eggs are kept at a temperature of around 28°C (82°F), but there is no closely defined incubation period and you should not be in too much of a hurry to discard a clutch that has not started to hatch.

The young snakes can be housed together once they emerge from their eggs, as they will not feed until after they have shed their skins for the first time. After this, though, they will need to be separated because of the risk of cannibalism. Ventilated plastic lunchboxes would make suitable accommodation for the young snakes. Pinkies (dead day-old mice) can be used as a rearing food, although these may have to be macerated before being fed to smaller, newborn hatchlings.

◆ ABOVE
Equipment needed to rear a young hatchling snake: ventilated plastic accommodation, substrate, a retreat and a container for water.

◆ RIGHT
Rearing a young hatchling snake. Keep a watch on the appetite of a hatchling. Young snakes should soon start feeding once they have sloughed their skin for the first time.

LIZARDS

Lizards are a very diverse group of reptiles, both in terms of their appearance and requirements. Always consider the needs of a species with particular care, therefore, to ensure that you will be able to fulfil them. Most lizards are insectivorous in their feeding habits, with a few being carnivorous, while some require a vegetarian diet. Smaller lizards are likely to live for perhaps six or seven years, with larger species having a lifespan of up to 15 years.

INTRODUCTION

♦ BELOW LEFT AND RIGHT
Some lizards have sharp claws (*left*), while others have have expanded toe pads (*right*).

Lizards are found in many different habitats, ranging from desert areas to the edge of the Arctic circle, in spite of their cold-blooded (poikilothermic) reptilian natures. A highly adaptable group, their appearance is very variable, ranging from the seemingly legless slowworm (*Anguis fragilis*) to the quick-footed gecko and the dramatically colour-changing chameleon.

As pets, some lizards, such as geckos, can be easily accommodated thanks to their relatively small size, whereas others, such as green iguanas and water dragons, which can reach 1 yd (1 m) or more in length, require more spacious accommodation. A few lizards, particularly bearded dragons, are pets with real personality and are now being bred on a large scale to reflect their growing popularity. Green iguanas, too, are popular on this basis, but mature males in particular can become rather aggressive and may be difficult to manage; neutering can help with this problem.

Handling lizards can present particular problems. Geckos, for example, can be especially difficult to catch if they escape from their quarters. Worse still, if roughly handled, they may shed their tails, which is a natural defence mechanism designed to draw potential predators away from the head end of the lizard. This is why the tails of many small

♦ LEFT
The bearded dragon has become very popular as a pet, thanks to its friendly nature, although be sure to start out with a young hatchling, which can be tamed relatively easily.

One of the features distinguishing the slow-worm as a lizard is its eyelids, which snakes do not possess. The body of these lizards is also relatively smooth.

♦ RIGHT
It may look like a snake but, in fact, the slowworm is actually a legless lizard. The legs here have virtually disappeared.

lizards are colourful, compared with their bodies. The tail, when separated, twitches for a time, but the lizard itself appears to suffer no pain or blood loss. The tail will regrow to some extent, although it rarely reaches the same length as the original. Such individuals are then described as "stub-tails".

CHOOSING A LIZARD

If you intend to purchase a lizard as a household pet, especially one that is to be allowed out of its quarters on a regular basis, then it is vital to start with a young hatchling, which you can tame yourself. This will allow the reptile to grow up with you so that it feels secure in the home. Research has shown that it is quite possible for these lizards to recognize individuals, and they do form quite strong bonds with their owners.

If you are seeking breeding pairs, starting out with young lizards has the advantage that you can be sure of their age, although distinguishing the gender of young stock is often more difficult. When it comes to assessing whether a lizard is in good health, animals should be relatively plump, particularly over the hindquarters, and alert and lively by nature in the case of the smaller species. Any obvious difficulties in moving around may be indicative of skeletal weakness; a vet will be able to confirm this for you.

♦ ABOVE
Slowworms need to be handled with care. Like many lizards, the ends of their tails are very fragile and will break off readily, although they will then regrow slowly.

Coloration is also significant, with a brightly coloured individual likely to be in good state of health. Darker coloration is not necessarily a sign of illness, however, but could simply indicate an individual that is being bullied by a dominant male – lizards are territorial by nature. The skin will also darken prior to a moult.

Before you buy, think about the type of pet you want and whether you can meet its particular requirements. The bizarre appearance of many lizards, such as chameleons, for example, has helped to ensure their popularity, and a better understanding of their needs means that they are easier to keep now than in the past. However, chameleons have specialist requirements. A large green iguana is an imposing lizard, and trying to win its confidence once it is adult will be virtually impossible. You could end up being badly scratched by its claws, while its tail can inflict a painful blow.

♦ ABOVE
It may look rather fierce, but this spiny-tailed dab lizard feeds almost entirely on plant matter.

◆ BELOW
A leopard gecko. These lizards lose their banded
appearance as they grow older, developing a
leopard-like patterning. Unlike many geckos,
they are not agile climbers.

SPECIES

The lizards on these first two pages
are the smaller breeds, which will not
require particularly spacious vivaria.

LEOPARD GECKO

The leopard gecko (*Eublepharis
macularius*) is one of the most popular
of all display lizards, thanks to its
attractive patterning and compact
size. These geckos can be kept in pairs
or preferably trios, comprising a male
and two females for breeding
purposes, and they rank among the
easiest lizards to breed in a vivarium.
They grow to 25 cm (10 in) in length.

There is a distinct difference in
appearance between young and adult
geckos, however, with hatchlings
being strikingly banded, displaying
chocolate- and sandy-coloured stripes.
As they mature these bands break up,
giving rise to the speckled appearance
of the adults. Colour variants are now
being bred as well, although these are
relatively scarce at present. Leopard
geckos do not require a tall vivarium
as, unlike most geckos, they do not
climb. A sandy substrate, with rocks
and retreats such as cork bark, suits
them well. One corner should be
kept damp to encourage
egg-laying. The
temperature under

the spotlight can be up to 40°C
(104°F), with a temperature gradient
across the vivarium, while at night
the temperature can be allowed to
fall back to 20°C (68°F).

DAY GECKO

The day gecko (*Phelsuma* species)
is one of the most colourful of all
lizards, and its brilliant emerald green
coloration is patterned with striking
markings of red, blue and gold,
depending on the species concerned.
The largest is the Madagascan
(*P. madagascariensis*), attaining a
length of about 25 cm (10 in) when
adult. All require similar care: a tall
vivarium, heated to about 28°C
(82°F), falling back only very
slightly at night. As for all
lizards, lighting is

absolutely essential, both to maintain
their appetites and to ensure bone
condition and a healthy skeleton.

These geckos also feed on small
invertebrates, such as crickets,
which should be dusted with a
suitable vitamin and mineral powder
beforehand. In addition, they will
enjoy a little honey water or bird
nectar, which must be changed daily
to ensure its freshness. Sexing is
straightforward, and egg-laying will
occur in bamboo or similar tubes of
a suitable diameter. Gecko pairs must
be housed on their own, as males
especially can be very aggressive.

GREEN LIZARD

The green lizard (*Lacerta* species)
originates from temperate climes
and is sometimes housed in outdoor

◆ LEFT
Day geckos are an attractive group of lizards.
They can be prolific when breeding. Females
only lay two eggs per clutch but they will
produce these at regular intervals.

◆ LEFT
A common wall
lizard basking on
a rock. These are
very active lizards by
nature, scampering
around their
quarters. Retreats
and basking facilities
are vital for them.
Adults may measure
20 cm (8 in) long.

◆ BELOW
In spite of their name, green lizards are
quite variable in terms of coloration. This
is a mature male in breeding condition, as
shown by the blue area on the chin. Green
lizards can reach 40 cm (16 in) in length.

◆ LEFT
There are a number
of different wall
lizards, all of which
require similar care.
This is Danford's
wall lizard. They
are agile reptiles
by nature, and
are primarily
insectivorous,
feeding on crickets
of suitable size.

◆ BELOW
Various factors can affect the coloration of
lizards, with young green lizards being less
striking than adults. Cooler temperatures
will cause them to darken in colour.

vivaria in the summer months, which
need to be secure and yet adequately
ventilated to prevent overheating on
hot days. The green lizard takes its
name from its coloration: green
predominates although other colours,
such as blue spots on the flanks, are
also common. The colour patterning
differs between individuals, and can
be a reflection of regional variation –
it does not provide a means of
distinguishing the species.

Once mature, green lizard males
can be recognized by their larger, more
colourful appearance. The young, in
comparison, are a duller greyish-green.
It will take three years for them to
mature, although they will need to be
separated before this stage as males
are aggressive towards each other.

WALL LIZARD

The wall lizard (*Podarcis muralis*)
is also a member of the
lacertid group, and
will thrive in a similar
set-up, receiving full-
spectrum lighting.
They require an arid
environment, with
plenty of retreats for
hiding purposes, as well as basking
spots. The typical temperature in the
warmest part of the vivarium should
be up to about 31°C (88°F) during the
day, and reduced to about 17°C (63°F)
at night. Females often lay two
clutches of eggs in the summer
period. The diet for wall lizards should
consist mainly of invertebrates, with
the occasional offerings of sweet fruit.

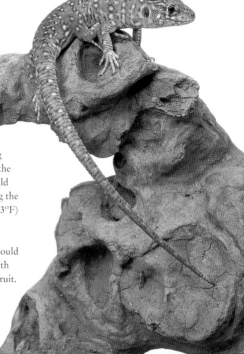

BEARDED DRAGON

The bearded dragon (*Pogona vitticeps*) is now one of the most popular lizards in the world, thanks to its friendly personality and rather primordial appearance. Hatchlings are widely available, and they can become sufficiently tame to feed readily from the hand. They will grow to about 51 cm (22 in) in length. Their beard of spines under the chin, which form part of an inflatable throat pouch, may look fearsome but, in reality, these projections are soft and harmless.

A number of localized colour variants have been recorded in the wild, and as domestication has taken place breeders have also concentrated

◆ ABOVE AND TOP
The bearded dragon is so-called because of the spines on its throat and under the chin. They are quite prolific, with females laying clutches of up to 30 eggs.

◆ ABOVE
The green iguana makes an impressive pet, but its temperament is not as reliable as a bearded dragon, for those seeking a lizard that can be handled regularly.

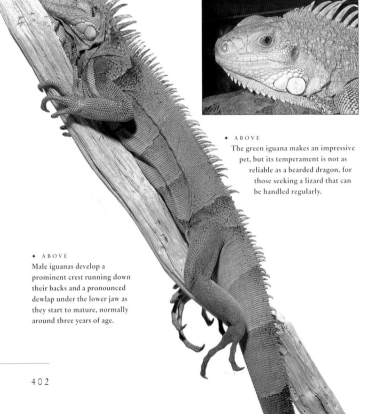

◆ ABOVE
Male iguanas develop a prominent crest running down their backs and a pronounced dewlap under the lower jaw as they start to mature, normally around three years of age.

on developing these shades. Red and golden strains are probably most widely kept at present. These lizards live well in groups, but, especially with hatchlings, it is important to check that they all have enough to eat, as weaker individuals will have to wait in order to feed.

There are now prepared foods for bearded dragons or, alternatively, they can be fed a wide range of plant matter, including dandelions, nasturtiums, and similar leafy plants. Carrots and even a little fruit can be supplied, augmented with a vitamin and mineral mix. Small invertebrates should also form part of the diet, especially for juveniles, which grow very rapidly. They are likely to be mature by a year old. A hot vivarium, plus full-spectrum lighting are essential for these lizards, which naturally bask for long periods.

GREEN IGUANA

Although hatchlings look cute, it is important to bear in mind that adult green iguanas (*Iguana iguana*) can become difficult to handle, especially as they become mature. They also require plenty of space, and it is better to prepare for this at the outset by starting out with the correct sized accommodation for this species. They can easily grow to a total length of 1.8 m (6 ft), with their powerful tail making up roughly half of this figure.

Green iguanas are quite arboreal by nature, and they require branches fixed securely in their quarters; this also allows them to bask under a heat source, protected with a grill, without burning themselves. Full-spectrum lighting for 12 hours a day is also necessary, helping to guard juveniles

◆ LEFT
The Asian water dragon is another large lizard that will need spacious accommodation. The banded patterning on the tail often disappears after maturity.

◆ RIGHT
A panther chameleon. The ability to change their coloration to blend in with their surroundings is well known in chameleons. They also display in this way as a threat to others of their kind.

◆ BELOW
A veiled chameleon. The casque on the head indicates that this is a male. Some chameleons reproduce by eggs, whereas others give birth to live young. Most average 30 cm (12 in) long.

in particular from the effects of metabolic bone disease. Their diet, too, is important for this purpose. It is very difficult to sex young green iguanas by sight, but males develop a distinctive crest extending down their backs as they grow older.

ASIAN WATER DRAGON

The Asian water dragon (*Physignathus cocincinus*) is similar to the green iguana – it will grow to about 91 cm (36 in) overall – although it is a member of the agamid family. But, whereas green iguanas are essentially vegetarian in their feeding habits, these lizards require a diet based on invertebrates and some fruit. As their name suggests, they are found close to water and their vivarium should incorporate a pool area for bathing. These lizards originate from the tropics, so the temperature in their quarters must not be allowed to dip below 24°C (75°F) at night. Water dragons like to climb, and will also need full-spectrum lighting.

CHAMELEON

Chameleons rank among the most fascinating of all lizards, thanks to their colour changes, amazing eyes and hunting agility, which allows them to

◆ BELOW RIGHT
A Yemeni chameleon. Note how the tail is carried curled up. It can be used for grasping branches.

catch flies with a strike of the tongue. Their requirements are specialized, however, and, most importantly, they are solitary by nature and can suffer severe stress – losing their appetites if closely confined together. The Yemeni chameleon (*Chamaeleo calaptratus*) is one of the most commonly bred species at present, and it is relatively easy to look after. A vivarium for these arboreal lizards must have branches for climbing purposes. The vegetation should be sprayed with water, as chameleons are often reluctant to drink from a water bowl. Offer a choice of invertebrates for their food.

HOUSING

Lizards tend to be housed in an enclosed vivarium, often with a melamine interior, the surface of which can be wiped over easily. Ventilation grilles should be incorporated into the design, along with a door giving easy access to the interior. If required, you can make a vivarium of this type, with sliding glass or perspex doors at the front. Supply heating by means of a spotlight, located in the roof of the vivarium, where it should be set in a wire cage to exclude climbing lizards coming into direct contact with it.

Ceramic infra-red heaters, with a reflector around them, are a popular choice, emitting no light. The heat output can be controlled quite easily by means of an adjustable thermostat, enabling you to lessen the heat output overnight, for example. Using ordinary light bulbs to provide heating is possible but the constant resulting light output can be harmful to the lizard's well-being, while the bulbs

✦ RIGHT
Lighting equipment for a lizard vivarium, including a control unit. Spotlights for basking purposes are very important, but ensure arboreal species cannot burn themselves.

✦ ABOVE
Special fluorescent tubes are available that emit the vital ultraviolet rays necessary for the lizard's calcium metabolism and growth.

✦ BELOW
The decor in the vivarium should match the natural habitat of the lizard. This set-up is suitable for a tropical forest species, but not for one of desert origins.

themselves tend to have a shorter lifespan when hanging downwards.

Ultra-thin heat mats, in various sizes and wattages, can also be used for heating. Although these mats are traditionally placed under the vivarium, they can be attached to the sides, though they do detract from the appearance of the vivarium here.

Another option that provides localized heating for small terrestrial lizards is to use what are normally described as "hot rocks". In the past, these have had a bad press because they would overheat, causing burns, but today's models should be safer – check the temperature control method prior to purchase, however.

LIGHTING

Correct lighting is absolutely vital in a vivarium for lizards. It is not a matter of using an ordinary light bulb or fluorescent tube, however, because these do not emit light of the same wavelength as sunlight, specifically light from the ultraviolet (UV) part of the spectrum. There are two components that are of significance to the well-being of reptiles – UVA, which acts as an appetite stimulant and generally encourages activity, including the onset of breeding behaviour, and UVB which is vital for the synthesis of Vitamin D3. This is vital in regulating the body's calcium

◆ LEFT
Height is an important consideration of vivarium design when housing arboreal lizards. Be sure to provide them with adequate climbing opportunities here.

stores, and helping to ensure this mineral remains in the correct ratio with phosphorus.

Special full-spectrum fluorescent tubes can be fitted into the vivarium for this purpose. Their ultraviolet light output will decline over a period of time – most tubes need to be replaced after nine months of usage, even though they may appear to be still working. Black lights are also sometimes used in vivaria for lizards, but these do not have an adequate UVB output.

VIVARIUM LAYOUT
Provide hiding areas for your lizards, and make sure that the substrate used matches their needs. A wide range of bedding options are available. Lizards

◆ ABOVE RIGHT, TOP
Substrates for a vivarium housing lizards. Fine gravel is not recommended for vegetarian species as it may be ingested with their food.

◆ ABOVE RIGHT, BELOW
Retain the moisture in a tropical vivarium by including tree fern and peat slabs, which can be sprayed with water.

◆ RIGHT
A piece of cork bark makes a good retreat for smaller lizards.

that are desert dwellers can be kept on calcium sand, which will be safe even if ingested with food. Chipped bark, in various grades, is suitable for lizards from forested areas as it is dark in colour. Other items, such as branches and living plants, can be included in the vivarium, if required, and these will respond well to the lighting. Never include any which could be hazardous though, such as cacti, and bear in mind that vegetarian lizards are likely to eat any live plants placed in their quarters.

FEEDING

♦ BELOW
Crickets are one of the most widely used livefoods today. Being available in a range of sizes, they are valuable for small and large lizards alike.

♦ BOTTOM
Invertebrates form a major part of the diet of many species of herptile. They are usually swallowed headfirst, as shown by this bearded dragon eating a locust.

There are various prepared diets available for the most popular types of lizards, such as green iguanas and bearded dragons. These diets are often in pelleted form and, although the foods can be fed in a dry state, they often prove to be more palatable to the lizards if they are moistened with water beforehand. Even so, it is still a good idea to offer a range of fresh foods on a regular basis, as these will add bulk and fibre to the lizard's diet. A good selection of fresh foods, ranging from sprouting pulses, such as mung beans, to alfalfa, can be grown quite easily even if you do not have access to a garden.

Other vegetables that can be fed to reptiles include carrots and cabbage in small quantities. Green lettuce contains little in the way of nutrients,

however, compared with red-leaved variants. Some lizards will eat fruit, including grapes, apple and melon, but avoid rhubarb, which could be toxic because of its oxalic acid content.

While larger lizards can munch whole leaves, food should be cut up into pieces, which can be swallowed

without difficulty, particularly in the case of carrot. Provide the food in a bowl that cannot be tipped over easily. It is also a good idea to sprinkle over a vitamin and mineral supplement to maintain the nutritional value. Read the labelling: overdosing is harmful, especially over a period of time.

◆ RIGHT
Some lizards, such as this skink, will feed mainly on fruit and greenstuff. Wash fresh foods thoroughly; it may be advisable to peel them if they could have been sprayed by chemicals.

INSECTIVOROUS LIZARDS

Catering for insectivorous lizards requires the use of a supplement as these foods are known to be deficient in terms of their calcium: phosphorus ratio, and this can be a cause of metabolic bone disease. There are now various ways of improving the nutritional values of the main types of livefoods to compensate for the nutritional deficit. One effective way of doing this is known as gut loading. This involves feeding smaller livefoods to the lizards' standard invertebrate livefood diet. The benefits should then

be passed on to the lizards when they eat their regular food. Similarly, crickets can be sprinkled with a nutritional balancer prior to being fed to lizards. Crickets are available in various sizes, and it is possible to choose a suitably-sized cricket to meet the requirements of the lizard. This can be useful when rearing young lizards as they can then be fed on an ever-increasing size of food as they develop and grow.

Mealworms also range in size from the mini-mealworms through to giant mealworms, which are actually a different species. The giant type is only suitable for the biggest lizards, such as fully grown water dragons,

but the smaller sizes will be eaten by a variety of lizards. Their tough outer-body casing means they may not be easily digested in some cases, especially by small lizards.

Waxmoth larvae are also very popular as a diet for lizards, and these are particularly valuable for rekindling the appetite of a sick individual and helping it to regain condition. The waxmoth larvae need to be kept cool to delay their pupation. If the larvae are allowed to develop, they will emerge as moths and can be fed to various lizards, such as chameleons, which will enjoy being able to catch their dinner themselves if the moths are emptied into the vivarium.

◆ LEFT
Water dragons will eat a diet based on invertebrates and some fruit. The substantial size of these lizards means that they will feed happily on giant mealworms.

◆ LEFT
Special nutritional balancers are available to compensate for shortcomings in invertebrate livefoods. These may be sprinkled over the invertebrates or added to their foods.

◆ BELOW
Crickets, like other livefoods, are low in calcium.

GENERAL CARE

The diversity in the size and shape of lizards means that there is no standard way of handling them. The tails of small species are fragile, whereas those of iguanas, for example, are strong and can cause a painful blow. Some lizards have sharp claws and can inflict deep and painful scratches. For these species it is always best to wear a pair of leather gloves and to avoid handling them with bare arms. Some lizards may even bite if they feel seriously threatened.

CATCHING LIZARDS

In the case of smaller species, such as geckos, the simplest means of catching them is to use a plastic container, such as the type used for transporting lizards, and gently steer the reptile into it. Place the lid over the top once the lizard is inside. Never try to catch several lizards at the same time as this will be near impossible; always concentrate on catching each of your pets individually.

A net, as used for catching tropical fish, can be helpful, especially in the case of any escapes into the room.

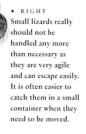

♦ RIGHT
Small lizards really should not be handled any more than necessary as they are very agile and can escape easily. It is often easier to catch them in a small container when they need to be moved.

♦ LEFT
Large lizards, such as this green iguana, need to be handled carefully because they can scratch, bite and inflict a painful blow with their tails.

♦ RIGHT
Restraining small lizards, such as this day gecko, carelessly could easily result in tail loss.

You must shut the door as a priority before attempting to recapture the lizard, as it could quickly dart out and disappear elsewhere in the home. If you do need to hold a small lizard directly, then try to cup it in your hand, and do not restrain it tightly.

When it comes to catching larger lizards, both hands will be needed. First, restrain the head, using your left hand (if you are right-handed)

Male green iguanas develop a prominent dewlap as they mature. They can become more aggressive at this stage, and neutering may be advisable in some cases.

and then hold the tail and hind quarters with your free hand. This should help to stop the lizard struggling badly. If an iguana proves reluctant to return to its vivarium when allowed to roam around the room, the immediate solution will be to restrain it with a blanket or similar material. Avoid constantly chasing lizards if they prove hard to catch as this can be stressful for them and might even prove to be fatal.

MOULTING

There will be times when the lizard starts to moult, with the skin starting to lift from the body. In most cases, this doesn't cause a problem but, on occasion, difficulties may arise, especially with geckos. The old skin may stick around their flattened toes, and start to constrict here, and if it is not removed then the affected digit will be lost. Raising the relative humidity level in their quarters may help to overcome this problem.

PRACTICAL MATTERS

A vivarium is kept clean by removing soiled areas of substrate on a regular basis. It needs to be completely stripped down and washed out every two or three months on average; much will depend on the occupants.

If you go on holiday (vacation), you will need to find someone to look after your lizards. If transporting the vivarium to the helper's home – provided this is done quickly – there is no need to remove the lizards from their quarters; just take out water and food bowls and any heavy decor. Provide a spare heating element, in case this fails in your absence, as well as a supply of food.

♦ ABOVE
Pay close attention to a moulting lizard, in case it has problems shedding its old skin.

♦ BELOW
Keep the vivarium decor clean by washing it thoroughly in a special disinfectant solution.

♦ ABOVE
A tail that has been shed will usually regrow, but it may not reach its previous length.

♦ BELOW
Spot-cleaning the substrate means the removal of soiled areas. Wear disposable gloves.

BREEDING

♦ BELOW
Various herptiles give birth to live young, rather than laying eggs. In addition to lizards, certain snakes also reproduce in this way, as may some salamanders.

♦ BELOW
Various herptiles give birth to live young, rather than laying eggs. In addition to lizards, certain snakes also reproduce in this way, as may some salamanders.

The smaller species of lizard generally represent the best prospects for breeding in vivarium surroundings, simply because they do not require such spacious enclosures, unlike green iguanas, for example. Although there are a number of specific features that allow the sexes to be distinguished in particular cases, there are also general guidelines that can be useful for sexing lizards.

Males are frequently brighter in colour, often with crests or head embellishments not seen in females. Geckos in general can be sexed by examining them from beneath in a clear-bottomed container. This allows the femoral pores, which extend down their hind legs, to be distinguished easily. These pores are indicative of a male lizard.

In many cases, male lizards are highly territorial, which is why they must be kept apart from each other. Even if there is no direct conflict, the weaker individual may be bullied to the extent that its condition may deteriorate. Its growth rate, for example, is often significantly slower as it will be kept out of favoured basking sites and is unlikely to have the pick of the food on offer.

As with snakes, cooling during the winter followed by an increase in temperature in the spring will serve as a breeding trigger for lizards from more temperate areas, whereas other factors, such as increasing humidity in the case of rain forest species, and even keeping pairs apart for periods, will be significant in some instances.

Most lizards engage in a mating display, which involves head-bobbing and similar movements. Mating itself can be quite aggressive in some cases

♦ LEFT
A container with sand provided for a female bearded dragon, who is laying a clutch of eggs here. The container can then be removed so that the eggs can be incubated.

♦ RIGHT
A tokay gecko hatching from its egg. When it comes to purchasing herptiles, younger, smaller individuals are invariably cheaper than adult breeding stock.

as the male anchors himself by biting the skin of the female's neck. This may result in some loss of scales, but should not cause significant injury.

A few lizards, notably some chameleons, give birth to live young but the majority lay eggs. These may have either a parchment shell or a calcerous hard shell, which influences the way in which they should be incubated. The female will start to swell with the eggs as these develop in her body. Some lizards seek to bury their eggs whereas others, such as geckos, stick their eggs around their quarters. It will be obvious when the female has laid by the change in her appearance, as she will become much slimmer at this stage.

The eggs should be transferred carefully to an incubator where they can be hatched, hopefully under optimal conditions. Damp vermiculite, available from garden centres, is commonly used as the hatching medium and care must be taken to ensure it does not dry out. This will

enable parchment eggs to absorb water during the incubation period, but hard-shelled gecko eggs can be hatched without vermiculite.

Again, there is no set incubation period, even for a clutch of eggs, so do not discard them in a hurry. This can

last five weeks to ten weeks or more. The incubation temperature is known to be significant in a number of species as it can influence the gender of the hatchlings. Some experimentation will be necessary, with the incubation temperature generally being set around at the 30°C (86°F) mark.

Remove the young as they hatch to rearing quarters. At first, they will digest the remains of their yolk sacs and so will not need feeding. A separate vivarium is also recommended for the young of live-bearing lizards, which could otherwise be tempted to prey on their offspring. Correct lighting and a balanced diet are vital for their subsequent healthy development in all cases.

TORTOISES, TERRAPINS AND TURTLES

With their distinctive shells and relatively slow, ambling gait, members of this group of reptiles are instantly recognizable. They are very popular as pets, often appealing to people who may not like other reptiles, such as snakes. The ease of their care depends to a degree on where you live, and whether you are intending to keep a tortoise, a terrapin or an aquatic turtle. Most can be tamed quite easily, to the extent of feeding from the hand.

INTRODUCTION

The names given to this popular group of reptiles can be confusing. Collectively, they are known as chelonians, since they belong to the order Chelonia. While the description of "tortoise" is usually reserved for those that live on land, the use of the term "turtle" is more varied – in the United States and Canada it is used for all aquatic chelonians, whereas elsewhere it is used to describe marine species, and these are not kept as pets.

This group of reptiles are sometimes housed outside for part of the year, even in temperate areas, but care needs to be taken to ensure they do not become chilled. Tortoises, in

◆ ABOVE
The hingebacks are African tortoises characterized by the hinge which allows them to draw the hind part of their shell forward, protecting themselves against attacks from behind.

◆ LEFT
In sunny climates, this group of reptiles can be allowed to remain outdoors in safe accommodation for much of the year. Indoor housing is more usual in the temperate areas of the world.

particular, are vulnerable to respiratory diseases when kept at sub-optimal temperatures, and these can frequently progress to a fatal pneumonia. Advances in our understanding of the reproductive behaviour of these reptiles means that captive breeding of tortoises is now becoming commonplace with a number of species, but these young chelonians require rather different care from mature adults, needing to be housed in vivaria for most of the time.

The shells of chelonians are probably their most distinctive feature, offering them good protection from predators, with their skeletal system being encased beneath the shell. It is usually possible to distinguish between tortoises and aquatic chelonians on the basis of their shell shape; in most cases, turtles have relatively flat shells, whereas those of tortoises are more domed in appearance. In many cases, the shell is attractively patterned with highly individual markings. It is not true that the numbers of rings on the tortoise's shell give an exact indication of its age, however, as these do not correlate with all the years of its life. There will be more in the young tortoises, and then in older individuals the shell becomes much smoother, with the

rings having been worn down. Tortoises, in particular, may have a lifespan that is equivalent to or even in excess of human beings.

TORTOISE OR TERRAPIN?

The choice between keeping tortoises and terrapins may depend on where you live since, if you do not have access to a garden, your tortoise will have to spend its time in a vivarium, rather than being able to roam freely outdoors on a lawn. If you have no garden, it may be better to choose a terrapin, but bear in mind that these can grow quite large, and may require a small indoor pond rather than a tank.

While terrapins in general are predatory in their feeding habits, tortoises are mainly vegetarian, and will require relatively large volumes of food as a result. Tortoises rely heavily on beneficial bacteria and other microbes in their digestive tract to help them to break down their food, and this can make them more vulnerable to digestive disturbances if their diet is suddenly changed – you should bear this in mind at the outset.

Eurasian tortoises such as Horsfield's tortoise (*Testudo horsfieldi*) spend part of the year hibernating underground. It is, therefore, important to ensure that tortoises are in a reasonable state of health before hibernating, and that their hibernation conditions are suitable. Otherwise, they can become seriously weakened and may even die during this vulnerable period.

◆ BELOW
The attractive mottled patterning of leopard tortoises is variable, allowing individuals to be distinguished easily by their markings. They can grow quite large.

TORTOISE SPECIES

Tortoises have a wide distribution through the warmer parts of the world, but for many years the Eurasian species have tended to be most commonly kept as pets.

MEDITERRANEAN SPUR-THIGHED TORTOISE

Originating from the countries bordering the Mediterranean Sea, the Mediterranean spur-thighed tortoise (*Testudo graeca*), as its name suggests, is found on the opposite shores in both North Africa and Europe. Individuals are easily identified by raised areas, called tubercles or spurs on each side of the body between the hind legs and the tail. Their shell length can be 30 cm (12 in).

◆ ABOVE
The Mediterranean spur-thighed tortoise. The patterning of tortoises is as distinctive as fingerprints, with some displaying more darker blotches than others.

◆ LEFT
A Hermann's tortoise. These and Horsfield's tend to be slightly smaller than the spur-thighed.

HERMANN'S TORTOISE

Hermann's tortoise (*Testudo hermanni*), whose distribution in Europe and Asia is constant through Spain, Turkey, Bulgaria and Greece, looks similar to the Mediterranean spur-thighed when viewed from above, but it lacks the spurs and is slightly smaller in size. The tail is much more elongated, particularly in the case of males, and terminates in horny tips.

HORSFIELD'S TORTOISE

Horsfield's tortoise (*Testudo horsfieldi*) has the most northerly distribution of any tortoise, ranging into parts of the former Soviet Union, as well as other Asiatic countries including Pakistan and Iran, and extending eastwards to China. It has not been widely available in the past, but is now quite extensively kept and bred with increasing frequency. As in

◆ LEFT
Horsfield's tortoise has especially powerful front legs with strong claws for digging purposes.

◆ LEFT
An attractively patterned leopard tortoise. These tortoises feed on herbage and grow fast under favourable conditions.

◆ BELOW RIGHT
A juvenile red-footed tortoise. These are tropical rainforest tortoises originating from South America and can grow to 50 cm (20 in). Fruit should predominate in their diet.

◆ BELOW LEFT
A red-eared terrapin. Tortoises can be recognized by their domed shell, while the terrapin shell is much flatter.

(*K. belliana*). The carapace in this case is domed at the back, forming a protective flap, and the shell coloration is highly variable, from plain brown to variegated with cream blotches. Other hingebacks are Home's (*K. homeana*), with its strange

other species, males have longer tails and a relatively concave base to the shell, known as the plastron. The feet of these tortoises are very strong and the upper surface of the shell, called the carapace, is relatively flat, allowing these tortoises to burrow, in order to escape from the blistering sun and freezing winters that prevail in the areas from where they originate.

LEOPARD TORTOISE

With increasing concerns about the wild populations of many tortoises, those available today are generally bred in captivity. Under suitable conditions, pairs can prove to be quite prolific and, as a result, Leopard tortoises (*Geochelone pardalis*), which occur over a wide area of Africa, are also often available. As their natural habitat is further south than the Eurasian species, they are only suitable for housing outdoors in the warmest weather in temperate parts of the

world, as they are especially prone to chilling. Their plastron is very attractively marked with a combination of striking dark and light blotches. As Leopard tortoises grow quite large – their shell can grow to a length of 40 cm (16 in) or more – accommodating them indoors as they grow can often be difficult.

HINGEBACK TORTOISE

The other group of tortoises from Africa which are seen occasionally are the hingebacks (*Kinixys* species), particularly Bell's hingeback

indented shell, and the eroded (*K. erosa*), which has a shell of a reddish shade. These are tropical forest tortoises with highly specific requirements. They need a more omnivorous diet than other tortoises, and must have an accessible container of water where they can immerse themselves. A relatively high level of humidity is necessary in the vivarium.

◆ BELOW
Hingebacks have a protective flange that can be lowered to protect their hindquarters. The hinge of softer tissue is present above the hind legs. The shell itself is 20–25 cm (8–10 in) long.

TURTLE SPECIES

SOFT-SHELLED TURTLES

Turtles vary quite widely in their requirements. Some, notably soft-shelled turtles (*Trionyx* species), are highly aquatic by nature, spending virtually their whole lives in water. This behaviour needs to be reflected in the design of their enclosure. They are also very territorial and aggressive, and even if you acquire two hatchlings at the same time then, almost inevitably as time passes, one will start to grow at a faster rate, and will start to bully its companion. Fights can often prove to be fatal because these leathery-shelled turtles are very susceptible to fungal infections if they sustain damage to their bodies. They are more aggressive than other turtles, and are carnivorous in their feeding habits. Adults will frequently reach more than 30 cm (12 in) long.

SIAMESE TEMPLE TURTLE

Much more placid by nature is the Siamese temple turtle (*Siebenrockiella crassicollis*), which is an attractive, gentle Asiatic species. It is black in colour, with large, pale yellow spots on each side of its head. The shell, in particular, is of an appealing ebony shade, with the skin being a greyish colour. These turtles are also aquatic by nature, especially as hatchlings. They are relatively small in size, even when adult, attaining a shell length of approximately 20 cm (8 in). Their accommodation should incorporate a basking area where they can come out on to land, even though they are largely aquatic. Feeding is quite straightforward. As Siamese temple turtles grow larger, it is possible to distinguish the sexes. Males have larger, chunkier heads than females, with the space from the base of the tail to the ano-genital opening being longer than in the female.

AMBOINA BOX TURTLE

Originating from south-east Asia, the Amboina box turtle (*Cuora amboinensis*) has yellow stripes extending on the sides of its face. The shell is blackish and paler on the underside, with two flaps here that enable these reptiles to seal themselves into the shell entirely if danger threatens. Once they are used to being picked up, however, they will stop behaving in this way. These turtles

◆ LEFT
A three-striped box turtle. They grow to a similar size to other box turtles, with a shell length of about 18 cm (8 in).

◆ LEFT
The American snapping turtle has a bad reputation. It's shell can measure 48 cm (19 in) in length.

◆ BELOW LEFT
The jagged shell turtle is an Asiatic semi-aquatic turtle, which may attain a shell length of nearly 20 cm (8 in).

◆ BELOW
Marine turtles such as this olive Ridley are
only likely to be seen in zoological collections.
All seven species of marine turtle have highly
specialist requirements for their care.

will spend considerable periods of
time on land as well as in water,
and this should be reflected in their
accommodation set-up.

NORTH AMERICAN TURTLES

The North American box turtle
(*Terrapene* species) can be recognized
by its brown coloration. It spends
much of its time on land, although
there are a number of more aquatic
turtles in parts of North America,
where they are bred on turtle farms.

Among those that are quite
regularly available as hatchlings are
the painted turtles. There are four

distinctive forms. The southern
(*Chrysemys picta dorsalis*) is the most
distinctive, with a bright orange stripe
running down across the centre of
the top of its shell. The western
(*C. p. belli*) can be recognized by
its yellowish markings here, and the
mottled coloration on the underside
of the shell. The colour of the plastron
also serves to separate the other two
types of painted turtle. The midland
(*C. p. marginata*) has a dark stripe
running down the centre of the shell.
This same area is coloured clear yellow
in the case of the eastern (*C. p. picta*).
These turtles will all require a housing

set-up which provides swimming water
and an adequate land area, where they
can bask and move around. *Chrysemys*
turtles may grow up to 25 cm (10 in).

Map turtles are so-called because,
in the case of hatchlings especially,
the lines on their shells look like the
contours on a map, although the lines
may fade with age. Some types of map
turtle also have knobbly tops to their
shells, so they are often referred to
as sawback turtles. Map turtles need
similar housing to painted turtles – a
reasonable amount of land and water.
Mature females can grow to 23 cm
(9 in) – twice the size of their mates.

◆ ABOVE LEFT
A red-bellied turtle
sunning itself. It
may be possible to
house some of these
Chrysemys turtles
outdoors in escape-
proof ponds during
the summer months
when the weather
has become warmer.

◆ RIGHT
A red-eared turtle,
identifiable by the
red flashes behind
the eyes. This is
a male, as shown
by the long front
claws, used for
display purposes.

HOUSING

♦ BELOW
When it is fine and warm, Mediterranean tortoises can be allowed outdoors to browse on a lawn; make sure that the lawn has not been recently treated with garden chemicals.

The type of accommodation for this particular group of reptiles will depend very much on where your live, as well as on the species concerned.

TORTOISE HOUSING

In the case of tortoises, it is especially important to ensure they do not become chilled, as this can often lead on to a fatal pneumonia, particularly if the conditions are damp as well. Young tortoises are therefore normally kept in a vivarium in temperate parts of the world for much of the year, only being allowed out into a sheltered outdoor run when the weather is set to stay warm and sunny during the day, before being brought inside again at night.

The vivarium must be sited to give the tortoises access to shade from the sun, allowing them to adjust their location according to their body temperature. It is possible to let a tortoise roam freely around a garden, but under these circumstances, it is likely to escape unless the boundaries have been made secure. Some tortoises

♦ BELOW
A typical set-up for young terrapins. Note the basking lamp suspended over the rock, which provides easy access to and from the water; keep the water level low.

are also very adept at climbing and may slip away over a low wall in this fashion. Even if your tortoise has not actually escaped, you may still have difficulty in locating it on occasions if it is roaming freely outdoors, particularly should the weather turn unexpectedly cold during the day. This will cause the tortoise to dig itself in and, with its shell providing very effective camouflage, the tortoise can be very hard to spot.

INDOOR HOUSING

When housed indoors, smaller tortoises can be accomodated in a typical vivarium, equipped with a heat pad beneath part of the enclosure, and a spotlight. A natural-spectrum fluorescent tube will be necessary to ensure the healthy development of the tortoise's shell and its appetite. A hide, to give the young tortoise somewhere

to retreat to, should also be included. There should be a temperature gradient across the vivarium, and good ventilation is also important.

Old newspapers, which will be absorbent and are easy to change when soiled, make an adequate floor covering. However, if the newspaper becomes wet and the tortoise is being fed damp greens directly on the floor of its quarters – a practice not to be recommended – it may also consume the newspaper. Of the alternatives, wooden bark can be difficult to clean, while special sand can sometimes irritate the tortoise's sensitive eyes if it attempts to burrow into the substrate. Larger tortoises will require a tiled area as a base, with stout walls to their enclosure, plus a heat lamp suspended at one end of their quarters.

TERRAPIN HOUSING
Terrapins are usually accommodated in an aquarium, with a heat pad positioned under the tank, set under thermostatic control. The water temperature needs to be 25°C (77°F). A standard heaterstat for aquaria can be used, but is less suitable for larger turtles in particular who may damage it. While gravel can be included, it will make the tank harder to clean,

although it is essential for soft-shelled turtles who will burrow into it. There must be easy access from the water on to an area of dry land where the turtles can bask under a spotlight. A fluorescent lighting tube here is also important. Using a power filter in the

aquarium will help to keep the water clean, and adding a dechlorinating product to the water is recommended before filling the tank. There is really no point in adding any plants, even if you put in gravel, because the turtle will dig them up as it swims.

+ ABOVE LEFT
Any aquatic plants growing in the aquarium substrate are likely to be uprooted by terrapins as they swim. Floating plants can be used for basking purposes.

+ ABOVE RIGHT
Some terrapins, such as this red-eared, will spend long periods sunning themselves on land. This activity helps to ensure a healthy bone and shell structure.

+ LEFT
A secure run will be essential to prevent tortoises disappearing in, or escaping from, the garden. A retreat and a water bowl must be included in the enclosed area.

FEEDING

There are a number of different prepared diets on the market in the form of pellets and foodsticks but, especially in the case of tortoises, it is important not to change their diets suddenly. This is because tortoises are very dependent on beneficial bacteria and other microbes in their digestive system to digest their food, and any sudden dramatic change can lead to a fatal diarrhoea. Introduce any new foods to your tortoise very gradually over a couple of months.

TORTOISE FOODS

The tortoises covered in this book are primarily herbivorous in their feeding habits but, in general, fruit should not be offered to them. Instead, provide a wide variety of vegetable matter, including wild plants, such as dandelion leaves and flowers, or chickweed and cultivated crops, such as alfalfa, tomatoes and cabbage. While ordinary lettuce contains little other than water,

◆ LEFT
Tortoises can prove to be quite clumsy when feeding, and a heavy-weight food bowl that they will not be able to tip over easily is to be recommended.

◆ BELOW LEFT
Variety is important in the diet of these reptiles, but bear in mind that although some tortoises are mainly herbivorous, those from tropical forests must have fruit.

the red varieties of lettuce have a much higher nutritional content.

Always provide the food for tortoises on a low-sided tray, such as those used as plant stands, to prevent it being dragged around the vivarium and contaminated on the substrate. It will also be easier to remove uneaten

food before it can start to turn mouldy. Tortoises generally need feeding on a daily basis as they are browsers, eating throughout the day, and then resting before feeding again. If you are relying on a diet consisting of fresh food, then the use of a special vitamin and mineral mix will be essential as a supplement, especially for young tortoises.

Should you decide to use a complete food, it will not be necessary for you to add a supplement as well – indeed, this could even be harmful. Always read the instructions on the food carefully and, if in doubt, contact the manufacturers directly or ask your vet for advice. The palatability of dry foods can be improved by soaking them in a little water to soften the texture. Any leftovers will then need to be removed at the end of the day. You will soon be able to estimate quite accurately how much food your new tortoise needs on a daily basis, and this will help to prevent wastage. A heavyweight bowl of drinking water should be accessible in the vivarium at all times, but ensure that the design

of the bowl is such that the tortoise cannot fall in and drown. In older tortoises, particularly if they are eating mainly soft food, the edges of the jaws can become overgrown, and this will require veterinary treatment.

TERRAPIN FOODS

A prepared diet is essential to keep terrapins in good health. In the past, owners were forced to rely on raw meat and similar items which, aside from being nutritionally unbalanced, are likely to be a possible source of *Salmonella* infection for the terrapin. Complete diets have a further advantage over meat in that they do not pollute the water after each feed. Match the amount of food offered to the turtle's appetite to avoid wastage. Although turtles, generally, will not feed on land, it is quite possible to persuade them to feed from the hand in water. Always take care not to be bitten: while chelonians do not have teeth in their mouths, they do have sharp edges to their jaws which can inflict a painful nip on a finger.

◆ ABOVE
A wide range of prepared diets are available in pellet form for both tortoises and turtles; particularly with tortoises, be sure to offer them plenty of fresh vegetable matter as well, although avoid feeding fresh fruit to most tortoise species.

◆ RIGHT AND INSET ABOVE
Fresh vegetables and other plants help to provide the necessary bulk and fibre in a tortoise's diet. A vitamin and mineral supplement will help to increase the nutritional value of the food.

GENERAL CARE

Chelonians are not particularly difficult to handle; you can pick them up placing your fingers on either side of the shell, but take care to avoid their feet, which may scratch you. The claws of turtles, as well as young tortoises, are sharp because they have not yet been worn down by contact with the ground, as in the case of older tortoises.

A vivarium needs daily cleaning, along with the feeding tray and water bowl, which should be both washed and rinsed. A terrapin tank should have its water changed once or even twice a week. Wear rubber gloves when doing this as there is always a slight risk of harmful bacteria, such as *Salmonella*, entering the body through minor cuts on your hands. It is vital to switch off the heating system before placing your hands in the water, and always leave a heaterstat to cool down for a few minutes before lifting it out of the water. Tortoises, terrapins and turtles can be transferred to a reasonably spacious, temporary plastic container – which they should not be able to climb out of – while their quarters are being cleaned.

CLEANING THE TANK

Never try to empty the tank by sucking water through a length of rubber tubing. If you want to use a siphoning method, fill the tube with tap water, and place one end in the tank, keeping your finger in place over the other, before releasing this and triggering the flow into a bucket. Alternatively, you can obtain a special aquatic siphon for this purpose. Rinse the cartridge of the power filter in this tap water as well, squeezing the foam out to remove the debris which will have been sucked in here. In the case of a small tank, you may be able simply to tip the water straight down a drain. Never use the kitchen sink for this purpose because of the risk of introducing harmful bacteria. When filling the tank again, check the water temperature with a thermometer first, ensuring that it is at the correct temperature before allowing the turtles back into the tank.

In the summer it will be beneficial, particularly as they grow bigger, to allow turtles outside on warm days. Rocks, for basking purposes, should again be included in an outdoor tank.

♦ ABOVE
Handling a chelonian safely. Beware, as they do have strong feet and sharp claws.

Although it may seem a nice idea to allow the turtles into an outdoor pond, this will need to be escape proof around the edges, preferably with a central island where they can emerge on to land. The turtles should always be brought inside again at night.

HIBERNATION

In temperate areas, Eurasian tortoises will instinctively want to hibernate as the days become shorter. It is important that they are in satisfactory health for this purpose, and have put on enough weight over the summer months to sustain them through their winter fast. A veterinary examination may be advisable to estabish their condition. The two key measurements are the tortoise's weight, which can be gauged simply by placing it carefully

SIPHONING THE TANK

1 Fill the tube with water. You will also need a bucket within easy reach. Ideally, you should wear protective gloves for this task.

2 Use your thumbs to cover both ends of the tube. One end must be below the water level, with the other extending into the bucket.

3 Release the thumb over the end in the tank first, and then take your thumb away from the other end to start the water flow.

PREPARING FOR HIBERNATION

1 Prepare a cardboard box lined with sheets of newspaper. Fast your tortoise beforehand, so that its digestive tract is empty.

2 When the tortoise is ready to settle down for hibernation, it will not move around very much when placed in the box.

3 You will also need a tea chest that can be lined with straw – avoid using hay as this contains fungal spores that could cause an infection.

4 Leave a space at the top of the tea chest so that you can place the tortoise and its box here. Do not seal the box.

5 To ensure that your tortoise cannot climb out of the tea chest, and to protect it from possible predators, fit a mesh lid.

6 The lid should fit snugly into the opening at the top of the tea chest, being hinged in place here and fitted with bolts.

7 Wrap sheets of newspaper around the tea chest to provide further insulation, holding them in place with string.

8 A blanket or polystyrene can also be used for insulation purposes but it is important to make sure there is an adequate air supply.

♦ A B O V E
Fluid as well as weight loss occurs during hibernation. Tortoises that have recently woken up will benefit from regular baths and having their eyes bathed.

in a stout plastic bag and lifting this just a short distance off the ground with a spring balance, and its length, measured in a straight line across the top of the shell.

Cut up clean newspaper into strips to form bedding, avoiding the use of hay, which is full of fungal spores and could infect the tortoise while it sleeps. The temperature is critical; if the location is too warm, the tortoise

will not settle down and will use up its fat stores prematurely; if it is too cold, it could literally freeze to death. A hibernating tortoise should be maintained at a figure of 4°C (39°F), and will emerge in the early spring as the temperature starts to rise again.

The tortoises' eyes may be sticky at this stage, and placing it in tepid water up to the edge of its shell will allow it to bathe and also to drink. Adding a

supplementary vitamin preparation to the drinking water should help to encourage the tortoise to become more active again and this, in turn, will rekindle its appetite. Any tortoise that is not eating again within about ten days of emerging from hibernation should receive a check-up from the vet in case it is unwell.

BREEDING

◆ BELOW
Accurate temperature control is not just vital
for hatching tortoise and turtle eggs. It can also
directly influence the gender of the resulting
hatchlings as well.

Most tortoises and terrapins can be
sexed quite easily by examining their
underparts. The tails of males are
generally longer and often narrower
than those of females, with the ano-
genital opening being closer to the
base of the tail in the case of a female.
In some cases, the underside of the
shell is also more curved in the male,
particularly in tortoises, helping them
to balance on the female's shell when
mating. There are also more specific
indicators in some species as well, such
as the longer front claws, seen in the
case of male red-eared (*Trachemys
scripta elegans*) and related turtles.

Courtship in chelonians can be
an aggressive encounter. In the case
of tortoises, the male will often snap
at the female's legs to slow her down,
and then battes her shell from behind,
before climbing up on to her shell
once she is stationary. Turtles may
start displaying in a more gentle
fashion, with male red-eared sliders,
for example, using their claws to fan
the water in front of the female's face,
but, when they actually start mating,
the male will bite at the loose folds of
skin on the top of the female's neck,

anchoring himself in place. Serious
injury is unlikely, but if this attention
is persistent then separate the
chelonians for a period to prevent the
female being constantly harried by her
intended partner. Once mating has
occurred successfully, the female will
be able to produce fertile eggs for over
a year without having to mate again.

All chelonians reproduce by
means of hard-shelled eggs. These
are buried in a hole in the ground
or the substrate so, in vivarium
surroundings, there should be a tray
of sand provided specifically for this
purpose. Occasionally, turtles may lay
their eggs in water and, provided that
the eggs are undamaged, there is no
reason why they cannot be hatched
there satisfactorily. In the case of
tortoises, females tend to become
increasingly restless as the time for
egg-laying approaches, and will spend
time constructing their nests in the
afternoon. Do not disturb the female
when she is engaged in this process,
but wait for her to lay her eggs and
then cover the nest site. When the
eggs are covered she will then take
no further interest in them.

It is usually necessary to remove
the eggs to an incubator before they
hatch, certainly if they are laid

◆ LEFT
A young spotted
turtle breaks free
from its egg, using
a structure known
as the egg tooth
on its nose to cut
through the hard
shell. This disappears
soon afterwards.

A young spur-thighed tortoise emerges from its egg. It is a miniature of the adult at this stage, but lacks the growth rings on its shell when newly born. The shell appears quite smooth.

outdoors. A garden trowel will help you to dig out the soil carefully and reach the eggs. These should be lifted out carefully, taking care not to turn them over. Leave the eggs in the same position after laying.

There are various methods of incubating the chelonian eggs; many breeders prefer to set them in damp vermiculite in an incubator. The surface of this material needs to be kept moist. Although the eggs discolour during the incubation period, this will not affect their hatchability. It is now clear from studies that the gender of many chelonians will be influenced by the incubation temperature, although there are no set rules in this respect – it depends very much on the individual species. The aim is to maintain a constant temperature of about 29°C (84°F), with a relative humidity reading of 75–80 per cent.

There is no set incubation period. When the time for hatching approaches, the young chelonian will start to cut its way out of the shell using its egg tooth – a temporary structure on its snout, which disappears soon after hatching. After emerging from the egg it will be nourished for the first days of its life by the remains of its yolk sac, which can be seen on the underside of the shell. It is then likely to start seeking its own food. Do not allow aquatic chelonians access to deep water at this early stage as they are not yet strong swimmers.

It is not uncommon for young chelonians to be more colourful than adults, as shown by these two gopher tortoises. The precise markings of each individual are unique.

425

FROGS AND TOADS

Colourful, bizarre and often quite straightforward in their requirements, frogs and toads deserve to be more popular vivarium subjects, particularly as many species can be persuaded to spawn successfully in such surroundings.

Some can even become sufficiently tame to take food from your hand. Even so, these anurans are not to be handled on a regular basis, since their skins are delicate and careless handling can cause fatal infections.

INTRODUCTION

Frogs and toads collectively form the tail-less groups of amphibians, with this feature helping to distinguish them from newts and salamanders. Amphibians have a very different lifestyle from reptiles, which means that they have to stay close to water because, otherwise, they face the very real threat of death as the result of dehydration.

In general terms, frogs are more closely tied to water than toads: some species are almost entirely aquatic by nature, whereas others will only return here to breed. In terms of appearance, frogs generally have smoother skins than toads, and they are more athletic by nature. The tree frogs, as a group, have evolved to have a mainly arboreal existence, clambering around in the branches of trees.

The colour of most frogs is such that it enables them to blend in against their background, with hues of green often predominating in the case of many species. Those that are brightly

♦ LEFT
Amphibians in general are found in damp surroundings, often immersing themselves for at least part of the day in water.

♦ LEFT
Toads have grown used to terrestrial life. They are better-suited to walking on land than most frogs, which progress by hopping.

♦ BELOW LEFT
The orange-sided tree frog has adapted to arboreal living. The swollen toe pads will help them to maintain their grip.

coloured, however, such as poison dart frogs, may appear highly attractive to our eyes, but their striking appearance warns of their deadly skin secretions. Although not directly harmful, these frogs must be handled very carefully – wearing thin gloves – on the occasions when they do need to be caught. Handling should be avoided if

possible though, because of the risk of damaging their sensitive skins.

Toads usually have a stockier appearance, frequently with wart-like swellings over their bodies. In spite of popular folklore, these warts are not transmissible to human beings, but there are prominent glands, especially on the sides of the head, that produce toxins so, again, handling should be carried out carefully.

Frogs and toads have colonized many areas of the planet, in spite of the fact that they are dependent on

The southern toad is a North American species.
A period of cooling over the winter months is
thus likely to encourage spawning activity in
the springtime.

The American green tree frog, originating from
the south-eastern part of the United States,
is a very attractive species that does well in
a tall-sided, planted vivarium.

The marine or cane toad is the largest toad in
the world, growing to approximately 20 cm
(8 in) in size. It will feed on small vertebrates
such as pinkies.

water for breeding purposes. They are
insectivorous by nature, and some of
the largest species may even prey on
small rodents and young birds. It will
therefore be necessary to provide
them with invertebrates although,
on the whole, frogs and toads are
not expensive to keep.

Breeding of anurans is achieved
quite easily, often by cooling them
down for a period during the winter
months, in the case of those species
found in more temperate areas.
The breeding cues in those from the
tropics are more complex, which often
necessitates keeping them in drier
surroundings for a period of time,
before the start of the rainy period.

Females lay jelly-like eggs, in the
form of threads in the case of toads,
with frogs' eggs being clumped. The

This Spurrell's leaf
gliding frog originates
in the tropical forests
of Costa Rica.

young frog or toad starts to develop in
the centre of the egg, emerging in due
course as a tadpole with feathery gills
on the sides of the head, which serve
to extract oxygen from the water.

Gradually, the tadpoles start to
grow legs, their tails become shorter
and their gills start to disappear as
they are transformed into miniature
anurans. They will spend longer at the
water surface, often resting on rocks
as they start to breathe atmospheric
air, before finally emerging on to land.
Young toads in particular may have
a long lifespan in front of them – over
20 years in some cases.

The spring peeper, so-called because
of its calls at spawning time, is
another North American species. It
is hardy, grows to over 2.5 cm (1 in)
long and has a call like a whistle.

The bony-headed tree frog, like
others of its kind, can use all its
limbs to maintain its balance. Flies
are a useful food for tree frogs,
which do not hunt on the ground.

SPECIES

Requiring similar conditions to tropical fish, dwarf clawed frogs make very attractive occupants of a small heated aquarium, often spawning in these surroundings.

It is important to match the type of set-up carefully to the type of frog that you are keeping, as their requirements can be quite different.

DWARF CLAWED FROG

This frog (*Hymenochirus boettgeri*) is an ideal choice if you are looking for an aquatic species. The small size of these frogs, which average about 3.5 cm (1½ in) long, means that they can be accommodated easily, compared with their larger relatives known as African clawed frogs (*Xenopus laevis*). These can reach a size of 13 cm (5 in) or more and are far more disruptive within an aquarium, with their flattened body shape and powerful legs meaning that they will uproot any planted decor.

The water in the aquarium needs to be heated to 24°C (75°F), and should be relatively shallow. An undergravel filtration system is recommended, along with decor such as bogwood, to provide retreats for the frogs. Java

♦ BELOW LEFT
The markings of grey tree frogs differ between individuals, so that once a pair have spawned, you should be able to recognize the male and female. They grow to about 5 cm (2 in) long.

♦ BELOW RIGHT
The camouflage provided by the grey tree frog's patterning is very effective. Decorate a vivarium for them with cork bark, branches and other decorative vegetation.

moss (*Vesticularia dubyana*), growing on the wood, and floating plants at the surface should be included. Male frogs have large glands behind the front legs and they call loudly when in breeding condition. The eggs must be removed from the aquarium, and will hatch after five days. Tadpoles will change into frogs after about two months.

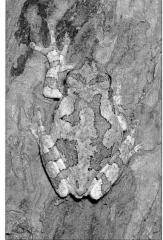

◆ LEFT
The stunning appearance of the red-eyed tree frog. Tropical tree frogs are more demanding in their requirements than those from temperate areas. It measures 7.5 cm (3 in) in length.

WHITE'S TREE FROG

The White's tree frog (*Litoria caerulea*) is an easier proposition to care for, although its large size means that it should be housed in a vivarium with stout-leaved plants, which will support its weight. Again, heated surroundings are essential, although this tree frog requires slightly lower levels of humidity – around 80 per cent – compared with the red-eyed species. The coloration of the White's tree frog is typically green, sometimes with a bluish hue, although piebald individuals, with green and prominent areas of white are also known. These are bold, lively frogs and they can become quite tame. Adults will eat larger invertebrates and pinkies. For breeding, reduce the humidity in their quarters to 70 per cent for one month before raising it again.

◆ BELOW
White's tree frogs can reach 11.5 cm (4½ in) long. Females may lay up to 300 eggs twice a year, with tadpoles leaving the water at five weeks.

An attractive albino form of the dwarf clawed frog has also been bred and is quite widely available. It will require identical care.

GREY TREE FROG

There are a number of tree frogs available, and it is important to determine where they originate from, as not all are of tropical origin. The grey tree frog (*Hyla versicolor*) is a species found in the United States, and this needs slightly cooler and less humid conditions than its tropical cousins. The mottled grey coloration varies between individuals, with orange areas usually apparent on the thighs and a small cream-coloured area below the eyes. A tall aquarium set-up, incorporating cork bark as well as stout plants for climbing purposes, will be needed for these frogs.

RED-EYED TREE FROG

This frog (*Agalychnis moreletii*) is one of the most striking of all the tropical species, thanks to the stunning coloration of its eyes, offset against its bright green body colours. The fact that these frogs are nocturnal in their habits means that they are not as conspicuous as some frogs. Their care is also more specialized: include a small waterfall operated by an aquarium pump in their quarters to maintain the humidity level. Adult males are smaller than females.

HORNED FROG

It is definitely not a good idea to house frogs or toads of different sizes together, because the smaller individuals may be eaten by their larger companions. While this is the case for most species of frogs and toads, some are more cannibalistic than others, with the horned frog (*Ceratophrys* species) being one of the worst offenders. In spite of this, the cute appearance of horned frogs means that they have become popular as vivarium pets.

The horns from which the species takes its name are actually enlarged areas above the eyes. These frogs are easy to accommodate. They require a vivarium with a thick layer of moss on the floor in which to bury themselves, remaining here for long periods, with just their faces evident, and snapping at any invertebrate within reach.

Breeding these frogs presents more of a challenge. The males are identified by darker markings on their throats. The temperature in their vivarium

◆ ABOVE AND INSET
The predatory nature of the horned frog is reflected by its very large mouth. It spends much of its time on the floor of the vivarium, partially hidden from view, and grows up to 12 cm (5 in).

◆ BELOW LEFT
Golden mantellas vary in terms of their coloration, from a reddish shade to orange.

should be reduced to approximately 20°C (68°F) for a maximum period of three months, before increasing the humidity level. Providing an area of water may also encourage spawning.

GOLDEN MANTELLA

The popular and attractive golden mantella (*Mantella aurantiaca*), which originates from Madagascar, can vary in appearance from shades of yellowish-orange through to reddish-orange. These are small frogs, measuring about 3 cm (1¼ in) when adult, and they should be housed in a vivarium with damp moss on the floor and plenty of hiding places.

The Oriental fire-bellied toad is an attractive species that can be easily maintained. Males grip the females by their hind legs when spawning is occurring. They grow to 5 cm (2 in) long.

The golden mantella is an example of a species that should be housed together with other frogs if spawning is to take place – sexing these frogs by sight is difficult as their coloration is not a reliable indicator. A cave with water in it should be provided as it is here that the mantellas will spawn. Their eggs are sensitive to light and need to be kept in darkness until the tadpoles have hatched. The tadpoles metamorphose in about six weeks. Females lay several times throughout the year, with relatively small clutches, comprising fewer than a dozen eggs.

FIRE-BELLIED TOAD

The fire-bellied toad (*Bombina orientalis*) is an easy species to keep and breed, and is an ideal choice for someone who has not kept anurans before. These toads are hardy and they do not require artificial heat in the home, orginating as they do from the temperate areas of Asia. In fact, allowing the temperature in their quarters to drop to 10°C (50°F) in winter will stimulate breeding behaviour the following spring. These toads benefit from an aqua-terrarium with an accessible area of water. They enjoy foraging on land, and will feed on invertebrates out of the water. Males call loudly at the start of the breeding period, while females increase in size due to their eggs.

GREEN TOAD

A number of toads make popular vivarium subjects and can become quite tame. These include the green toad (*Bufo viridis*), which is not to be confused with the American green toad (*B. debilis*). Their patterning is green and reddish rather than the green and black of their African cousin.

Toads require a spacious terrestrial environment with a moss floor, as well as retreats and an area of water. Provide an aquatic set-up for breeding. Males are smaller than females, and can be distinguished by their croaking calls in the springtime. A female may lay thousands of eggs, and cannibalism is common among tadpoles. Even when the young toads have emerged on to land, it is a good idea to keep larger and smaller individuals separate for this reason.

The variable markings of the Eurasian green toad can be seen by comparing two individuals. Their care in vivarium surroundings is straightforward, and they will eat a range of invertebrates. They are larger than their American counterpart, growing to about 15 cm (6 in) when adult.

HOUSING

The same type of basic equipment used for reptiles can be useful for amphibians as well. If possible, however, it is better to use acrylic containers rather than those made of glass or other materials because these are easier to move and clean. In some cases, though, especially with tree frogs, you may have little choice because these enclosures may have to be specially constructed, using sheets of glass stuck together with an aquarium sealant. Most herptile shops can offer this type of service.

The sensitive nature of the skin of these creatures, coupled with the fact that they generally require much lower temperatures than reptiles, means that

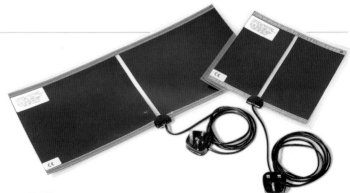

✦ ABOVE
Heater pads in various sizes to correspond to that of the tank are invaluable for a set-up for tropical amphibians. The heat output can be controlled thermostatically.

✦ BELOW
Not all frogs are tiny, as shown by this tree frog. The vivarium needs to correspond to the natural habitat in which the species occurs.

spotlights in their quarters will not be required. Instead, heat pads are used to a much greater extent for frogs and toads, even in the case of aquatic species. It is not a good idea to use a standard aquarium heaterstat, which could burn the amphibian's sensitive skin, while the relative low water level in the vivarium means that siting the unit would also create problems, as it has to be kept submerged. In addition, a heat pad is more versatile, serving to warm both the water and the air, operating under thermostatic control.

Both frogs and toads are quite secretive creatures by nature, and they should not be exposed to unnecessarily bright lighting. In fact, there have been suggestions that protracted exposure to ultraviolet light may be harmful to them, while tungsten bulbs will emit a relatively large amount of heat, and this too can be damaging. The best solution will be to use a full-spectrum fluorescent tube, which has a maximum output of no more than two per cent UV light. This should be sufficient to meet the requirements of those frogs and toads that are active during the day and may benefit from some exposure to this type of light, as well as helping you to have a clear view

◆ BELOW
A beautiful mantella frog found only on the
island of Madagascar. A number of these species
are now well established in collections, breeding
regularly in vivaria.

Plastic substitutes can be used for
decoration, and these will not damp
off and turn mouldy, as can often
happen with their living counterparts,
especially if the ventilation within the
enclosure is poor.

It is vital to fit the vivarium with
a ventilated cover – which will often
be included as part of an acrylic set-up
although they do not include any areas
for the attachment of lights. Frogs
and toads can not only jump well in
most cases, but they are also able to
climb up the corners of their quarters
– particularly in a vivarium set-up –
and then slip out through the roof
area, so a secure hood will be essential
for their safety.

of the vivarium occupants without
having to raise the temperature
within the enclosure.

Great care needs to be taken,
however, to ensure that water does
not come into direct contact with
the electrics when it is vital to spray
the substrate to maintain the relative
humidity level. Therefore, the type
of lighting set-up recommended for
aquaria is very important in this case.

Take care when siting the vivarium
in the room, bearing in mind that the
temperature within is likely to rise
rapidly if it is placed close to a window
when the sun is shining. A secure side
table, near a power point, is the best
locality, away from a radiator, which
could also affect the temperature
within the tank.

You can buy a range of items
from herptile shops, including
retreats and containers suitable for
use as water receptacles, and different
substrates. Bark, in various grades,
and moss are most suitable for use as

substrates, while a plant sprayer can
be used for misting the vivarium. You
may want to include living plants such
as ferns, which are most likely to
thrive in this type of environment.

◆ BELOW
The stunning golden mantella is considered to
be one of the most attractive of all amphibians,
but its bright coloration gives a warning about
its toxic skin secretions.

FEEDING

The feeding requirements of frogs and toads differ through their life-cycle, with tadpoles being partly vegetarian in their feeding habits. Adult animals, in contrast, require a variety of invertebrates to form the basis of a nutritional diet, with some of the larger toads being capable of eating small vertebrates.

INVERTEBRATES

You can purchase a suitable selection of invertebrates from pet stores, or by mail order from suppliers listed at the back of specialist publications. Crickets are especially useful for frogs and toads. They are available in a range of sizes and can be fed to the amphibians in one size or another as they grow larger. The crickets can be dusted with a nutritional balancer to improve their feeding value.

The movement of crickets also means that they will attract the attention of a frog or toad readily, and the fact that they will jump and climb (unlike mealworms) means that they are also ideal for tree frogs, which may otherwise be reluctant to descend to the ground in order to hunt for food. The only other way to feed frogs and toads is to place a shelf on the side of their quarters within easy reach, placing other food items on it for them to eat.

It is a good idea to offer some variety in the amphibian's diet to allow you to provide them with other items on occasion. Worms are often favoured by toads although, if you dig these up in the garden, collect them from ground that has not been treated in any way with chemicals. The worms should be left to empty

their intestinal tract for a couple of days, in damp grass, before being offered to the vivarium occupants. In the case of the smaller species, you can offer green aphids as a change, brushing these off garden or wild plants with a clean paintbrush.

If you are keeping more than one frog or toad in the same enclosure, it is important to check that all of them have adequate opportunity to feed properly, and that the dominant individual is not taking all the food. Avoid overfeeding as this can be very harmful, with toads in particular becoming obese over a period of time. Amphibians should be eager to feed, although the amount of food that they need will vary, depending on their size and the time of year. Temperate species, for example, will have larger appetites when they first emerge from a period of winter inactivity, needing to replace the stores of body fat that they will have lost over this time.

SMALL VERTEBRATES

When offering dead day-old mice, known as pinkies and sold in frozen form by specialist suppliers, make sure they have thawed out thoroughly; simply dipping them in hot water may not be sufficient for this purpose, and you should allow adequate time for defrosting. You will need to persuade the amphibian to take the inert prey: waving the mouse slightly to one side of the amphibian's face should be sufficient to encourage it to strike, but take care to keep your fingers out of the way. Although amphibians do not have teeth they can inflict a painful nip and, once attached to a finger with their jaws, they will usually be reluctant to let go.

+ BELOW
It is not a good idea to keep large and small specimens of the same species together, because in the case of amphibians, such as these toads, the smaller individual may fall victim to its larger companion.

Mealworms can be purchased in a variety of sizes, with mini-mealworms being valuable for smaller herptiles. Keeping them cool will slow their development.

Giant mealworms may be too large for some herptiles, but they are often favoured by bigger species. Their nutritional value can be improved by feeding them special foods.

Waxmoth larvae are especially useful for herptiles that may not be in top condition – after illness, for example – as they provide excellent nutrition.

COLLECTING LIVEFOODS

You can usefully augment the diet of your amphibians by collecting invertebrates if you have access to a garden or woodland, and if you are sure they have not been exposed to harmful chemicals. Greenfly can be dusted off roses, for example, and they are very valuable for recently-metamorphosed amphibians. Earthworms, too, are easy to acquire, and these are often favoured by toads, as well as axolotls and adult salamanders. If the ground is dry, watering a patch of earth will attract the worms back to the surface.

♦ BELOW
Choose your pet's food according to its particular species, and always ask the advice of the breeder from whom you bought your pet if you are unsure about its nutritional needs.

♦ ABOVE
Crickets can be obtained in a variety of sizes. Matching the size of crickets to that of the herptiles is important, particularly when prey is being swallowed whole.

GENERAL CARE

Frogs and toads generally require relatively little care, although it is important to change the water in their quarters regularly. Use a water conditioner to remove the chlorine-based chemicals present in fresh tap water, as these might be harmful to the amphibians. In the case of aquatic species especially, be sure that the temperature of the new water is similar to that of the water removed from the tank, using an aquatic thermometer for this purpose. There is no need to remove all the water under these circumstances because of the presence of the undergravel filter. Instead, take out about one quarter of the total volume.

Every month or so, it will be a good idea to replace the substrate in the quarters of the more terrestrial species and, in order to do this, you will need to catch the vivarium occupants. As a result, it is worthwhile keeping the plastic containers in which you brought your pets home, as these will make useful, escape-proof, temporary accommodation while you

◆ LEFT
Always handle frogs and toads with disposable gloves, especially if you have any cuts on your hands. The yellow-bellied toad, seen here, is a close relative of the fire-bellied toad and needs similar care.

◆ LEFT
Always bear in mind that frogs and toads are surprisingly agile and can leap out of their quarters when the lid is off. They can also climb up the sides, so always open the lid with care.

◆ BELOW LEFT
The strawberry poison dart frog is beautiful to our eyes, but its bright coloration serves as a natural warning that its skin contains potent toxins.

clean their quarters. Wear disposable rubber gloves for this task, just in case you have any cuts on your hand, which could be irritated by the amphibians' skin secretions. Generally, however, it will not be necessary to handle them directly as you can usually shepherd them into the plastic containers with your hands.

Try to match the quantity of invertebrates you are offering as food to the amount the amphibians will eat within half an hour. It is not a good idea to leave invertebrates for any length of time, as they may escape into the room, with aphids then infesting

♦ LEFT
Fire-bellied toads will benefit from being
maintained at a lower temperature over winter,
to encourage breeding the following spring.

♦ BELOW
In the case of frogs or toads in the water, the
simplest way to catch them is by scooping them
up with a fish net of suitable dimensions.

♦ BOTTOM
You may also be able to use a net to catch frogs
or toads on land, but it is often simpler to
persuade them to hop into a container.

household plants, while crickets are
likely to drown in large numbers in
the water bowl. It is better to remove
the bowl, or to cover it with a small
sheet of perspex (Plexiglas) while you
are feeding the amphibians, to prevent
the invertebrates gaining access to it.

If you do need to catch small frogs
in particular, then a net as sold for
catching aquarium fish will be useful.
Dip it into the water first, to prevent
the risk of causing injury to the mucus
covering on the amphibians' skin
when you catch them. Again, it is
better to persuade them to hop into
the net than to pick them up by hand,
although in the water you can scoop
them up safely with the net.

There will be times when you may
see the skin of a frog in the water.
Frogs will shed their skins at irregular
intervals, and it is a normal process.
In some cases, the discarded skins
may be eaten by the frogs themselves.

When spraying the vivarium, use
only dechlorinated water. You may
need to wipe over the vivarium glass
if it starts to develop algal growth,
caused by the high humidity in
tropical set-ups. Never be tempted
to use commercial spray to clean
the glass, or in the room housing
the vivarium, because these can be
potentially fatal to amphibians.

BREEDING

Although it is theoretically possible to sex frogs and toads on the basis of their size, this is actually harder in practice, unless you can be sure that that they are of roughly the same age. Otherwise, one could simply be a younger individual of the same sex. As the breeding season approaches, so it becomes easier to distinguish the sexes. Males develop what are known as nuptial pads – swollen areas present on the forelegs, and often on the digits. Wrinkled, more darkly pigmented skin over the throat area is another indicator of a male anuran, with the loose skin here being inflated as part of the courtship display when the amphibians are calling.

Just having a pair, however, is no guarantee that they will breed. Conditioning is vital for this purpose. In the wild, there are a number of changes that occur in the amphibians' natural environment, and these stimulate the breeding process. In the case of species found in temperate parts of the world, temperature is an important trigger,

◆ LEFT
Calling is a natural prelude to mating in the case of frogs and toads. This oak toad is inflating his vocal sac.

◆ BELOW LEFT
The characteristic embrace when frogs or toads pair off is called amplexus, with the male fertilizing the eggs as they are laid by the female, who is often larger in size.

◆ BELOW RIGHT
The calls of frogs, such as this squirrel tree frog, are most likely to be heard in springtime, after rain and at dusk.

and reducing this in their quarters in the winter will serve this purpose. The reproductive triggers for anurans from tropical areas, where the temperature is constant throughout the year, are related more to changes in humidity than to temperature. Making the

vivarium slightly drier for several weeks of the year, and then raising the humidity level again, should trigger reproductive behaviour, although it is obviously important that the amphibians themselves are in good health. In some cases, artificial

◆ LEFT
The prolific spawning of many frogs and toads reflects the fact that in the wild only a small percentage of the resulting tadpoles will survive to breeding age themselves.

hormones have been used to condition frogs and toads for breeding purposes, although these should always be used with care.

When the time for egg-laying is near, most frogs and toads will spend longer in water, where the female will lay her eggs. The eggs are normally fertilized by the male externally as they are laid, with the male clasping the female with his legs in an embrace described as amplexus. A few species lay their eggs on land. In the case of the red-eyed tree frog, the eggs are attached to a leaf overhanging water so that, when the tadpoles wriggle free, they will fall into the water where they can continue their development.

The number of eggs varies greatly, from just ten or more in some cases through to thousands in others, where only a small proportion of the offspring will survive.

The transparent, jelly-like material around the egg helps to protect the developing tadpole from fungi until it hatches, although infertile eggs often suffer fungal attack while among those that are developing normally. It is not usually necessary to treat the eggs but, once the tadpoles have hatched, the remaining eggs should be removed. At first, the tadpoles will be inert, using up the remains of their yolk sacs but, within a few days, they start to swim and feed on tiny particles in the water.

It is important to provide tadpoles with plenty of space as they grow, partly to reduce the likelihood of cannibalism; tadpoles become more carnivorous as they grow larger. Powdered fish flake is a valuable addition to their diet at this stage, and will be less likely to pollute the water than pieces of raw meat. Water quality is vital, and partial water changes must be carried out as the tadpoles grow.

Gradually, the legs of tadpoles will start to develop, along with their body shape, and the tail starts to shrink. Provide an area, in the form of a rock in their quarters, where the young amphibians can emerge on to land as their lungs start to function. Soon afterwards, they can be transferred to an aqua-terrarium to roam on land, with an area of water also accessible. Small invertebrates should now form the basis of their diet.

◆ BELOW LEFT
Male frogs develop nuptial pads on their forelegs. This can help to distinguish the sexes.

◆ BELOW RIGHT
A metamorphosing Trinidad leaf frog tadpole. The strong legs and frog-like body shape have already developed by this stage.

NEWTS AND SALAMANDERS

This group of amphibians are distinguished from frogs and toads by the fact that they have tails. They are rather shy and secretive creatures in most cases, whose environmental needs centre around water. Most show the amphibian cycle of reproduction, laying eggs which hatch into tadpoles and metamorphose into miniature adults. Some give birth to live offspring. Others display a remarkable degree of parental care by guarding their eggs.

INTRODUCTION

◆ BELOW
A smooth newt on a rock. These amphibians return to water to breed in the springtime.

This group of amphibians include the biggest members of the group, which are the endangered giant salamanders found in parts of China and Japan. They can reach at least 1.5 m (5 ft) in length, but are not likely to be seen outside zoological collections. Others are much smaller in size, rarely exceeding more than 30 cm (12 in) in length.

It can be difficult to distinguish between newts and salamanders since there are no clear differences between them. In general terms, however, newts are more dependent on water than salamanders, especially for breeding purposes. Both groups have a wide distribution in cooler parts of the world, being rather secretive and shy by nature. The brilliant skin coloration of many salamanders is, again, an indication of their highly toxic skin secretions.

◆ BELOW LEFT
A brightly coloured European fire salamander. The bright coloration serves as a warning to predators about the toxic skin secretions produced by these amphibians.

◆ BELOW RIGHT
A marbled salamander. Although the basic colour scheme of these amphibians is the same, it is possible to identify individuals quite easily by their skin markings.

◆ BELOW
An adult red-spotted newt. Males develop a
broad tail fin rather than a crest at the start of
the breeding period. Also, unlike most newts,
pairs grip together when mating.

◆ BELOW
A young red-spotted newt, which has recently
emerged on to land. It is highly colourful at this
stage, often being described as a red eft. Its
appearance gradually changes as it matures.

An unusual phenomenon associated
with salamanders is that of neoteny.
Like other amphibians, their life-cycle
begins with an egg which hatches into
a larva or tadpole. The larvae then
develop and lose their gills, emerging
on to land as miniature adults. In the
case of the axolotl, the larvae do not
metamorphose into adult salamanders
but continue to grow, with the result
that they can then breed in the larval
state. This can be related to a shortage
of iodine in the diet, which is
necessary for the manufacture of the
thyroid hormones that help to trigger
the change into the adult form. Often,
however, if the water level is allowed
to drop back, then the axolotl will
transform into an adult salamander,
and will breed in this state.

The reproductive behaviour of the
salamander is generally less dependent
on water than is the case with many
other amphibians. Some populations
of the fire salamander, for example,
give birth to live tadpoles rather than
lay eggs.

All newts and salamanders are
predatory in their feeding habits,
catching their prey both on land and
in water. The care of most salamanders
and newts is very straightforward and,

in some cases, it is possible to keep
them in outdoor vivaria for at least
part of the year. If you decide on this
approach, however, you need to ensure
that their quarters are escape-proof,
because allowing non-native species
to escape is not only likely to be illegal
but could also have serious effects on
local wildlife if the escapees establish
themselves in your neighbourhood.

However, it may be possible to
hatch the eggs of any newts which you
find in the part of the country where
you live, and allow these to build up a
population in your garden. There may

be restrictions on transferring
wild newts or salamanders to new
environments, however, so check on
this beforehand. It is also possible to
obtain eggs of such amphibians from
breeders who have surplus stocks.
Most breeders with regular stock on
offer will advertise in the specialist
herpetological magazines. A local
newt society may also be able to help.

◆ BELOW
The yellow phase of the fire salamander is
more common than the orange variety shown
opposite, although both colour forms can result
from a single spawning.

SALAMANDER SPECIES

FIRE SALAMANDER

Variability in appearance is a feature of the fire salamander (*Salamandra salamandra*), which is found over a wide area of mainland Europe in the wild. Some populations display yellow spots, set against a black background, whereas others have yellow stripes and some even have fiery orange, rather than yellow, markings. There is also some variability in size, and individuals can range from 20–30 cm (8–12 in) in length when adult. Fire salamanders are easy to house in a spacious vivarium, with plenty of retreats.

Perhaps surprisingly, fire salamanders cannot swim at all well, and the water container in their quarters must be not only shallow, but must allow easy access both in and out of the water. A cool environment is another important consideration, particularly during the summer months when the temperature indoors can rise rapidly; fire salamanders should be kept at a maximum of 20°C (68°F). It may, therefore, be necessary to move the salamanders outdoors to a vivarium in a shaded corner of the garden, out of direct sunlight.

MARBLED SALAMANDER

The marbled salamander (*Ambystoma opacum*) is found in eastern parts of the United States. This species can be kept outdoors during the warmer summer months. It grows to a maximum size of 11 cm (4¼ in) and is black in colour, with silvery markings, which are whiter and brighter in the males. Mating is unusual in that it takes place on land in the autumn. The eggs are laid in a dried-up pool, and the female stays with them over the winter until they hatch.

♦ LEFT
An example of the fire salamander, found in the Cantabrian region of Spain. This is one of the populations where the discontinuous spots have merged to create stripes running down the sides of the body.

♦ LEFT
Spaghnum moss makes an ideal substrate for salamanders like the marbled, seen here. Spray the moss as necessary, using dechlorinated water, to prevent it from drying out.

It is possible to encourage axolotls to change into adult salamanders by allowing the water in their tank to fall. Their gills will then start to recede as a result, to the extent that they will disappear altogether; if the water level is topped up again, then the gills will grow back in due course. As a result, the axolotl is sometimes known as the "Peter Pan of the amphibian world". Females may lay as many as 300 eggs at a single spawning, draping these around aquatic plants. Hatching will usually take about two weeks.

SPOTTED SALAMANDER

The range of the spotted salamander (*A. maculatum*) extends down the eastern part of North America, from southern Canada. These salamanders are recognizable by the clearly defined pattern of yellow or yellowish-orange spots extending down their bodies in two distinctive rows. They grow to a size of about 20 cm (8 in) in total, and require moist surroundings compared with the marbled salamander. An outdoor enclosure will suit them well, although they are shy by nature and will be hard to spot outdoors.

AXOLOTL

The axolotl (*Ambystoma mexicanum*) ranks as one of the most bizarre and distinctive of all amphibian species. It can grow up to 30 cm (12 in) in length, and is confined in the wild to two Mexican lakes, although it has been bred for many generations in private collections, in spite of its endangered status. Only the dark brown form occurs in the wild; the albino mutation has been developed from captive stock. There are also piebald variants, which have black and white coloration, plus rarer individuals which are a golden shade.

As tadpoles, axolotls must be kept in aquatic surroundings, thriving in water kept at room temperature. They are inactive by nature, but if kept together they may fight, sometimes even to the extent of biting off a companion's limbs. Remarkably, however, this may regenerate to form a completely functional limb, providing the water is clean and fungus does not attack the wound.

NEWT SPECIES

◆ BELOW
When in breeding condition, a male Alpine
newt has blue areas on the flanks and a low crest
on the back. His underparts are also brighter
than those of the female.

JAPANESE FIRE-BELLIED NEWT

Part of the reason for the popularity
of the Japanese fire-bellied newt
(*Cynops pyrrhogaster*) is the fact that
it is almost entirely aquatic, and can be
housed in an aquarium with unheated
water throughout the year. These
newts grow up to 12 cm (4½ in), and
take their name from their fiery red
underparts, with black markings.

To encourage breeding, allow the
water temperature in the aquarium
to fall in the late winter. This species
will distribute its eggs in true newt
fashion, carefully attaching each egg to
the underside of the leaves of aquatic
plants. The young should be reared in
more terrestrial surroundings, once
they have lost their gills, until the age
of about six months, when they can be
returned to an aquatic set-up.

ALPINE NEWT

The Alpine newt *(T. alpestris)*, as
its name suggests, is found in
mountainous areas of Europe, and

◆ BELOW
A young marbled newt. Both juveniles and
females of this species display the orangish
vertebral stripe down the back, whereas
breeding males develop a crest.

some forms are more aquatic by
nature than others. They are
sufficiently hardy to be kept in
outdoor enclosures throughout the
year, although the enclosure must
incorporate land areas. Growing
to a length of about 13 cm (5 in),
these newts rank among the most
colourful European species, with
males in particular developing a much
more vibrant shade of blue on their
backs and sides than females, while
their underparts are a rich shade of
pure orange. Females are easy to
distinguish by the brown coloration
on their upperparts.

MARBLED NEWT

Another colourful species is the
marbled newt (*T. marmoratus*), which
originates from south-west Europe.
This species is terrestrial in its habits,
and this needs to be reflected in the

◆ BELOW
The red eft – the immature form of the
red-spotted newt – may not return to water
for several years, although it will stay in damp
surroundings, growing to 12 cm (5 in) overall.

◆ BELOW
A smooth newt tadpole hatches from its egg.
The gills at the sides of the head allow young
amphibians to take oxygen from the water
until their lungs develop.

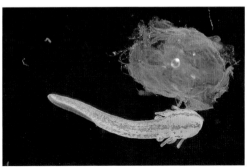

design of its vivarium. The set-up
should comprise an area of sphagnum
moss lining the floor, with adequate
retreats, as well as a shallow dish of
water that is accessible to the newts.
Following a period of winter dormancy,
the newts require an aquarium of
water for spawning, before returning
to their terrestrial lifestyle. They may
grow to 17 cm (7 in) in length.

RED-SPOTTED NEWT
The red-spotted newt (*Notophthalmus
viridescens*) is one of the most striking
of the North American species, and
is extensively found on the eastern
side of the continent. There are slight
variations in appearance between
individuals, as there are three
distinctive types among their wide
range. Even so, the distinctive red
spots, highlighted by black circles on
the sides of their bodies, are clearly
apparent in all cases. The number
of spots varies, depending on the
individual, and the remainder of
the upperparts are brownish with
tiny black spots in adults, who have
yellower underparts.
  The newly metamorphosed
red-spotted newts are the most
dramatically coloured, and are known

as red efts. As well as displaying the
distinctive spotted appearance of
adults, they also have a body colour
which varies from bright orange to
red. They retain their colour for the
time that they remain on land, which
can be up to three years before they
switch back to an aquatic lifestyle to

breed, acquiring their adult coloration
at this stage. The female is likely to lay
up to 200 eggs, in small batches, over a
period of three weeks or so.

◆ BELOW
A crested newt tadpole, with its feathery gills
and legs clearly evident. It will now be preying
on a variety of small water creatures.

HOUSING

The set-up required by newts and salamanders is not only influenced by the species which you are keeping, but also by the time of year. Salamanders by nature are more terrestrial in their habits, and so they will benefit from an enclosure which has a large floor area, compared with its height. It needs to be lined predominantly with damp moss. There are acrylic enclosures of this type available, which come complete with a ventilated and secure roof covering, incorporating a feeding hatch.

Unfortunately, the moss is unlikely to grow in these surroundings, and ultimately will need to be replaced. Suitable retreats will be essential in the enclosure, as salamanders often like to burrow away under logs. These should always be lifted carefully as a result, to avoid any risk of injuring amphibians which may be hiding there. A dish of water which allows the salamanders to submerge themselves is also important, with a rim that merges with the surrounding substrate. Smooth pebbles which allow the amphibians to climb back out again are essential, but these must be firmly supported in the tank.

When filling the water container, it helps to use a large jug (pitcher) for the purpose. Fill this with water from the cold tap, which must then be left to stand for at least 24 hours to remove any chlorine-based chemicals; alternatively, you could use a dechlorinator. This also applies in the case of water that is used to spray the moss. Since the water will need to be changed regularly, try to position the container so that you can lift it out easily without causing a major disturbance in the vivarium.

You may want to add a couple of sprigs of water plants to the container. Elodea or Canadian pondweed *(Elodea canadiensis)* is a good choice for this purpose, particularly if there is a likelihood of the vivarium occupants breeding as it is popular for egg-laying purposes, especially with female newts. Living plants in the substrate are harder to establish, although small ferns in pots may thrive in these surroundings. They can also give an indication of poor ventilation if they start damping off and turning mouldy, which is likely to have an adverse effect on the amphibians' health.

Axolotls need an entirely aquatic set-up if they are to remain in a larval state. Their housing needs are very basic, however, and they can be kept in a large acrylic tank or a standard glass aquarium. They are unlikely to climb out of their quarters so a cover may not be essential, but it will protect the axolotl from falling prey to a determined cat, and should help to stop potentially harmful chemicals from wafting in. In the interests of cleanliness, and as axolotls require a meat-based diet, it is better not to include any gravel on the floor of their aquarium, to make it easier to keep their environment clean.

Newts will need to be transferred to aquatic surroundings in the springtime for breeding. An aqua-terrarium, divided in two by means of a partition, is ideal for this purpose but check that the top of the partition is smooth and will not damage the newt's skin. There must be easy access in and out of the water by means of rocks which are securely supported, to prevent them falling over and injuring the newts. An undergravel filter will maintain the water quality. Plants set in gravel are essential for spawning purposes.

SETTING UP A VIVARIUM

1 It is important to create a humid yet well ventilated set-up. Cork bark provides an attractive backdrop, with the plant providing cover.

2 Place the plant towards the back of the tank, where it will be possible to disguise the pot more easily, while still allowing you to see the occupants.

3 A plastic water container is very important to allow the vivarium occupants to bathe and, hopefully, spawn. Use bark chips as the substrate.

4 The moss should be kept damp by regular spraying, as the amphibians will often retreat here. Only use dechlorinated water in the vivarium.

FEEDING

◆ LEFT
A whiteworm culture.
Not all forms of livefood
are sold in commercial
quantities. Some have to
be purchased as starter
cultures, which can be
harvested regularly.
Feeding herptiles on
home-produced food
proves to be
inexpensive.

Newts and salamanders eat livefoods but it may be possible to persuade them to eat small goldfish pellets when they are living in water. This is a safer option than other aquatic livefoods available from fish-keeping outlets. Tubifex worms, for example, are likely to introduce unpleasant bacteria into the water, while daphnia, or "water fleas", may bring parasites or even predatory insects with them, and these could attack tadpoles. The best option when providing livefood is to breed your own.

Although daphnia can be cultured in a water tank outdoors, there will be less risk of disease if you use terrestrial livefoods such as whiteworm (*Enchytrae* species). These can be bred at home with little effort, and can be used when these amphibians are both on land or in water. You cannot buy supplies of whiteworm in the same way as other livefoods, such as mealworms, but you can usually acquire starter kits.

To cultivate whiteworms you will need a clean plastic container with a lid, such as an empty margarine tub. Half fill the tub with a peat substitute and then, with a pencil, dab some holes in the peat. The holes should be partly filled with damp bread, which has been moistened in milk and will act as nourishment for the worms. Divide the culture up and cover the worms, placing the lid on top to prevent it drying out too quickly. If kept at a temperature of 20°C (68°F) it should be possible to harvest from the culture after about one month. Lift out the worms with tweezers and drop them into a saucer of dechlorinated water, which will keep them apart from the substrate, and offer them to the amphibians. Whiteworms are a very nutritious food and are especially valuable for young amphibians.

For a supply of uncontaminated aquatic livefood, leave a bucket of water outdoors in the summer. This should attract a variety of gnats and similar creatures to lay their eggs in it, which will soon hatch into larvae. These can then be sieved out with a tea strainer and transferred to the tank. Avoid offering more food than the amphibians will eat or you may find your house becomes invaded by gnats.

Larger salamanders, in particular, require bigger prey, and worms of various types are suitable for this purpose. These are available from livefood suppliers, and represent no danger to the amphibians' health, compared with garden worms.

Species such as fire salamanders may even be persuaded to eat pinkies (dead day-old mice), but since it is the movement of their food which attracts them to it, you will have to offer the mouse by hand. Avoid using forceps, particularly sharp-ended ones, as these can cause injury if the amphibian snatches at its food.

Axolotls are often fed on raw meat but this pollutes the water rapidly, and it soon starts to smell unpleasant. Persuade them to eat other foods, such as mealworms, since these are less of a pollutant, and are cheap enough to keep in good supply.

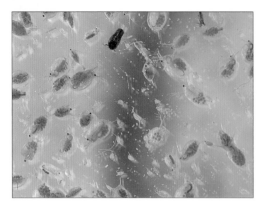

◆ LEFT
Daphnia, also called water fleas because of their shape, are a valuable food for aquatic amphibians. They can be cultured in a pond or large aquarium, and are caught easily with a sieve or fine net.

BREEDING

◆ LEFT
The appearance of
male newts alters
at the start of the
mating season. In
many species, the
male will develop
prominent crests,
which are only
visible at this
time of the year.

Distinguishing between male and female newts and salamanders is the first step towards successful breeding, and this is most easily accomplished in the spring, when the differences between the sexes will be more pronounced. Male newts, for example, will generally become much more colourful at this stage and will often develop prominent crests along their backs. Females swell with eggs and start to look rather stocky, compared to their mates.

Examining them from beneath in a clear container can also be valuable at this time to highlight the difference in the appearance of the cloacal region, which becomes far more swollen in the case of males. Male salamanders often display swellings on the front feet, rather like the nuptial pads seen in frogs and toads.

A range of display behaviour is likely to be seen in the spring, with the male newt following the female closely, often fanning the water with his tail. This releases a scent which encourages her to mate. He releases a packet of spermatozoa, known as a spermatophore, which the female picks up and takes into her cloaca. The eggs are laid in among aquatic vegetation, and after she has done this the female will take no further interest in them. Remove the eggs at this stage, before they hatch, or the tadpoles may be eaten by the adult newts.

Salamanders as a group do show more varied breeding behaviour than newts. Some species, for example, mate directly, and a number display

parental care towards their eggs, with the female staying with them until they hatch. Although most salamanders lay in the water, some will produce their eggs on land. Check on the individual breeding habits of your chosen species.

It is again possible to watch the development of the tadpoles through the eggs. The young hatch with feathery gills which allow them to take oxygen from the water. With eggs of newts being laid over the course of several weeks, it is important to keep the young in groups of similar size to reduce the likelihood of cannibalism. Good water conditions are vital.

Change 25 per cent of the volume of the water in their quarters each week, replacing it with dechlorinated water which has been standing for a day to reach room temperature. Small livefoods are needed to rear the young.

As they start to resemble miniature adults, lower the water level and allow them on to land. A platform is useful, and a damp, mossy substrate is an ideal hiding place for the young amphibians when they first emerge. They can then be offered small terrestrial livefoods, and should grow rapidly. For axolotls there is no need to make these changes, but you must allow them more space as they grow larger in size.

◆ RIGHT
Some newts are more aquatic in terms of their
lifestyles, but all species will return to the water
at the beginning of the breeding season.

GENERAL CARE

Salamanders, in particular, need to be handled with care because their bright coloration is actually a warning sign that they produce toxic skin secretions, which could enter through a cut in your hands and make you feel unwell. It is not a good idea to handle them anyway, however, because you are likely to damage their delicate skin, and this will predispose them to skin infections. A net, as used for aquarium fish, will make it easy to catch them in the water but, on land, wet the net first in the water container, again to protect the amphibian's sensitive skin.

The secretive nature of this group of amphibians may mean that often they are not easily seen, especially when housed in an terrarium rather than an aquatic setting. Even so, you should inspect their quarters carefully each day to ensure that nothing is amiss if you cannot see the amphibians moving around. Try to establish a

✦ ABOVE
Although they like to remain close to water, most amphibians require a largely terrestrial set-up. Different surroundings will often be needed for breeding purposes.

✦ LEFT
Catching a fire salamander with a fish net. Place your hand over the top of the net to prevent the salamander from climbing out and, possibly, falling on the floor.

routine, as far as possible, by feeding them in the evening after spraying their quarters. This is most likely to bring the amphibians out in to the open to seek their food.

When a group are being housed together in the same accommodation, it is important to ensure that they are all receiving an adequate supply of food. If you are feeding them in the water, aim to separate the amphibians as far as possible using a net because, otherwise, there is a possibility that one will seize the limb of another in a feeding frenzy, confusing it with its prey, and could bite it off.

Some species need to be allowed to overwinter at a relatively low temperature if they are to breed in the following spring. Only those which

◆ BELOW
Adding a dechlorinator to water for
amphibians. Products of this type, sold for
fish-keeping purposes, will be necessary. Always
take care to measure out the correct volume.

◆ BELOW
An Alpine newt walks over lichen. Mosses are
often used on the floor of an amphibian set-up
and will only require regular spraying with
water to remain in good condition.

are healthy and well fed should be
allowed to have a period of winter
dormancy for a couple of months.
Reduce the amount of food offered
beforehand so their guts can empty.
A dense layer of moss should be
provided in the vivarium, allowing
them to burrow down into the
substrate of their quarters. It is
preferable to lower the temperature
gradually, rather than plunging them
suddenly into a cold environment.

Overwintering can usually be
accomplished more easily in an
outdoor set-up, which has suitable
areas for hibernation purposes. It is
important that the enclosure here is
escape-proof, and there is an area of
higher ground within so that there
is no risk of heavy wintertime rain
flooding the amphibian's quarters.

In the event of heavy rains, you may
need to bale out the pond at intervals,
to prevent it from overflowing.

In the spring, the amphibians will
gradually emerge from their sleeping
places and should then make their way
back to the water. In the case of newts,
spawning will occur soon after their
return to the pond.

Very little is required in the way
of maintainance for an outdoor
enclosure for newts and salamanders.
The grass can be allowed to grow quite
long although, if you do decide to
cut it back, you must take great care
not to harm the vivarium occupants.
You must also be very careful about
using horticulatural chemicals nearby
in the garden. If these filter through
the soil into the pond water, they
could prove deadly for the amphibians.

INVERTEBRATES

The invertebrates, meaning creatures without backbones, represent the largest group on the planet. They come in many weird and wonderful forms, some of which are highly colourful, whereas others, such as stick insects, blend very effectively into the background. A number are predatory, and can give painful, even fatal, stings and bites, while many live on a vegetarian diet, sometimes having evolved powerful mouthparts for this purpose.

INTRODUCTION

Many people use the terms "insects" and "invertebrates" as if they are the same. In fact, insects are just one of the groups within the invertebrate category. They are distinguished by their three pairs of legs, whereas the arachnids, incorporating spiders and scorpions, have a different body structure with four pairs of legs. Invertebrates are distinguished from all the other groups covered in this book by the lack of a backbone. This has not prevented them from becoming the most numerous category of creatures on the planet, however, colonizing virtually every available habitat. As a group, invertebrates are exceedingly diverse in both lifestyle and appearance and, although they will not become tame in the same sense as many other pets, their behaviour is fascinating and keeping them can be highly rewarding.

◆ LEFT
Invertebrates such as the praying mantis are effective hunters, grabbing their prey with their forelegs.

◆ BELOW LEFT
Invertebrates have evolved to blend with their surroundings as shown by this leaf-mimic katydid from Malaysia.

◆ BELOW RIGHT
Another leaf katydid, from Costa Rica. Note the difference in its appearance.

Some invertebrates, such as leaf-cutter ants, are social by nature, living in tightly structured communities, but the sheer size of such groups means that they are very difficult to accommodate satisfactorily in the home. Others, by contrast, are highly aggressive by nature, and need to be kept on their own. Introducing two praying mantis, for example, is likely to end with one being decapitated.

Tarantulas, one of the most popular group of invertebrate pets today, are also highly aggressive towards each other. They have venom that allows them to overcome their prey, and they may also bite if you try to pick them up unexpectedly. These spiders also have irritating hairs on their bodies, which can stick into the skin or even enter the eyes if you hold them too close to your face. Coupled with the

◆ RIGHT
The ability to use
vegetation for their
camouflage is seen
in a wide range
of invertebrates.
This example is a
leaf-mimic moth.

fact that tarantulas are extremely
delicate creatures by nature – their
bodies can rupture easily as the result
of a fall – you can see why they are
not pets to be handled regularly, but
are better admired from outside their
quarters. Scorpions also possess a
painful and dangerous sting, and
they are not to be recommended as
childrens' pets for this reason.

Stick insects, better known in the
United States and Canada as "walking
sticks", are a much better choice for
children. These creatures are entirely
herbivorous in their feeding habits and
can be handled quite safely, especially
in the case of the larger species,
although some do have protective
spines on their bodies. The only
drawback, perhaps, is that, as with
other invertebrates, the reproductive
rate of stick insects is such that you
will very soon be overrun with eggs.

The prolific nature of these
invertebrates is a reflection of the
fact that, in the wild, they have a very
precarious life and, out of many
hundreds of eggs, just a handful of
the resulting young invertebrates
will themselves survive for long
enough to breed.

The potential for invertebrates
to reproduce rapidly, under suitable
conditions, and build up a population
of plague proportions means that

keeping certain species may be
outlawed in some countries. This is
the case with the giant land snail.

Not all invertebrates live on land.
There are some species that are found
in freshwater ponds and lakes and
even in the sea. These species tend
to be kept less often as pets because
of the difficulties of accommodating

them successfully in the home.
However, some of those that live
partly out of the water, such as various
crabs, are occasionally seen for sale in
larger pet stores. As with any other
pet, so long as you are aware of their
needs and can provide the necessary
habitat, there is no reason why you
should not consider keeping them.

◆ TOP RIGHT
Mantids are
generally coloured
to blend in with
their surroundings,
but their shapes can
differ, as shown by
these Costa Rican
leaf mantids.

◆ LEFT
Leaf insects are
quite commonly
kept. They have
evolved on different
lines compared with
stick insects, but still
rely on their shape
and coloration to
remain concealed.

STICK INSECT AND LEAF INSECT SPECIES

These insects are sometimes described collectively as phasmids. This name comes from the ancient name for a ghost, and refers to the amazing powers of mimicry of these creatures. In the same way that stick insects are named after the tree branches that they resemble, leaf insects get their name from tree and plant leaves. The similarity is such that blowing gently on a stick insect will cause it to rock back and forth, just as a twig would sway in a breeze. Phasmids have a wide distribution around the world, with the greatest concentration being in warmer climates.

INDIAN STICK INSECT

The most commonly kept member of the phasmid group is the Indian or laboratory stick insect (*Carausius morosus*), which grows to a length of about 10 cm (4 in). If you intend to breed your stick insects, there is no need to worry about sexing them – males of this species are extremely rare, and females lay fertile eggs without mating. It is possible to recognize males by the red coloration of their middle body segment, called the thorax. Indian stick insects have a life expectancy of about one year.

◆ LEFT
The Indian stick insect is very easy to cater for in the home, and will almost inevitably produce fertile eggs without mating. The young hatch as miniature adults, growing through a series of moults.

◆ BELOW
Asian stick insects can be maintained successfully like most other species on bramble leaves. The safest way to pick up adults is by placing fingers each side of the body.

GIANT PRICKLY STICK INSECT

A much larger species is the giant prickly stick insect (*Extatosoma tiaratum*), which originates from Australia. Mature females grow up to 20 cm (8 in) long, while males are smaller, at 15 cm (6 in), and less bulky with functional wings, although they rarely fly. Females can be handled easily, but they must have stout

◆ BELOW
A pair of giant prickly stick insects, with the large green female on the right and her smaller partner on the left. The wings of the male are folded along his back.

branches of bramble
to support their
weight. In this
case, it is possible
to distinguish young females by
the presence of spikes on their
abdomen. Once mature, they lay
hundreds of eggs in small numbers,
expelling them with considerable force
from their abdomens.

GIANT SPINY STICK INSECT

Occurring on New Guinea and
neighbouring islands, the giant spiny
stick insect (*Eurycantha calarata*)
differs significantly from the previous
species, since it is terrestrial in its
habits – a fact that must be reflected
in the layout of its accommodation.
A large floor area, rather than height,
is important in this case. Males grow
to about 12.5 cm (5 in) long, being
slightly smaller than females, and can
be distinguished by the presence of a
long spine on the upper part of their
hind legs. In contrast to other species,
giant spiny stick insects will often eat
fresh grass. They must have a shallow
container of drinking water on the
floor of their enclosure. The females
will bury their eggs in the substrate,
with the nymphs, which are miniatures
of the adults but green in colour,
emerging five months later.

PINK-WINGED STICK INSECT

The pink-winged stick insect
(*Sipyloidea sipylus*) is a delicate species
that is able to glide long distances.
The wings, as with other stick insects,
are usually kept furled up, but it is a
good idea to cut off sharp thorns from
bramble that is provided for food, to
reduce the likelihood of damaging the
wings. Adult females are slightly larger

than the males, and
will grow to about 10 cm
(4 in) in length. Rather than
scattering their eggs in their quarters,
they stick them around carefully, with
the small nymphs emerging about
40 days later.

JAVANESE LEAF INSECT

The Javanese leaf insect (*Phyllium
bioculatum*) is a typical example of the
leaf insect group, which should all be
kept at a temperature of 24°C (75°F).
High humidity is essential, and
bramble is used for feeding purposes.

◆ ABOVE
An immature giant
prickly stick insect,
described as a
nymph. Given their
relatively short
lifespan, it is better
to obtain pet stick
insects as nymphs,
although these are
one of the longer-
lived species, with
a life expectancy of
around two years.

◆ LEFT
A leaf insect on
bramble. Their
requirements are
very similar to
those of stick insects
from tropical areas.
A heat pad can be
used to provide
them with warmth.

TARANTULA AND BABOON SPIDER SPECIES

MEXICAN RED-KNEE TARANTULA

The large spiders called tarantulas are found in the warmer parts of the world. The Mexican red-knee tarantula (*Brachypelma smithi*) is the best known of this group. It is recognizable by the orange-red coloration at the top of its legs, which is offset against its predominantly black body colour. The sexes are alike in coloration, but males can be distinguished by the

◆ RIGHT
The Mexican red-knee is a particularly striking tarantula. Young captive-bred spiderlings of this species are readily available, although it will take several years for them to attain maturity. When adult, their bodies measure about 6 cm (2½ in) – about 2.5 cm (1 in) bigger than the other tarantulas shown here.

◆ LEFT
Tarantulas differ in terms of their temperament, although they are not pets to be handled. The Chilean rose has proved to have a relatively placid disposition.

◆ BELOW
Not all tarantulas live on the ground. The pink-toed is an arboreal species, found in tropical forests of South America. Its housing must be designed accordingly.

on account of its attractive pinkish coloration and its relatively docile temperament, which has helped to ensure successful breeding. Males of the species may have slightly larger legs than females when mature. Aim for a relative humidity of about 75 per cent in the terrarium for this tarantula; the temperature should be maintained at around 25°C (77°F).

presence of their palpal bulbs, which look like miniature boxing gloves on the end of the palps near the mouth. It is a burrowing species and this must be reflected in its accommodation, with a suitable retreat being provided.

CHILEAN ROSE TARANTULA

Originating from further south in the Americas, the Chilean rose (*Grammostola cala*) has become a popular species over recent years,

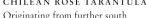

PINK-TOED TARANTULA

The pink-toed tarantula (*Avicularia avicularia*) occurs in the Amazon region of South America, and so it will require a slightly higher temperature and a humidity of about 80 per cent in its quarters. A humid environment is vital to the well-being of these spiders. The pink-toed is also an arboreal species, at home in the treetops rather than burrowing on the ground. A tall, well ventilated enclosure will be needed for these spiders, with branches for climbing purposes. Males are smaller in size than females, and are coloured black overall, apart from the tips of their legs, which are pinkish-white. There is also a yellow-toed tarantula (*Avicularia juruensis*), although this is far less commonly available. It requires similar care.

INDIAN BLACK AND WHITE TARANTULA

There has been increased interest in Asiatic tarantulas over recent years, thanks to their impressive markings. The Indian black and white tarantula (*Poecilotheria regalis*) has become a popular member of the group, in spite of the fact that its sting is more potent than almost any other tarantula. The Indian black and white requires a relative humidity of 75 per cent and a temperature of 25°C (77°F) in its quarters. Breeding these spiders is not especially difficult. Males are smaller, without the females' rounded form.

BABOON SPIDER

These spiders originate from Africa, and have a reputation for being aggressive, rearing up when they feel threatened, and biting if given the opportunity. They can also move very

◆ LEFT
Baboon spiders are of African origin, often occurring in arid grassland areas. Provide water at all times, however, as dehydration can be a major insidious killer of pet tarantulas.

◆ BELOW
The Indian black and white tarantula, and related Asiatic species, have become popular over recent years. They do have an unpleasant bite, and will need to be handled with particular care.

quickly and it is important not to allow them an opportunity to escape while you are attending to them. As with similar species, the baboon spider has a potent venom, and you should avoid handling it. Always wear gloves when handling is required.

Many baboon spiders originate from grassland areas rather than tropical forests, and they do not require high humidity. The substrate can include dried grass, with a water container included. The temperature should be as for other tarantulas.

OTHER INVERTEBRATE SPECIES

♦ BELOW
An emperor scorpion. These invertebrates can
be sexed by viewing from beneath in a clear-
bottomed container. Males have larger pectineal
teeth and grow to 15 cm (6 in) in length.

SCORPIONS

These close relatives of the tarantula
have a painful, if not deadly, sting
on their tails, and they need to be
handled with extreme care. In fact,
these arachnids are best left in their
quarters, with special forceps being
recommended for moving them safely.
Those that are kept as pets are

♦ LEFT
A praying mantis. During courtship, a male is
at risk of being decapitated by his larger female
partner. Feeding her well beforehand can help to
protect him. They reach about 10 cm (4 in) long.

Scorpions often originate from
hot, dry areas of the world but the
imperial is a rainforest species
and must have a warm, humid
environment if it is to thrive. The
substrate in the imperial's quarters
must also be loose, to allow it to
burrow. Retreats, provided by cork
bark, are also important. A secure
ventilated lid over the terrarium is vital
for all species, although lighting is not
important – scorpions are nocturnal
and are most likely to emerge from
their hiding places when the light level
is low. Scorpions feed on invertebrates.

PRAYING MANTIS

Another predatory invertebrate kept
as a pet is the praying mantis (*Mantis*
species). There are a number of

species, and it can often be difficult
to distinguish between them. Their
common name comes from the way in
which they rest, with their front legs
folded as if in prayer. The legs grab at
passing prey at lightening speed, while
the mantis remains immobile, relying
on its camouflage for disguise. Crickets
can be used as a food. Mantids must be
housed on their own because of their
predatory habits. The female has six
segments on the underside of the
abdomen, while the male has eight.

GIANT MILLIPEDES

Giant millipedes belong to the family
Sphaerotheriidae. These creatures can
produce toxic secretions to protect
themselves, which they squirt from
pores on their bodies, and because of

generally larger members
of the group, such as
the imperial scorpion
(*Pandinus
imperator*), which
originates from West
Africa. Their appearance is
impressive because of their large
pincers; large pincers are an indication
that the sting is less potent than that
of scorpions with smaller pincers.

♦ OPPOSITE BOTTOM
Rainbow crabs can be
housed in an aquarium
with a shallow area of
water. Check the salt
concentration needed.

♦ ABOVE
Giant millipedes may look
inoffensive, but they do need
to be handled with care.

this they must be handled with care; it is always preferable to wear gloves when handling them. The tropical millipedes that are popular as pets can grow to over 25 cm (10 in) long. These millipedes are inhabitants of tropical rainforests, and this climate must be reflected in their accommodation. Millipedes feed on vegetable matter.

GIANT LAND SNAIL

Another large species that is widely kept in Europe – but is illegal in the United States and Canada because of fears that it could become established in warmer areas there – is the giant land snail (*Achatina fulica*). This snail is a native of Africa. It can grow to a length of more than 20 cm (8 in), and is easy to cater for, with a heated propagator often being used as accommodation. Assorted vegetable matter will form the basis of the diet for these snails, but they should also be offered cuttlefish bone as an additional source of calcium for their shells. Since they are hermaphrodite, keeping two snails together will invariably result in fertile eggs being laid. The eggs can be found stuck on to the sides of the snails' quarters.

LAND HERMIT CRABS

Various types of crab can be kept as pets, particularly land hermit crabs (*Coenobita clypeatus*), which are found on the sea shoreline rather than in deep water. These crabs need a covered terrarium since they are able to climb well, in spite of the bulk of their shell. Their surroundings must be kept humid with a container of shallow salt water, using sea salt as used in marine aquaria. As they grow, these crabs abandon their shells in search of new ones, leaving them scattered around the floor. Hermit crabs are natural scavengers, and will eat animal rather than vegetable foods; formulated foods are also available. Other crabs may require a more aquatic home, with dilute salt water provided, to mimic their estuarine habitat. The water level should be low to allow them access to dry areas in the tank. A temperature of 25°C (77°F) will be necessary.

HOUSING

Most of the popular invertebrates kept as pets require heated surroundings as they originate from tropical parts of the world. This can be accomplished in various ways, using equipment developed for use in other fields, such as an electric propagator or heat pads under thermostatic control, with the temperature in the vivarium monitored with a thermometer. The shape of the enclosure is a very important feature, and is influenced by the lifestyle of the invertebrate as well as by its size.

The majority of invertebrates are not especially active by nature, often displaying a tendency to remain inert and avoid the attention of predators. In the case of stick insects, which generally live off the ground, a tall vivarium will be the most appropriate for their needs. While smaller nymphs can be housed in temporary accommodation – such as glass jars with ventilated, screw-top lids – they will need to be transferred to permanent surroundings as they grow larger.

Although not aggressive by nature, stick insects will often nibble at the legs of their companions if their quarters become overcrowded. This can, ultimately, have fatal consequences because stick insects rely heavily on their legs to support themselves as they climb around in the branches. In the case of a young nymph, the loss of a leg will not necessarily be catastrophic as it is likely to grow back at the next moult.

A wide selection of acrylic containers, in a range of sizes and

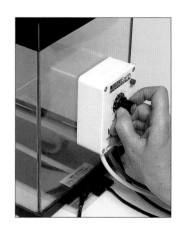

◆ ABOVE
Various lightweight plastic containers can be used both to transport and house a range of herptiles. They are suitable for both aquatic and terrestrial species.

◆ LEFT
Height can be an important consideration in the design of vivaria for terrestrial invertebrates, including some tarantulas. Special sizes can be constructed quite easily.

◆ BELOW
The heat output in a vivarium should always be under thermostatic control. Modern thermostats can be easily adjusted.

◆ BELOW
Some vivaria can incorporate living plants, making them an attractive focal point in the home. Lighting and ventilation are important for successful plant growth.

shapes, can be used for housing invertebrates. The substrate used will depend very much on the occupant and its particular requirements. A moisture-retentive substrate, such as vermiculite, may be useful for cases where high humidity is required. Nevertheless, the vermiculite needs to be damp but not soaked to the extent that stale water accumulates in the substrate. This is not only likely to be harmful for the occupant but can also result in an unpleasant odour being associated with the vivarium.

Many invertebrates will burrow into the substrate and, for these species, a thick layer of bark may be needed in their enclosure. The decor is also important to provide retreats for terrestrial species. In the case of burrowing tarantulas, a plastic flower pot, cut and angled well down in the substrate, is recommended; this will be disguised by the substrate above. Tarantula species that are arboreal will also appreciate retreats rather than being left exposed on the bark. Use cork that is curled, so that the spider can retreat round under the curve of the trunk.

Decor to match the creature's natural environment will enhance the appeal of the vivarium as a focal point in the room. A sandy base, made using sand sold for reptile vivaria, is recommended for land hermit crabs. The sand can mimic a beach and, if decorated with small pieces of driftwood and scattered shells, it will create an interesting view.

You will need to be careful when lighting enclosures for invertebrates, however, because many are shy and will not emerge under these conditions.

With a tungsten bulb in particular, there is also a real possibility that the additional heat will not only cause the vivarium temperature to rise, but will also cause the relative humidity to fall back. This can be very harmful to the occupants. If you are using a

converted aquarium, the best compromise is to choose a fluorescent tube that simulates natural daylight. This will be out of reach of the occupants in a sealed unit, and it is unlikely to affect the temperature in the vivarium.

FEEDING

Invertebrates vary widely in their feeding habits, with some being vegetarian while others are active predators. In most cases, you will need to provide the food yourself as there are very few prepared foods sold commercially for this group of pets. It is therefore important to make adequate provision in advance, particularly for those, such as stick insects, which are quite specific in their feeding habits. Thankfully, most stick insects will eat bramble readily and this can be collected quite easily, even in urban locations, or else it can be cultivated without difficulty.

PREPARING BRAMBLE

To cultivate bramble at home, simply dig up some wild bramble roots and plant them in a suitable container of

soil, keeping them moist. The shoots will grow rapidly, particularly in the spring, and it can be useful to transfer the container directly into the stick insects' quarters once the shoots are well developed. When the insects have eaten the leaves, the plant can be replaced with another and, especially if pruned back, it will soon sprout again.

This method means that it is not necessary to cut fresh bramble every few days, as would otherwise be necessary. This can prove to be difficult during the winter when the leaves often shrivel up and become brown around the edges. If you do provide bramble, place it in a narrow-necked container of water, stuffing the sides with tin foil to prevent the stick insects from falling in and drowning. Similar arrangements work well for leaf insects. Should bramble become impossible to obtain, then privet may make a suitable substitute.

FRUIT AND VEGETABLES

Giant millipedes will prefer to feed on fresh fruit and this can be sprinkled lightly with a herptile vitamin and mineral supplement to improve its nutritional value. Chop fruit into small chunks and provide it in an

✦ ABOVE
A giant millipede and its food. Provide only a small quantity, which the millipede can eat before the food starts to turn mouldy.

✦ LEFT
Crickets taking moisture from the cut surfaces of a carrot. Crickets will often drown in open containers of water.

♦ OPPOSITE TOP
A commercially produced vivarium for stick insects. The bramble serves not just as a food source, but it also allows them to climb. Note the ventilation panel in the roof.

♦ ABOVE
During the winter months, it can be hard to find bramble with fresh leaves. Trim back brown edges to make the green areas more accessible.

♦ ABOVE
Prolong the life of bramble shoots by keeping them in a jar of water. Cover the neck of the jar, to prevent the stick insects from drowning.

live for long in a tarantula's enclosure because they require different conditions. You will quickly learn how much food is needed but start off cautiously and feed according to the invertebrate's appetite.

Since crickets have to be purchased in quantity, it will be useful to have a separate set-up where they can be maintained until required. A typical acrylic set-up, with grass and flour as food, should be provided. It needs to be kept reasonably warm, with a shallow container of water, lined with a sponge to prevent the crickets from drowning, being included.

Mealworms are even easier to look after and will require only a container lined with chicken meal, with a few slices of apple on the surface of the food to provide them with moisture. Keep the worms cool to delay their change into pupae and then mealworm beetles. Once they do become mealworm beetles, they are likely to lay eggs, and these will hatch into another generation of mealworms.

easily accessible container, wedged firmly into the substrate. Be prepared to change the contents every day, before the fruit can turn mouldy.

Giant land snails are far less demanding in terms of their feeding requirements, as they will eat almost anything that is of vegetable origin. Peelings and discarded leaves from household vegetables can therefore be offered to them, with vegetables being

preferable for this purpose. Cabbage is often a favourite. You can even grow suitable foods, such as bean sprouts, at home to guarantee a fresh supply of food every day.

In the case of those invertebrates that prey on others, then crickets or mealworms should be offered, depending on their size. It is important not to provide too much food – for example, crickets will not

PREPARING BRAMBLES IN A BOTTLE

1 Start with a narrow-necked bottle, which will help to keep the stems in a relatively upright position. This will ensure the stems always remain below the water line.

2 Foil is ideal for wrapping around the stems and using to form a cover over the top of the bottle. Beware of catching your fingers on any sharp thorns at this stage.

3 This bramble is now ready to be transferred into the stick insects' quarters. The foil helps to hold the stems in place and prevents the insects from falling into the bottle.

GENERAL CARE

◆ BELOW AND INSET RIGHT
Tarantulas can inflict a painful bite, possessing
fangs on the underside of the body which they
use to overcome their prey. These spiders need
to be handled very carefully.

Invertebrates are pets to be admired
from a distance rather than handled
regularly, not just because of the
toxins produced by some groups,
but also because their bodies are
frail, especially in the case of young
individuals. It is often much cheaper
to start out with young individuals,
particularly in the case of tarantulas
where spiderlings sell for a fraction
of the price of a mature individual.

In the case of some invertebrates,
such as stick insects, you may even
purchase eggs that you can hatch at
home. In terms of handling hatchlings,
though, you should not attempt to
pick them up directly as you can
damage them very easily. Instead, use
a clean paintbrush, as used for picture
painting. It is usually quite easy to
persuade a young stick insect nymph
to step on to the end of the brush so
that you can move it elsewhere.

◆ BELOW
A Mexican blonde tarantula. In spite of their
large size, all tarantulas are quite fragile
creatures and they can be easily killed as the
result of a fall.

With stick insects, it will help to
line the floor of their quarters with
newspaper, with the vessel or pot
containing bramble standing on
top. You can then change the
floor covering very easily, once
or twice a week. Relying on
newspaper rather than a loose
substrate also means that as the stick
insects mature, you will be
able to spot their eggs
more easily.
The accommodation for
tarantulas and scorpions
needs very little
attention. In contrast,
giant land snails need to have
their quarters cleaned out frequently,
and their food replaced each day.
Much depends on the size and the
number of individuals being housed.

The environment outside the
invertebrates' quarters can also be
hazardous for them, even though they
are not roaming here. You must take
particular care not to use any sprays
that could be harmful if particles of
chemicals are wafted on air currents
into their quarters. Fly sprays are
one of the more obvious hazards,
but other preparations, such as flea
treatments for dogs and cats, can be
equally dangerous. Take care to treat
other pets elsewhere.

The moulting period can be
difficult for invertebrates, especially
if they have not been kept in ideal
surroundings. In the case of stick
insects, for example, they need to be
able to hang off branches to their full
length so they can split their skin
easily and wiggle free. This is why a

◆ BELOW
An East African tree millipede. This is an arboreal species and its quarters need to be designed accordingly, with suitable branches being provided for climbing.

◆ BELOW
A pill millipede. As is obvious from this individual, millipedes do not have a thousand legs, as their name suggests. They can be kept quite easily.

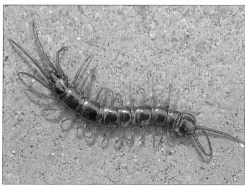

tall container is especially important for stick insects, particularly as they grow bigger.

Increasing the relative humidity in the vivarium as the time for moulting approaches can be helpful. For tarantulas, the most obvious sign of an imminent moult is that the spider loses its appetite, its body colour becomes darker and it may spin a web, called a moulting cradle. The spider will then lie on its back in its web, and the skin will start to split, enabling the tarantula to free itself from its previous skin. At this stage, the new skin will be soft but it soon hardens, and the spider will regain its appetite. Young tarantulas are likely to moult every three months or so, up to the age of about two years old, after which time they can be expected to moult about twice a year.

◆ BELOW LEFT
A large tropical millipede. Beware of holding millipedes in your hands because they may produce toxic skin secretions. These are highly secretive creatures by nature.

◆ BELOW RIGHT
An emperor scorpion. This species relies more on its powerful claws rather than its venom to defend itself. Extreme care is needed when handling any type of scorpion.

BREEDING

A young pink-toed tarantula. Invertebrates, including tarantulas, will usually produce large numbers of offspring, and you will need adequate space for rearing them.

While it is highly unlikely that invertebrates such as crabs will breed successfully in the vivarium, the prolific nature of other species, such as stick insects and tarantulas, means that, potentially, you could be faced with hundreds of offspring. In the case of the Indian stick insect, it is impossible to avoid having eggs laid, even if you have just one individual. This is because of a remarkable phenomenon known as parthenogenesis. Females lay eggs that are effectively clones of themselves, without the need to mate. Some other stick insects also display this feature although, generally, eggs produced as a result of mating have a higher hatchability rate, and the nymphs will hatch more quickly from the eggs.

Stick insect eggs are usually scattered randomly around their quarters and resemble seeds in

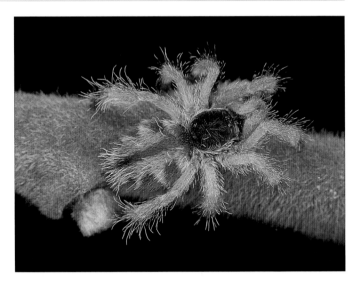

◆ BELOW
Young spiderlings bear a strong resemblance to adults, as shown by this four-month-old tarantula. The young will often have a more feathery appearance than their elders.

appearance. The eggs can be easily collected if newspaper is used to line the floor of their quarters because, unlike the droppings, the eggs will roll off the paper into a container such as a clean margarine tub. Attach a plastic bag with some air holes punched into it at the top, holding it in place with an elastic band. Keep the eggs out of direct sunlight and away from a radiator while they complete their development. It can take anything from a few weeks to a year or more for the eggs to hatch. There is no set period, and the eggs will often hatch over a long period of time. The young nymphs are miniature adults and, as they hatch, they should be transferred carefully to accommodation where bramble is readily accessible to them.

Giant land snails also breed readily, although these do need to mate. Since they have both male and female sex organs in their bodies, keeping two snails together will invariably result in

◆ BELOW
Scorpions display a remarkable degree of
parental care, with the female carrying her
offspring around with her on her back for
the first week or so of their lives.

eggs, which are laid in a jelly-like
substance stuck around their quarters.
The young snails are tiny replicas of
the adults when they hatch, and their
individual shell markings will soon
become apparent.

Breeding tarantulas is a more
involved process but, potentially,
it can result in a large number of
offspring. It is usual to introduce the
male briefly to the female's quarters
for mating purposes. This needs to be
supervised as it could develop into an
aggressive encounter. She may not lay
for several months – if she moults
beforehand, then she will no longer be
fertile, as the seminal pouch where the

sperm is stored will be lost as well.
If mating is successful, the female
produces her eggs in an egg sac of
silk, and she will guard this structure
containing her young ferociously.

The young hatch after an interval
that is likely to extend over nine weeks
or more. They are often whitish but
recognizable as miniature spiders at
this stage. The female must then be
transferred elsewhere as she is likely
to prey on her young. Tiny livefood,
such as wingless fruit flies and
microcrickets, can be used for rearing
the young spiders, which will also
need to be separated from each other
to prevent cannibalism.

The male praying mantis suffers a
grisly fate when he mates – his partner
is likely to rip off his head – but this
does not stop the process. The female
produces an egg sac, and this may
contain as many as 500 young. These
need to be reared in a similar way to
young tarantulas.

Female scorpions are dedicated
parents, with the female giving birth
to live offspring two to eight months
after mating. These are white and
helpless when born, and will be carried
on their mother's back for the first
week of life. Once they are moving
around on their own, separate them
from their mother.

HEALTH CARE

Veterinary knowledge of herptiles and invertebrates has grown significantly over recent years, thanks in part to the increasing popularity of this group of creatures as pets. Those illnesses which are most often seen can frequently be linked to nutritional deficiencies or environmental shortcomings, such as inadequate lighting or incorrect relative humidity in the creature's quarters. The good news is that these factors are easily corrected.

REPTILE HEALTH

It is not always easy to determine when a reptile is sick, but perhaps the most significant indicator is a loss of appetite. This, in turn, could be a reflection of the creature being kept at a sub-optimal temperature, or it might be a sign of bullying by a companion, as often happens with male lizards. Weight loss and lack of interest in its surroundings are other signs that all is not well with a reptile.

Diagnosis of the exact problem will usually require the assistance of an experienced herptile vet and, probably, some laboratory tests as well. In many cases, ill-health in reptiles has a parasitic involvement, with unicellular protozoa in the digestive tract often being responsible for severe, if not fatal, illnesses, particularly in snakes and tortoises. Digestive problems can usually be detected from faecal samples, with appropriate treatment then given. This sampling should also detect any sign of *Salmonella*, which can be acquired by human beings from reptiles.

COMMON DISORDERS
A reptile's loss of appetite may result from mouth rot, which is especially common in tortoises that have recently emerged from hibernation, and also in snakes. In extreme cases, it may be necessary to anaesthetize the reptile, so that the mouth can be cleaned and the treatment given.

◆ ABOVE
Dullness, depression and loss of appetite are common indicators of illness with these species.

◆ ABOVE
Snake mites can easily become established in a vivarium, resulting in progressive debility.

External parasites can also present a problem, with the small size of snake mites making them very difficult to spot. Worse still is the fact that these parasites can survive for months within a vivarium, and so a number of snakes can be infected in sequence. The risk of infection is often far greater in pet stores selling these reptiles than in home vivaria. Provided that the cause is recognized, then a treatment to kill the parasites safely can be obtained from your vet.

Ticks are much larger than snake mites, and they swell up as they penetrate beneath the scales and feed

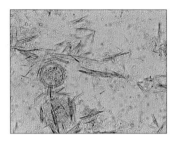

◆ ABOVE
Round unicellular microbes, called protozoa, are parasites commonly found in the intestinal tract of reptiles. They can cause illness or death.

◆ ABOVE
Mouth rot often develops in reptiles which are already debilitated. Urgent treatment is needed to allow the individual to feed normally.

on the snake's body fluid. Ticks
can spread microscopic blood parasites
when feeding in this way. As a result
of their complex life-cycles, ticks
cannot be spread directly from snake
to snake, and they are most likely to
be encountered in recently imported
individuals. Treatment is straightforward. The ticks can be persuaded
to drop off by smothering them with
petroleum jelly, which will block
their breathing hole. Ticks can also
sometimes be a problem in tortoises,
congregating in the soft tissue beneath
the shell.

Fungal infections are most likely
to afflict terrapins. These infections
develop most commonly at the site
of wounds, but they can usually be
treated effectively using veterinary
medication. Nutritional problems
also sometimes afflict terrapins, and
these will cause swollen eyes and
soft shells. Making changes to the
diet – boosting the Vitamin A level
in the case of eye inflammation, and
checking on the Vitamin D3 and
calcium : phosphorus ratio – will be
necessary to ensure a healthy shell.
On occasion, a tortoise may fall and
injure its shell. This may bleed, and
there can be a deeper fracture within.
Repair of this type of injury is
possible, but healing will be slow and
the shell is likely to show signs of
permanent damage.

Snakes and lizards may suffer from
moulting problems, especially when
newly rehomed. In the case of snakes,
the spectacles that cover the eyes
may be retained. If this occurs, it is
important to seek specialist help from
a herptile vet, with careful bathing and
the use of forceps being required to
remove the spectacles.

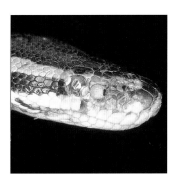

◆ ABOVE
A snake tick anchored to the head. These
parasites swell in size as they feed and there is a
danger they will transmit microbes to the snake.

◆ ABOVE AND INSET
A retained spectacle – the transparent covering
over the eyes – being removed. This problem
occurs when the snake hasn't moulted properly.

TREATING SHELL ROT IN A TORTOISE

1 This is a case of shell rot in a Hermann's
tortoise. The diseased tissue is being removed
while the tortoise is anaesthetized, and then the
repair work can begin.

2 The areas which have had to be removed are
now filled in with calcium hydroxide. A
similar technique can also be used in cases of
shell damage on tortoises, turtles and terrapins.

3 *(right)* In the
final stage of the
shell repair process,
the treated area is
then covered with
a synthetic hoof
material, which will
provide a tough
outer casing.

AMPHIBIAN HEALTH

◆ BELOW
Poor environmental conditions will predispose amphibians to illness. They must be kept in damp surroundings, with the humidity being maintained by regularly spraying with water.

Amphibians are very easy to maintain in good health, and when cases of illness do occur their cause can often be traced back to something that is wrong in the way they are being kept.

FUNGAL INFECTIONS

Since they spend much of their time close to or in water, they are very vulnerable to fungal infections, particularly following an injury to their bodies. This may not even be evident in some cases – rough handling, which strips away the protective covering of mucus on their bodies, can be sufficient to allow fungal microbes to invade.

The signs of a fungal infection of this type will be most apparent when the amphibian is in the water. Depending on the type of fungus, it may create a halo effect at the site of infection, or a more obvious cotton wool- (cotton ball-) type growth. Fungi spread rapidly, especially in the case of an amphibian that is already weakened, and so rapid treatment will be necessary.

A specific anti-fungal cream, available from your vet, which can be applied to the affected area, will

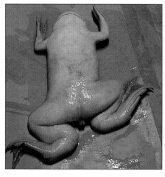

◆ ABOVE
Red leg is a bacterial illness especially common in frogs. It usually creates a reddish, inflamed appearance, and is worse under the hind leg.

be useful for treatment. It will also help if the amphibian is temporarily transferred to a slightly drier environment, although this will not be possible with axolotls, which cannot be transferred out of water.

In such cases, one of the fungal treatments sold for tropical fish, often based on dyes such as methylene blue, may be helpful if added to the water. Simply changing the water in the aquarium can be beneficial as this will reduce the number of fungal organisms present in the water, and will improve your pet's chances of making a recovery.

◆ ABOVE
Jagged rocks and dirty conditions in an aquatic vivarium can damage the sensitive skin of frogs, causing soreness, which can become infected.

◆ ABOVE
An amphibian may have to be confined to a small bath if the treatment involves it being immersed in a medicated solution.

◆ ABOVE
The most common problems associated with amphibians such as this alpine newt are caused by unsuitable housing conditions.

Good ventilation is vital in a vivarium housing tropical species such as this White's tree frog. Otherwise, fungal microbes will thrive in these damp, warm conditions.

Keep a watch on the amphibian's appetite and body condition. A poor appetite, weight loss and duller than normal coloration will often be a sign that your pet is ill.

Breeders may use this approach if they find that amphibian eggs are being killed by a fungus before they can hatch, but this is unusual. Eggs are normally protected by a natural immunity and it is only those that are infertile that will be affected by fungi. Even so, once the young tadpoles have hatched it is a good idea to transfer them to a tank away from the other eggs, to lessen the risk of them developing fungus. Do not place them in newly dechlorinated water, as this will not contain the microscopic food particles present in water that has been allowed to stand and is showing signs of algal growth.

When catching or moving sick amphibians, remember that microbes will be transferred on the net, so that dipping this in a solution of aquarium disinfectant is recommended. Always clean out and disinfect the tank, even if any other amphibians present are unaffected by signs of illness.

RED LEG

It is not just fungal infections which can strike when an amphibian's sensitive skin is damaged. Frogs are especially susceptible to a condition described as "red leg", owing to the signs of reddish inflammation which become evident on their hind limbs. This is usually caused by insanitary surroundings, and a complete water change will serve to protect any other frogs that are sharing the same accommodation. The substrate should also be replaced entirely. The treatment of red leg is difficult, but sometimes the use of antibiotics in a bath for affected individuals can lead to a recovery.

Injuries caused by sharp branches or rocks in your pet amphibian's set-up will often cause skin infections, so be sure the furnishings in the vivarium are safe.

INVERTEBRATE HEALTH

It may seem that there is little that can be done to assist a sick invertebrate but it is possible to correct even life-threatening problems in some species, especially in the case of tarantulas. This is significant because, although most people think that invertebrates only have a very short lifespan, this is not always the case – female tarantulas can live for more than half a century if housed in suitable conditions.

TARANTULAS

The main enemy of tarantulas in the home is dessication. Although a number of these spiders come from arid areas of the world, dew forms at the entrance to their burrows each day, raising the humidity level and providing the spiders with drops of water. It is essential to provide a shallow container of water in the terrarium of all tarantulas.

The biggest threat of injury to tarantulas is incorrect handling.

TREATING DEHYDRATION IN A TARANTULA

1 Dehydration is a major killer of tarantulas. This individual is in poor condition, being shrivelled and emaciated and showing signs of hair loss on the abdomen.

2 In serious cases like this, your vet may be forced to try to rehydrate the spider by administering fluid directly into its body, using a syringe and needle, as shown here.

In the worst cases, this can result in the spider falling to the floor and rupturing its body, which in turn can lead to the seepage of haemolymph, which is the spider's blood. This is a life-threatening situation.

Applying a plaster is not a viable option because of the hairs on the spider's body, but some success at stemming the flow of haemolymph has been claimed from sprinkling the wound with flour and applying rice paper over the damaged area. More permanent sealing of the wound can be achieved with dental cement. Spiders that have been injured in this way may then encounter more difficulty at their subsequent moult, however, and further assistance from the vet may be required at this stage.

◆ ABOVE
Healthy tarantulas have a good covering of hairs on their bodies. Any bald patches, notably over the abdomen, may be an indication of rough handling or old age.

◆ LEFT
Stick insects may sometimes lose a leg as the result of an injury or overcrowding, with a companion nibbling off another's leg. The leg should regrow at the next moult, however.

◆ RIGHT
It can be difficult to provide treatment to some invertebrates, since so little is known about their illnesses. In general, however, millipedes prove to be quite healthy creatures.

Tarantulas sometimes lose their limbs, like stick insects. This is far less serious as the joints of the limbs seal off effectively, rather like when a lizard sheds part of its tail. The limb may regrow at the next moult. The same applies if a tarantula has a bald area on its abdomen, and new hairs will regrow.

On occasion, particularly with recently acquired tarantulas, the spider may encounter difficulties in shedding its skin, and it will need help if it is to survive. The best way to resolve the situation is to prepare a solution of glycerine, made using 15 ml (1 tbsp) added to 150 ml (⅔ cup) of water at room temperature. Then, with a dropper, drizzle this mixture over the spider; take care to avoid the book lungs – the hairless patches on the underside of its body, which enable it to breathe.

The glycerine will soften the spider's exoskeleton so that it should have freed itself several hours later. You need to be extremely careful about trying to interfere directly in these circumstances. Do not prise the old body casing off, because you could very easily damage the new skin beneath, causing a fatal loss of haemolymph. Even when the spider has moulted, do not handle it for two weeks, to avoid the risk of injury.

LAND HERMIT CRABS

These can become dessicated easily, and if you have one that appears to be less active than normal, it could be that it is dehydrated. If this is the case, it will benefit from a series of salt water baths. Normally, a healthy individual will withdraw rapidly into its shell if touched, and you should take note if it does not.

◆ LEFT
Body posture can help to indicate an invertebrate's state of health, as in the case of this giant millipede. Curling up in this way suggests that it is quite healthy.

◆ BELOW
A plump body, bright coloration and a full complement of legs are signs of health in tarantulas. Yet these spiders may appear off-colour just prior to the moult.

FISH

Fish are found in a wide range of aquatic environments, having adapted successfully to live in both fresh and saltwater. They survive in these habitats by very different mechanisms, since in fresh water, there is a risk that vital body salts will pass out of the body into the less concentrated water around them.

As a result, freshwater fish produce a large volume of urine, with salts being absorbed from the kidneys to minimize losses from their bodies. Marine species, however, face the problem of losing fresh water from their bodies into their environment. Because of this their urine is very concentrated, to retain fresh water in their bodies.

All fish generally require a stable environment if they are to thrive, although some species are more resourceful than others. Guppies, for example, are far more adaptable in their needs than fish that live on tropical reefs. This in turn is reflected in their care in aquarium surroundings, with guppies being among the easiest tropical freshwater fish to keep and breed here.

✦ OPPOSITE
The common goldfish is the most widely kept fish in the world. Colourful and hardy, these attractive fish can be kept in the home in an aquarium or outdoors in a pond.

✦ LEFT
A tuxedo rainbow delta guppy – just one of the many highly distinctive and colourful ornamental strains of this free-breeding tropical fish which exist in aquaria today.

GOLDFISH AND OTHER COLDWATER FISH

GOLDFISH

The goldfish, in its many forms, is
the most commonly kept fish in the
world, partly because of its versatility,
as it can be housed in both garden
ponds and indoor aquaria. All goldfish
are descended from dull green carp
living in southern China. The earliest
records of these fish acquiring golden
coloration date back to about AD 400,
after which the local people started to
breed them selectively. Goldfish were
introduced to Europe in the 1600s and
they now exist in a range of varieties.

It is not just their coloration which
has changed, but also their body shape,
as well as the shape of the fins in some
cases. The common goldfish is a sleek,
orange fish, frequently growing to
20 cm (8 in) or more, especially in
pond surroundings. These are hardy
fish, as are the shubunkins which have
a distinctive mottled blue coloration,
broken with black and gold areas. The
London shubunkin has a more angular
tail fin than its Bristol counterpart.
The comet is another sleek variety,
which is often red and white in colour,
with a pointed tail. Its active nature
means that it is more suited to life in
a pond than an aquarium, particularly
in the case of larger individuals.

◆ ABOVE
Long-bodied and sleek, the comet is an active
goldfish originating from the United States.

◆ ABOVE
A red and white lionhead, so-called because of
the fleshy swellings on its head.

◆ ABOVE
A Bristol shubunkin. These attractive fish can
be exhibited, as can most other goldfish varieties.

◆ ABOVE
A chocolate oranda. These goldfish have a hood
on their head and a recognizable dorsal fin.

◆ ABOVE
A butterfly moor. Matt-black coloration serves
to distinguish these goldfish.

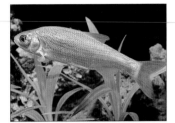  

The so-called fancy goldfish are far more suitable as aquarium pets since they are not especially hardy. They can be recognized by their more corpulent body shape. It is important when buying these goldfish to check that they are swimming properly and are not lying at an abnormal angle in the water, which is indicative of a swim bladder disorder. Examples of fancy goldfish include the moor, which is instantly recognizable by its black coloration. Pearlscales, too, have become more popular over recent years, with raised scales resembling tiny pearls on their bodies.

Changes to the shape of the tail fin have given rise to varieties such as the fantail, while the lionhead actually has no tail on its back. This feature serves to distinguish it from the oranda, with both these types of fancy goldfish having raspberry-like swellings on their heads, called hoods, which develop to their maximum extent over the course of several years. These two fish are bred in a variety of colours, including blue and chocolate, while red-capped orandas with white bodies are also very popular.

Other commonly available coldwater fish, such as the golden orfe (*Leuciscus idus*), are generally more suited to outdoor life in ponds. These are active fish that need well aerated water and thrive best in groups. Blue as well as silver variants are also sometimes available.

KOI

These ornamental carp can grow up to 90 cm (3 ft) in suitable surroundings. They have been kept for centuries as a food source, initially in China, and then in Japan, where the first colour sports occurred in the 19th century. Today, they are no longer eaten.

The term "koi" is an abbreviation of their full name "nishikigoi", which literally means "colourful carp". Koi varieties are described under their native Japanese name, with some varieties such as the ogon being a single colour – golden in this case – whereas others, like the kohaku, are patterned, with this variety being reddish-orange and white.

Although prize-winning koi can sell for huge amounts of money, koi fish at much more reasonable prices are widely available. These will grow very rapidly and they need to be kept in large ponds, equipped with a filtration system to deal with their corresponding high output of waste. They are quite hardy, provided they can overwinter in a deep area of a pond where the water will not freeze.

CARE IN AN AQUARIUM

♦ BELOW
Once established, regular maintenance of the aquarium and some equipment will be required to ensure that everything functions well and the fish remain healthy.

Setting up a suitable aquarium for a goldfish is very straightforward, but it is still a good idea to include a filtration system of some kind, as this will help to maintain the water quality. Although you can use a power filter, you may prefer to use an undergravel filter, which will be less obtrusive. The decision of what type of filter to use will be influenced to some extent by the choice of tank since, in order to be effective, this type of filter needs to cover the entire floor area. Most undergravel filters are, therefore, rectangular in shape, but they can be cut down in size, if necessary, to fit a particular area.

It is important to choose a large aquarium at the outset, so that there will be space for the goldfish as they grow. This will be particularly important if you intend to keep more than one fish together. Do not be tempted by circular designs, modelled on the old-style goldfish bowl, because, although these may be satisfactory for a single small individual, they are soon likely to be outgrown.

If you obtain a glass tank, do not forget to stand this on a level surface, on a sheet of polystyrene, to eliminate any unevenness in the surface which could put pressure on the glass and cause the tank to spring a leak. Lay the filter plate in place and then prepare the gravel. This should be reasonably coarse, with a particle size of about 5 mm (¼ in), as it is between the pieces of gravel that the beneficial bacteria which break down the goldfish's waste will develop. You can use ordinary gravel, but there are a number of more striking alternatives now available, although these need to be chosen

carefully. White gravel will enhance the appearance of most goldfish, even the moor, but avoid blue gravel as this effectively drains the colour from these fish.

Allow on average about 1 kg per 4.5 litres (2¼ lb per imperial gallon), as you need to build up a covering of gravel to a depth of approximately 7.5 cm (3 in) above the undergravel filter. Wash the gravel thoroughly in batches, using a colander, since it will inevitably be dirty even if it is prewashed. Otherwise, if tipped into the tank in this state, an unsightly scum, which will be hard to eliminate, will form on the water once the tank is filled. You may want to include some decorations but, generally, try to leave an uncluttered area where the fish can swim. In terms of planting, you can include some sprigs of Canadian pondweed (*Elodea canadensis*), the ends of which simply need to be weighed down in the gravel, although there is a chance these may be dug up by the fish.

A calibrated watercan will be useful for filling the aquarium as you will

need to add a water conditioner, which will neutralize chlorine-based chemicals present in tapwater that are toxic to fish. These products also help the fish to settle in their new environment, protecting the delicate covering over their gills.

The addition of a biologically active product, containing beneficial bacteria to seed the filter bed, is also recommended. The other piece of equipment which will be required is an air pump of a suitable size for the aquarium. This sits outside the tank and needs to be set up so that water cannot be inadvertently sucked into it once it is operating.

Special goldfish food should be offered to the fish, once they are settled in their quarters. Feed small quantities about three times a day to avoid polluting the tank. On average, about a quarter of the volume of water in the aquarium should be changed every week or so, certainly for the first two months until the undergravel filter is fully established. After this, the interval between water changes can be shifted to once per fortnight.

ASSEMBLING AN AQUARIUM

1 The undergravel filter needs to be fitted first, lying directly on the bottom of the tank, and covering the entire area here. The air uplift, attaching to the filter plate, is on the left.

2 Positioning the rockwork is important not just so that it looks attractive, but also so that it is safe and will not topple over. Some fish will spawn on rocks such as slate.

3 The gravel must be thoroughly washed before being added to the tank, as dirty gravel will cause a scum to form on the surface of the water once the water is added.

4 Bogwood is a feature of some aquaria, especially those containing fish from the Amazon region. It serves to provide hiding places, and these are favoured by catfish in particular.

5 The air feed runs to the air pump. Be sure to fit a non-return valve near the pump outlet, to prevent any risk of water running back into the pump along this tubing.

6 Once the basics are in place, the next stage is to add water. Using a bowl, as shown, will ensure that the gravel is not disturbed when you pour in the water.

7 It is easier to put the plants in place once the tank is filled, but do not connect and switch on the heaterstat while your hands are in the water. This could be dangerous.

8 You can buy collections of plants recommended for aquaria of specific sizes. Always aim to include the smaller plants at the front, with larger ones at the back.

9 Fitting a splash shield reduces the risk of water coming into contact with the electrics, or causing corrosion. It also helps to prevent evaporation of water.

CARE IN A POND

♦ BELOW
An attractive garden pond. This set-up is ideal for goldfish, but koi tend to be kept in a less naturalistic setting, often having a filtration system to keep the water clear.

Setting up an outdoor pond, especially for koi, is likely to be a costly and time-consuming exercise. Even so, the availability of new materials and particularly butyl liners, with a life expectancy of perhaps 50 years or more, means that this task is now considerably easier, and the results more durable than in the past. The major advantage of creating a liner pond is that you can make this to a suitable size for the fish, whereas many of the pre-formed ponds on the market are simply too small, and not deep enough for overwintering fish, where a minimum depth of approximately 1.2 m (4 ft) should be the aim.

If you have a young family, however, great thought needs to be given to the design of the pond: toddlers can drown in just a few inches of water. It may well be better to construct a raised pond, built above ground level, which young children will not be able to fall into without climbing up on top of the structure first. As an additional precaution you can cover the top with a removable mesh-clad framework.

When siting the pond, it is obviously pleasant if it can be easily seen from inside your home, but it must not be overhung by trees, as the leaves are likely to pollute the water when they fall. Tree roots can also potentially damage the liner, even to the extent of causing a leak by

Pond filtration system

perforating it. This can be a problem with some aquatic plants too, which is why those on the floor of the pond are best grown in containers.

When it comes to working out the amount of liner required, there is a very simple formula for this purpose. You need to take twice the maximum depth figure and add this to both the width and length figures, to give you the dimensions needed for the liner. You will also need an underlay to place in the hole under the liner, having removed any protruding sharp stones or roots from this area first. It also helps to bed moulded

Goldfish flakes

Fish pellets

Frozen pond food

ponds down on an underlay of some sort, as they should not move at all. Always check, using a spirit level and a plank of wood, that the shell is level in the ground before starting to fill it with water.

Allow the pond at least a week or two to settle down before adding any fish. This will also allow plants an opportunity to start growing if you construct the pond in the spring. Koi are often destructive towards vegetation, and so only a few waterlilies are usually recommended for their ponds, particularly if the fish are quite large. These fish are usually kept in clear water, and a pond filter, of the appropriate turnover relative to the volume of the pond, will be essential for them.

In the case of goldfish, however, oxygenators such as Canadian pondweed (*Elodea canadensis*) can be included in weighted bundles, along with some marginals which can add colour and interest in the shallower area around the side of the pond. If you want to add a fountain, this will benefit the fish by improving the oxygenation of the water, but keep it away from waterlilies, which will grow better in a part of the pond where the water is calm and still rather than splashing.

The appetites of pond fish can be directly related to the temperature of the water. As this falls with the approach of winter, so a change to an easily digested, low temperature food is recommended. This can be used in the spring as the fish start to eat again after their winter fast. Floating pellets are a good choice, because this will attract the fish up to the surface for their food, and koi in particular can be tamed to feed from the hand.

◆ ABOVE LEFT
Plants are not only decorative in a pond, but can also be beneficial to the fish, providing cover, as here, or spawning localities. Not all waterlilies are hardy.

◆ ABOVE RIGHT
A group of koi being fed by hand. A fish's appetite varies through the year in temperate areas, and special easily digested foods are recommended when the weather turns colder.

◆ BELOW
An outdoor pond offers tremendous scope from a decorative standpoint, depending on the size of your garden.

BREEDING COLDWATER FISH

It can be very difficult to sex these fish easily, particularly when they are small and also when they are out of breeding condition. Mature male goldfish can be distinguished by the tiny white pimples which develop on their gill plates behind the eyes, extending along the adjacent pectoral fins on each side of the body. These should not be confused with the parasitic disease, known as white spot, which covers the entire body. As the time for spawning approaches, so the males will start to chase females relentlessly, which in turn will have become swollen with their spawn.

Mating is likely to occur during the morning, once the early rays of the sun have started to warm the pond water. The eggs will be scattered around the pond, falling down into the weed. This can be very important, because the pond growth helps to conceal the eggs from the fish, which are otherwise likely to eat them, as well as providing protection for the tiny fry when they first hatch. This

can take a week or so, depending on the temperature of the water. Although hundreds of eggs may be produced at a single spawning, only a very small number of young fish are likely to survive in the pond.

If you want to rear a larger number of fish successfully, then you will need to transfer them to an aquarium filled with pond water. This is important because it contains micronutrients, called infusoria, which the young fry will eat as their first food. There are also commercial substitutes available, after which the small fish can be introduced to powdered flake food as they grow larger. Immediately after

♦ RIGHT
Male goldfish in spawning condition can be distinguished by the appearance of white spots, which are evident on the gills and along the edges of the pectoral fins.

hatching, however, they digest the remains of the yolk sacs attached to the undersides of their bodies before they become free-swimming.

Young goldfish tend to be greenish-bronze at first, resembling their wild ancestors in colour; it is only later that they acquire their distinctive golden hue. This change may not occur until the fish are over a year old, and a few individuals may never actually alter in colour during their lifespan, which can be 20 years or more.

Koi are difficult to sex visually until they grow to about 23 cm (9 in) long, by which stage the ovaries of the female fish give their bodies a more rounded appearance. Again, rising water temperature in the spring serves as an important breeding trigger. Rather than allowing the eggs to be scattered so they fall to the bottom of the pond – where they will be hard to collect and are likely to end up in the filtration system – special spawning mops, made from nylon, are dropped into the pond at this stage, with the eggs sticking to them.

These mops are then removed elsewhere, with the young koi swimming freely about 10 days later. The young koi can be reared in aquaria at first, but groups must be divided up to prevent overcrowding as the fish grow bigger. Their potential lifespan is even longer than that of goldfish; koi will frequently live for 80 years or more. When it comes to breeding those koi where bodily markings are significant, there is no guarantee that even a top-quality pair of fish will produce a high percentage of similar offspring. This is what helps to sustain the high prices paid for the best examples of these fish.

♦ ABOVE
A shubunkin male driving the female. She will release her eggs for the male to fertilize. It is an exhausting process for both fish.

♦ LEFT
These shubunkin fry hatched 48 hours after spawning. They absorb the remains of their yolk sacs before swimming free.

TROPICAL FRESHWATER FISH

Many people like to keep a community aquarium, housing a number of different tropical fish together, but it is vital to check at the outset that the fish which you are thinking of buying will be compatible with each other. Some shops operate the so-called "traffic light system", which helps to identify fish that are likely to be aggressive, indicating these on tanks with a red dot. Those which are recommended for community set-ups are indicated in green, and those which may have special requirements are shown in orange.

It is not just a matter of whether the fish will agree well with each other which needs to be considered, though, because different species may have widely differing needs in terms of water chemistry, making them incompatible on this basis. Tetras, for example, living in rivers swollen by rain, require soft, acidic waters, whereas cichlids, from the Rift Valley region in eastern Africa, need hard water to mimic that of their native surroundings. The growth rate of the fish may also be significant in

◆ ABOVE
Tiger barbs should be kept in shoals. They can be disruptive, and must not be mixed with long-finned companions, as they may nip their fins.

◆ BELOW LEFT
The panther catfish is a member of the *Pimelodus* group. These catfish are active and predatory by nature, so they should not be mixed with smaller companions.

◆ BELOW RIGHT
The knife-edge livebearer produces live offspring rather than eggs. These fish will thrive in a community tank.

determining their compatibility. It is sometimes suggested not to house angelfish (*Pterophyllum* species) in a set-up alongside barbs and similar fish. The trailing fins of the angelfish are likely to be nipped by the barbs while they are small, but the rapid growth of angelfish means that they may turn on their tormentors in due course. It is also worth bearing in mind that fish do differ in temperament, to the

♦ BELOW
The lyretail killifish requires soft, slightly acid
water, and will spawn in special spawning mops.
A peat-based substrate in their aquarium is
often recommended.

♦ BELOW
Colour variants now exist in the case of
a number of popular tropical fish. This is
the golden form of rosy barb, which is
distinguishable by its orange coloration.

extent that some individuals may
prove to be more aggressive than
others of the same species.

There is also the possibility that,
although they may be quite amenable
towards different species, they will not
agree well with others of their own
kind. This applies in the case of the
red-tailed black shark (*Labeo bicolor*),
which is a very popular occupant of
the community tank, provided that
only one such fish is kept in the
group. Outbreaks of aggression are
most likely to develop not when
you first set up the aquarium but
subsequently, once the fish are
established and their territorial
instincts are coming into play. Any
overcrowding at this stage will worsen
the situation, and it is not just the
number of the fish which is significant
in this respect but the area of the tank
which they inhabit.

In a community tank, aim to include
a selection of fish which live close to
the surface and on the bottom, as well
as mid-level occupants. This will lessen
the risk of bullying as the fish will
space themselves out naturally.
Including fish, such as catfish, that are
likely to be active after dark rather
than during the daytime, will also help.

Some aquarium fish, especially
those which grow large such as the
oscar (*Astronotus ocellatus*), need to
be housed on their own, partly
because keeping a group together
is impractical in terms of the space
required. Be prepared to invest in
a large aquarium with an efficient
filtration system at the outset. This
is likely to prove cheaper in the long
term than purchasing a series of
aquaria as these fish increase rapidly
in size. Housing such fish will
inevitably work out as being more
expensive than setting up a
community aquarium.

♦ ABOVE
The neon tetra is one of the most popular
tropical fish. It is suitable for a mixed aquarium,
and looks impressive when kept in shoals.

♦ RIGHT
The glowlight tetra requires similar conditions
to the neon. Females have a more rounded body
shape than males and are slightly larger.

A Selection of Tropical Freshwater Fish

In terms of a community aquarium, it is a good idea to group fish which come from the same part of the world so that you will be able to match them in terms of water quality. Fish that originate from the freshwater rivers of the Amazon region are very popular in this respect.

TETRA

There are many different types of tetra suitable for the community aquarium but, undoubtedly, the most colourful is the cardinal tetra (*Paracheirodon axelrodi*). It can be distinguished easily from the brightly coloured neon tetra (*P. innesi*) since the red stripe extends along the full length of the lower side of its body, rather than being confined to the rear. These fish should be kept in shoals, which should also mean that you have pairs for spawning purposes. Sexing is relatively difficult, however, although the females tend to have slightly broader bodies.

◆ ABOVE
A Myer's hatchetfish. The upturned mouth and flat top to the body indicate these fish live close to the surface, with their narrow bodies minimizing water resistance.

◆ BELOW
A corydoras catfish. These catfish are found near the bottom, as suggested by their down-pointing mouths, allowing them to feed here, as well as by their flat underparts.

GUPPY

Guppies (*Poecilia reticulata*) and their relatives, such as platies and swordtails (*Xiphophorus* species), are also popular fish for a community aquarium. They have been bred in a dazzling array of colour varieties, and sexing is quite straightforward since females are larger and duller in coloration than males. The breeding habits of these fish are unusual, in that they are livebearers rather than egg-layers, which increases the chances of at least some offspring surviving in a densely planted aquarium. It may be better to keep them in a group on their own, however, as they often prefer slightly brackish water conditions, particularly the black molly (*P. sphenops*).

CATFISH

Although many catfish grow too large, or are unsuitable for a typical community aquarium, the corydoras group will usually thrive in these surroundings. They are quite small, typically averaging around 7.5 cm (3 in) in size, and will spend most of their time on or near the floor of the

◆ LEFT
Silverlip tetra. The roughly symmetrical upper
and lower curves to the body and the central
position of the mouth indicate that these fish
occupy the middle water level.

(*Brachydanio albolineatus*) are another
social fish from this part of the world.
They display an attractive violet sheen
on their bodies, with males being more
brightly coloured than females.

Members of the group to avoid
include the tinfoil barb (*Barbus
schwanenfeldi*), because it will rapidly
outgrow a community aquarium, and
the tiger barb (*B. tetrazona*), as this
will nip at trailing fins, such as on the
Siamese fighting fish (*Betta splendens*).
These fish belong to the anabantoid
group, also known as bubblenest
breeders because they construct a nest
of bubbles where the female lays her
eggs. Another fish that is suitable for
mixed housing is the dwarf gourami
(*Colisa lalia*). Some gouramis are too
large for a community tank, however,
and may fight with small companions.

◆ BELOW
Catfish with long barbels, like this beautiful
tiger shovelnose, usually have predatory natures
and will not make good aquarium mates.

aquarium, frequently resting on wood
or slate here. Female corydoras can
sometimes be recognized by their
slightly larger size and, for breeding
purposes, it is better to keep them
in smaller groups consisting of a
male and two females. The bronze
corydoras (*Corydoras aeneus*) is one
of the most commonly kept species
in the world.

OTHER SPECIES

There are a number of cyprinids from
Asia which are popular aquarium
occupants, including the rosy barb
(*Barbus conchonius*). These are an
attractive reddish shade overall,
with females being recognizable by
their transparent fins. Pearl danios

SETTING UP
A TANK

✦ BELOW
A wide variety of heating and lighting
equipment, as well as thermometers, are now
available for fish-keeping purposes. Tank size
will often influence your choice.

✦ BOTTOM
A range of the different types of filter is shown
here. In all cases, it is important to seed the
filter bed with beneficial bacteria, which will
break down the fishes' waste.

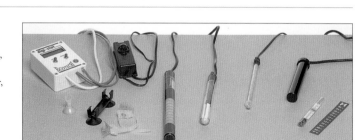

A tropical freshwater tank will need
to be set up in a similar way to that
recommended previously for goldfish,
with an undergravel filter and a layer
of gravel on top. In addition, however,
a heaterstat will be required in order
to maintain the water temperature
at around 25°C (77°F) for the fish.
These differ in their power output,
with about 100 watts being needed in
an environment at room temperature
for every 100 litres (22 imperial
gallons) of water in the tank. You can
work out the volume of the aquarium
easily: multiply the length, depth and
width measurements together in
millimetres, and then divide by 1000
to give a figure in litres, from which
you should subtract approximately
10 per cent to allow for the volume
occupied by decor such as rockwork.

In addition to the undergravel
filter, a small power filter can also be
recommended, partly to assist with the
circulation of water in the tank. It has
a foam cartridge, drawing particulate
matter into the unit. This will then be
trapped in the filter and broken down
by the bacteria which will become
established here. There are also other

types of filter which can be used,
but always check on the cost of the
filtration media as these may work
out to be expensive if they need to
be changed regularly.

Items are available to decorate the
aquarium and these can help to create
an attractive aquascape, especially if
you add a decorative sheet outside
at the back of the aquarium, which
will emphasize the natural setting.
A selection of plants can be grown in
a tropical aquarium, and it is important
to follow a planting scheme to
create the best effect. Leave
an unplanted area at the
front of the aquarium
where the fish can
swim and will be
clearly visible.

You can place a large impressive
plant in the centre, with smaller plants
around the sides. Put these in place
when the tank is half-full, otherwise
they are likely to be displaced as you
add the water. It may be better to keep
them in pots, disguised by the gravel
and the decor in the tank, so that their
roots will not block the undergravel
filter bed. Floating plants can be added
once the tank is full.

If you choose living rather than
plastic plants, then good lighting in
the tank will be essential. Lighting
should be set in a hood so there is
no risk of condensation affecting
the contacts. Lights, which help the
growth of the plants and also enhance
the colour of the fish, are available
from aquatic outlets.

✦ BELOW
The choice of gravel
is important, not
only for the correct
functioning of an
undergravel filter,
but also because it
could affect the
water chemistry.

CLEANING A FILTER

1 When cleaning out a filter, have a bucket to hand, where you can tip out the water. The filter media may sometimes need replacing, so remember to check for this.

2 If possible, it is better to wash out the foam cartridge rather than discarding it, because you will be throwing away the beneficial bacteria here at the same time.

3 Should you replace the foam, then it will take time for a new bacterial population to become established on the new cartridge, and this is likely to affect the filter's efficiency.

4 Only use dechlorinated water, such as that removed from the tank, to wash the parts of the filter, because the chlorine in tapwater will kill the beneficial bacteria.

Suitable safe rockwork, obtainable from an aquatic shop, can be included. It needs to be free from calcium, which will otherwise dissolve in the water and affect the water chemistry. Bogwood is also available, and can be used to add further retreats for the fish. It must be prepared by being soaked in a bucket of water, with the contents being changed regularly to remove the tannins which will leach out of the wood and turn the water a brownish colour. Alternatively, there are synthetic substitutes available, designed to resemble bogwood in appearance.

When you fill the tank pour the water in carefully, preferably on to a saucer placed on the gravel, so that it will cause less disturbance to the substrate. It must be treated with a water conditioner to remove harmful chlorine-based chemicals and help the fish to settle in their new environment. Special bacteria added to the tank to seed the filter bed will also be helpful. These can be bought from good fish suppliers and simply need to be sprinkled into the water.

CHANGING THE WATER IN A FRESHWATER TANK

1 A gravel cleaner plus a bucket will be needed. Fill the tube with dechlorinated water, keeping a finger over each end, and placing one end in the bucket with the other in the aquarium.

2 By releasing your finger from the lower end of the tube last, water will flow into the bucket with the gravel cleaner stirring up the mulm, which is removed in the water.

3 When topping up the aquarium, be sure the water is at the same temperature as that already in the tank, and add a water conditioner, before pouring it in carefully.

GENERAL CARE AND FEEDING

If possible, always allow a new aquarium to settle down for a few days before adding any fish. This will give you an opportunity to monitor the temperature of the water, ensuring that the heating system is working correctly (a digital thermometer is usually attached to the outside of the tank for this purpose).

SETTLING IN

When you acquire the fish, take them home as quickly as possible, and allow the bags in which they have travelled to float on the surface of the aquarium water for 15 minutes, to allow the temperature to rise again. This will make it less stressful for the fish when you release them into their new home.

It is not a good idea simply to pour the fish and water in the bags into the aquarium, as this can introduce parasites, such as white spot, which may be present in the bag water. Instead, net the fish from the bags

and transfer them directly into the aquarium, disposing of the bag water. Nets in a range of sizes are available from aquatic stores. When using a net, scoop the fish up from beneath, as this is usually the easiest way to catch them.

As a precaution, place your hand over the top of the net to prevent the fish jumping out, before lowering the net back into the water. It will be easier and safer to catch the fish individually. When releasing them

Flaked food

Basic tropical flake

Floating green pellets

Plant diet

Carnivore flake

Floating red pellets

into the aquarium, allow them to find their own way out of the net. Some, such as loaches can have spines which may occasionally catch in the mesh. They will usually free themselves easily by wriggling in the water, but you can help by inverting the net so that the fish sinks out of it. Avoid handling fish directly, certainly with dry hands, because you may damage the mucus covering their bodies.

Keep the lights off at first and allow the fish to settle overnight. You can then start feeding them the next day.

SUITABLE FOODS

A wide range of commercial diets are now produced for tropical fish, with specialist foods, such as catfish pellets, available for specific varieties. Pelleted foods sink to the bottom of the tank, whereas flake foods float on the surface, which makes them especially valuable for surface-feeding fish.

Although these foods will keep the fish in excellent health, it does help to vary their diet. The provision of livefoods will help to trigger breeding behaviour. Although aquatic livefoods such as tubifex worms can be provided, there is a risk that they will introduce disease. It is safer to feed livefoods such as tubifex in a

◆ RIGHT
Frozen and freeze-dried foods are a safe and convenient way to feed livefoods.

◆ TOP LEFT
Catfish often feed at the bottom of the tank, and are regarded as scavengers for this reason.

◆ TOP RIGHT
Corydoras can be given catfish pellets, which sink readily to the floor of the aquarium.

◆ ABOVE
Beware of wasteful overfeeding as decomposing food can affect the fish's health badly.

freeze-dried state; food prepared in this way can also be stored for longer. Alternatively, you can purchase frozen fresh livefoods, which should be defrosted before being fed to the fish. Never overfeed with this food because it will quickly decay in the aquarium if left uneaten.

If you need to be away from home, there are slow-release food blocks that can be left in the aquarium without polluting the water. If you will be away for long, it is better to arrange for someone to check the aquarium daily, in case the fish fall ill or the equipment fails in your absence.

Freeze-dried bloodworms (*top*) and tubifex worms (*below*).

Frozen food

491

BREEDING

♦ BELOW
Distinguishing between the sexes is easier
in some fish than others. Male guppies, for
example, are more colourful and smaller in
size than females.

One of the fascinations of keeping
tropical fish is the possibility of being
able to breed them successfully in
the home aquarium. Fish will display
a remarkable range of breeding
behaviour and, although many species
simply lay large numbers of eggs and
take no further interest in them – even
eating them in some cases – others
display remarkable parental concern,
brooding the eggs in their mouth and
providing a refuge here for the young
fish once they hatch.

Perhaps not surprisingly, it is the
livebearers such as the guppy which
generally prove the easiest to breed
successfully in aquarium surroundings.
The eggs, in this case, are retained
within the body of the female fish,
and develop up to the point of
hatching, with the young fish bursting
out of their egg cases just as they
emerge from their mother's body.
Unfortunately, they are at risk of
being cannibalized by larger fish in the
aquarium, and it will be essential for

the aquarium to be densely planted
if the young fish are to survive the
critical early weeks of life.

The other alternative is to move
the pregnant female into a separate
tank, housing her in what is known
as a breeding trap. This will keep her
confined while her young can swim

off into an annexed tank. Once she
has produced her brood, the female
can then be returned to the main tank,
leaving the young to be reared on their
own. Livebearers generally produce
fewer offspring than egglayers, with
a typical guppy brood consisting of
about 100 young fish.

♦ ABOVE
The anal fin of livebearers is modified into
a copulatory organ, called the gonopodium,
which helps to differentiate the sexes.

♦ LEFT
Selective breeding has resulted in stunning
strains of livebearers, especially guppies.
These fish are blonde cobra guppies.

These may be guarded by the adult
fish for a time but, ultimately, it will
be necessary to remove the eggs so
they can be hatched elsewhere.

Hatching typically only takes a
day or two, and the young fish will
then rest for a few days, absorbing
the remains of their yolk sacs before
they start to swim freely around the
aquarium. A special fry food intended
for the young of egg-laying species
can then be offered to them, followed
by larger food such as brine shrimp as
they grow older. A gentle foam filter
will be important to keep the water in
good condition, with regular partial
water changes, along with the use of
a water conditioner, which at this stage
is necessary for the well-being of
the young fish. They will need to be
separated into smaller groups as they
grow larger, to prevent overcrowding.

◆ BELOW
Some fish allow their young to dart inside
their mouths if danger threatens, as shown
by this golden Mozambique mouthbrooder.

Sexing livebearers is usually very
straightforward, because males are
invariably smaller and often more
colourful than females. If possible,
choose the biggest females on offer,
because they will produce the largest
number of offspring, but if you are
particularly interested in breeding
your own guppies, for example, you
will need to start out with young
females. This is because these fish
only need to mate once in order to
remain fertile for their entire lives.

It can be harder to distinguish
between the sexes in the case of
egg-laying fish, but the differences
often become clearer as the time for
spawning approaches. Males often
become more colourful, while females
swell with spawn at this stage. A
separate spawning tank will give the
greatest likelihood of success, with
the adult fish being transferred back
to the main aquarium once they have
finished spawning.

The design of the spawning set-up
depends on the fish themselves.
A stack of marbles used as a floor
covering will allow the eggs to fall
down between them where they
will be out of reach of the fish.
Alternatively, plastic mesh of the
appropriate size, draped over the sides
of the tank and trailing into the water,
with the edges held in place with
masking tape, can be used to protect
the eggs as they are laid. Some
fish, such as catfish, will spawn on
rockwork and other tank decor.

MARINE FISH

Setting up a marine aquarium is more complex and costly than most freshwater aquaria but, thanks to modern technology, it is quite straightforward to maintain fish in these surroundings. Most marine aquaria feature coral reef fish from the warmer parts of the world, such as the Red Sea and the Caribbean. These are often brightly coloured and sometimes bizarrely shaped, which adds to their appeal but, again, it is important to ensure that they are compatible, because some can prove to be aggressive.

ANEMONES

The anemone fish, also called clown fish because of their appearance, are one of the easier groups to care for in a marine aquarium, and they can also be bred successfully. The coloration of anemone fish can vary – there are a number of similar species which are mainly orange with white stripes, while others, such as the chocolate or yellow-tailed anemone fish (*Amphiprion clarkii*), are a darker shade. These fish have a close relationship with the Radianthus group of sea anemones, and it is important to include one of these

◆ ABOVE
A regal tang swims past a fanworm. Keeping invertebrates alongside fish in the aquarium can be difficult because they are likely to be eaten.

◆ ABOVE
A striking orange anemone fish. In this case, the fish will benefit from being housed with a sea anemone, with which they normally associate in the wild.

◆ LEFT
A yellowhead wrasse. Some wrasses change dramatically in appearance from juveniles to adults.

invertebrates alongside them. The fish will retreat within the stinging tentacles of the invertebrate for protection if danger threatens.

The damsels are closely related to anemone fish. They are predominantly blue in colour and relatively hardy, and they are often recommended for introducing to a marine aquarium in the early stages. It is not easy to sex them, and take care not to overcrowd them because males, especially, are territorial by nature.

TANGS AND SURGEONS

These fish, so-called because of the sharp spines which can be raised on each side of the base of the tail, have a flattened, yet tall, body shape. They are often beautifully coloured but they can be aggressive towards each other, and it may be better to house them separately. The yellow tang (*Zebrasoma flavescens*) can be kept in a small group in a large aquarium, but the powder blue surgeon (*Acanthurus leucosternon*), which can potentially

◆ RIGHT
A black patch
trigger. Active and
solitary by nature,
these fish should not
be mixed with others
of their kind in an
aquarium set-up.

grow to 25 cm (10 in) long, is far
less social. These fish are primarily
vegetarian in their feeding habits,
browsing on marine algae and
vegetable foods, although young
individuals may also eat livefoods.

TRIGGER FISH

This is another boldly-coloured group
which reaches a similar size to tangs
and surgeons. Trigger fish have powerful jaws and must not be housed with
marine invertebrates, which they will
eat in the wild. The clown trigger fish
(*Balistoides conspicillum*), with its bold
white spots and mainly brown and

yellow body colour, is popular, as is
the Picasso trigger (*Rhinecanthus
aculeatus*), with its markings and
coloration recalling the artist's work.

OTHER SPECIES

Puffer fish have similar feeding habits
to trigger fish, and while some species
will live in brackish water, inhabiting
estuaries in the wild, others live in the
ocean. Their bodies are often covered
in spines. Other fish with a similar
compact body shape include box fish,
which can be dangerous if stressed as
they can release a toxin into the water
which poisons the other inhabitants.

One of the most popular members
of this group is the long-horned cow
fish (*Lactoria cornuta*), with bony
projections on its head that resemble
horns. Their slow swimming style
means that they may not be able to
keep up with faster tankmates when
obtaining food, so check that they
receive their share.

Avoid keeping the cleaner wrasse
(*Labroides dimidiatus*) with puffer fish
because it may harass them, causing
them to release their deadly toxin.
Wrasses, in general, are colourful fish
and are relatively easy to maintain in
a tropical marine aquarium.

One of the most appealing of all
tank occupants is the seahorse, with
its unique breeding habits. Males
brood their young in a pouch on the
front of their bodies. Seahorses feed
mainly on live brine shrimps. Their
slow, inoffensive nature means that
they are best housed as part of a
mainly invertebrate set-up.

◆ ABOVE
A seahorse, revealing its ability to merge into
its background, anchors on to coral here.

◆ RIGHT
A yellow dogface puffer, showing its powerful
jaws. Its teeth can give a painful nip.

SETTING UP A MARINE TANK

It is vital that all equipment used in a marine aquarium is made of glass or plastic, rather than metal, which is likely to be corroded by the salt water in the tank.

◆ ABOVE
Correct lighting is very important for the well-being of the inhabitants of a marine aquarium, especially where anemones are present.

TANK DECOR

In contrast to freshwater set-ups, a marine tank looks rather bare. An undergravel filtration system is to be recommended, however, but with a thick layer of cockleshell serving as the filter bed, often with a covering of coral sand on top. Suitable decor to provide retreats for the fish will again be required, and these can support a range of invertebrates in tanks where they will not be harmed by the fish. It is often recommended to add "living rock" to a marine aquarium, consisting of rockwork which features a range of established invertebrates. This, too, should only be put in place once the system is running properly.

When planning the aquarium, ensure that you have a good view of the fish, with decorations being concentrated towards the back and around the sides of the tank. Aside from living rock, you can incorporate tufa rock which, with its loose structure, provides plenty of nooks and crannies where small invertebrates can establish themselves. Check that the rocks will not affect the pH reading of the water, which should be on the alkaline side of the scale, between 8.0 and 8.4.

WATER

Once the decor is in place, you can fill the tank with water. Only use water from the cold supply to avoid the risk of copper being introduced to the aquarium, as this can be toxic, especially to invertebrates. Add a set volume of water to a plastic bucket before stirring in the recommended quantity of sea salt, bought from specialist suppliers, and ensure that the salt dissolves completely before pouring the solution into the tank.

Once the tank is full, switch on the air pump, to ensure that the salt has dissolved, because this will assist in circulating the water, as well as the heating system. Check on the concentration of salts in the water by measuring the specific gravity figure with a hydrometer. This needs to be set against the water temperature to give a reading; the temperature needs to rise to approximately 25°C (77°F). The reading should be approximately 1.023, but it may take several days to stabilize when the tank is first set up. This is why it is important not to add fish to a marine aquarium immediately, but to allow the system time to settle down for perhaps a week beforehand.

LIGHTING

If you are including invertebrates such as corals and sea anemones, the lighting above the tank will be very important. These invertebrates often have living algae present in their bodies, and they will only thrive if there is adequate light in order to photosynthesize and produce their own nutrients. Special high intensity lights are available from aquatic stores for this purpose – try to locate a specialist fish supplier for the best selection – and these will need to be suspended over the water. Their light output, for maximum benefit to the invertebrates, should be towards the blue end of the light spectrum.

◆ LEFT
Coral sand (far left) is the favoured substrate for marine aquaria, but coarser crushed tufa rock (left) may be used as a base. The coral sand can then be added over a gravel tidy to create the impression of a sandy base.

SETTING UP A MARINE TANK

1 Fitting a decorative back sheet will greatly enhance the overall natural effect of the finished tank. These seets are obtainable in various lengths and designs to suit different tanks.

2 The undergravel filter must cover the entire base of the floor of the tank if it is to function effectively. These can be purchased to fit various sizes of aquarium and can be cut if necessary.

3 The substrate chosen, which in this case is coral sand, should then be tipped in to the tank and spread out evenly over the filter, where it will serve as the filter bed.

4 Choose suitable rocks to decorate the tank and provide hiding places for the fish. Ensure that these are chemically safe, like tufa rock, and cannot be dislodged because this could have catastrophic results.

5 You can infill between the rockwork with additional substrate if required. Plants are not a feature of marine tanks, so the decor may appear to be rather sparse, although you will be able to see the fish more clearly.

6 If you want to add extra colour and interest in the tank, then it is possible to obtain items such as pieces of coral for this purpose. These should be cleaned as necessary beforehand.

FEEDING AND GENERAL CARE

Your marine aquarium will need occasional maintenance to ensure the welfare of the fish, but as long as the set-up is adequate and a good care routine is established, you should not encounter many problems.

◆ LEFT AND RIGHT
Living freshwater plants will not survive in marine aquaria, but plastic substitutes can be used if required.

◆ BELOW
Air pumps and related equipment are important for the successful functioning of the marine aquarium.

MARINE DIETS

The range of specialist foods now available makes feeding marine fish straightforward. Formulated foods are available for some marine invertebrates. It is important that the food matches the dietary needs of your fish. You may need to use different types if you have vegetarian and more omnivorous species sharing the tank.

Feeding small quantities, several times a day, is recommended to prevent food being wasted and polluting the water. In some cases, as with seahorses, you will need to set up a brine shrimp hatchery to maintain a constant supply of food. Brine shrimp are obtainable in the form of eggs, which are then hatched in a well aerated aquarium of heated water.

WATER CONDITION

It takes time for the filtration system to reach maximum efficiency, so restrict the number of fish for the first

◆ LEFT
Visiting an aquatic outlet specializing in marine fish and invertebrates is the best way to obtain suitable decor for your aquarium.

◆ ABOVE
A selection of processed foods now available for marine fish from fish-keeping stores.

◆ LEFT
A marine cleaner shrimp. These small invertebrates can be added to the tank.

two months to nitrite-tolerant species.
This is because the level of nitrite
may rise higher at this stage, until the
bacteria are present to convert this
chemical to nitrate as part of the
nitrogen cycle. If you overfeed the
fish, then the level of pollution
caused by the breakdown of the
uneaten food will rise as well.

Since a coral reef is such a stable
environment, marine fish from these
areas of the world must be kept in
similar water conditions. Partly as
a result of the heat of the lighting,
however, water will evaporate from
the tank, leaving the salt behind and

therefore increasing its concentration.
Regular hydrometer checks are very
important, with dechlorinated water
being added to the tank to correct the
concentration as necessary.

WATER TESTING
Checks on other aspects of water
chemistry, such as the nitrite level
and pH, will also be required. Use a
pipette to extract water samples from
the aquarium. Using a test kit, you
can compare the colour change in
your water sample to an accompanying
chart to determine the result. Should
the pH fall below 8.0, then you will

need to replace a quarter of the
volume of water, checking the
specific gravity as well.

The nitrite level will give a good
indication of the efficiency of the
filtration system, and a filter
maturation product is helpful for this
purpose. It will peak at a figure of
about 15 parts per million (ppm) and
should then fall back to zero to
confirm that the chemical is being
converted to nitrate. Watch the fish
first introduced to the tank, as they
will be vulnerable to developing signs
of the parasitic illness known as velvet
disease, which may be triggered by
relatively high nitrite levels.

BREEDING
The likelihood of breeding marine
species within an aquarium is less than
with tropical freshwater species, but
a range of species, from clown fish
to seahorses, are now being spawned
increasingly successfully. There are
recommendations for each species –
an increase in the duration of lighting
can help with clown fish, for example.

USING A WATER TEST KIT

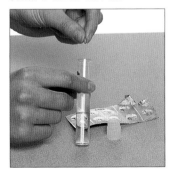

1 Test kits of this type are easy to use and
reliable, giving trustworthy readings of water
chemistry. The first step usually entails adding
water and then the reagent.

2 Place the cap on the tube, and then wait for
the reaction to take place. You may have to
shake the tube several times, turning it up and
down, to mix the solution.

3 In most cases, the result is easily read by
comparing the colour of the solution in
the tube with that on the accompanying chart.
Regular checks are advisable.

HEALTH CARE

Since fish are normally housed in groups rather than individually, it is important to transfer any sick individual to separate quarters with a view to safeguarding the health of the other fish as far as possible. Effective treatment for many fish ailments can be obtained from aquatic and specialist fish-keeping stores. These products can be used at home, but be sure to use them strictly in accordance with the manufacturer's instructions.

FISH HEALTH

♦ BELOW
A typical tank set-up which can be used for treating sick fish. Note the bare base to the tank.

Many of the common diseases that affect fish can be traced back to poor water quality, which leaves them vulnerable to developing infections.

Recently acquired fish are the most at risk, particularly if they have suffered any damage to their scales or fins during the move, as this will make it easier for fungi and other harmful microbes to penetrate the body. Since it is possible to introduce diseases into the established aquarium when new fish are added (for example, if the water in their previous tank was contaminated), it is worthwhile using an isolation tank for a couple of weeks to check the new arrivals are in good health and feeding well. Many of the formulated fish foods now available contain Vitamin C, and this may help to boost the immune system of the fish at this stage.

♦ BELOW
A typical tank set-up which can be used for treating sick fish. Note the bare base to the tank.

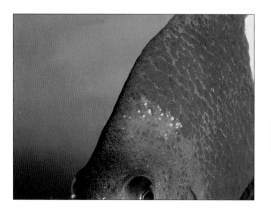

♦ BELOW LEFT
If fish are not isolated before being introduced to the aquarium, they can introduce parasites such as white spot, which will quickly affect other fish and will be harder to control.

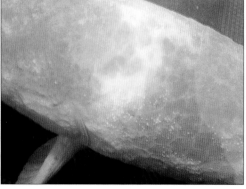

♦ BELOW RIGHT
Another case of white spot, this time of the freshwater variety, in a koi. Diseases in pond fish are hard to spot until they are well-advanced – by which time it could be too late.

◆ A B O V E
A very severe case of fungus smothering a black moor goldfish. Fungus in fish is often linked to the more superficial injuries.

◆ A B O V E
Fin rot which has spread from the tail up the caudal peduncle of a young koi. Poor water conditions often result in this type of infection.

An isolation tank can be converted easily into a treatment tank, should a fish fall ill. A sick fish should be removed at the earliest opportunity from the main aquarium to avoid infecting the others and to improve its chances of recovery. Signs of illness will vary according to the specific condition but loss of colour and appetite are typical, along with a difficulty in swimming.

In the case of many parasitic diseases there may be obvious signs. Fish leeches and anchor worms stick to the fish's body, often causing irritation so that the fish rubs against rockwork. They should not be pulled off directly from the body because this increases the likelihood that the resulting wound will be infected by fungus. These particular parasites are especially common in coldwater fish.

The parasite commonly known as white spot or "ich" (as a result of its scientific name, *Ichthyophthirius multifiliis*) can strike any fish, and spreads very rapidly within an aquarium, thanks to the fact that each individual white spot can contain thousands of the microscopic tomites which are released into the water of the aquarium or pond. These are the intermediate stage in the life-cycle, so removing a fish at this stage should

lessen the likelihood of the infection spreading. Treatments can be used to kill off the free-swimming stage in the life-cycle before the tomites are able to bore into the fish's body.

A similar parasite encountered in marine fish is Oodinium, which causes velvet disease. Outbreaks are often precipitated in this case by a high level of nitrite in the aquarium. If left untreated, the fish will become weak and succumb to fungus, particularly in the case of freshwater species, with the fungal spores being ever-present in the water. Under normal circumstances, the fish will have sufficient resistance to fight the infection, but beware of those which may have suffered fin damage – for example, coldwater fish

in ponds outdoors – for their immune system will not function as well during spells of cold weather.

Signs of an infection of this type depend not only on the part of the body affected, but also the type of fungus. There may be a halo-like effect in some cases, or the fungal growth may appear like strands of cotton wool (cotton balls). Treatment should be carried out in a separate tank, using a proprietary remedy. It is important to use a sponge filter rather than a box-type design, as any carbon here may inactivate the remedy. It is also vital to take care when treating fish in tanks containing invertebrates, as copper-based remedies may assist the fish but are likely to kill their companions.

◆ L E F T
The cause of some parasitic illnesses in fish can be clearly seen, such as anchor worm, which is affecting this goldfish. Always try to check new fish for such parasites.

COMMON ILLNESSES

DROPSY

It is not always possible to treat fish ailments successfully, and the illness known as dropsy is particularly hard to counter. It is often seen in goldfish, with infected individuals suffering from a swollen abdomen which causes them to have difficulty in swimming. Not all cases seem to have infectious origins, but affected fish lose their appetites and, in the case of infectious dropsy, death will follow rapidly. Dropsy is often the result of a bacterial disease, although the illness does not seem to be highly infectious, and it rarely reaches epidemic proportions.

PISCINE TUBERCULOSIS

This is probably the most serious bacterial illness encountered in fish, and it can be spread to people. There are no clear-cut symptoms, but bulging eyes, loss of weight and widespread mortality in a tank can

◆ LEFT
The raised scales seen in the case of this ten-year-old koi are indicative of dropsy, which is often known as "pine cone disease" because of its appearance. The cause in this case was a liver tumour.

be indicative of an outbreak, which can only be confirmed by an autopsy. As a general precautionary measure, it is always sensible to wear rubber gloves when attending to the fish's needs, and this will give effective protection against piscine TB as well. This disease causes an unpleasant skin infection in human beings, usually on the hands where they have been in the water, although it can be treated.

OTHER DISORDERS

Bulging eyes are a feature of some fish, and are often associated with some varieties of goldfish, such as the moor. In other cases, bulging eyes can be a sign of illness or injury, particularly if just one eye is affected. There is usually nothing that can be done to correct a problem of this type, and it is often fatal. The same applies in the case of a swim bladder disorder, which will cause the fish to have difficulty in swimming properly. Fancy goldfish are particularly vulnerable to this condition, which causes them to lose their buoyancy. In the case of tropical fish, swim bladder disorder is often linked with old age.

A less serious disorder, however, is constipation. This is often identified by a long strand of droppings, rather like a length of cotton thread, trailing down from the underside of the fish. Constipation in fish may be related to the feeding of dry food only. Offering a more varied diet, and including livefoods in a suitable form for the type of fish, should help to resolve the problem naturally, as may the addition of fresh greenstuff to the diet of vegetarian species.

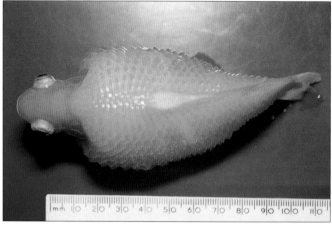

◆ ABOVE
A goldfish displaying signs of dropsy and pop-eye (exophthalmos), which causes the eyes to bulge abnormally. The symptoms in this case were the result of kidney disease.

SUDDEN DEATH

One of the most worrying situations is when most, if not all, of the tank occupants are suddenly found dead. This may be due to an environmental factor rather than an outbreak of illness. Check the water chemistry for signs of a sudden shift in the chemical concentration. In any event, change up to a quarter of the volume of water without delay to stabilize the condition of any remaining fish.

Check the functioning of the tank equipment, as it could be that the filtration system has failed or the heaterstat has stopped working. The heater may have continued to warm the water, and this should be obvious by checking the thermometer. A drop in the water temperature, perhaps as the result of a power cut, is far less severe. Once the power is switched back on, the water temperature will gradually rise again.

Poisoning from a source outside the tank is another possibility. A number of common household products, including insecticides which may be sprayed on to houseplants, and flea preparations for other pets, can be deadly for fish. These could be drawn into the water via the air pump. Never be tempted to use such products in a part of the home, or next to a pond, where they could indirectly cause harm to the fish.

◆ LEFT
Some fish are more susceptible to certain ailments than others. Discus are especially at risk from the parasitic illness known as "hole in the head" disease.

◆ ABOVE
Ulcers caused by bacterial infections can be common in young koi. Look for such signs prior to purchasing these fish, checking both sides of their bodies.

GLOSSARY

Abscess collection of pus forming a painful swelling.

Acquired disorder condition or illness that develops after birth.

Acute condition occurring suddenly and rapidly. *See also* Chronic.

Agamids group of lizards, none of which are represented in the Americas.

Agouti a coat pattern seen in mammals, where each individual hair is banded with two or three colours.

Albino lack of pigment melanin, causing white fur and pink eyes.

Amphibian creatures dependent on water for breeding purposes. Most lay eggs here, which hatch into larvae known as tadpoles.

Amplexus mating grip adopted by frogs and toads, when the male holds on to the female using his front legs.

Anurans collective name for tail-less amphibians: frogs and toads.

Aqua-terrarium housing provided for herptiles or invertebrates which includes both water and dry land.

Bay characteristic bark of a hound.

Bird characterized by the presence of feathers on the body; reproduces by means of hard-shelled eggs.

Bitch female dog.

Boar male guinea pig.

Breed domestic variant, usually a colour form, created by selective breeding.

Buck male rabbit.

Caecum large, blind-ending sac at the junction of the small and large intestines. Significant in rodents and rabbits; contains bacteria and protozoa essential for the digestive process.

Calling the noise a female cat makes when she is ready to mate.

Cannibalistic tendency of some creatures, especially herptiles, fish and invertebrates, to prey on their own kind.

Carapace top half of the chelonian shell.

Carnivorous feeding on animal matter.

Castrate to surgically remove the male reproductive organs.

Caviomorph a group of rodents; confined to the Americas. Includes guinea pigs and chinchillas.

Cavy alternative name for a guinea pig, derived from the generic name of *Cavia*.

Chelonian collective name for tortoises, terrapins and turtles.

Cold-blooded unable to regulate the internal body temperature independently of the environment. A feature of lower vertebrates such as herptiles.

Crop part of the avian digestive tract at the base of the neck where food is stored before being passed down the digestive system.

Cubs name given to the young of certain species, including rats.

Dam mother of a litter of puppies.

Dew claw extra toe on the inside of a dog's leg above the paw. Often removed by surgery when a puppy is a few days old.

DNA deoxyribonucleic acid, the substance that makes up chromosomes, from which all life is made.

Docking cutting a dog's tail for medical or cosmetic reasons when a puppy is a few days old. Docking for cosmetic reasons is illegal in many countries.

Doe female rabbit.

Fancy selective breeding to display traits for exhibition purposes.

Feral domestic animals that have reverted to a wild state.

Finch seed-eating bird.

Flake food prepared food for fish which is light and floats on the water's surface.

Full-spectrum lighting artificial lighting which corresponds in its wavelength output to sunlight.

Gait style of a dog's movement.

Gestation period the length of time that a female mammal carries her young prior to birth.

Gills organs which enable oxygen to be extracted from water. Located on the sides of the head, these may be external or internal, covered by a membrane.

Herptile collective term for reptiles and amphibians.

Herpetology the study and keeping of reptiles and amphibians.

Hexapod an animal with six legs, such as an insect.

Iguanids group of lizards.

Incisors upper and lower front teeth.

Infusoria microscopic plant and animal life occurring in water; forms the natural diet of young fish as they start to feed.

Insect invertebrate with six legs.

Insectivorous feeding on invertebrates.

Invertebrate creature without a backbone.

Kittens name given to the young of some mammals, including cats and rabbits.

Kits name given to young chinchillas.

Lagomorph collective name given to rabbits, hares and pikas.

Malocclusion failure of the teeth in the upper and lower jaws to meet correctly. A common problem in rodents and lagomorphs, which can lead to starvation.

Mammals group of vertebrates which suckle their young. Most give birth to live young, with very few laying eggs.

Marsupial group of mammals where the young are born in an immature state, and are reared in their mother's pouch where they can suckle.

Mastitis inflammation of the mammary glands seen in nursing mammals.

Metamorphosis change from one state to another as part of the life-cycle.

Mongrel dog of unknown parentage.

Myomorph major grouping of rodents; includes rats, mice, hamsters and gerbils.

Neuter to castrate males or spay females to prevent reproduction and unwanted sexual behaviour.

Neoteny ability of some amphibians to breed in their immature larval state.

Outcrossing pairing to avoid inbreeding between a male and female.

Pedigree a record of ancestry, showing a family tree over several generations.

Plastron underside of a chelonian shell.

Poikilothermic cold-blooded; unable to regulate body temperature independently of environment.

Protozoa microscopic single-celled organisms; can be beneficial as aids to food digestion in herbivores, or can cause various diseases.

Rabies fatal viral disease affecting nervous system. Usually transmitted through a bite from an infected animal.

Rex mutation resulting in a curly or crinkled rather than straight coat.

Ringworm fungal disease seen in small animals; can be spread to human beings.

Rodents biggest group of mammalian species; distinguished by their dentition pattern, particularly the sharp incisor teeth at the front of the jaws.

Scurvy effect of Vitamin C deficiency, resulting in skin problems.

Self a solid-coloured variety of mammal, with no pattern or shading in the coat.

Show standard description of the ideal example of a breed, used for judging purposes; specifies not just the physical appearance but also other features, such as coloration, for which points are awarded.

Sow female guinea pig.

Spay to surgically remove a bitch's ovaries and uterus to prevent oestrus and unwanted pregnancy.

Spermatophore packet of spermatozoa produced by male newts, which females use to fertilize their eggs.

Stud an entire male that has not been neutered (altered).

Tabby striped, blotched, spotted or ticked coat markings, usually seen in cats.

Tadpole aquatic larval stage in the life-cycle of amphibians.

Terrapin freshwater turtle that regularly comes on to land.

Terrarium enclosure which does not contain a large area of water.

Tipped the colouring of a mammal's fur at the very tip of each hair shaft, the remainder of the fur being pale.

Tortie an abbreviation for a mammal with tortoiseshell coat colouring and marking.

Tortoise terrestrial member of the chelonian group, generally distinguishable by its domed shell.

Type description of a creature's physical appearance; used in show circles, especially for small mammals and birds.

Turtle name used in North America to describe both freshwater and saltwater chelonians; name used elsewhere for marine species only.

Vivarium housing for herptiles and invertebrates.

Vocal sac area under the lower jaw inflated by male frogs and toads in the display to attract breeding mates.

Weaning gradual change in a young animal's diet from its mother's milk to solid food.

White spot protozoal fish disease, resulting in white spots over the body.

Yolk sac part of the egg which provides nutrition prior to and immediately after hatching.

ACKNOWLEDGEMENTS

The authors, photographers and publisher would like to thank the following for their help and co-operation in making this book:

Ian Abercrombie, John Ainley, J. Ansley, S. & R. Badger, S. Bagley, Harriet Bartholomew & Flora, Jonathan Bartholomew, Stephen Bartholomew, G. Black, P. Beaven, S. L. Bond, S. Bradley, Jane Burton, J. & P. Canning, William Church, Ian Cinderby, M. Clark, Peter Curry, Paddy Cutts, P. J. Daniels, Carley Deanus, Lauren Deanus, Dawn Deanus, Vanessa Dyer, Jill Fagg, Sue Fisher, Emma Freeman, C. Fry, Dr M. Hackelsberger; Alison Hay, James Hay, V. A. Harris, Wade & Kirby Heames, H. Hewitt, Debra Hodson, B. Hollandt, J. & D. Johnson, Duane Joy, A. E. Kensit, Simon Gardner, L. Graham, Jo King, Graham Knott, Simon Langdale, Jenny Lavender, Rosie Lowen, Jeanette Marina, M. J. McLellan, M. Peacock, L. & A. Piatnauer, B. & L. Riddy, Mary Rodriguez, Jackie Roswell, Steve Rudd, Britta Stent, Kevin Stevens, Wendy Stevens, Antonia Swierzy, N. P. Tabony, Anne Terry, B. Terry, Trevor Turner, J. Ward, Angela Warrell, A. Wells, Cathy Whitehead, Charlotte Whitehead, Stuart Worth.

Thanks are also due to the Sherfield family, Canine Partners for Independence, Colin Clarke Veterinary Practice, Celia Cross Greyhound Rescue, Pampered Pets of Godalming, and Sue and family at Burntwood Kennels, Dunsfold.

With thanks to the following cat breeders:
Persian: S. MacHale, Isabella Bans, Lynn Lincoln, Jo and Nick Bolton, Maxine Fothergill, Carol Gainsbury, Rose Lovelidge; **Turkish Van:** T. Burnstone, Joyce Johnson; **Somali:** Jane Bean, Celestine Hanley, Rosie Lowen; **Maine Coon Cat:** Mr and Mrs Badger, Daphne Butters, Sue Deane, Bill Griffiths, Jackie Huddlestone; **Ragdoll:** Belinda Bright, Dawn Davies, Janet Edwards, Dianne Mackey; **Exotic Shorthair:** Mr and Mrs J. Clark, Rosemary Fisher, Maxine Fothergill, Carol Gainsbury, Shelagh Heavens; **British Shorthair:** Brenda Hollandt, Paulette Larmour, Celia Leighton; **Oriental Shorthair:** Carolyn Fry, Mr and Mrs Funnell, Monica Harcourt, Sheena Manchline, Lynn Studer, B. Reece; **Russian Blue:** Val Price; **Burmese:** Maria Chapman, Dr Kim Jarvis, Naomi Johnson, Mrs Marriott Power, Mr and Mrs P. Webb, S. Williams-Ellis; **Siamese:** E. Corps, Sheena Manchline, Lynn Studer, B. Reece; **Balinese:** Mrs P. Browning, Mr and Mrs Cleland, Luisa Jones, Mr and Mrs Meerings, Mrs Pinnington; **Bengal:** Sandra Bush, Helen Hewitt; **Cornish Rex:** S. Luxford Watts; **Devon Rex:** Stephanie Cole, Chris Franks.

With thanks to the following dog breeders:
Afghan: Mrs Pascoe; **Beagle:** P. Walden; **Deerhound:** S. Finnet & H. Heathcote; **Pointer:** Mr & Mrs M. Welsh; **Irish Setter:** M. Gurney; **Golden Retriever:** C. Fry; **Labrador Retriever:** C. Coode; **English Cocker Spaniel:** B. Harris & S. Oxford; **English Springer Spaniel:** Mr & Mrs D. Miller; **Field Spaniel:** Mr & Mrs N. R. & J. Park; **Weimaraner:** Mrs Schall & Mrs B. Adlington; **Shih Tzu:** Mrs V. Goodwin; **Dalmatian:** Miss C. Hicks; **Airedale Terrier:** Mary Swash; **West Highland White Terrier:** Mr R. Wilshaw; **Staffordshire Bull Terrier:** Alec Waters; **German Shepherd:** Miss L. Graham; **Dobermann:** Miss K. Le Mare; **Border Collie:** F. Cosme & J. Collis; **Cavalier King Charles:** Mrs J. Read; **Yorkshire Terrier:** O. A. Sameja.

PICTURE CREDITS
t=top; b=bottom; c=centre; l=left; r=right

Animals Unlimited: 14t, 18t, 25t, 30t, 38t, 38bl, 39br, 40t, 44b, 46t, 46b, 50t, 52b, 54c, 59tr, 58c, 58b, 63c, 65t, 68t, 68c, 76t, 77br, 81c, 126, 132 bl, 132br, 134t, 134bl, 137t, 142c, 84t, 85t, 85b, 87c.

Dennis Avon: 350, 351, 352, 353t, 354t, 354c, 354b, 355t, 355c, 355b, 356t, 356bl, 357t, 357b, 363b, 364t, 365t, 367b, 368b, 370b, 378t, 378b, 379t, 379br, 381bl.

BBC Natural History Unit: Niall Benvie 2, 268t; Bernard Castelein 417tl; John Cancalosi 399tl; Jim Clare 332b; Georgette Douwma 416c; Hanne and Jens Eriksen 340b; Jeff Foott 445tl; Jürgen Freund 304c, 158t; Andrew Harrington 269t; Fabio Liverani 440bl; Vivek Menon 417tr; Steven David Miller 341t, 341b; Chris O'Reilly 268b, 440t; Pete Oxford 332t, 333b, 389t, 430b; Tony Phelps 399tr; Rico and Ruiz 414c; Doug Wechsler 441tr; David Welling 417b; Andrey Zvoznikov 286br.

Janet Boswell: 41br, 47b, 50b.

Gilly Cameron Cooper: 15c, 28br, 39bl, 52t, 75c, 77tr, 103tl, 114br, 114c.

Chanan Photography, C. A.: 45c, 47t, 70t, 105b.

Bruce Coleman Collection: Ingo Arndt 411b; Trevor Barrett 481b; Jen and Des Bartlett 465bl; Erwin and Peggy Bauer 312t; Jane Burton 286t, 298b, 299t, 330t, 331b, 334b, 335tl; 425t, 443bc, 443br, 446, 481tl, 492br, 494t; John Cancalosi 425b, 449b, 467; Bruce Coleman Inc. 482t; Jeff Foott 499t; Sir Jeremy Grayson 464t, 464tr; Werner Layer 334t, 443t, 482b; Joe McDonald 407bl; Robert Maier 303t, 313tr, 335tr, 444t; Hans Reinhard 322t, 322b, 331tl, 419tr, 476t, 493t; Marie Read 441tl, 450t; Alan Stillwell 466t, 466b; Kim Taylor 302b, 323t, 445tr, 445b, 446b, 465tl, 465br, 473c, 473b; Uwe Walz 480t; Jörg and Petra Wegner 289t, 290t, 290c, 290b, 291t, 291c, 291b, 300t, 303b, 331tl, 344b; Rod Williams

415cl, 433t, 433b; Günter Ziesler 286bl.

Camfauna UK: 409cl, 410bl, 410br, 411t, 412t, 413b, 421b, 421bl, 471tl, 471tr, 472cr, 473t.

John E. Cooper: 470c, 470bl, 470bc, 472tl, 472tr, 473t.

FLPA: 8, 10, 17c, 41bc, 42bl, 42br, 48, 50br, 54t, 55b, 76bl, 78t, 79bl, 80br, 91b, 111t, 114tl, 114tr, 114bl, 118b, 120t, 128t, 132t.

Marc Henrie: 12, 15t, 98c, 134cl, 134br, 135b, 82, 95t.

Cyril Laubscher: 353b, 356br, 358b, 359, 364b, 366t, 367t, 368t, 369t, 369b, 371t, 374t, 375t, 375b, 381tl.

W. G. V. Lewis MRCVS: 342br, 343tr.

Mac on Mac Design: 24b; 43t.

Dermod Malley FRCVS: 342t, 342bl, 343tl, 343b, 344t, 344c, 345t, 346t, 346br, 347t, 348t, 349t, 377bl, 377br, 378tr, 378c, 379bl, 380t, 380b, 380bc, 381br, 468tc, 468tr, 468bc, 468br, 469tl, 469tc, 469tr, 469cl, 469cr, 469b.

Chris Mattison: 384b, 385c, 386c, 386bc, 387tc, 387tr, 387bl, 388tc, 388tr, 388c, 388br, 391tl, 391tc, 391bl, 391br, 392t, 393br, 395t, 396c, 397tl, 397tc, 397tr, 398tr, 399c, 399b, 400t, 401tl, 401c, 402ttc, 402c, 403c, 404c, 404b, 405tr, 405cr, 406b,

408br, 410t, 410br, 412b, 413t, 415cr, 416t, 416b, 419tl, 419b, 420b, 421t, 422t, 422bl, 422bc, 422br, 424t, 424b, 426b, 427tl, 427tc, 427tr, 427c, 427b, 428t, 428br, 429b, 431t, 432b, 435tr, 435b, 436b, 438t, 438bl, 439br, 439t, 439bl, 439br, 441b, 442c, 442b, 444b, 447tl, 447tr, 447bl, 447br, 448b, 449t, 452t, 452bl, 452br, 453t, 453tr, 453b, 454t, 454br, 455c, 457b, 459t, 460t, 460br, 461, 462t, 462c, 462b, 465tr, 473t.

Papilio Photographic: 11tl, 11c, 11br.

Photomax: 474, 475, 476cr, 476bl, 476bc, 476br, 477tl, 477tc, 477tr, 477b, 481tr, 483t, 483c, 483b, 484t, 484bl, 484br, 485tl, 485tr, 485bl, 485br, 486t, 486b, 487t, 487b, 490t, 491tl, 491tr, 491c, 492t, 492bl, 493b; 494c, 494b, 495t, 495bl, 495br.

Planet Earth: 11bl.

Warren Photographic: Jane Burton 14b, 19, 20t, 23, 25b, 34t, 34br, 35b, 36, 38cr, 39t, 41t, 41bl, 58t, 43b, 50c, 53tl, 53r, 55t, 57bl, 57br, 58t, 59br, 60, 62t, 62bl, 62br, 64b, 68bl, 68br, 69tr, 69c, 69b, 75bl, 77tl, 79tr, 80t, 80bl, 81tr, 81b, 86b, 87b, 92, 98t, 100t, 100bl, 100br, 101t, 101b, 102t, 102b, 105t, 106, 111b, 116, 117, 120b, 123bl, 123bl, 123br, 124, 125, 127,155bl, 155br, 159tl, 170t, 170b, 171t, 171c, 172t, 172c, 173t, 182b, 190b, 191, 207, 217r, 267, 298tl, 298tr, 312b, 313tl, 313b, 316c, 316bl, 321tl, 321tr, 321cl, 321br, 335br, 339tc, 339tr, 339c, 339bl, 339br, 345b, 504.

William H. Wildgoose: 500c, 500bl, 500br, 501tl, 501tr, 501b, 502t, 502b, 503tl, 503tr, 503bl, 503br.

INDEX